THE RAJAH OF RENFREW

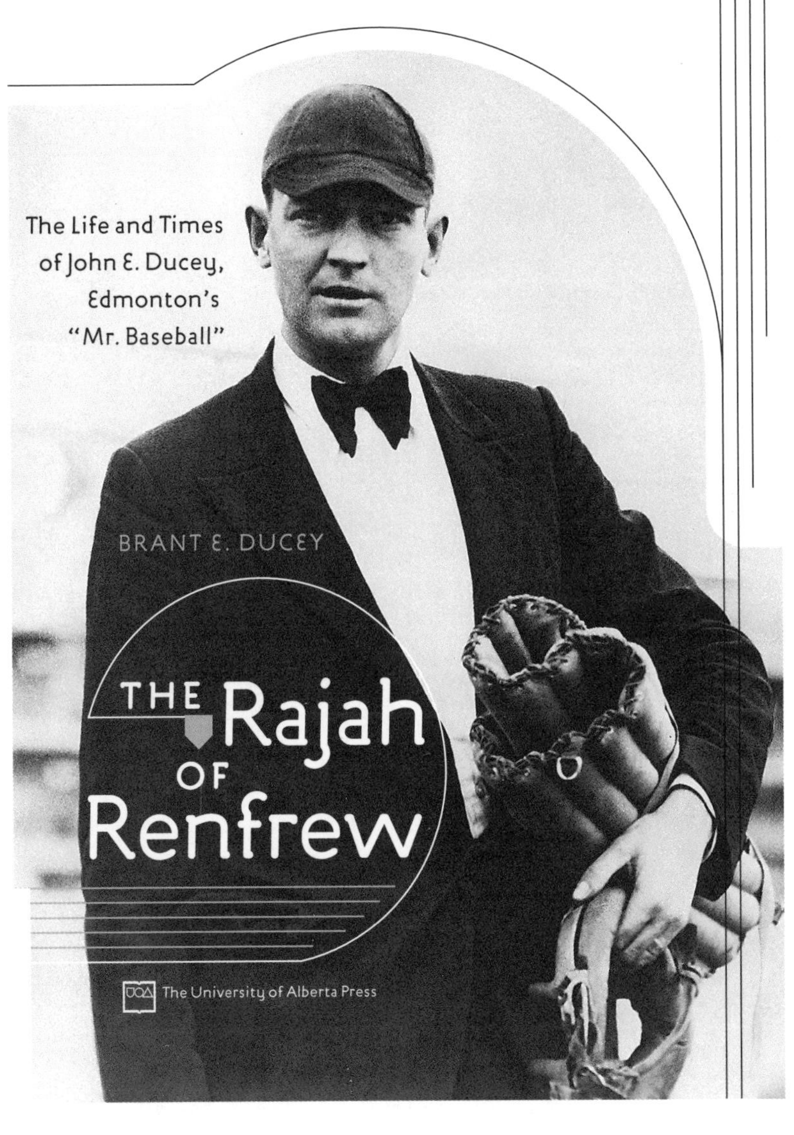

The Life and Times
of John E. Ducey,
Edmonton's
"Mr. Baseball"
BRANT E. DUCEY
THE Rajah
OF
Renfrew
The University of Alberta Press

Published by
The University of Alberta Press
141 Athabasca Hall
Edmonton, Alberta T6G 2E8

Printed in Canada 5 4 3 2 1

ISBN 0–88864–314–4

Canadian Cataloguing in Publication Data

Ducey, Brant E. (Brant Eugene), 1936–
The Rajah of Renfrew

Includes bibliographical references and index.
ISBN 0–88864–314–4

1. Ducey, John E. 2. Baseball—Alberta—Edmonton—Biography.
3. Baseball—Alberta—Edmonton—History. I. Title.
GV865.D82D82 1998 796.357'092 C98-910696-9

∞ Printed on acid-free paper.
Printed and bound by Friesens, Altona, Manitoba.
Photographs scanned by Screaming Colour Inc., Edmonton, Alberta.

The University of Alberta Press acknowledges the financial support of the Government of Canada through the Book Publishing Industry Development Program for its publishing activities. The Press also gratefully acknowledges the support received for its program from the Canada Council for the Arts.

Contents

Acknowledgements

THE BULK OF THE MATERIAL USED IN THIS BOOK COMES FROM SCRAPBOOKS, ARTICLES, PHOTOGRAPHS, AUDIO TAPES, AND LETTERS INCLUDED IN THE JOHN DUCEY COLLECTION AT THE ALBERTA ARCHIVES.

Other material comes from the City of Edmonton Archives and the Glenbow Museum Archives. For their professional help, I would like to thank David Leonard, formerly of the Alberta Archives; Wendy McGee of the Alberta Archives; and the team of June Honey, Paddy Lamb, and Bruce Ibsen of the City of Edmonton Archives. Paddy Lamb shared his own insights about Deacon White's achievements and unearthed several unpub-

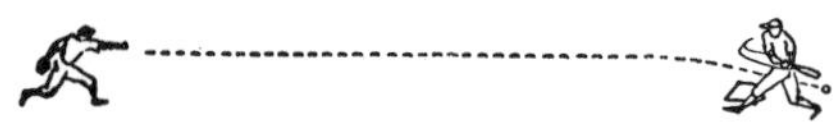

lished Edmonton baseball photographs. Much of the Calgary perspective about the Big Four League comes from a scrapbook assembled by Dorothy and Dick Noon of Medicine Hat. I would also like to acknowledge University of Alberta law student Angela Weaver's work on the 1907 Federal *Act Respecting The Lord's Day*.

Several people gave interviews about their experiences with baseball and John Ducey. They include former players Des O'Connor, Cliff Johnston, Doug Darrah, Dick Noon, Frank Finn, Ralph Vold, and Wayne Tucker, as well as Brian O'Hanlon, who worked with my father for several years. Early memories of John Ducey were supplied by my late mother, Grace Ducey; his sister, Mary Broderick; and the late Riley Mullen, one of his boyhood friends.

Valuable personal insights were provided by the Honourable Justice Allan Wachowich, a keen student of Edmonton's baseball history; Cecil "Tiger" Goldstick; former Edmonton alderman Ron Hayter; Kenny Awid; and of course, Don Fleming, much of whose writing from the *Edmonton Journal* forms the basis of game reports and background material. I am also indebted to Messrs. O'Connor, Fleming, and Wachowich for struggling through the first draft of the manuscript and suggesting improvements. Edmonton author Tony Cashman gave me helpful advice on the structure of the book at a time when I desperately needed it.

Researching a book based on events on Edmonton while living in Vancouver and Kelowna was made easier with help from friend Richard Hyslop, my sister, Duane, and her husband, Peter Quily. I am indebted to my patient wife, Dagmar, who not only did all the microfilm copy work of hard-to-read newspapers, but who gave up many sunny days on the golf course while I worked on this project over several summers.

Finally, I would like to express my gratitude to three people who helped bring this book to a successful conclusion: Glenn Rollans, Director of the University of Alberta Press, who believed in the project and rescued it at a critical point; baseball researcher Owen Ricker, who added professional discipline and insight; and editor Leslie Vermeer, who took to her first exposure to the technicalities of baseball history with enthusiasm, accuracy, and a demand for proper perspective, all of which helped bring about a more readable book.

Introduction

MANY MONTHS AGO, WHEN I TOLD A SCHOLARLY FRIEND IN THE EAST THAT I WAS ABOUT TO START WRITING A BOOK ON THE HISTORY OF SEMI-PRO BASEBALL IN EDMONTON, HE ASKED, "WHY EDMONTON?"

I answered that it was because baseball was central to my family life when I was growing up there and that it had also been important to a good many Edmontonians in the 1940s and 1950s.

What I did not know at the time was that baseball had been important in Edmonton from the time the town became a city and the capital of the new province of Alberta in 1905. By the 1920s, Edmonton was reputed to have been the busiest baseball centre west of Toronto, with dozens of leagues and scores of teams at play. It had all begun back in May 1884, when a group of young men got together to organize a "base ball" team. By 1905, Edmonton had a semi-pro baseball team named the Capitals in honour of the city's new status.

Baseball was also very much a part of Edmonton's social fabric during the decades of the city's rapid growth. Diamond Park, Boyle Street Park, and Renfrew Park provided citizens from all parts of the growing city and the surrounding environs with a sense of community. On weekdays and Saturdays, you saw your friends from around town when you went to the City Market to shop. On Sundays, you saw them at the ball park—although they were rarely as tranquil and neighbourly at the ball game.

A visit to the ball park was one way people coped with some turbulent periods of our history. Through two great wars and the Korean War, during the land booms and busts, in the grime of the Great Depression, and into Edmonton's post-war growth years, baseball brought the city's people together. It gave them a common reason to rally civic pride. Visiting teams and fans also provided economic stimulus to the city during some tough times. Gazing out at those white uniforms against a green field provided a temporary escape from life's cares. Yet it became anything but peaceful once the umpire bellowed "play ball"—particularly when the bitter rivals from Calgary were visiting!

It was far from the big leagues. In fact, it was the "bush leagues." Yet Edmonton was a hotbed of professional and semi-professional baseball throughout the first half of this century. One of those who established the modern foundations for baseball and other major sports in Edmonton was an American, William Freemont "Deacon" White. This book documents his contribution to baseball in Edmonton, which was merely one of his many sporting occupations. The man who took up where White left off,

John Ducey, was also an American, for whom there was no other sport but baseball.

My father never told me much about the early years of baseball in Edmonton. He was too busy trying to scratch a living from the game each day to talk about its past, so I had to discover the history for myself. What I discovered was that John Ducey was at the centre of the sport in Edmonton for several decades. Then, in the 1960s, after long distances and bad weather forced him to give up, senior inter-city baseball literally disappeared from Edmonton for twenty years.

During those lean years, he did his best to keep alive his dream of professional baseball returning to the city. He continued to predict that someday Edmonton would get a triple-A franchise—the closest classification to the major leagues.

In 1981, that prediction came true. A few years later, Calgary joined Edmonton in the Pacific Coast League, rekindling the fierce rivalry that had sprung up in 1906 and died away in 1954.

This book is about the period in Edmonton's baseball history that laid the foundation for the sophisticated level of professional baseball that followers of the Edmonton Trappers enjoy. They now watch the game in what is acknowledged to be one of the best ballparks in the minor leagues. It wasn't always so comfortable, but Edmonton's three former baseball parks helped sustain the game over eight decades. The story of how it happened is told as a background to the career of one man. Nonetheless, many others played important roles and some of their contributions are reflected in the story that follows. They all had one thing in common: they loved the game.

Edmonton's "Mr. Baseball"

As the Great Depression ended, John Ducey had become one of Edmonton's best-known baseball personalities. By then he was coaching junior baseball and umpiring in several leagues. A city boy all his life, Ducey began

playing baseball in the fourth grade at Grandin School in 1918. He was actively involved in the game for most of the next fifty years, developing, supporting, and promoting baseball in Edmonton. Ducey was among the legions of dedicated people who made a contribution to baseball far from its centres of fame and power. He cited the usual reasons for loving the game, but deep down, his attachment to baseball, like that of his colleagues, had grown out of the boyish fun of playing a competitive game with good friends. In baseball, he was fond of saying, there was always a winner and always a loser, never a tie. He would also point out that no clock could end the game and spoil the fun...well, except on Sundays, at six o'clock, when the Lord's Day Act forced play to cease.

In August 1983, just as his life was ending, Ducey was named to the new Canadian Baseball Hall of Fame, then in Toronto. He was one of the first six people to be so honoured and the only one in that group from western Canada. His nomination capped a life-long romance with baseball. Baseball dominated Ducey's life for more than sixty years and in Edmonton, Ducey dominated baseball.

A player, umpire, coach, and general manager, he became well known throughout professional baseball as a skilled administrator and devoted student of the game. In his time, most major-league baseball officials knew where Edmonton was because Ducey was there. His contacts in organized baseball were wide and reached throughout the major-league level. Yet his baseball career remained centred in Edmonton, far from the big leagues that had captured his interest as a young boy and shaped his approach to the game throughout his life. A perfectionist with a professional approach to playing, umpiring, and presenting baseball, Ducey would often apply the disparaging term "bush league" to any performance that did not measure up to his standards of professionalism. In the end, he had to admit that mainly through choice, his entire baseball career had been spent in the "bush leagues" of professional and semi-professional baseball. But that was just fine with him.

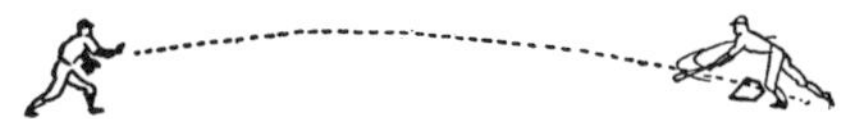

This book is about John Ducey's life in baseball and some of the influences on his career. A good deal of it examines the foundations of early Edmonton baseball in an effort to establish the city's strong baseball tradition and to recognize the role played by W. F. "Deacon" White. It is not intended to be a history of baseball in the city, but it is about some of the forces, people, and events that shaped Ducey's forty-plus active years in baseball. It focuses on the professional and semi-professional ball played in three Edmonton parks: Boyle Street, Diamond, and Renfrew. It does not fully recognize the many Edmontonians who laboured on behalf of baseball in the city and surrounding communities during the period of Ducey's involvement. Yet for many years, he provided them with focus and support. In return, they called him "Edmonton's Mr. Baseball."

I

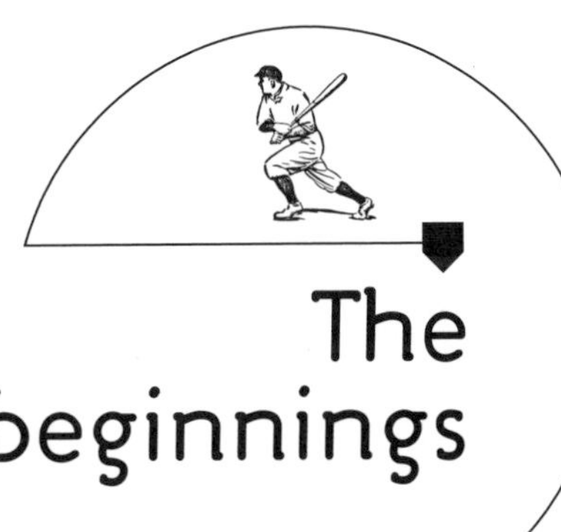

The beginnings

THE CAMERA HAS CAPTURED THEM IN THEIR PRIME, THEIR YOUTHFUL FACES FROZEN IN TIME. Edmonton baseball teams have been posing proudly for more than a century. Fading pictures represent the many who played on Edmonton's dusty diamonds through the years. There are the early Alberta boys who played the game for fun, later turned to men, still playing their games and still having fun. There are smiling faces, serious faces, nearly all white faces. With them are coaches and sponsors, posing with a dignified air.

The earliest known photograph dates back to 1892, some eight years after baseball was first organized in Edmonton. Another shows the Edmonton Baseball Club of 1900, posing on a rough diamond on the outskirts of "the bush," between 103 and 104 streets, just north of Jasper Avenue, on what

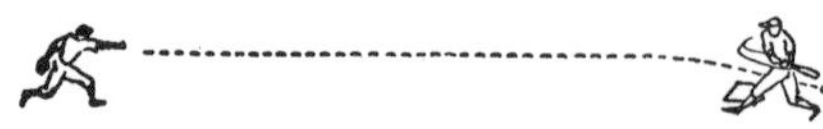

Identified as Edmonton's 1890 "base-ball" team, this is probably the earliest photograph of an Edmonton baseball group extant. Several experts believe it may have been doctored, however, as some of the heads look too big for the bodies. Courtesy of the Edmonton Archives EA 10-16.

was then part of the Hudson's Bay Lands. That is where Edmonton baseball was played until new grounds were developed soon after 1900, down on what was then known as Ross Flats. Another photo shows Edmonton's first professional baseball team of 1907, made up of older, veteran players from eastern Canada and the United States. There is a picture of the dressy 1910 Edmonton Eskimos, including pitcher George Dell, the first Edmonton player to go on to the major leagues. There are photographs of Deacon White's 1920 and 1921 professional teams, the latter with two future big-league stars. These players are bigger and many are older men, with the air of accomplished veterans. White himself stands tall and neat, in shirt-sleeves and tie, wearing a straw "boater" hat. There is husky Reg

Godson, wearing his civilian cap, posing with his 1924 Red Sox...and there's coach John Ducey, outfitted in a jaunty fedora and belted overcoat, standing with his 1932 Arrow Busses.

The usually grey, ill-tailored uniforms on raw-boned prairie boys of the 1920s and 1930s contrast sharply with the neat, well-pressed Yankee pinstripes on the clean-cut American college players who largely made up Ducey's semi-pro Eskimo teams of 1955–59. The American service teams who played at Renfrew Park in World War Two are also pictured, usually flanked by a captain in U.S. military dress. Then there are the Big Four League clubs with local players still remembered from post-war years: McGill, Morgan, Brant, Belter, Ryan, Darrah, Johnston, Brockie, Stewart, O'Connor, Ornest, Price, Seaman, Superstein, and others, along with a sprinkling of American players.

The earliest photographs make us wonder just what drew those turn-of-the-century players to the baseball diamonds in far-off Edmonton. Wasn't baseball an American game? Most of us were brought up to believe that the game was invented in Cooperstown, New York in the spring of 1839 and that it spread from there. Historians now say baseball as we know it began in New York City in 1842, a derivative of "town ball," which had begun decades earlier. The driving force of modern baseball was Alexander Cartwright, who organized the New York Knickerbocker Base Ball Club in 1845, setting the stage for today's game.

In his book *Diamonds of the North*, William Humber, Canada's pre-eminent baseball historian, argues that Canadians can legitimately claim "the great American pastime" as their game too. He documents the early nineteenth-century development of a distinct, Canadian version of the game, including one of the earliest and most famous baseball games played in Canada. It is believed to have taken place 4 June 1838 in Beachville, Ontario—almost a year before the legendary fathering of baseball by Abner Doubleday at Cooperstown.

Baseball scholars now generally agree that a variety of historical bat and ball game antecedents, including the English game of "rounders"

and several early American versions such as "town ball" and "cat ball," led to the rise of baseball under several different rule systems in various locations in the 1830s and 1840s. In *Northern Sandlots*, his definitive study of baseball in the Maritimes, Colin Howell confirms that a form of "town ball" was played in St. John, New Brunswick as early as the 1830s and that baseball was played there, alongside cricket, in the 1840s. Danzig and Reichler's 1959 book *The History of Baseball* names Alexander Cartwright the "Father of Organized Baseball." Drawing strongly on the reflections of noted nineteenth-century sports-writer and scorekeeper Henry Chadwick, they explain how Cartwright drew up new rules and laid out the ninety-foot diamond in the 1840s. The first recorded use of Cartwright's new rules was 19 June 1846, in a game between the New York Club and the Knickerbockers at the Elysian Fields in Hoboken, New Jersey.

Bill Humber illustrates how the Canadian version of the game, first played in 1838, gradually gave way to Cartwright's new rules in the late 1850s. He traces the spread of "base ball" through the Ontario heartland in the 1860s and early 1870s. Canada's first professional league was formed in April 1876 and included teams from Guelph, London, Toronto, Hamilton, and Kingston.

Bill Phillips, born in St. John, New Brunswick in 1857, became the first Canadian to play major-league baseball, joining Cleveland, then in the National League, in 1879. Phillips played 1,038 games over a 10-year career. James "Tip" O'Neill of Woodstock, Ontario was the first Canadian to become a noteworthy major-league star, in 1887. That year he was the best hitter in the major leagues, batting .442 for the St. Louis Browns.

Baseball comes to western Canada

In far-off western Canada, the first baseball clubs in Edmonton and Calgary were playing by 1884, a year before the Riel Rebellion. How did baseball get to Edmonton so early, when it was still a small outpost in the Northwest Territories? In fact, baseball was late in coming to Edmonton.

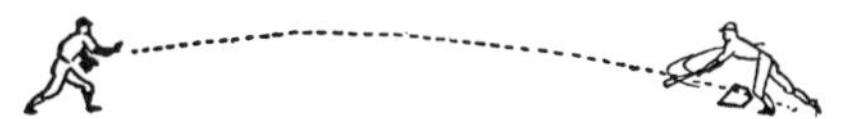

Humber describes early Canadian baseball developing in several distinct regions, with strong south-to-north alignment. In the last third of the nineteenth century, teams in the Maritimes, Quebec, Ontario, the Prairies, and British Columbia frequently played teams from neighbouring states. At the same time, however, baseball's popularity in Canada was spreading east-west as the country developed.

The arrival of the railway in Manitoba late in the 1870s, and in Saskatchewan by 1882, hastened the spread of the game in both territories. Manitoba historian Morris Mott says baseball was played at Winnipeg as early as 1870. He documents the story of the Manitoba Baseball League of 1886, the first professional league formed on the Canadian prairies. Saskatchewan historian David Shury's research shows the first baseball game, played in what would become his province, took place in 1879.

British Columbia historian Geoff LaCasse links the game's development in B.C. to Alexander Cartwright's arrival in San Francisco in 1849. After establishing baseball there, Cartwright went to live in Hawaii. But baseball quickly made its way up the coast to B.C., well before Canada's confederation. LaCasse found the first recorded baseball game in that province took place at New Westminster on 24 May 1862. The sport moved rapidly through the B.C. interior with the eastward construction of the Canadian Pacific Railway (CPR) in the early 1880s. Building westward, the CPR reached Calgary in 1883, and the line was joined at Craigellachie in the B.C. interior in November 1885. The first baseball activity in both Edmonton and Calgary was reported in the summer of 1884, and the game developed quickly, even though the Edmonton area did not get a rail link with Calgary until 1891.

Unfortunately, we still know little about the very early Edmonton baseball teams. Who organized those teams, built the diamonds, and put up the money so these young men could play, back in the days when winters were six months long and summers only three? What fortunes of chance brought them together in 1884 to play on the race track behind the old Methodist church, in an area that later became the centre of downtown

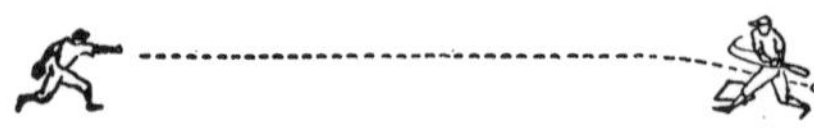

Edmonton? Who, by 1900, had the idea to move the first baseball park from the Hudson's Bay Lands on 102 Street north of Jasper Avenue, down to the Ross Flats fairgrounds near Edmonton's present baseball stadium? And who were those proud-looking players who posed for pictures well before the existence of Edmonton's old Diamond Park, Boyle Street Park, and Renfrew Baseball Park?

Baseball and society

If we know a great deal more today about *how* and *when* baseball developed in Canada, we also know a lot more about *why* baseball came about. Sociological analysis reveals the links of modern sport to work, leisure, and social conditions; certainly, the emergence of baseball was tied to each of these factors. In the early part of the nineteenth century, sport in Canada was considered a frivolous diversion, restricted to the middle and upper classes and frowned upon by the church.

As Canada's natural and agricultural resource-bases grew, stimulated by developments in transportation, communication, and massive immigration, sporting activity began to develop throughout the country. Unlike the imported British sports of soccer, cricket, and rugby, which dominated Canada during most of the nineteenth century, baseball developed as a wholly North American pursuit. With interest spurred on by local newspaper coverage of major-league baseball, the game became Canada's predominant sport by the early 1920s.

In *Canada Learns to Play*, his study of Canadian sport up to World War One, Alan Metcalfe identifies several characteristics that distinguish baseball from other nineteenth-century sports. These included its American influence; an early intrusion of the professional element (which brought both good and bad to the game); the lack of local, provincial, and national organizations to give it stability; and the groups who played baseball. Early intra and inter-city leagues were plagued by a lack of stability, although this did not hinder baseball's rapid growth. The turn of the cen-

Baseball was a social occasion for rural communities early in the twentieth century. At Bowden, Alberta, dressed in their Sunday best, a group of citizens gathers for baseball in the early 1900s. Courtesy of the Provincial Archives of Alberta H 764.

tury saw a massive expansion of amateur organizations and the arrival of professional players, teams, and leagues. Of those early baseball years Metcalfe writes, "If 'Canadian' is to be measured by number of teams and presence throughout Canada, then baseball must truly be called the Canadian game."

Metcalfe describes a clear difference between the development of urban and rural baseball. While urban ball quickly turned to a professional game, rural play remained a form of competition, mirroring both the origins of the game and the realities of rural life. The seasonal demands of farming and the lack of organized free time restricted rural baseball largely to communal celebrations and expressions of community spirit, such as Queen Victoria's birthday, Dominion Day, and Labour Day. On those festive occasions, baseball tournaments—with a variety of prizes, from ribbons to money—played a featured role in villages and small towns. Rural baseball was also characterized by exhibition and "chal-

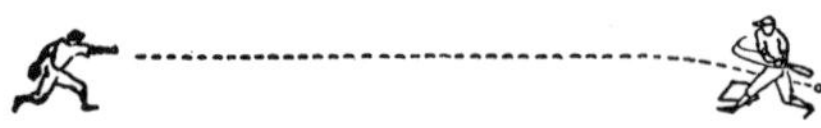

lenge" matches against other communities—although this was also a feature of urban ball. "A second team chosen from the base-ball players of the town herewith challenge the Edmonton team who played at Sturgeon River on Her Majesty's Birthday, to a friendly game of baseball on Monday evening next," read one such a challenge in the *Edmonton Bulletin* of 25 May 1900.

It was not long before "the money problem" surfaced in prairie baseball centres. Competitions among villages and towns soon came to involve prize money, and before long, professional players from the United States were not only being imported to play on Canadian clubs but were individually drifting across western Canada looking for opportunities to play. "A new man from Grand Forks, North Dakota also showed up last night who has the style, shape and action of a ball player and a suspicion of diamond dust about his uniform," observed a *Bulletin* reporter in 1906. Roving professionals were soon followed by promoters and league organizers, usually packing a strong desire for financial gain.

Betting quickly became an accepted feature of baseball. "Betting was indulged in," said the *Bulletin* of a game played on Dominion Day 1884. The chance to make easy money led to a clear distinction between professional and amateur baseball early in the twentieth century. Professional baseball was linked with serious gambling, while amateurs played a friendly game, with occasional wagering only a side-product. The Chicago "Black Sox" scandal of 1919 shook professional baseball to its foundations, finally forcing the game to clean up its act under the imposition of authoritarian rule by its new Commissioner, Judge Kenesaw Mountain Landis.

Professional prairie ball was characterized by instability, due to some fundamental problems. Metcalfe identifies the lack of organization at the national and provincial levels as a basic problem. However, the isolation of smaller western population centres and the harsh weather at either end of the ambitious summer schedule also played critical roles in bankrupting many endeavours. The citizens of Lethbridge could occasionally take advantage of a chinook blowing in from the west, and they prided

A mid-winter game with Calgary at Lethbridge on 27 January 1906—the earliest game of the year. The next year, the record was broken when the same two clubs played on 26 January. Courtesy of the Glenbow Archives, Calgary, Canada, NA 1276-1.

themselves on getting in a ball game on 26 January 1907, thus beating the 27 January record of the previous year. The poor souls further north in Wetaskiwin and Edmonton, however, considered themselves lucky if frost or spring rain held off long enough to get in an opening game on 24 May. And while the railways stimulated the spread of inter-city play in Alberta, the province's first professional four-team league of 1907 faced crippling railway costs, which totalled more than $7,000 for the season's travel.

Despite such challenges, baseball blossomed on the Prairies, albeit in fits and starts. Although the game had returned to the orbit of amateur sport by 1915, largely due to World War One, it was described by Metcalfe as "the most widely played game in Canada." In their 1969 study *Sports and Games In Canadian Life*, Nancy and Maxwell Howell wrote much the same thing: "Perhaps the most popular sport on the Canadian scene during the first twenty or more years of this present century was the game

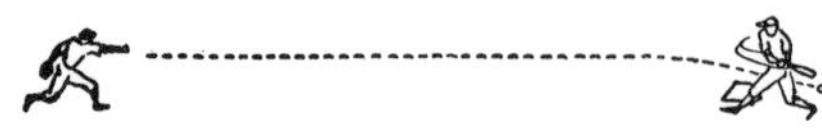

of baseball. Amateur, professional, and semi-professional teams flourished and competed in countless leagues. Every city, town, and village boasted of its teams." The fact that baseball prospered in the face of competition from so many other summer sports, while hockey had no rival except curling, led Metcalfe to conclude that "Baseball was truly Canada's national sport."

In *Northern Sandlots*, Colin Howell outlines the cultural similarities and divisions that characterized the maturation of baseball. Baseball cut across class divisions in early Canadian society as unions, commercial and professional organizations, fraternal and political groups, churches, and schools sponsored teams. Its early and universal acceptance differed from ice hockey and Canadian football, which came later and were created and developed by middle and upper-class anglophones in Montreal and Toronto. On the other hand, baseball was quickly seized from its early origins among the middle and upper classes and became the sport of the working class. Yet even within the working class it was fragmented by ethnic, religious, racial, and gender divisions: the game reflected the social cleavages of turn-of-the-century society. Yet at the same time, Howell observed, "working men often turned to baseball in order to demonstrate their physical ability and manly prowess in what appeared to be a more egalitarian environment than the workplace." Gender lines in baseball were well defined, and women were largely shut out of either watching or playing the sport in its early years.

Bill Kirwin, editor of the scholarly baseball journal *Nine*, has compared the early growth of the professional minor leagues in western Canada with the concepts of imperialism and colonialism. He describes the Western Canada Baseball League of 1912 as "a colony within a colony," with the western "hinterland" dependent upon the eastern "heartland's" demand for commodities (players). For Kirwin, western subservience in both baseball and commerce gives rise to "a sense of remoteness and alienation from industrial Canada and indeed the world." He maintains that to combat such alienation, prairie towns engaged in communal

rivalry: "boosterism and nefarious activities such as drinking, brawling, baseball, and gambling."

Baseball and Boosterism

To one degree or another, Kirwin and other contemporary historians identify two major factors which brought about the early development of professional baseball in western Canada. The first is "boosterism," the concept of home town pride which was used to promote the economic and social advances of a community or a town. Its manifestations of local exuberance—such as parades, exhibitions, and athletic tournaments—made citizens feel good about their towns and themselves. A 1906 report in the *Calgary Herald* claimed that from a tour of the Calgary baseball team as far east as Winnipeg two years earlier, "Calgary got more publicity than it did from any other source." The *Edmonton Bulletin* of 3 May 1907 carried a report from the *Cedar Rapids Times*, noting that "...Medicine Hat is the name of a city in the Western Canada Baseball League. The city is sending out the team as an advertising scheme for the town."

In 1907, the Calgary baseball club proposed that the city finance sending a civic booster with the team on a pre-season exhibition swing to Saskatchewan and Manitoba. A local report supported the idea:

> Considerable care will have to be exercised in the selection of a man for the position. He will have to be conversant with western conditions, and particularly have information concerning the city at his finger ends. ...[the City] must pick out a good booster to let the easterners know what Calgary has to offer to the world in the way of a place to work and make a home in.

The *Edmonton Journal* thought this such a good idea that it ran the story for its own readers and asked, "Why not do it here?"

The other strong influence on the rise of early professional baseball was profit-making, which could take the form of gate receipts, the sale of players to senior leagues, or gambling. In Edmonton, however, the introduction of professional baseball had more to do with boosterism than with profit-making. A sense of alienation from the national government and eastern power centres, its remote location, and the lack of an early main-line rail link all combined to foster a strong sense of rugged individualism in early Edmonton. The northernmost of the early western cities, Edmonton was further isolated by the North Saskatchewan River, which prevented the CPR's direct link from Calgary to Strathcona from entering the capital until the High Level Bridge was built in 1912. Edmonton's early boosters had to work harder and talk louder to get the recognition that came easily to more geographically blessed centres, such as Calgary.

Edmonton's earliest and most effective booster was Frank Oliver, who first published the *Edmonton Bulletin* in 1881 and later became a federal cabinet minister, a post he used to help get his town its due. His newspaper could not resist chiding rival Calgary as the new capital was preparing to celebrate the inauguration of the province of Alberta in 1905:

> Boosters of Calgary and the other less-deserving towns seemed to think Frank Oliver being in the Cabinet had given Edmonton some kind of an advantage.

The Calgarians were certainly correct. In *Edmonton: Life of a City*, urban historian Gilbert Stelter observes that although Calgary got the first transcontinental railway, Edmonton, largely led by Oliver's efforts, got the provincial capital as well as the university. These developments spurred an intense rivalry between the two cities which has been played out between their sports teams throughout the twentieth century.

Donald Ross, an industrialist contemporary of Oliver, was another Edmonton booster. From his land holdings on the river flats, Ross pioneered a good deal of Edmonton's late nineteenth-century growth in his

varied roles as a coal miner, hotelier, and horticulturist. The enterprising Scot remained a driving force behind the eventual 1912 entry of the CPR from Strathcona into Edmonton and the bridge needed to carry the railway over the North Saskatchewan. Ross also played a role in the move of Edmonton's early baseball activities away from the Hudson's Bay lands down to the river flats—a location conveniently adjacent to his Edmonton Hotel.

Boosterism was clearly a factor in the development of inter-city baseball rivalry in Alberta. Yet the very influences that gave rise to boosterism in Edmonton—the city's remote setting and its transportation challenges—crushed virtually any chance of baseball profit-making there. It seems that inter-city baseball came to Edmonton because it provided necessary social and athletic outlets like those of the rural, amateur game. However, it was largely a personal dedication to the game that sustained the efforts of men who had grown up with baseball, men like Deacon White, Henry Roche, and John Ducey. Their love of the game nurtured the strong baseball heritage of Edmonton and surrounding communities.

2

Edmonton's early innings

When Thomas James Ducey stepped off the train at Strathcona station just south of Edmonton on a wintery day in March 1906, it was the end of a lengthy journey to the city that would be home for the rest of his life.

Edmonton then had a population of 11,500 people and was in the midst of a real estate boom. Another 3,000 people lived across the river in Strathcona, where the boom was less pronounced but equally promising. Real estate

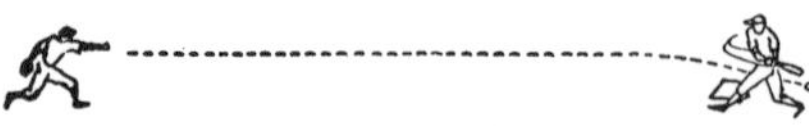

Thomas Ducey and Mary Normile in Buffalo, New York on their wedding day, 31 August 1904. They moved to Edmonton in 1906 but returned to Buffalo briefly in 1908 for the birth of their son, John. Courtesy of the Edmonton Archives EA 524-1.

had drawn Thomas Ducey and his wife Mary to the Edmonton area. Tom, and others like him, chased a potential bonanza. The huge Hudson's Bay land holdings north of the city, which made up part of that company's fur-bearing empire, were rumoured to be ready for release for commercial and residential development. The new Glenora subdivision was under development, with 50 by 140-foot lots selling for $125. A residential lot could be bought in Westmount, then just outside the city limits, for $100 to $250; just to the northwest, in the Sherbrooke subdivision, lots were selling for $75. "Real estate is the basis of wealth," proclaimed an advertisement in the *Bulletin* of 1906.

Thomas Ducey was a Canadian but had spent his adult life in the United States. One of thirteen children, he was born in Lindsay, Ontario to Irish immigrant parents on 11 August 1871. Fifteen years later, his father Daniel decided to leave Canada and follow his former neighbours to the plains of Nebraska, where they had been lured by the promise of free, productive land. In Platte County, about seventy miles west of Omaha, they claim-staked large farms around a village centre which they named Lindsay, after their Canadian home.

Tom Ducey left the family farm in Nebraska at age twenty-one to start a career as a railway telegrapher. Trained in Wisconsin by Charles Parker (who was then in the process of inventing the Parker fountain pen), Tom found work as a telegrapher in Buffalo, New York. He soon took a better-paying job as a fireman with the New York Central Railway. He met his future wife in Buffalo in 1901. She was Mary Elizabeth Normile, born in Corry, Pennsylvania, to Irish immigrant parents who later moved to Buffalo. Mary and Thomas were married 31 August 1904. Her son John would later take immense pride in the fact that she was a first cousin to Henry "Hank" O'Day, a former major-league ball player and manager who served with distinction as an umpire in the National League from 1895 to 1927.

In Buffalo, Tom Ducey was soon looking for more opportunity than he felt the railway could offer. The formation of the new province of Alberta in 1905 caught his attention, as he was still a Canadian citizen. That fall, he took leave from the railway and convinced his brother Daniel to travel to Edmonton with him to look at real estate opportunities.

Unlike industrial Buffalo, the Edmonton of 1905 had a "boom town" air. Some city lots were still selling for $25, while in the Norwood area, new residential lots were being offered for $60 and up, with terms of $10 cash and $5 per month. The young city offered any man with an enterprising spirit the chance to share in the prosperity. Although a bit rough around the edges, Edmonton seemed a nice place to raise a family. It even had its own baseball team, the Edmonton Capitals. Tom was sold on it instantly.

He returned to Buffalo and convinced his skeptical bride to leave her home and family and settle with him in Edmonton. She reluctantly

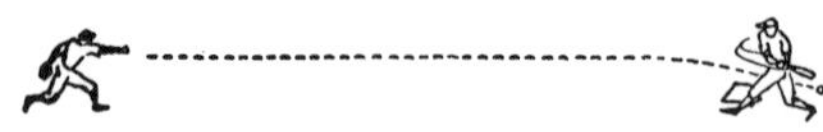

agreed. Tom's brother Daniel followed, homesteading south of Winterburn for some twenty years before moving to California.

The young couple settled in Strathcona, where Tom turned to the buying of land and the selling of residential lots. The real estate business was wide open in Strathcona, which was in a growth phase. During that first summer of 1906, Tom and Mary were delighted to find both junior and senior baseball thriving in Edmonton, as it was throughout Alberta. Edmonton's selection as the provincial capital had also provided fresh impetus to a lively baseball rivalry with Calgary, and the game would take a major turn late that summer when a barnstorming ballplayer named William Freemont White arrived in the city.

Except for a brief sojourn back in Buffalo for the birth of their first child, Edmonton became the Duceys' permanent home. Mary Ducey insisted her first child be born on American soil, so Thomas took her back to Buffalo for five months in June 1908. Their son was born on 31 August, their wedding anniversary. Three weeks later he was christened John Eugene Normile Ducey in Buffalo's Immaculate Conception Church. He was born and baptized a left-hander.

The family of three arrived back in Strathcona in October, but because of the winter isolation in the years before the High Level Bridge was built, Mary Ducey prevailed on Thomas to move to the north side of the river. They moved into a home on what was then Kinistino Avenue (now 96 Street) and settled near Immaculate Conception Church. Mary quickly made friends in Catholic social circles. Over the next several years, as an active realtor, Tom was asked by the Archbishop to help religious orders such as the Sisters of the Good Shepherd and the Sisters of Charity to find permanent quarters as they came to Edmonton. As a result, the family socialized with educated nuns and priests, many of them teachers, allowing young Ducey to thrive in an atmosphere of sophisticated conversation. Politics, religion, and baseball were frequent topics of discussion in the Ducey household. Both his parents were avid baseball fans, and

their interest was emulated by young John, who quickly learned how to talk baseball with anyone who would listen.

In the Ducey household, three important holidays drew a stream of visitors. One was Christmas, with all its religious significance, ceremony, and socializing. The second was American Thanksgiving, which Mary and Thomas celebrated with American friends and visitors. Thomas always bought the biggest turkey he could find at the City Market for the late November occasion. The third was St. Patrick's Day, when there was always a party at the Ducey home, and anyone who even pretended to be Irish was welcome.

When John's only sister, Mary Elizabeth, was born in 1912, the Duceys needed larger quarters. To be closer to Tom's south-side real estate business, the family returned to Strathcona, where Tom built a large, two-storey home on 117 Street, a few blocks south of Saskatchewan Drive. By that time, he owned most of the property in what is now Edmonton's Windsor Park area. John later recalled his father's fascination with the land business:

> One morning in the late spring of 1913, my father told my mother that it was about time to sell out his holdings in Edmonton and return to Buffalo. My mother was very pleased and had built herself up to a state of excitement by the time he got home that evening, ready to make plans with him to go back to New York. He arrived home that night rather quiet, and sheepishly explained to her that he had just bought another ninety large lots in Windsor Park. Just over a year later he lost everything in the land crash of 1914. They never went back to Buffalo.

Mary Ducey was never completely happy back in Windsor Park, so the family spent most of the next two winters in apartments on the north side, where life seemed a bit more socially civilized in those days. Partly because of his wife's discontent and partly because of the land crash of

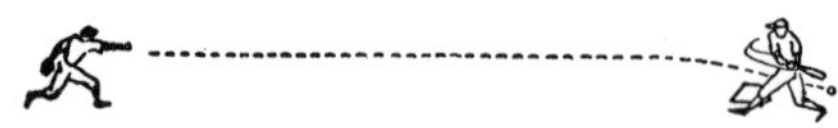

1914, Tom soon had to give up the big house in Windsor Park. He moved the family to smaller quarters north of the river, near St. Joachim's church. They were also close to the Tenth Street School where John was enrolled in the fall of 1914. A few blocks away sat what would be the new Grandin School, then under construction; it opened the following year. More importantly, for Ducey's mother, the location was central to the growing Catholic community, and she became an active participant in church social affairs at St. Joachim's. The elder Duceys would live in or close to that section of Edmonton for the rest of their lives, later taking an active role in St. Joseph's Parish once the Cathedral opened in 1925.

Edmonton was still a fort when Frank Oliver and his first partner, Alexander Taylor, published Volume 1, Number 1 of the weekly *Edmonton Bulletin* on 3 January 1881. It reported that few Indians were camped around the fort over the winter and that buffalo were in scarce supply. Yet the holiday period had been comparatively mild. On that New Year's Day, a crowd of about 200 people, "including several ladies," had gathered at the Edmonton Race Track on the Methodist Church property to see the horse races. A purse of more than $100 had been made up for prizes, an indication of Edmonton's early sporting (and gambling) spirit. As he would do down through the years, Oliver concentrated his first editorial remarks on the federal government, chiding them to establish a badly needed money-order office in the town.

Oliver was always outward-looking in his editorial comments and berated the federal government and "the railway syndicates" for not doing enough on Edmonton's behalf. His antagonism led him to run for office as a member of the North West Council and eventually for a seat in the federal parliament. He campaigned on a platform of improving roads,

building bridges, and constructing other public works to benefit the district. He also took a strong interest in issues such as timber, land, and homesteaders' rights. A resident of Edmonton from 1877, Oliver won handily over two opponents and gained a North West Council seat in the spring of 1883.

By then, Donald Ross was advertising in the *Bulletin* that his Edmonton Hotel, "the pioneer house of entertainment west of Portage LaPrairie," had completed an extensive addition, which included a first-class billiard room for the enjoyment of its clients. Among the many travellers staying at his river flats hotel were surveyors busily engaged in setting up the surrounding townships for incoming settlers and, of course, real estate salesmen. Ross was named chairman of the big July sports day that year, but baseball had not yet arrived. Cricket was the main sporting attraction for the 200 spectators who also cheered on those involved in the horse races, pony races, and various foot races held for men and boys.

Baseball comes to town

The early history of Alberta baseball was documented by Arnold M. Enger in 1966, as part of his physical education studies at the University of Alberta. Enger found the first published newspaper references to the formation of baseball in Edmonton and Calgary occurred in 1884. One can assume, however, that the game was played even earlier on an informal basis. The *Bulletin* of 24 May 1884 reported on its front page that eighteen men had attended a meeting the previous Saturday to organize a ball team:

> A base ball organization meeting was held on Saturday evening last in Ross Brothers building for the purpose of organizing a base ball club. E. Lyons was elected captain, and Jas. Ross secretary-treasurer. The club now numbers 30 members and practice is to commence at once. Material was sent for by last mail.

The simple act of organizing a community athletic pursuit gave baseball its start in Edmonton. On that May holiday weekend, again dominated by a cricket match between Edmonton and Fort Saskatchewan, the *Bulletin* noted that the would-be "base ballists" had already given it a try:

> The base ballists also had a quiet game near the cricket grounds, but as it was not a match, the club was scarcely organized and the weather so hot, not much excitement was developed.

In June, Secretary-Treasurer James Ross published notices of regular weekly club practices "...on the race track in rear of the Methodist Church. Members of the club are requested to attend."

After the Dominion Day holiday, Frank Oliver bashed the federal government over the need to establish a railway to open up the Peace River area. The 5 July edition of the *Bulletin* also carried a report that the baseball club "had received by last mail a half dozen balls of the new league standard." Then Oliver made the first link between Edmonton baseball and boosterism:

> The Baseball Club turned out in good form and a very exciting match was played. The club is without a rival in the North West.

Given that it had not played a real game at that stage, his boast could not be disputed!

Enger notes that the first published report of baseball activity to the south quickly followed in the *Calgary Herald* of 9 July. It noted that the day before, a team made up of members of the police force defeated a team of Calgary citizens 31-28. After a flourishing start that first year, Enger found that "baseball and all athletics took a back seat in 1885 to the Indian uprising recorded in history as the Riel Rebellion." That significant event may explain why rifle competition got most of the summer sports coverage in the papers in 1885 and 1886, with almost no references to baseball.

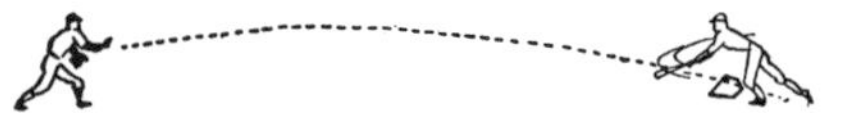

Edmonton baseball coverage was sporadic in the last years of the nineteenth century. A story from Calgary told of a game played in southern Alberta on Good Friday, 1886, when a North West Mounted Police squad was defeated by a team of Lethbridge citizens. In the late 1880s, most of the reported baseball activity took place in southern Alberta among Lethbridge, Medicine Hat, and Calgary teams. Enger attributes their early inter-city play to the fact that the three centres were linked by rail, which encouraged travel to exhibition and tournament play. The early spread of the game in southern Alberta was also stimulated by the large numbers of Americans who settled there.

Baseball disappeared from Oliver's *Edmonton Bulletin* for most of the next fifteen years, as he occupied his paper with his duties on the North West Council, the rights of masters and servants, Indian affairs, farming, attacks on the CPR "syndicate," and complaints about railway freight rates. This was a busy period for Oliver and the rapidly growing town. Edmonton made the transition from a fort, linked by stage coach to Calgary, to a bustling commercial centre, including a minor role as the northeast staging point for some of those rushing to find gold in the Klondike by 1898. Across the river, Strathcona was linked by rail with Calgary in 1891, and Edmonton boosters could see big things ahead for their town by the turn of the century.

Edmonton "base ballists," isolated by lack of a rail link, had to play against Strathcona and other neighbouring communities. The completion of the new CPR line from Calgary to Strathcona in 1891 brought about inter-city travel and sporting rivalry between Edmonton and Calgary. Cricket and football teams first exchanged visits in 1892. The first visit of a Calgary baseball team to Edmonton was part of a large front page announcement about the upcoming sports weekend in the *Bulletin* of 15 May 1893. There would be inter-city cricket, football, and lawn tennis matches on the first day, with the baseball clubs meeting on 24 May. At that time, however, Oliver's paper depended on the participants to report on such events, and apparently no one did, so we have no record of which

city won the first baseball game ever played between Edmonton and Calgary.

Two men named Patton and Pattison had got baseball going again in Edmonton during 1891 and 1892. In the latter year, Pattison led a team of married men against Patton's bachelors, but the two battled to a 13-13 tie in a Victoria Day game. By 1894, schools in Edmonton and surrounding communities had begun to form teams and play against one another. On 24 May 1894, Belmont School challenged the Edmonton Public School to a game on the race track grounds. The latter team thrashed the challengers 22-9 over six innings. But it was 1899 before senior baseball began to catch on permanently in Edmonton, with a north-side team crossing the river to defeat Strathcona as part of Dominion Day activities.

Baseball soon became identified with a variety of social classes, groups, and commercial interests, as well as the schools. Matches took place among teams of various business and professional men around town. Enger cites reports of a team of doctors playing a team of lawyers—the doctors prevailed, 35-25; of "McDougall and Secords" store beating the Hudson's Bay Co. team; of "the Professions over the Accountants," and "the 'all others' defeating the mechanics." Ross Brothers store, which had played a part in organizing the first team in 1884, still had teams playing in 1899 and 1909.

Edmonton gets serious

In February 1899, the committee formed by the Edmonton Board of Trade to seek a new location for permanent exhibition grounds announced a deal with the Hudson's Bay Company. For $7,000, the company would give Edmonton 55 acres on the river flats, south of 96 Avenue, between 101 Street and 104 Street. It was also a good deal for the Hudson's Bay: it meant the race track and baseball grounds could be moved off their land north of Jasper Avenue and the property subdivided for town lots. By July, the new race track had been graded, fencing was

Edmonton's 1900 club, dominated by the three Ball brothers, on the original baseball grounds located just north of Jasper Avenue between what is now 103 and 104 streets. Courtesy of the Edmonton Archives EA 524-2.

up, and the old grandstand had been moved down the hill and set up in its new location. Work was a little slower on the baseball diamond, and for part of the summer of 1899, the ball players continued to play on the original grounds. Occasional games were still played there over the next five years on a vacant plot of land.

In turn-of-the-century Alberta, baseball was quickly becoming the preferred summer sport. Around Edmonton, rural baseball thrived in towns like Wetaskiwin, Leduc, Spruce Grove, Morinville, Partridge Hill, and Ponoka. By May 1900, baseball had taken strong root in Wetaskiwin where "every evening there is a lively game and a good attendance of spectators." Edmonton's 1900 baseball team included the three Ball brothers—Billie, Frank, and Wallace—as well as Will McNamara, who later became mayor of Edmonton. They soon had enough players for two teams. The umpire for those early games, identified as "F. Grey," was probably Frank Gray, who a few years later became one of Edmonton's first real baseball

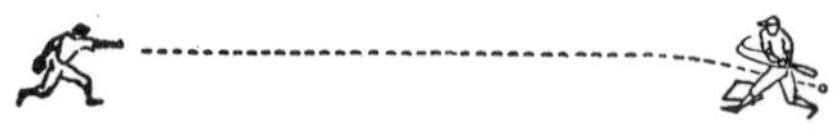

An early studio photograph of the 1903 Edmonton "base ball" club, with captain Will Inglis (kneeling, left). James McKinnon, in the dark suit, later became a member of the Canadian Senate. Edmonton's biggest rival was the team from Strathcona. Courtesy of the Edmonton Archives EA 45-1114.

promoters. The Edmonton boys agreed to take part in a big July sports day tournament but admitted in advance that they would be no rival for mighty Strathcona. They were right. Strathcona took the sports committee medals, winning 10-6, although Frank Ball struck out seventeen opponents, and the *Bulletin* proudly observed that the team "played better than at any previous time this season."

As the Edmonton team improved, the *Bulletin*'s baseball coverage began to increase. During this period, baseball travel between some of the smaller centres increased. Enger describes an early road trip in July 1901 when the Ponoka ball club visited Strathcona, then came over to Edmonton. To the delight of the home fans, the visitors lost both games, beaten 18-17 at Strathcona and 11-5 in Edmonton. That same year,

Baseball quickly became very popular among a variety of social and working classes. These members of the Edmonton Never Sweats and Thirsty Thugs, made up from a group of commercial travellers, played a well-publicized game on 18 August 1903. Courtesy of the Edmonton Archives EA 10-23.

Edmonton formed a tournament team called the Northern Stars. An unidentified sponsor put up the money to assemble a team to tour picnics and fairs, competing in any and all baseball tournaments. But the team failed to show up for a big 1 July game against Strathcona and disappeared from the sport pages into oblivion.

By 1903, there was talk of forming an Alberta Baseball League, with a Calgary promoter offering beautiful medals for the winners; there is no record that the idea ever made it from the meeting hall to the diamond. The main northern rivalry was still between Edmonton—whose captain, Will Inglis, opted for grey uniforms with black trim—and Strathcona, who were nattily garbed in red uniforms with white trim. In what was reported as "the best baseball that has ever been played in the North

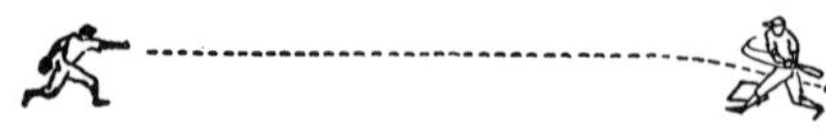

Country," Edmonton shut out Strathcona 6-0 in a June match, one of many between the two nines that summer.

A less sparkling account told of a rural game played later that month when the Partridge Hill team beat Beaver Hill 46-34. A report from Beaver Hill, carried in the *Edmonton Bulletin*, observed that early baseball was not a game for sissies: "Baseball is all the rage here now and the trade marks of the game are to be observed on the fingers and faces of the players." By then, commercial teams were being formed to play sandlot baseball, with names like the Punters, the Thirsty Thugs, and the Edmonton Never Sweats. The latter two teams were made up of commercial travellers and local men, who gathered at the diamond down on the river flats to play a much-noted game on the civic holiday of 18 August 1903. (The game was still being written about thirty-one years later in the *Edmonton Journal*.) Baseball was more advanced in the south, where semi-professional teams were being formed in towns from Calgary through the Crowsnest Pass. The seriousness of the competition is reflected in a report that the Macleod baseball club, bolstered by "five American imports," defeated Calgary 10-4 on 24 May 1903.

In 1904, the town of Edmonton was preparing for incorporation as a city. Anticipating that it would also be named the capital on formation of the province of Alberta in 1905, the Edmonton senior club was named the Edmonton Capitals. Harold Deeton, a young hockey player who had come west after playing for Brandon against Ottawa for the Stanley Cup that spring, joined the Capitals. He would play for Edmonton baseball teams for the next ten years. Frank B. Sommerville was president of the club, then managed by Percy Chapman, which played its first road game in Fort Saskatchewan on 24 May; the $75 purse was won by the home team. It was also the first Edmonton team to engage in regular rivalry against Calgary. Over the summer of 1904, the Capitals lost their series against the southern team, along with the $100 silver cup that had been put up by Arthur E. Cross of the Calgary Brewing Company. The Capitals got their revenge in 1905 when they made a major road trip to Wetaskiwin,

Innisfail, and Calgary. They beat Calgary 4-1 in the final game of the Calgary Fair tourney and brought the silverware back to Edmonton.

A road team of a different sort was called the "Hottest Coons In Dixie County." It was an informal team, composed from forty members of a coloured musical theatre group that was visiting Edmonton in late May 1905 to stage a three-act vaudeville show. The black ball players came complete with their own band. Leading the Edmonton Capitals and exuberant fans, they marched out from the Windsor Hotel to the old baseball grounds on the Hudson's Bay lands, where new bleachers had been built in anticipation of a large crowd. Hometown pride prevailed on consecutive days as the Capitals swept a two-game series, 10-9 and 18-6, and the visitors retreated to the vaudeville stage.

Perhaps due to its status as the new capital of a new province, Edmonton's interest in baseball became firmly established in 1906. The now-serious rivalry with Calgary sparked additional interest in the sport. Baseball became front-page news in the *Bulletin* as the local boys "gingered up" at practice, awaiting the arrival of the Strathcona club:

> The home team was out last night for the first time under the new manager, and as Commodore Rooks gazed over the mechanics of the diamond and selected with Napoleonic eye the performers who were going to make good, the boys threw more ginger and voltage into their play than has been apparent at any previous time this summer. Berry was practising last night and is to become a fixture with the Caps, although Wetaskiwin wanted badly to keep him down there.

In addition to the former Wetaskiwin player, manager Tom Rooks was trying out an American who had previously played in Grand Forks, North Dakota. If he could import just one more player, Rooks was sure he could fill the rest of the "amateur" team with local boys.

In 1906, boosterism set the tone for baseball coverage in the *Bulletin* and became a permanent fixture of game reports:

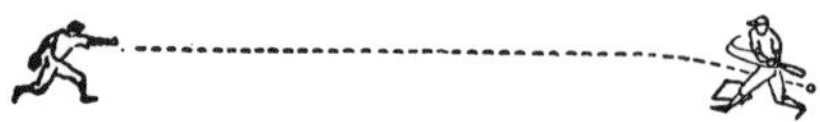

> ...Edmonton has the fastest bunch of amateurs in the Golden West. Rooks says that he will have a team on the diamond that will rattle the slats off anything this far north, or west, or north-west or straight up or straight down or anything else in the country.

Boosterism was also thriving in Calgary, where the *Herald* reported that "baseball men say a successful ball club would give the city a great deal of the very best kind of advertising." That summer, Frank Goode, proprietor of the Imperial Hotel, made a serious bid to organize Edmonton's first professional baseball team by selling $10 shares to local citizens. His initial effort brought in $1,060 toward his target of $3,000, much of it from fellow hotel operators. The money was targeted for permanent baseball grounds, the building of club houses, promotion of baseball and other sports, and the acquisition of a professional baseball franchise. Goode and his friends eventually sold 309 shares, then formed a limited-liability athletic company. Half the money was to be used to get the new club started and the rest to retire debts of the previous club.

After Goode delayed his organizational meeting in deference to a Board of Trade dinner, the baseball boosters urged the mayor and the council, as well as the Young Liberals, to "hurry the proceeding as much as possible," so the ensemble could get around to discussing organization of the new athletic set-up. The *Bulletin* promised that the discussion would mark "a new era in the affiliation of athletics of all kinds for this city under one comprehensive and business-like head." Goode, team manager Tom Rooks, and a Mr. Field were appointed provisional directors of Edmonton's first athletic club. The club promised that the matter of permanent baseball grounds would soon be settled to everyone's satisfaction. The *Bulletin* was certain an enduring new athletic era was about to unfold:

> The success of baseball and like games now seems assured. With a company such as has been organized there should be no difficulty in making things go.

Just as Alberta's first provincial exhibition opened, the new team was ready to play its first series of games against teams from Strathcona, Wetaskiwin, Calgary, and Red Deer. The ever-exuberant *Bulletin* proclaimed, "it should be the greatest baseball ever pulled off in Edmonton."

In early July, citizens and visiting farmers flocked to the new fairgrounds down on Ross Flats to see such attractions as "Prof. Downie's troupe of dogs, starring 'Patsy,' the high-diving dog, Prof. White's performing donkey and Msle. Latena Downie on her marvellous performance on the revolving globe." But the biggest crowds were around "Baseball Park," then a temporarily fenced ball field. The Capitals emerged triumphant before a home crowd of 1,200 fans on 5 July, beating arch-rival Calgary 4-2. Two days later, the Caps beat Wetaskiwin in front of 1,000 happy fans. Over the summer, however, Calgary won eight of eleven games with Edmonton, causing the *Albertan* newspaper to observe, "Edmonton people started baseball first but have been caught and passed by Calgary." Enger reports that, stung by this boasting, "Edmonton brought in four new men and managed to split a double header before leaving the confines of the Calgary baseball park." The athletic rivalry between Calgary and Edmonton was entrenched.

Barnstorming Yankees

After returning from their first road trip to Calgary at the end of July, Rooks and his Capitals prepared for their next big series of the season, a visit from a touring ball club from the state of Washington. The Anacortes Baseball Club, managed by W. F. White, was a touring semi-professional team made up largely of college ball players. They billed themselves as "champions of the Puget Sound League." The Americans, who were the subject of a front-page cartoon in Bob Edwards' *Calgary Eye Opener*, had such a good time in Calgary that they missed the train and their first game in Edmonton, scheduled for Thursday, 2 August. In their absence, the Strathcona boys came over in a hurry and were drubbed 10-2 by the Capitals.

In a rare acknowledgement of the subject of sport, the Calgary Eye Opener *ran a cartoonist's view of the visit of Deacon White's Anacortes team to Calgary in early August 1906. The visitors had so much fun, they missed their train to Edmonton. Courtesy of the Edmonton Archives EA 524-3.*

Friday evening, 1,000 eager fans were down at the Edmonton baseball diamond to watch the visiting American team. Despite the partying that went on in Calgary, manager White confidently claimed that "his team was in good shape." Harold Deeton, now the captain of the Capitals, was equally confident that his club would prevail. The Edmonton fans were not disappointed, as the hometown club beat the barnstorming Yankees 5-1. Over the following three days, the Capitals took the series, tying 3-3, then winning 3-2 and 6-1. The Edmonton fans took to the Americans, largely because of their neat appearance and hustling play. Even the *Bulletin* was impressed by the opponents, the first semblance of a professional-looking team Edmonton fans had ever seen:

> The Americans are a tidy lot. They play good ball on general principles and do a few exceptional stunts occasionally. They play with their heads in the game at all stages. They are gentlemanly boys and there is no unnecessary noise about them. It was a treat for the citizens of the

"Base Ball To-Night" banner stretched across Jasper Avenue in 1906. It might have been promoting the late August visit to Edmonton of Deacon White's barn-storming team from Anacortes, Washington. Courtesy of the Glenbow Archives NA 303-20.

> Capitol to meet them and they showed their appreciation of the visitors by applauding roundly their special features.

The professional demeanour so appreciated by the Edmonton fans came from the Anacortes manager, twenty-seven-year-old William Freemont White. He liked Edmonton and Edmonton's baseball fans liked him. In fact, with some $1,500 still in their treasury, local baseball organizers prevailed on White to stay and help them get their professional team launched. Stay he did. An entrepreneurial spirit, "Deacon" White became the dominant influence on Edmonton sport for some two dozen years.

3

The Deacon White era

WILLIAM FREEMONT WHITE WAS BORN IN SHERIDAN, ILLINOIS ON 6 DECEMBER 1878. He graduated with a master's degree from Chicago's Northwestern University. While there is no record of him playing inter-collegiate sports there, he was said to have been an outstanding athlete, excelling in intramural track, basketball, rugby, and baseball. He began his working career as a mathematics professor at the University of Chicago, but baseball eventually took him to the West. The son of a preacher, he inevitably picked up the nickname "Deacon" (although it could have come from James "Deacon" White, a popular major-leaguer who played between 1876 and 1890).

City of Edmonton archivist Paddy Lamb assembles the missing links in White's early career in a monograph entitled *Deacon White: The Founder*

of Modern Sport in Edmonton. Lamb found that White coached the St. Alban's Military Academy in Chicago to a state baseball championship soon after his own college graduation. In 1903, he moved to Iowa where he continued to teach and coach baseball. He then went on to coach and manage teams in Wisconsin, Montana, and North Dakota. White took the Fargo team to Seattle in the fall of 1905 and remained there himself over the winter. In the spring of 1906, he played with Spokane of the North-Western League for two months, until sidelined with an injury. He then returned to Puget Sound and the port town of Anacortes, where he formed a team of young players and took them on a lengthy road trip into Canada. When their 1906 baseball tour ended, the Anacortes team went home while White returned to Edmonton. Soon after, in a letter to the sports editor of the *Winnipeg Free Press*, he explained that "the country and the climate about Edmonton has pleased me so much that I have cast my fortunes with Edmonton for the rest of the season and will remain here permanently."

It was more than just "the country and the climate" that drew White to Edmonton. He arrived at a most propitious time. The enthusiastic young city was hungry for professional baseball and its boosters had the money to get it started. In White, they saw the ideal man to help realize their ambitions. At twenty-seven, blonde, tall, and raw-boned, White exuded an air of reserved confidence well beyond his years. His knowledge of baseball and his experience with the professional side of the game impressed men like Frank Oliver, Frank Goode, and Frank Gray, who thought he was just what they needed to establish Edmonton as a baseball centre worthy of the capital city. White, who had the soul of a promoter, identified with the confident spirit of the Edmonton organizers and his new-found home. Although never averse to making a dollar, for these men, professional baseball was a sign of the city's growing maturity. Unlike Edmonton, the more sophisticated city of Vancouver was motivated wholly by finances, as Robin John Anderson describes in his article "'On the Edge of the Baseball Map' with the 1908 Vancouver Beavers":

> Beaver baseball was all about money and profit. League organization scheduling, player personnel, team performance, and the character and motives of many spectators were shaped by the drive to make money. All participants saw profit as a just reward of the game.

In Edmonton, money remained in the club treasury after Frank Goode's earlier sale of shares. A permanent site was picked on the flats for a new baseball park (near what is now a city park bounded by 98 and 99 avenues and 100 and 101 streets), and White set to work to get Edmonton into professional baseball. He quickly made contact with promoters in Calgary to organize a league for the following season. By early November, Bruce Robinson of Calgary had been elected the first president of the ambitiously titled Western Canada Baseball League. It was made up of Alberta teams, the others being the Calgary Chinooks, the Medicine Hat Gaslighters, and the Lethbridge Miners. Perhaps to distance himself from the semi-professional Capitals of 1905-06, White chose to call his club the Legislators. Each team put up a $400 guarantee that it would finish the season. Salary limits were set at $1,200 monthly, and the league applied for a Class-C designation. That, the *Bulletin* proudly noted, would put it on a par with Winnipeg of the Northern League or any of the state leagues on the other side of the border.

In mid-December, White received word from the national board of professional baseball that Edmonton had been officially recognized, allowing the *Bulletin* to trumpet that "Western Canada is on the baseball map of America." An official bulletin advised that the province of Alberta, as baseball territory, was now covered by a franchise issued to the Western Canada league. This protected the province from invasion by any other organized ball team. Deacon White then further endeared himself to local supporters by revealing he had turned down an offer of $200 a month to manage the Bloomington, Illinois team in the Three I league for the 1907 season.

In January 1907, the *Bulletin* devoted almost two-thirds of a page to White's reports of a meeting of the new league's officials and the proposed 1907 season schedule. White noted Edmonton's outlook was "as rosy as any of the other places," with seven or eight players already signed. Calgary had presented catcher "Kid" Ford with a diamond ring for his 1906 exploits, then club followers learned that White was trying to sign him. The gift was to no avail: White must have offered a more tempting attraction. He wanted Ford to catch noted spitball pitcher Charlie Crist, whom he had also lured away from Calgary. Nevertheless, the *Bulletin*'s baseball writer was not too impressed with some of White's early players, several of whom came from the western U.S.:

> ...most of them are old-timers. They may play as good ball as they did last year but they are not at all likely to play very much better.

This assessment would prove fairly accurate. A more optimistic topic on that date was the league approach to gambling: "No gambling will be allowed at league games, and the police on duty will be instructed to rigidly enforce this rule." White and his colleagues wanted to make sure that professional baseball's reputation for attracting a strong gambling element did not taint their new league. But there was really little they could do to stop fans from wagering among themselves. Such betting was openly discussed in the papers and wherever baseball fans met for the next several years.

New city, new team, new league

In 1906, the new city of Edmonton, enjoying a boom of its own, was also benefitting from a rapid rural land boom. The growth of a new western agricultural economy, sparked by the aggressive immigration policy of Laurier's Liberal government, was aiding rapid settlement throughout the western countryside. New villages and towns sprang up across the prairies

as large numbers of Ontario and European immigrants were drawn to free farmland by an aggressive campaign to promote the "Last, Best West." Edmonton's population grew from 2,626 in 1901 to 11,167 permanent residents in 1906, while the surrounding rural population included two to three times as many farmers as five years earlier. Immigration to Canada from the U.S. for the months of July through October 1906 totalled 17,790, compared to 12,664 for the same period in 1905. Americans, many of them actually returning Canadians like Tom Ducey, were pouring into the country, bringing with them a strong interest in baseball.

Edmonton's economy was dominated by real estate and railroads. Sixty-four real estate agencies and forty-three building contractors were at work as new neighbourhoods continued to be surveyed and opened for development. The CPR had built a parallel line from Winnipeg through Saskatoon to Wetaskiwin and by 1906 had gained access to the Alberta capital from Strathcona via the Calgary and Edmonton Railway, which crossed the North Saskatchewan River down at the flats. The previous year, Edmonton had gained its own spot on what soon would be a transcontinental line when the Canadian Northern Railway arrived from the east, just ahead of the Grand Trunk Pacific, which was chugging in from the west. Regular rail transportation accelerated the boom in the city and the surrounding area. Sawmills sprang up to meet growing building needs, and coal mines were developed for heat and fuel-hungry railway steam engines.

Clear social lines also began to develop with increasing immigration. Historian Carl Betke looks closely at the Edmonton of 1906 in his article "The Original City of Edmonton." Betke observes that while Anglo-Saxons dominated, with some eighty-five percent of the population, new ethnic groups were beginning to provide diversity to the city's cultural mix. Class lines were also represented in local geography, with prosperous English-speaking professionals and long-established French families dominating the immediate west end, south of Jasper Avenue. The area north of Jasper Avenue and east of First Street was largely populated by

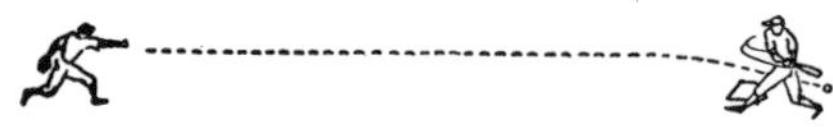

labourers, tradesmen, struggling businessmen, and ethnic newcomers. Boyle Street Park would later become their community baseball diamond.

It may have been entirely accidental to this division of population, but in 1907 Edmonton's new baseball park was located right on the dividing line of First Street, although down the hill from the city centre. White would ensure that his ball club attracted fans from all walks of society, but by virtue of his education and travel experiences, he was socially attracted to those in the ranks of Edmonton's civic and professional elite. One entry to this group was through the Liberal party, which dominated both federal and provincial politics. While amateur baseball was being played on school grounds and sand lots on both sides of the city, the men who wanted professional ball in Edmonton belonged to its well-connected business class. Frank Oliver, who had recently become a federal cabinet minister, and entrepreneurs like Frank Gray embraced the affable White because he held the key to an excellent boosterism opportunity. He got to know them early and well, and it was no accident that for want of a professional league in 1908, Deacon White ran Edmonton's Young Liberals amateur baseball club.

Betke describes the original Edmontonians and their neighbours in Strathcona as passive spectators of entertainment and sporting events. A herd mentality emerged. Fancy-dress skating carnivals, hockey games, and major curling bonspiels in the winter, and holiday athletic events in the summer, were intended to draw large crowds. Local businessmen strongly supported these events in an effort to bring in rural visitors, often on specially organized trains. The biggest event designed to attract visitors from far and wide was the first provincial exhibition of 1906. Although catering mostly to agrarian interests, like the other events, it was a symbol of civic pride and vitality—not to mention a producer of added economic benefits. Then on 26 December 1906, a crowd estimated between 1,800 and 2,200 people gathered in Strathcona as Edmonton took the opening game of the senior hockey league season, 7-5. Sports entertainment offered spectators the added dimension of teams carrying civic colours

and town pride. Inter-city hockey was extremely popular, although until then it had been based on exhibition and challenge matches, as league formation lagged behind that of baseball.

By 1906, Edmonton's two daily newspapers had established lively baseball coverage which extended far beyond local events. The *Edmonton Bulletin*, which had the city's readers to itself until the arrival of the *Evening Journal* in 1903, had reported on local baseball happenings since 1884. But its coverage of baseball outside of Edmonton was sporadic and depended on the small amount of space available for sports stories that came in by telegraph. For example, while there was no local baseball activity reported during the 1888 Dominion Day holiday, Edmonton readers were treated a week later to a report of a 1 July baseball tournament between Winnipeg and Grand Forks, Manitoba. Even during the first formal Edmonton baseball season of 1906, the *Bulletin* usually carried only a single column report on the Edmonton team. The *Journal*'s baseball coverage was similar.

Things changed quickly after the arrival of Deacon White that fall. The interest of both papers picked up when White went to the founding meeting of the Western Canada Baseball League in Lethbridge in November 1906. Soon after, White got busy with his own promotional schemes and began updating the newspapers of his progress. In January 1907, the *Bulletin* began devoting most of a regular page to sport. At first, it dealt mainly with hockey, curling, and wrestling; in this, its appearance probably reflected the evolution in sports coverage that had already occurred in daily papers elsewhere in Canada. The surprising aspect of the *Bulletin*'s sports page was that baseball quickly began to take over most of the coverage during the winter. As well as reports on White's own activities, the paper reported managerial appointments, player signings, and financial set-ups in the other league cities.

Before the winter was over, the *Bulletin* was carrying two full columns of regular feature stories on major-league baseball, covering such topics as salary costs (Cleveland topped the American league with an annual pay-

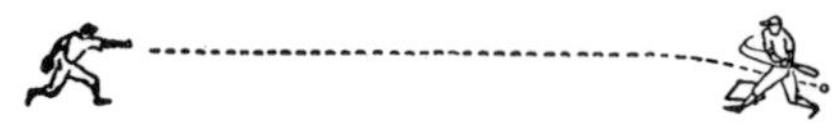

roll of $80,000; New York led the National league at $60,000), left-handed pitchers in the big leagues, rule changes for 1907, and reports on individual teams. In May, the sports page displayed some humour with a piece on "Advice to Young Players":

> The first thing a youngster has to acquire is a nickname. A ballplayer never became famous as William or Henry. Get to be "Mugsy" or "Trips" and your success is assured.
>
> . . .
>
> Remember umpires are your only friends and are meant to be abused. The umps must be made to take the blame every time you are called out and every good performer makes the umpire shoulder the blame for raw work on the bags.

Edmonton readers were now linked to the world of professional baseball on a daily basis, and the exploits of major-league stars were avidly followed by the local citizenry.

With the opening of the 1907 major-league season, Edmonton readers received a regular diet of American baseball names and reports that included not only the daily box scores from the big leagues but scores and stories from the Northern League, the Eastern League, and the American Association. By May, the *Evening Journal* had given its sports section a name, "The Field of Sport," which later became "The Sports of Summer." Both papers were then covering a full range of sports, including local cricket, football, hockey, and lacrosse, as well as North American events such as boxing, long distance running, automobile races, and U.S. collegiate rowing.

The winter of 1907 was extremely cold throughout Alberta. The *Bulletin* reported that additional trainloads of coal had to be shipped from Edmonton to Calgary, which was suffering an acute shortage of the fuel. In Edmonton, at least inside, things were warmer. White was organizing a minstrel show for early March to raise funds for new uniforms, expected

to be green with red trim and costing an estimated $300. He imported an impresario from Sarnia to handle the show and it played to turn-away crowds on three successive nights.

Despite a harsh winter and the latest spring in twenty-five years, Edmonton was in an optimistic mood in 1907. A full-page real estate advertisement in the *Bulletin* described Edmonton as "the Chicago of the North," as it touted choice lots adjacent to the site of the big, new packing plant in the east end, all offered at "easy terms at workingman's prices." Another large announcement for lots ranging from $125 to $350 in Strathcona also featured river-view lots at $1,000 each. Building permits were forecast to reach $7,000,000, and work was ready to begin on the construction of a permanent YMCA building and a street railway that would run down Jasper Avenue. A *Bulletin* investigation trumpeted that with the exception of housing rents, the city had achieved a cost of living that did not exceed any of the eastern cities.

As spring drew near, the Western Canada League schedule was expanded to forty-three home games for each club. Calgary manager Al "Hoss" Fiddler had estimated the three northern teams would rack up some 3,800 rail miles, with Medicine Hat having to travel more than 4,500 rail miles. This, calculated an enterprising reporter, meant the league would pour more than $7,000 in travel expenses into despised railway coffers. It also ensured that the clubs made little or no profit by the time the season ended.

While the *Bulletin* offered a regular diet of feature stories on major-league baseball, attention in Edmonton soon focused on the new baseball park. The fence around the old park on Second Street was torn down and briefly stored until an exact new location was selected. By mid-April, both the football and lacrosse clubs had agreed to use the new baseball grounds for practice and some of their games. For twenty-five percent of their gate receipts, the ball club also agreed to build them a dressing room under the stands. Such administrative matters were handled by club president John Mills, while White concentrated on forming the league and his

own team. As May began, White gathered nine ballplayers at Lewiston, Idaho for spring training. It was reported that another twelve would be invited for tryouts by 20 May when the team opened the season at Lethbridge.

The baseball club directors announced that the new baseball grounds would be built "near the centre of the city, a matter of three to four hundred yards from Jasper and First." They then secured a ten-year lease for land on which to build athletic fields. It came from acreage that had been a part of Donald Ross' garden property. Ross was praised by the *Bulletin* for the public spirit he had shown in the matter. The baseball grounds consisted of an entire block of land, ringed with a twelve-foot fence. A covered grandstand would seat 500, and bleachers down first base would provide for 1,000 more. Club director Frank Gray was given the initial $6,000 contract to build the park.

Professional baseball arrives

Meanwhile, White's team easily won all their exhibition games in Idaho, but the *Bulletin* writer questioned the quality of their early opponents. As an Edmonton booster, however, he picked the hometown boys to finish ahead of Lethbridge, Medicine Hat, and Calgary. On 21 May, Edmonton's professional baseball debut at Lethbridge was called on account of darkness after six innings, with the home team leading 4-2. About 600 people witnessed the game in cloudy, cold weather. Edmonton gained a measure of revenge the next day, winning 4-0. The scenario was repeated a few days later in Calgary when the Chinooks scored four runs in the first inning to take their first encounter 6-4. Edmonton won the second game 9-4, behind spitballer Charlie Crist.

In Edmonton, Frank Gray and his men were working flat out to get the new ballpark ready for the 29 May opening. The fence, grandstand, and bleachers were finished just hours before the scheduled ball game. The grounds and diamond were graded to professional standards, and the

Edmonton's first professional baseball team, Deacon White's 1907 Legislators. Catcher "Kid" Ford (front right) had been lured away from Calgary to catch star pitcher Charlie Crist (front left), who also left the Chinooks. Edmonton finished second in the four-team league; Calgary, last. Courtesy of the Edmonton Archives EA 524-4.

outfield was seeded with a mixture of Kentucky blue grass, wild oats, and white clover. Edmonton, assured the *Bulletin*, would have "one of the best, if not the best diamond and grounds in the West." With the game to start at 6:45 p.m., club directors made arrangements with all the hotels and cafes put dinner on early to enable everyone to get down the hill to see the game. Season admission prices were set at 50¢ for grandstand seats and 25¢ for the bleachers and standing room; however, the directors charged a flat $1 per head on opening day, "a practice observed by all other league clubs," in an effort to help defray the heavy expenses involved in securing and putting up the new grounds.

On opening day, White and his team were pictured in a formal studio portrait on the *Bulletin* sports page, the first sports photograph the paper had published. The front page carried a feature story on the event. Three

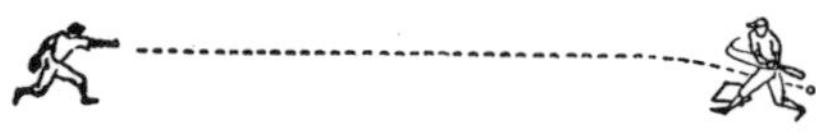

marching columns of Elks club members from Edmonton and points surrounding acted as escorts for the teams and invited guests, including Lieutenant-Governor Bulyea and Mayor Griesbach. Promptly at 6:00 p.m., they all marched out of the Alberta Hotel, down Jasper Avenue to Second Street, countermarched back to First, then made their way over to McDougall Hill and down the hill to the new ball park. The parade was led by Edmonton's newly organized city band—so new they were still without uniforms. But that mattered little with the entourage and onlookers in high spirits.

There was a slight hitch at the ballpark where 1,000 eager fans had taken almost every available seat. Priest, the official league umpire, missed the train from Calgary and failed to turn up. White had to name two of his non-starters, Bennett and Barnstead, to act as umpires and this almost resulted in a crowd uprising. According to the *Bulletin*, "Those thousand were there to boost the home team and if necessary, kill the umpire—and this almost befell the man with the indicator." Bennett got into trouble for failing to call the game because of darkness, with Edmonton leading 9-4 after seven innings. As light began to dim in the top of the eighth inning, Calgary scored four times. Bennett almost succumbed to the clutches of the frustrated crowd when he went up into the grandstand to confer with club directors. The two clubs stumbled through the bottom of the eighth inning, and Bennett called the game in Edmonton's favour 9-8, after the first Calgary batter was retired in the ninth. The hometown crowds went home happy. With umpire Priest in control of home plate the next two evenings, the fans cheered their boys on to 7-4 and 7-6 victories as the Legislators chased the Chinooks out of town.

After the initial euphoria, the crowds ranged between 400 and 700 fans. In a bid to increase attendance, Deacon White introduced "ladies' day" in Edmonton, a gimmick invented by Charles A. Powell in New Orleans in 1887. But attendance waned during weekday games when only the most avid fans showed up. Professional baseball in Edmonton was still

very much a social event, which only drew crowds on the weekends—if the weather was good.

Although he started the season at third base, Deacon White stayed on the sidelines and managed for most of the schedule, playing the occasional game near the end of the season. The league was run informally, with players coming and going as itinerant ball players travelled the Prairies from city to city, looking for the best financial deal.

Near the end of August, the Legislators were almost late for the start of a double-header at Medicine Hat. The details were wired to the *Bulletin* by Deacon White:

> The train was late in arriving; we jumped off the train and onto the diamond. Erickson pitched wild and high. Umpire Priest called Wessler out for not touching second base when Harper hit a home run. It was a raw decision. Priest robbed us of [the] second game....It certainly looks like no chance to win. We have to beat the umpires and the crowd too.

Edmonton lost the first game 7-6, and the second was called a tie in the sixth inning and cancelled due to darkness. Medicine Hat then moved in front of Edmonton and stayed there.

Just before the season ended, last-place Calgary switched its final three home games to Edmonton for lack of fan support and "a handsome offer" made by the Edmonton club to move the series to the northern city. Lethbridge and Medicine Hat protested the move without success. White's Legislators were always in contention, led by pitcher Charlie Crist and catcher "Kid" Ford, a talented backstop who was expected to progress upwards in professional baseball. Edmonton and Medicine Hat battled for the league lead near the end of the schedule, but White's boys could not catch the Gaslighters, who took the pennant five-and-a-half games ahead. Calgary beat Edmonton 4-2 in the final league game at Diamond Park and the season ended there as it had began—umpire

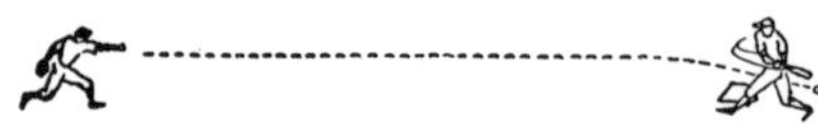

Priest failed to show up and two players were pressed into service. A summary of that season from the President's report to the National Baseball Congress was overly optimistic:

> While the new league met with very little encouragement from the general public, we are proud to say that we came through the entire season without making a change in any one of our teams and without any one of the teams losing any money to speak of. The standing of the teams was such as to keep people up to fever heat during the whole season, each of the teams having led some time during the season....

The Young Liberals at Diamond Park

White managed to turn a slight profit by selling Kid Ford's contract for $500. Reports, which were often just rumours, had it that he was sold to Philadelphia of the American League and sent to a west coast club. Still, for some reason connected with a failure to report, he was suspended from organized baseball for the 1908 season. Despite the optimism of the league office, it seemed doubtful professional baseball would return to Edmonton the next year. Overall public support had been weak. Edmonton and Calgary were unhappy with the long rail trips to Medicine Hat and Lethbridge. White wanted to reduce travel costs and talked of a league made up of Edmonton, Calgary, Wetaskiwin, Strathcona, and Red Deer. Professional, or at least inter-city, baseball was the only game that would satisfy the citizens, said Deacon White, boosting Wetaskiwin's entry:

> The past season has shown the fans there that league baseball is the drawing card. In fact the people will not go to see anything else. Professional baseball has killed the attraction in the amateur game and the people of Wetaskiwin realize this. As a result they are willing to put a team in the league and support it. Already one gentleman there has offered to contribute $1,000 toward starting a team there.

Deacon White (seated, centre) could not organize a professional league in 1908, so he formed a four-team league called the "Twilight League" because games began at 5:45 and 6:00 p.m. His Young Liberals included hockey player Harold Deeton (centre-right) and Walter Campbell (on White's left), who later joined him in hockey promotion.

But White could not convince his own friends to risk their money on another year in professional baseball. In the end, he had to settle for an inter-city amateur league in 1908, made up of Edmonton's Young Liberals, Camrose, Wetaskiwin, and Strathcona. (Vegreville was supposed to be in the league but did not field a team.) As manager of the Liberals, White played first base, and two men who later became life-long Edmonton residents, hockey player Harold Deeton and Walter S. "Shorty" Campbell, joined the club. White drew up a fifteen-game schedule and was elected acting president until R.L. Rushton of Camrose took the league helm in late May. It was called the "Twilight League," with game times moved

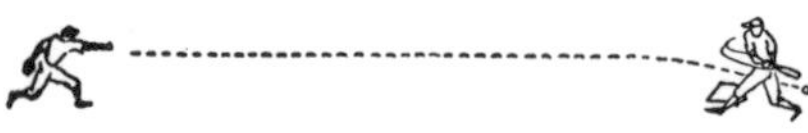

Diamond Park, Edmonton's first permanent baseball facility, was built in 1907 across the street from the Edmonton Hotel on what was them called the Ross Flats. Land for the park came from property of Donald Ross, who also owned the hotel. Courtesy of the Glenbow Archives, Calgary, Canada, NA 4696-2.

ahead to 5:45 or 6:00 p.m.—except on Sundays, of course. White likely didn't even notice that on 1 March 1908 the federal government introduced *An Act Respecting The Lord's Day*. Among other things, the Act prohibited the playing of commercial sport after 6:00 p.m. on Sundays.

With lower operating expenses, White convinced the club directors to make further improvements to the ball park. The first thing they did was give it a name: Diamond Park. Part of the first-base bleachers was eventually covered with a roof, giving the impression the park was larger than it was. Standing room remained along the fence behind the third-base foul line. Seating capacity was gradually increased to 4,000, a large facility for a city of 25,000 people. Commercial signs covered the outside front of Diamond Park and its fences. Diamond Park would serve as the centre of senior and professional baseball in Edmonton for twenty-five years.

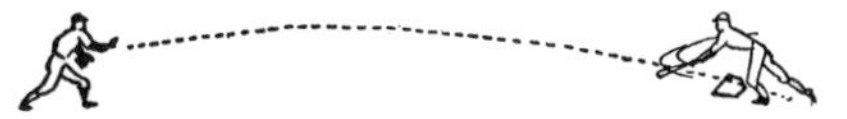

The opening of the 1908 senior league was set for the evening of 2 June. According to the *Bulletin*, it would be a gala event. It was also the park's "official opening," as the rush of building it in 1907 had left little time for official celebration:

> With the blare of trumpets and all the pomp and splendor of a parade, the baseball season will be opened on Tuesday, June 2 by a league game between the Edmonton Liberal Club team and Strathcona on Diamond Park. The game is called for 6:30 and the two teams will parade from the Liberal Club rooms down Jasper Avenue to the baseball grounds. Premier Rutherford will pitch the first ball. Deacon White, manager of the team, will hold down first base.

As was so often the case, the variable spring weather interfered: Diamond Park's official opening was postponed twice. As a result, White took the Edmonton team, now outfitted with new, light-blue uniforms and red caps, to Camrose, where they played their first game 9 June, more than a week after they were supposed to open in Edmonton. The weather finally cleared enough to open at home on 15 June, and by this time Edmonton was ready. The managers of the King Edward, Alberta, and Windsor hotels arranged a special 5:30 sitting so that fans could take in the game "without rushing their meal." Those patrons who bought their ball tickets at the top of the hill were given free passage down to the park on the incline railway. Ladies were admitted free, and a band entertained fans at the ball park. The fun was short lived, however. In the midst of a downpour and increasing darkness, the game had to be called in the sixth inning, with Edmonton leading Camrose 6-4. It was an inauspicious start to what became a permanent battle between weather and baseball in Edmonton.

Diamond Park never dried out that month, and by the last week in July, the team was forced to play its games on a grassy field over at Victoria Park. As the weather gradually improved, Edmonton was leading

In 1907, horse teams were the main form of transportation up McDougall Hill *from Diamond Park (left), unless a baseball fan paid five cents to ride the new incline railway. Courtesy of the Edmonton Archives EA 10-247.*

the league with seven wins and one loss, but attendance remained light. It picked up when a series of exhibition games was arranged between Edmonton and Calgary. The Calgary team now included the popular Charlie Crist, who had been White's star pitcher in 1907. Crist had returned south for more money in the spring of 1908. He briefly left for a try-out with Seattle in mid-July but was soon back in a Calgary uniform. The *Bulletin* was glad to see him again:

> The weeds still adorn the fence corners on Diamond Park, a challenge for the batters to lose the ball if possible. Charlie Crist is certainly there with the goods in all his old time form. It did the hearts of the fans good to see him in the box once more.

Edmonton sportswriters referred to Calgary as "the cow camp," "horse country," or "the little village beside the Bow," never missing an opportu-

nity for insult. Calgary writers shot back with insults about Edmonton's frigid weather, referring to its residents as "Esquimeaux." White became fascinated with the name "Eskimos" and his professional baseball teams of 1909-11, and later his hockey and football clubs, were all called the Edmonton Eskimos. Edmonton author and historian Tony Cashman credits the origin of the name to a Calgary sports-writer's 1903 reference to a team from the oft-frozen northern city. Others claim the name was first given to the Edmonton football teams, who began travelling to Calgary in 1892 and 1893. Initially bestowed in derision, as Cashman noted, "it had the advantages of alliteration, neatness, uniqueness, and a certain amount of truth. It stuck." In later years, Edmonton newspapers also sometimes referred to White's teams as the Esquimeaux but the club never officially used that spelling.

In 1908, Edmonton could brag about the marvellous new incline railway that had just opened. It carried the more affluent baseball fans up and down McDougall Hill for five cents a passenger. The *Bulletin* used it to take a shot at Charlie Crist and the visitors from Calgary:

> The boys from the southern village rode up on the incline railway last night and tried not to look self-conscious. When they saw the paved streets and car tracks already laid, however, they gave up and stared at the sights with mouths open.

Edmonton beat the turn-coat Charlie Crist on that first visit of the 1908 season, sweeping Calgary in a doubleheader, 3-1 and 6-1. A few days later, White's Young Liberals were also declared champions of the Twilight League, placing ahead of Camrose and Wetaskiwin. (Strathcona had dropped out of the league before the season ended.) At the league meeting soon after the season, the board took steps to stop the habit of borrowing players for key games and declared that in future, "a recognized player of one club cannot play with any other in championship games."

White builds a sporting foundation

Having secured the Twilight championship, helped to construct a new ball park, and re-kindled interest in baseball among the residents of his newly adopted home, White could have taken a well-earned rest over the winter. But he was already turning his interest to the Canadian game of ice hockey. White had quickly become established in Edmonton. With his former baseball team-mate, Walter S. Campbell, he played a prominent part in the development of the Edmonton hockey scene and then added Canadian football to his pursuits. His Edmonton Thistles hockey club unsuccessfully challenged for the Stanley Cup in 1908 and again in 1910. He also staged professional boxing matches, importing fighters from eastern Canada and the United States. When the old Thistle hockey rink on 102nd Street north of Jasper Avenue burned down in October 1913, White quickly recommended to the Edmonton Exhibition Association that its new livestock arena, nearing completion, be redesigned to accommodate hockey. White's suggestion was accepted, and he and Walter Campbell staged the first hockey game to be played in the Arena on Christmas Day, 1913. Edmonton hockey teams played there over the next sixty years.

In the spring of 1909, White brought professional baseball back to Edmonton, joining the Western Canada Baseball League in its second season. The sprawling league included Calgary, Medicine Hat, Lethbridge, Winnipeg, Moose Jaw, Regina, and Brandon—the first and only league to embrace all three prairie provinces—and operated through the 1911 season. The Eskimos finished dead last in 1909, well behind the champions from Medicine Hat. With higher travel expenses, the Class-C League was not a financial success, but each team finished an ambitious one hundred-game schedule and would start again in 1910.

Distance and weather combined to undercut any chance of financial success for the extended league. As the minor leagues expanded south of the border, fewer American players would come to Canada without a

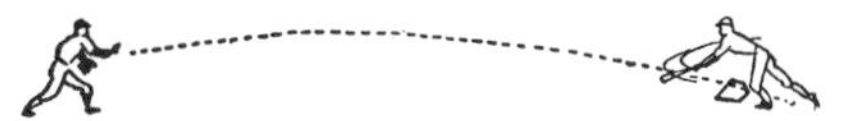

Deacon White's Eskimos finished second to Calgary in the 1910 Western Canada League. White is fourth from right. At far right is George "Wheezer" Dell, the first Eskimo to go on to the major leagues, pitching in the National League in 1912 and 1915-17. Courtesy of the Edmonton Archives EA 524-5.

guaranteed deal. As a result, the level of play was less appealing to the fans. The Medicine Hat and Regina clubs could not be sustained in 1910 and dropped out. Calgary beat out Edmonton in both halves of the schedule, but a Calgary demand that the entire seven-game series take place in that city led to their cancellation; President Eckstrom awarded the championship to Edmonton by default. The league shrank to six teams in 1911, then collapsed.

Somewhat disillusioned with the league after the raucous 1910 season, White left baseball at the end of the 1911 season, after managing both the baseball club and the Eskimos rugby team. With a partner, Howard Singleton, he opened Deacon's, a fancy nine-table pool hall and cigar store on Jasper Avenue, just east of First Street. One of its prominent features was a posting of the latest baseball and hockey scores, and the place quickly became a gathering spot for players and sports fans. White later renamed it the Eskimo Pool Hall.

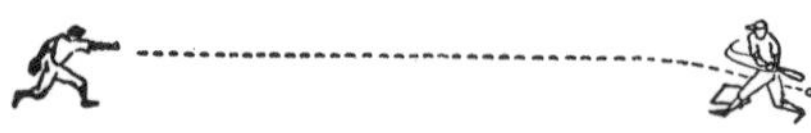

Amateur baseball thrived across the prairies in the early twentieth century. Edmonton had dozens of local leagues. This Edmonton City Dairy team was the city junior league champion in 1913. Courtesy of the Edmonton Archives EA 524-6.

Entrepreneur Frank Gray had been financially backing the Edmonton baseball club for three years but his worst experience, now without White, came in 1912. He renamed the Edmonton team the Gray Birds, and in 1912 the team played in a two-tiered professional league with Calgary and the small towns of Red Deer and Bassano. In his article "A Colony within a Colony," baseball scholar Bill Kirwin documents how Bassano, with its population of 1,400 (described by *The Sporting News* of the day as "the tiniest town in organized baseball"), embraced baseball as a boosterism tool, even naming its ball club the Boosters. The four teams struggled to finish the season, and Edmonton fans stayed away from the ballpark in droves.

Later that fall, it was revealed that the Edmonton franchise had lost $29,000 in its four seasons in the Western Canada League. Gray withdrew as a baseball sponsor, and he and other interests prevailed upon White to return to the challenge of professional baseball. White agreed on the condition that the city accept his proposal to subsidize Diamond Park's operating costs. There was some opposition, but the city came to baseball's aid and largely gave White what he wanted. In return, he began to promote the formation of an amateur athletic association for the city. It was White's sincere belief that such an organization would stimulate all sports and provide proper training and opportunities for boys and young men. With full civic support, the Edmonton Amateur Athletic Association was duly incorporated in February 1913 with initial capital of $250,000. White and Harold Deeton, along with aldermen Driscoll and Tipton, made up the management committee of the new joint-stock company. Having helped establish a secure foundation for the city's amateur sports pursuits, White turned his attention back to professional baseball.

The Edmonton of 1913 was a confident city. Augmented by its merger with Strathcona, the population had grown to 67,000 and the city and surrounding area continued to boom. Baseball seemed ready for a rebound. There was intense activity at the amateur level that summer, with twenty-two teams playing in Edmonton under the capable administration of Frank Drayton. Baseball was also enjoying unprecedented popular support throughout rural Alberta, much of it was brought about by boosterism. Sociologist Paul Voisey's study *Vulcan, Making of a Prairie Community*, while crediting much of the rural baseball boom to the large influx of Americans into the southern part of the province, notes that boosterism and local gambling were often the formative influences on teams in small centres.

Gambling and baseball was anathema to White. Off the diamond he was a well-known card player, often playing for extremely high stakes. Yet there was never a suggestion that he mixed his gambling on cards, to

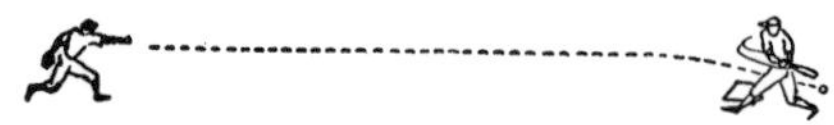

which he openly admitted, with his sports. When White returned to the ball club in 1913, he kept the name "Gray Birds," and Frank Gray served as league president. This version of the league included Edmonton, Calgary, Medicine Hat, Regina, Saskatoon, and Moose Jaw. Trouble arose between Saskatoon and Moose Jaw during the playoffs, leading to their cancellation after one game. Nonetheless, a report by the National Baseball Congress at the end of the 1913 season was highly optimistic about the Class-D league:

> Base Ball has established itself so firmly in Western Canada, north of our middle western states, that there is little doubt as to its permanent success.

White renamed the Gray Birds as the Eskimos in 1914, but as in previous years, he was unable to guide the team to a first place finish—despite having two players of major-league calibre. Dave Skeels, whose pitching with Moose Jaw and Regina in 1910 had earned him a one-game appearance with the Detroit Tigers that fall, played briefly as an outfielder with the Gray Birds in 1913. Skeels finished the season with Calgary and had a combined batting average of .307. In 1914, White enjoyed the starry services of outfielder Kenny Williams, who led the Eskimos with forty-two stolen bases and hit .315. He went on to play fourteen seasons in the majors and compiled a career .319 batting average. Although Edmonton suffered a serious land crash in 1913, Edmonton fan support reached new highs, and some 5,000 people crowded into Diamond Park for the 1914 home opener. But success was temporary.

War broke out in 1914 and the league was disbanded at the end of the season. Many of the players, including White, left the prairies for far-off places with the Canadian Expeditionary Forces. White joined the Canadian army at the end of 1915 and served with the 49th Canadian Battalion in France for two years, until demobilized in March 1919. He saw active duty and was involved in hand-to-hand combat on the German

front. When he turned forty, in December 1918, he was assigned to organize baseball games and conduct clinics among troops behind the lines. He also coached his army team to a Canadian Corps amateur championship.

4

Edmonton's "King of Sports"

THE EDMONTON OF 1919

WAS A SOBER PLACE.

The slaughter of young manhood in World War One signalled the frontier capital's entry into the realities of a new, international society. Of the 45,000 Albertans who served overseas, more than 6,000 did not return, casting a pall across the province. Dreams of a renewed boom after the war quickly faded as an economic recession took hold in Alberta. Wheat prices dropped and drought reduced incoming settlement; in hard-hit southern areas, these factors drove farmers from the land. Business was bruised by slow growth and was forced to return to boosterism and promotion to draw more people into the province. It would take the first half of the 1920s before Alberta began a healthy recovery, which would carry it up to the Great Depression in a relatively strong position.

Before the arrival of radio broadcasts, fans in many cities would "watch" the World Series on boards like this one, set up on the Edmonton Journal *building. On 13 October 1923, a big Sunday crowd gathered in front of the* Journal *as the Yankees beat the Giants 8-4 at the Polo Grounds. The Yankees went on to win the series four games to two. Courtesy of the Glenbow Archives, Calgary, Canada, ND 3-2130.*

Technology helped drive the eventual recovery, with everything from farm equipment to factories becoming much more productive. Automobiles and airplanes supplemented an overbuilt railway system as Canadians became more mobile. Radios, telephones, and movies began to expand popular culture, especially from south of the border. These technological advances were mirrored in—and indeed helped to augment—what became the "Golden Age of Sports" in the 1920s. Major-league baseball and hockey stories, along with professional golf and tennis reports, were regular features in Canadian daily newspapers. Camrose educator Stacy Lorenz documents the proliferation of professional sports coverage in

Baseball was popular with Edmonton women in the 1920s, before the advent of softball. This team represented the district of Namao in 1920. Courtesy of the Provincial Archives of Alberta A.3115.

western Canada newspapers, most particularly baseball. Lorenz notes that the early 1920s sports information network brought western Canadians into daily contact with baseball happenings in U.S. major-league cities, turning major-league ballplayers into "larger-than-life figures on both sides of the border."

In those years, no one American event, including presidential elections, so caught the attention of Canadian sports fans as did the World Series, brought live into western prairie cities by telegraphic reports. According to Lorenz,

> In the 1920s, it was not uncommon for sports enthusiasts to gather in front of newspaper offices during the World Series to receive regular updates of the game in progress. Large crowds watched games charted on illuminated model diamonds, while an announcer with a megaphone described the action from the telegraph wire.

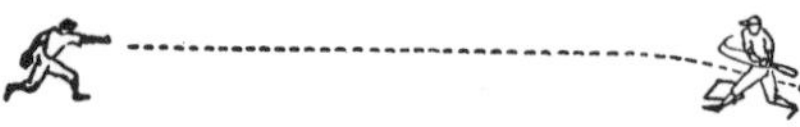

Reg Godson and his 1921 senior Edmonton All-Star team, provincial champions. Courtesy of the Edmonton Archives EA 524-10.

The *Edmonton Journal* was one western daily that brought the World Series to local fans in this manner. The proliferation of news about professional baseball simply stimulated the growing local popularity of the sport. The rise of community league, school, and church-sponsored sports organizations added impetus to baseball's dominance as Alberta's summer sport.

In March 1919, Deacon White was welcomed home from the war by more than one hundred local businessmen and sports enthusiasts who staged a huge banquet in his honour at the Hotel Macdonald. Cheers of "good old Deac" and "the king of sports" were heard throughout the room as Mayor Joe Clarke toasted the man of the hour. White was widely

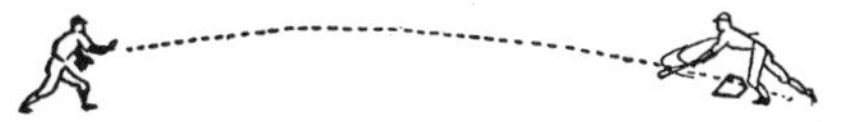

acknowledged as the founder of modern sport in Edmonton, and his fellow enthusiasts were glad to have him back. In his response, White said professional baseball would return to Edmonton, providing Calgary came in as well. Before the year was over, White was again running teams in hockey, football, and baseball.

Just before the baseball season began, White returned to Chicago for a brief visit with his parents, whom he had not seen since the war began. White took in his first big-league game in eighteen years with the opening-day crowd as the Cubs beat the Pittsburgh Pirates 5-1. He wired the *Bulletin* with his impressions of the game, noting that he had not learned any new opening day tricks because cold weather had kept festivities to a minimum at old Weeghman Park in Chicago. But White revealed his literary talent as he described how the Cub's great star Grover Cleveland Alexander, just returned from France, threw a ceremonial first pitch to mark the opening:

> He threw that first ball with the ease and grace of a master. You wouldn't have to be an expert on baseball to know that this man was on the top rung of his profession. Just as standing before the work of a Prexiteles or Raphael, the humblest layman has a feeling of awe and recognizes superior excellence without knowing why, so the most ignorant plebeian on baseball, in the presence of Alexander on the mound, realizes that he is in the presence of a master.

In Edmonton, however, there had only been time to organize a city league, bringing senior baseball back to Diamond Park. White's first post-war baseball club was made up largely of players returning from the war, so he called them the "Great War Veterans." They played with teams sponsored by the Knights of Columbus, the YMCA, and Dekan Grotto, a fraternal order whose fez-topped marching group appeared in the opening day parade. With Henry Roche on the organizing committee for the opening, Edmonton was reminded that Calgary had turned out an esti-

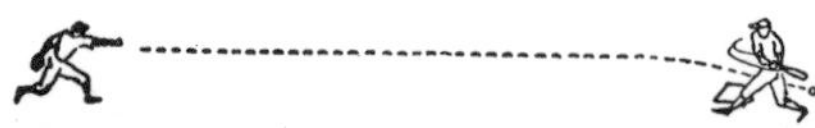

A view from the bleachers at old Diamond Park sometime before 1920. Courtesy of the Edmonton Archives EA 500-229.

mated 8,000 fans to start the season. Perhaps it was the end of the war, perhaps it was Deacon White's return, but that spring Edmonton mounted one of the greatest opening day extravaganzas ever seen, with the *Bulletin* writer as excited as any schoolboy that baseball was back in town:

> This afternoon starting a 1:45 o'clock on 102 street, the grandest, greatest, longest, noisiest, most spectacular parade ever held in western Canada will take place. In it there will be every species of public attraction ever brought into captivity or constructed out of the fertile imaginations of the accumulated ingenuity of all the showmen that ever told a lie. In it

> there will be bands, boys, bugles, banshees, automobile horns, white hordes and red-haired women; governmental dignitaries, civic authorities, the military and the ex-military; members of the Dekan Grotto in all the paraphernalia of their order, fezzes large and small, prophets grand and little and high priests and priestesses of all kinds; citizens and citizenettes, people large and small, fat and thin; young and old, important and unimportant, but mostly important, and many other things too numerous to mention.

Taking a bit of an edge off the celebrations, Jack Starky's offer to have his Crown Coal company supply gold and silver medals for the winning teams was turned down in favour of bronze, which the league felt was more in keeping with its amateur status and "the new principle of the conduct of amateur sports in Alberta."

Diamond Park's grandstand had been reserved for ladies and wounded war veterans, but the field was a mess. Wet weather, which delayed the opening game until the first weekend in June, persisted. While the grand parade went off without a hitch, only 1,405 fans turned out on a cold, windy day to watch Dekan Grotto beat the Knights of Columbus 4-0. With Con Bissett in left field and Jack Starky switching from the Knights to the Veterans, White's club won both halves of the split schedule. As they mowed down the opposition, they became known on the sport pages as "White's gang of assassins."

When White was nearing the end of his military service, he saw a young soldier by the name of Gordon "Duke" Keats playing baseball in an army camp. White did not think too much of his baseball skills, but his quick judgement of Keats' natural athletic ability proved that White had an eye for talent. In the fall of 1919, White prevailed on Duke Keats to come to Edmonton and join his Eskimo hockey team. Keats agreed and played centre Edmonton hockey teams for seven seasons. He also became a part-owner of Edmonton's entry into the new Western Canada Hockey League in 1920. A measure of the calibre of play in that league was shown

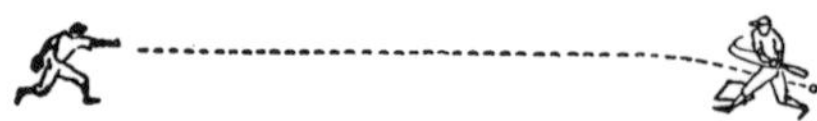

when Keats, who later admitted his best playing years were in Edmonton, went on to the NHL to play in Boston, Detroit, and Chicago. Keats became a hockey legend and was elected to the National Hockey League Hall of Fame in 1958.

Keats moved to the NHL when Frank and Lester Patrick sold the Western Canada Hockey League to National Hockey League clubs in 1926-27—a sale that also caused White to enter an Edmonton team into the newly formed Prairie League the same season. Keats later returned and revived both the WCHL and the Eskimo hockey team in 1931-32; he sold the team to sports promoter Henry Roche in 1934. Like many other hockey players, Keats kept his hand in baseball during his later Edmonton days, pitching and playing second base. He even took a turn umpiring with John Ducey at Renfrew Park in the 1930s. Years later, Ducey reminded Keats that he had been one of his boyhood sporting heroes:

> I remember very vividly, Duke, the first time I saw you. It was either 1919 or 1920 and the Edmonton hockey club was detraining at the CPR station where a parade had been organized to honour the Eskimo players. I believe you were at the head of the parade, sitting in the side car of a motorcycle... From 1922 through 1926, I was one of the privileged to enjoy and relish the great hockey entertainment you furnished the people of Edmonton during the Golden Years of the Western Canada Hockey League.

Although widely known at the time for his many promotional efforts in baseball, hockey, boxing, and basketball, Deacon White's admirers claimed his real strength lay as a coach. In 1919, the *Bulletin* said, "Deacon has a knack of holding players together and bringing the best out of them." John Ducey later echoed that trait, describing him as one who

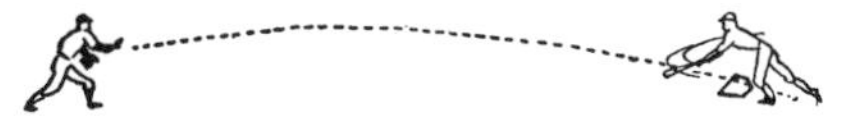

> had the art of getting the best out of his players, and although he never had an abundance of talent, his uncanny ability to diagnose plays and his knowledge of men, enabled him to get marvelous results.

Ducey's observations of White are echoed by Tony Cashman:

> He had a rare sort of honesty. He liked to win, and on at least two occasions, one baseball and one football, tried to use "ringers" to achieve victory. But when he was offered the position of head of physical education at the University of Alberta he declined. He said he played cards for money, and led a disorganized life and was therefore not likely to be a suitable instructor or a good example for university students.

White may have declined partly out of false modesty, because he was actually well organized and a good coach, although the card-playing part was true. In 1928, a reluctant City of Edmonton police officer laid an arrest warrant against White, who was found guilty of running a gambling house known as the Crocus Club. It was his only known transgression of the law, although in baseball he was not above the common practice of stretching the rules to bring in the odd professional "ringer" to stack a team's strength. Indeed, White *was* a man of principle, particularly where athletics were concerned. Cashman recounts a story about the time White boycotted an Edmonton baseball game:

> ...the only ball game Deacon White every missed. Along about 1921 a friend was surprised to see Deacon uptown while a ball game was raging below the hill at Diamond Park, between the Edmonton All-Stars and a semi-pro touring team from Regina. Deacon had refused to go because "Hap" Felsch, one of the figures in the "Black Sox" scandal, was playing for Regina.

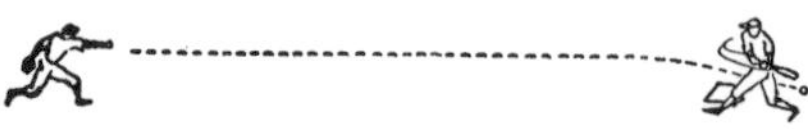

A Sunday afternoon crowd at Diamond Park after the new roof on the first-base bleachers was installed in 1920. Including standing room along third base, capacity increased from 4,200 to almost 7,000. Courtesy of the Edmonton Archives EA 524-7.

Organized baseball returns

In the same years that his football Eskimos enjoyed great successes and his hockey Eskimos won the Alberta Big Four league, White brought organized baseball back to Edmonton. As acting general manager, he organized and fielded the baseball Eskimos of the Class-B Western Canada League at Diamond Park in 1920 and 1921.

As tall as any of his players, White was a handsome man with lean, prominent features; when he occasionally joined the team in the dugout, he was smartly dressed in civilian clothes. Like Connie Mack of the Philadelphia Athletics, White usually wore a straw "boater" hat, white shirt, and tie. He demanded his players dress well on and off the field. "You may not be any good as a player, but you can at least try and look

This portrait of William F. "Deacon" White hangs in Edmonton's Sports Hall of Fame and in Red Deer's Alberta Sports Hall of Fame. White organized early "Eskimo" teams in baseball, football, and hockey, and is acknowledged as the founder of modern sport in Edmonton. Courtesy of the Provincial Archives of Alberta A.7286.

like one," White once told his charges. He ran all aspects of his clubs in a professional manner and was a stickler for gentlemanly comportment.

In the 1920s, gentlemanly comportment, as manifested by Deacon White, actually had little place on the playing field. Rugged competition was expected of all performers. Survival between the foul lines was the privilege of the fittest. In the same manner, to be an umpire and survive in that league, one had to be every inch as tough as the players. The young man listed as the league's official Alberta umpire in 1920 and 1921, John Edward Reardon, was one of that breed of hard-nosed characters. In the Calgary papers, he was first listed as Jack but in Edmonton, he was always known by his nickname, Beans.

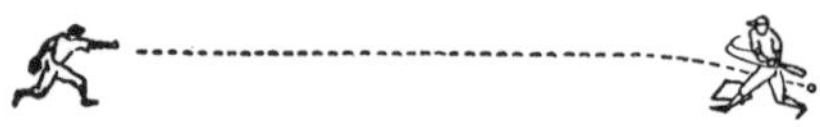

Former World War One flying ace "Wop" May dropped a ceremonial opening-day pitch on Diamond Park from his JN4 biplane. Usually identified as taking place in 1919, newspaper accounts indicate this event occurred in 1920. In any case, it was staged by promoter Deacon White. Courtesy of the Edmonton Archives EA 247-166.

When Calgary and Edmonton joined the Western Canada League at the start of its second season in 1920, its classification had been raised from Class C to Class B. The other clubs came from Regina, Winnipeg, Moose Jaw, and Saskatoon. The Eskimos were scheduled to play sixty-seven home games and sixty road games. Post-war Edmonton was excited about the return of organized baseball, and White responded with a gala opening. He arranged what was billed as a "million dollar parade of automobiles" along Jasper Avenue and down to Diamond Park. White also issued an invitation for every youngster with a bicycle in Edmonton to join the parade. Then he announced that Edmonton's favourite pilot, World War One flying ace Wop May, might make his first spring flight over the park just as the ball game started.

Deacon White (left) and his Edmonton Eskimos brought professional baseball back to Diamond Park in 1920. Construction of the Edmonton Journal *building is seen on the skyline. Courtesy of the Edmonton Archives 524-8.*

That spring the weather cooperated, and some 4,200 cheering fans squeezed into Diamond Park as Mayor Joe Clarke threw out the ceremonial first pitch. Then Wop May swooped over the field in his biplane and dropped another ceremonial baseball on the diamond. Excitement among the fans reached a fever pitch, but it was short lived. They left the park subdued as their new Eskimos were thrashed 11-4 by the Calgary Bronks. After losing the next two games to Calgary, White was reported to be "bringing in reinforcements" for his faltering club. Despite his efforts, the Eskimos could not catch Calgary.

Those 1920 professional Eskimos, who did not distinguish themselves, included player-manager Pete Standridge, a former Calgary pitcher who, in 1911 and 1915, had appeared in thirty-one National League games; Gus Gleichman; and a few local boys, including Cy Forsythe, Grover Brant, and Jack Starky. Starky was a legendary Edmonton athlete who later

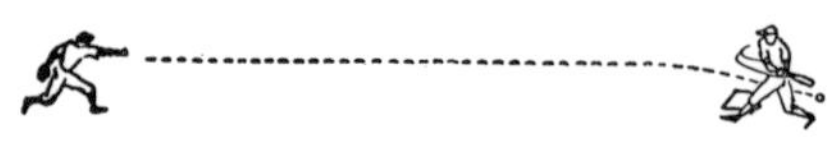

became a champion amateur golfer. He made his fortune in the Alberta coal industry. (Years later, Starky claimed he had once saved umpire Beans Reardon from a life-threatening beating from Eskimo team-mate Hunky Shaw: Shaw was upset over a decision and tried to attack Reardon under the Diamond Park stands between two games of a double-header.)

Regina and Calgary each won a split-season pennant and played for the league championship, with Calgary taking the seven-game series. The 1920 Bronks were led by Nelson "Chicken" Hawkes, who batted a league-leading .357 average, and Walter "Cuckoo" Christensen, who batted .345. Hawkes joined the New York Yankees for the balance of their 1921 season and returned to the majors in 1925 to play a single season with the Philadelphia Phillies. Christensen was with Cincinnati briefly in 1925 and appeared in 114 games in 1926.

White's Eskimos had little success that first season. They placed last in both halves of the one hundred-game schedule and only won thirty-seven games overall. They were also last in batting at a lowly .238, not much above White's own batting average during his playing years. Despite their struggles, Edmonton baseball was well supported in 1920, with the league reporting satisfactory financial results, but money troubles began to surface in 1921. White was determined to take a serious run at the league championship the second year. He had good relations with several major-league teams, which helped him attract a few talented young ball players who had already caught the interest of some big-league clubs. Ducey later said White was known as "a man of his word, who never had the need of a written contract in his dealings with major-league teams." White put first baseman Gus Gleichman in charge of the 1921 Eskimos and ordered him to come back from a two-week training camp in Crockett, California with a winning ball club.

5

Manush, Herman, and Reardon

FROM HIS HOME JUST ACROSS FROM GRANDIN SCHOOL, IT WAS AN EASY WALK FOR JOHN DUCEY TO THE BALL YARD DOWN ON THE ROSS FLATS. A skinny twelve-year-old who shagged balls down at Diamond Park, Ducey prevailed on Deacon White to let him do something of substance at the ball park in 1921. White was impressed with the youngster's determination and his love of baseball, and always had time to give him a few words of encouragement. The Eskimo general manager eventually agreed to let Ducey be batboy for the visiting clubs in 1921, then again in 1922. It was heady stuff for a kid who lived for baseball. He now had his own set of live heroes, and rubbing shoulders with them daily made a lasting impression on him. It was an experience

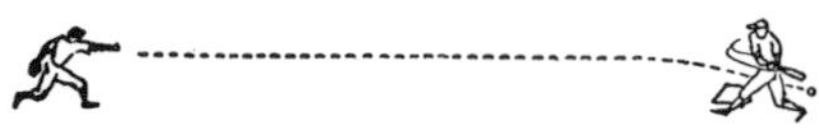

The 1921 Edmonton Eskimos at spring training in Crockett, California. Future Hall of Famer Heinie Manush stands fourth from left; seventeen-year-old "Lefty" Herman is sixth from left. Fred Snodgrass, the former New York Giants outfielder, stands to Herman's left. Courtesy of the Edmonton Archives 524-11.

most boys of his day could only dream about, a dream he lived for the better part of two wonderful summers. He was mingling with big, tough men who played baseball for fun *and* money. Despite the rampant gambling that pervaded major-league baseball and the revelation of the 1919 Chicago White Sox scandal in March 1920, every young baseball fan followed his big-league heroes in the sports pages and baseball magazines. Like many boys growing up in the 1920s, Ducey's favourite team soon became the New York Yankees. Led by the charismatic Babe Ruth, who had just been traded from the Red Sox to the Yankees in 1920 and responded with a record fifty-four home runs, the Yankees were just beginning to establish themselves as the big-league dynasty of the decade.

In April 1921, just before training camp was to open, manager Gus Gleichman injured his leg in an automobile accident. (Gleichman would lose his life in a car crash in the 1930s.) He was helped out of a jam by former major-leaguer Fred Snodgrass, to whom he was related by marriage. Snodgrass, a relatively good outfielder, had played for John McGraw's New York Giants from 1908 to 1915. He is forever remembered in baseball lore for dropping a third-out fly ball in the tenth inning of the deciding game of the 1912 World Series against Boston. That error cost the Giants the Series. Despite this ignominy, by 1921 Snodgrass had become a successful major-league scout. That spring, he was enthusiastic about two young players he had brought to Crockett for a tryout with the Edmonton club. Snodgrass, highly pleased with them after the first workout, described them cryptically for the *Bulletin*:

> ...big Herman at first; wonderful youngster; big future, hits long and hard; Manush, outfielder. Sick but working out; big powerful fellow, hits long and hard.

A pair of slugging Eskimos

Snodgrass certainly made no error in directing Floyd Caves "Lefty" Herman and Henry Emmett "Heinie" Manush, both first basemen, to the Edmonton camp that spring. When camp wrapped up, Gleichman picked the younger Herman as his choice for first base. Snodgrass insisted that the Eskimo manager take Manush to Edmonton as well, arguing that Manush was good enough to play the outfield if Herman won the first-base job.

The Snodgrass logic prevailed, and although Manush was injured much of that year, playing in only eighty-seven games, he still managed to hit a respectable .321 and lead the league with nine home runs. The seventeen-year-old Herman, who was moved to right field when Gleichman returned to the lineup, hit .330. Many years later, Ducey would tell a story about Herman's introduction to Edmonton baseball:

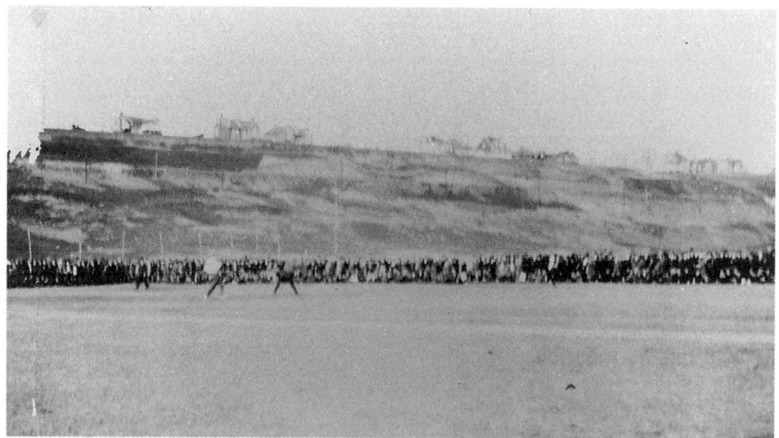

A good crowd gathers for an amateur game on the west side of the Victoria Golf Links in 1921. It was long a popular location for amateur baseball action and informal "pick-up" games. Courtesy of the Edmonton Archives EA 524-9.

Herman was installed in a boarding house on 113th Street and 99th Avenue. One afternoon soon after his arrival, he was taking a stroll and saw a baseball work-out in the river valley on the old cricket pitch. He walked down and stretched out in the grass to watch the fun.

Duke Keats, who had lined up the scrub game, needed another player and he asked the young kid if he wanted to play. The kid admitted that he "played some," so Duke told him he could play in the outfield "so that you won't get hurt." When it came time for the young fellow to come to bat, he smashed a pitch into the North Saskatchewan River. Duke, sensing undiscovered raw talent, rushed over and asked the kid for his name. Then "Babe," who went by the nickname of "Lefty" in those days, told him who he was and why he was in Edmonton.

It did not take long for Herman to become well known in Edmonton. Both he and Manush had inauspicious starts in Calgary, each hitting two singles in eight times at bat, as Edmonton split the opening doubleheader in Calgary. When the teams got to Edmonton the next day, young Herman announced his arrival in a big way. In front of 4,500 delighted fans, he belted his first professional home run over Diamond Park's right-field fence. He was the offensive star as the home team revenged the thrashing they had taken in the opening home game of the previous year, beating their Calgary rivals 9–0. In his first game in Edmonton, Herman went three for four and sparkled defensively by running into the crowd, which had spilled over onto the playing field, to make several catches. That day, Heinie Manush was limited to a single in four at-bats. Motion pictures of the opening game, and of the "monster" parade that preceded it, were taken by McDermid's Engraving and played the following day at the Pantages Theatre.

In the two summers he worked as a batboy at Diamond Park, young Ducey grew to worship Deacon White. Watching and being around White, he learned his early lessons about professional baseball conduct. Years later, Ducey modelled his own approach to baseball administration on the managerial integrity exemplified by Deacon White. The boy also struck up passing friendships with umpire Reardon and the youthful outfielder "Lefty" Herman in 1921. Despite the addition of the slugging pair of Herman and Manush, White's Eskimos only finished fifth in the first half of the season. Notoriously weak at second base and shortstop, they came a disappointing last in the second half of what had by then become

a four-team league. Lack of fan support caused the Regina and Moose Jaw clubs to withdraw after the first half of the season. Nonetheless, there were lots of hits and plenty of runs to entertain the fans. In the final five games of the season against Calgary, Edmonton won the first and last games 9-1 and 11-0, losing the middle three, 8-4, 6-5, and 12-7.

In the middle game of that series, Heinie Manush received a last, ignominious footnote in the *Bulletin* as an Edmonton Eskimo, thanks to umpire Beans Reardon:

> Although lacking in real fighting spirit, the game was an exceptionally good one and was enlivened considerably when Umps Reardon chased Manush from the park for throwing his bat against the grandstand after he had fanned in the sixth inning. It was lucky for Manush that the bat missed the batboy by inches.

Calgary was so happy with manager Joe Devine that he was presented with a gold watch when league play ended. He responded by coaching his club on to beat Winnipeg in the finals, winning the championship for the second year in a row. Devine's Bronks were the baseball powerhouse in Alberta during those years. When the season ended with the Eskimos in Calgary, Herman and Manush kept going. They drove through the Crowsnest Pass on their way back to California, stopping occasionally to play exhibition baseball for travelling money. The two slugging young outfielders, who had done their best for the Edmonton Eskimos, were soon on the road to baseball glory. Deacon White sold both of them to the Detroit Tigers after the 1921 season, and within a few years, they began long and illustrious careers as major-league stars.

While Herman and Manush were the most prominent, they were not the only Western Canada League players of that era to reach the majors (see appendix two). In addition to Art Haugher, who joined them in the 1921 Eskimo outfield, at least twenty others eventually played in the big leagues, three of them for several seasons. Oscar Melillo, the Winnipeg

Maroons' centre fielder in 1920 and 1921, hit .291 both years and joined the St. Louis Browns in 1926. He played with them for almost ten seasons before being traded to the Boston Red Sox, where he closed out his career in 1937 with a major-league batting average of .260. Weighing only 150 pounds on a 5'10" frame, he was nicknamed "Spinach," which he ate to counteract Bright's disease. Mark Koenig, who hit only .202 for Moose Jaw in 1921, compiled a .279 twelve-year career average after spending his first five major-league seasons with the powerhouse New York Yankees from 1925 to 1930. He was the Yankees' starting shortstop in the World Series of 1926, 1927, and 1928. Tony Kaufman, a right-handed pitcher for Winnipeg in 1920 and 1921, joined the Chicago Cubs at the end of the 1921 season and played for them for five years. His ten-year won-lost record in the majors was sixty-four and sixty-two.

Nick Dumovich, Bernie deViveiros, and Milt Steengrafe were among several who went on to shorter big-league careers. Dumovich pitched for Edmonton in 1920 and appeared in twenty-eight games for the 1923 Chicago Cubs. deViveiros played for Calgary in 1921. He was on the rosters of the Chicago White Sox in 1924 and the Detroit Tigers in 1927, but appeared in only twenty-five games. Milt Steengrafe pitched for Calgary in 1920 and 1922; he pitched a total of thirty-two innings for the Chicago White Sox in 1924 and 1926.

Floyd Caves "Babe" Herman played twelve years in the National League, six of them with the Brooklyn Dodgers. He finished his career by playing six very good seasons with Hollywood of the Pacific Coast League. Originally celebrated as a bit of a buffoon in baseball lore, his playing record shows him to have been one of baseball's most accomplished performers. The hopes of Brooklyn Dodger fans rose on his hitting and ebbed on his fielding. He compiled a respectable lifetime batting average of .324, and had 399 doubles and 181 career home runs. Ken Smith, former public relations director of the Baseball Hall of Fame, was one of several who later debunked the reputation of Herman as simply a clown. "The stories about 'Babe' and the rest of his Dodger team-mates were

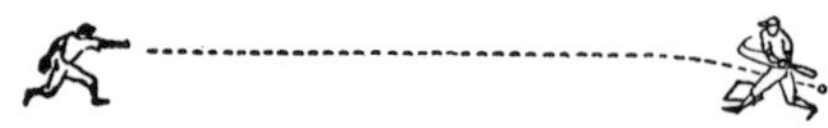

exaggerated," Smith told John Ducey. Herman never made it to the Baseball Hall of Fame, largely because a question mark hung over his defensive abilities. However they loved him in Brooklyn, and he was later enshrined as a star in the Dodgers Hall of Fame.

Herman had been born in Buffalo, New York five years before Ducey. When Herman joined the Brooklyn Dodgers in 1926, Ducey followed his major-league career with a passion. The two crossed baseball paths occasionally in the 1930s and then met again in Hollywood, California in 1939. They went on to become life-long friends and regular correspondents. Ducey later got Herman to partly confirm a local legend that the nickname "Babe" had first been hung on him by "some leather-lunged lady fan one afternoon at Diamond Park in 1921." According to Herman, the woman took to calling him "Babe" after Babe Herman, a popular champion flyweight prizefighter of the day. When the youthful Herman showed up at spring training with the Detroit Tigers in 1922, it was formalized by Dan Howley, one of Ty Cobb's coaches, who asked Herman if he had a nickname. The story was recounted in his biography, *Brooklyn's Babe*, by Tot Holmes:

> "What's your nickname kid?"
>
> "They called me 'Lefty' at home."
>
> "No, that won't do. Didn't they call you Tiny or Babe or something?"
>
> "There was a woman fan up in Canada who called me 'Babe' now and then."
>
> "Okay, from now on you're my Babe," said Howley.

It was most fortunate for Herman that it happened, because umpire Beans Reardon continued to call the gangly Herman "turkey neck" whenever the two met again in the National League. It was a nickname that might have stuck had he not been tagged earlier with "Babe." Herman's link to Edmonton was renewed again in 1953, when Ducey signed Herman's son

Don to play for the Edmonton Eskimos of the Western International League.

Henry Emmett "Heinie" Manush was without a doubt the most noteworthy graduate of the Diamond Park ballplayers. Until 1995, he remained the only former Edmonton player to be inducted into the Baseball Hall of Fame at Cooperstown, New York. Acknowledged as one of the great sluggers of major-league baseball, he was an accomplished outfielder. He hit .334 in his rookie year with the Detroit Tigers in 1923, under then-manager Ty Cobb. His .330 batting average over a seventeen-year career, along with 2,524 base hits and excellent fielding, got the Alabama-born Manush elected to the Hall of Fame in 1964.

John Edward "Beans" Reardon

Another Diamond Park friendship young Ducey struck up in that magical summer of 1921 would lead to a major turning point in his life. As the professional league opened for its second season, Beans Reardon was back in western Canada. Born in 1897 in Taunton, Massachusetts (near Boston), Reardon spent most of his boyhood in California. It was the proximity of his birthplace to Boston that occasioned someone early in his career to tag him with the nickname Beans. Just as Deacon White expected professional comportment in every aspect of the game of baseball, Reardon demanded respect on the diamond. If White represented the gentlemanly side of baseball, Reardon, equally professional, mirrored its tough, authoritarian side.

Reardon needed that toughness to survive in the rugged Western Canada League of 1920-21. Here Beans, whose heaviest umpiring weight didn't top 140 pounds in those days, recounts his early experience in Western Canada in a 1932 interview in *The Sporting News*:

> I also had to fight my way out of several situations when I was in the Western Canada league, where they had some tough players who

regarded all arbiters as doormats. Why up in that league, they had new arbiters almost every day.

When I signed with them, they guaranteed me my return carfare only in case I lasted through the season. When I asked why that clause was inserted, the president told me umpires had been running out on him so fast it was breaking the league treasury to pay their transportation home after a few day's service.

Reardon was only twenty-two when he got his first professional umpiring job in 1920, thanks to the recommendation of baseball friends in Los Angeles who had previously played in Canada. He was directed by league president Frank Miley to report to the owner of the Calgary club, Dr. J.H. Birch. When Birch first laid eyes on him he was astonished both at his age and his size:

"You can't be Reardon, the professional umpire. You're nothing but a schoolboy."

"That's who I am," said Reardon, "and I can umpire, doctor, don't worry about that."

In Larry Gerlach's book *The Men In Blue*, Reardon recalled how he firmly established himself with the players:

The night before my first game I went to see Joe Devine, the manager of Calgary, the home club, at his hotel. Devine was lying on the bed, talking to this guy. I said "Which one is Devine?" He said, "I'm Devine." So I said, "Mr. Devine, my name is Reardon. I'm going to be the umpire tomorrow and I don't want any arguments from anybody. Do you understand?" He didn't say anything, just looked at me. I could hear them laughing as I walked out. Hell, I was just a punk kid who weighed about 135 pounds.

> Nobody gave me any instructions. I just went out there and umpired. Hell, I was supposed to be a professional umpire, so they figured I knew how to umpire. So I went out there and ran the game.

It was an attitude he stuck with throughout his career.

Reardon worked the opening games in Calgary and in Edmonton in both 1920 and 1921, spending the full two seasons umpiring in the Alberta cities. His colourful style made him popular with both fans and sportswriters. He was also controversial. Once, when Reardon ruled a Calgary hit down the right-field foul line a fair ball—which proved to be the game-winning hit—angry Edmonton fans threatened to prevent him from leaving Diamond Park after the game:

> I caught all kinds of hell from both teams and the fans. After the game a crowd started gathering around the clubhouse. A policeman came in and said he'd show me how to sneak out of the park. I said, "I didn't sneak in and I won't sneak out."

He, in turn, stood up to them, ready to fight his way out if needed. While some fans jeered at him all the way up McDougall Hill and back to his hotel, no one dared to take him on. He was far tougher than two of his 1910-1912 Edmonton predecessors, according to George Macintosh of the *Journal*:

> Beans had his troubles with ball players here, but never had the experience of two other gentlemen in blue named Wheeler and Longnecker, both of whom, old-timers will remember, came charging up the McDougall steps with an irate mob at their heels, and pop bottles floating through the air perilously close to the umpirical ears.

Reardon's inner strength and absolute control of the diamond sustained him through his major-league career. He demanded hustle and respect

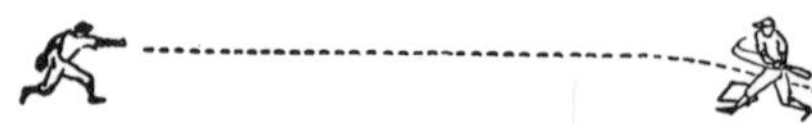

from the ballplayers. These traits were not lost on Ducey, the young visitors' batboy during that season of 1921.

Reardon moved up to the Pacific Coast League in 1922 where he had a couple of well-publicized fist-fights on the playing field. Nevertheless, he soon earned the respect of all sides. In Los Angeles, he got to know veteran umpire Hank O'Day, who wintered there during the latter part of his twenty-nine-year career in the National League. (O'Day was also a first cousin of Ducey's mother, Mary Normile, although this would have meant little to either man at the time.) Reardon and O'Day shared a passion for horse-racing and became good friends, with the latter passing his knowledge of umpiring on to Reardon. Reardon described O'Day in *The Men In Blue*:

> He was big and tough; guys didn't fool around with him. He told me not to try to imitate anybody. "Never mind what anybody tells you; you just go in there and umpire like you've been umpiring all the time." He told me that players would give a young umpire coming into the big leagues all the roughness he could put up with, but he said, "You're the boss out there. Don't let them tell you anything."
>
> And he told me, "Hustle all the time. Be on the top of every play, so you're in position to make the decision." He liked my work, so he recommended me to the National League. I was very fortunate to be able to learn from a great umpire like Hank O'Day. He was the best. At least he had the greatest influence on me.

Reardon went on to enjoy a sterling twenty-four-year career as a National League umpire and always prided himself on being his own man. He rejected the "organization men" of baseball and was, in the end, shunned by them. Ducey felt Reardon's record showed he had umpiring credentials equal to some of his peers who made it to the Baseball Hall of Fame. He later mounted a lobby to get Cooperstown officials to recognize Reardon in the "veterans" category, but with no success. He believed that

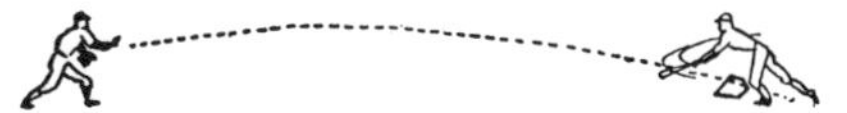

Reardon was "shut out of the Hall" because of his independent attitude toward club owners and league officials after his umpiring career had ended. Reardon, who quit baseball at the age of fifty-one to attend to his lucrative beer distribution business, pretended outwardly that it did not bother him. "I was in a position to tell everyone in baseball to go to hell," he later said.

And, although he was never "immortalized" in the Baseball Hall of Fame, perhaps Reardon did get the last laugh. While a handful of his umpiring peers got into the Hall, it is Reardon's image that is preserved forever in baseball art. He was the home plate umpire in Norman Rockwell's 1949 *Saturday Evening Post* cover of three umpires deciding whether to call off a game on account of rain. "Calling a game because of rain was the toughest call an umpire could make," Ducey reminisced years later, "and it was sweet justice that Beans Reardon got immortal recognition over that call, courtesy of Mr. Norman Rockwell." The original painting hangs in the Cooperstown baseball museum, and souvenir reproductions of it can be had in its gift shop.

On his initial visit to the Cooperstown baseball "shrine" in 1968, John Ducey's face visibly lit up with pride when he sought out and caught his first glimpse of the Heinie Manush plaque in the Hall of Fame. It had been forty-seven years since that unforgettable Edmonton summer, and the memories of Manush, Herman, Reardon, and White at Diamond Park came flooding back. At Cooperstown that day, John Ducey shed a joyful tear in front of the bronze image of Heinie Manush, ex-Edmonton Eskimo.

White tries again

Following the struggles with the Western Canada Baseball League in 1921, Deacon White led the organization of a new league alignment in 1922. This was the Class-B Western International League. With White as league president, it was made up of Edmonton, Calgary, Vancouver, and

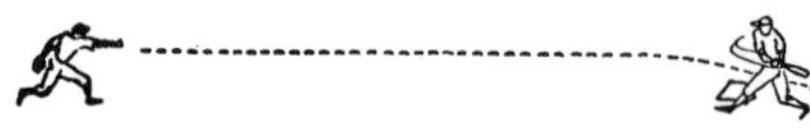

Tacoma. White took his Eskimos to Los Angeles for spring training, while Calgary went to Sacramento. Manager Gus Gleichman reported that the thirty men he had in camp were "a snappy looking bunch."

In Edmonton, on the afternoon of 16 May 1922, the baseball flag was flying at the top of the flagpole of the Metropolitan theatre on Jasper Avenue. This was the signal for fans that the game was definitely on and that they could flock to Joe Driscoll's hardware store between the hours of noon and four o'clock to buy their advance tickets, thus avoiding the lineup at the ball park. When there was no game, the flag was lowered.

It was opening day of the 1922 season, and young Ducey was at the ball park well before the 5:45 p.m. start, eagerly moving through his pre-game routine as batboy for the visiting team from Tacoma. It was his second year "in professional ball," and he was looking forward to another exciting season. The Tacoma team lost that opening game to the Eskimos 6-4, but it mattered little to him at the time.

Ironically, a few weeks later, the Tacoma club brought the season to an early end. The distant coastal city could not kindle fan interest for such a league and withdrew on 18 June. White saw the league could not continue with only three teams and reluctantly moved to cancel it, thus ending professional baseball in Edmonton for the next thirty years.

In 1922, White was preoccupied with the success of his football club. He had managed Edmonton football teams before the war, but his most memorable efforts were in 1921 and 1922 when his powerful Edmonton Eskimos won the Western Canada football championship and went east as the first western team to challenge for the Grey Cup. There they acquitted themselves well but lost the first two national Grey Cup games ever played. They were beaten by the Toronto Argonauts 23-0 in 1921 as

Lionel Conacher plunged for two touchdowns, and lost to Queen's the next year, 13-1. Just the same, as he had already done with the sports of baseball and hockey, White put Edmonton on the Canadian football map as a team to be reckoned with.

White also made a major contribution to Edmonton's basketball history. Impressed by the ability of the Edmonton Grads basketball team, coached by Percy Page, White put up the money to bring the claimants to the world women's championship, the Cleveland Favorite-Knits, to Edmonton in 1923 to play the Grads. It was a risky financial gamble, but ever the promoter, White turned it into a success. The Edmonton team won, gaining international recognition and beginning a brilliant chapter in Edmonton's basketball history. Years later, Percy Page would continue to credit the support of Deacon White in making the Edmonton Grads an international basketball success:

> The "Deacon" immediately saw the possibilities of big time basketball....It was the first time that a world's championship contest in any line of sport had been played in Edmonton and the response on the part of the citizenry was 'manna from Heaven,' to the 'Deacon' and the girls. After all expenses had been paid, there was a profit of around $2,800 to be divided on a 50–50 basis. History has it that the "Deacon's" share lasted him less than two weeks.

The "Busher King"

In 1924, White staged the "Busher King" tournament at Diamond Park. As a promotional effort to create fan interest, he named a committee of forty baseball fans who would select the "Busher King" at the end of a four-team tournament, involving the Edmonton Outlaws and teams from Tofield, Mirror, and Lamont. Among those whom White chose for the committee were the *Journal*'s George Mackintosh and Ken McConnell, hotelier Bob McDonald, Henry Roche, Joe Driscoll, Cap Speissmann,

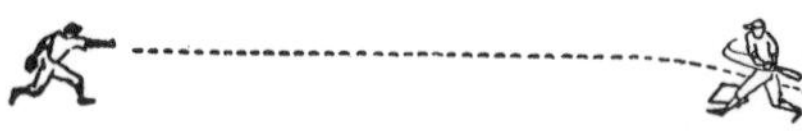

Reg Godson (back left) and his 1924 Red Sox, "Cap" Speissmann kneeling at left. Courtesy of the Edmonton Archives EA 524-12.

Frank Hughes, Duke Keats, Walter Campbell, and Henry Boulanger. Edmonton mayor Kenneth Blatchford was also a member, and among the prizes was a special gold medal that he donated on behalf of the city. White also arranged for scouts from the Detroit Tigers and the Brooklyn Dodgers to attend the tournament.

Edmonton was, of course, favoured to win. Its club featured former Eskimo professionals Jack Starky at third base, Chuck Henderson at first base, and Jim Enright in left field. On the mound for Edmonton were Norman Dodge and Lefty Long, a noted pitcher from Viking, Alberta. With White pulling all the promotional strings, the tourney got off to a glittering start on the evening of 31 July. Mayor Blatchford threw the ceremonial pitch to the premier of Alberta, the Hon. Herbert Greenfield, while the province's Lieutenant Governor, R.G. Brett, was catching behind

Deacon White with his Edmonton Outlaws, favoured to win the "Busher King" tournament of 1924. Local stars on the team included Chuck Henderson, Jim Enright, Norman Dodge, and Jack Starky. Courtesy of the Edmonton Archives EA 524-13.

the plate. Sadly, fans got to see only two innings of baseball between Edmonton and Tofield. At the end of the second, they were driven out of the park by a violent rainstorm that forced umpire Frank Drayton to cancel the game.

Things dried out a bit the next day and that evening Norman Dodge pitched a four-hitter, shutting out Tofield 7-0. George Mackintosh described the hometown club as "breezing through the game like big leaguers." However, when the 4 August civic holiday was over on Monday, "the miracle team" from Mirror had swept the tournament. The CNR-sponsored club won both games of a double-header behind the strong pitching of Cliff "Tiny" Turner. Turner was a tall, strapping young man whom Deacon White had brought down from Peace River in 1921 for an unsuccessful

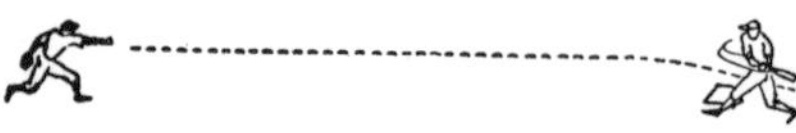

For his performance at the "Busher King" tournament, Cliff Turner (pictured here in 1923) was signed by the Detroit Tigers. But the Peace River pitcher died in Edmonton in 1925 of typhoid fever shortly after a spectacular rookie season at Paris, Texas. Courtesy of the Edmonton Archives EA 524-15.

tryout with the Eskimos. Turner was born in 1902 at Chilliwack, B.C.; soon after, his family moved to Calgary. His brother Charlie played baseball there, and another brother, Bill, played in Washington state. It was Cliff, however, then living in Peace River, who looked as if he would become the family baseball star.

By 1923, Cliff Turner was pitching for Mountain Park, a team on the Alberta Coal Branch. In 1924, bigger and stronger, he struck out sixteen batters in the first game of the "Busher King" tournament, as Mirror shut out Lamont 3-0. That evening, home favourite Norman Dodge was breezing along with a 4-0 lead over Mirror after five innings, and it looked as if Edmonton would take the Blatchford medal and the cash. But Turner came on in relief in the sixth and shut Edmonton out the rest of

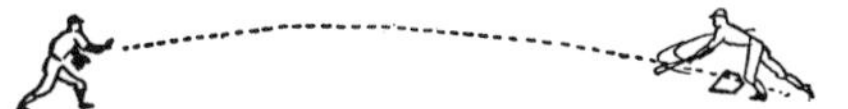

the way, striking out six. His team-mates began chipping away at the Edmonton lead with some timely clutch-hitting. A couple of Edmonton errors and two bad throws to first base by Jack Starky allowed the visitors to come roaring back to upset the home team 7-4.

"This Turner has a whole lot more pitching artistry than he needs to play in the bushes," wrote George Mackintosh as the committee crowned "Tiny" Turner "the King of the Bushers." Eddie Herr, the Detroit Tigers' top scout, enticed to cover the series by Deacon White, signed Turner to a professional contract then and there. He looked good at Detroit's 1925 spring training camp and was assigned to the Tigers' Class-C club in Paris, Texas to get some seasoning. He appeared in twenty-eight games and recorded sixteen wins and eight losses. Hopes were high that he would eventually reach the big leagues. But the hot Texas climate did not agree with him. Feeling ill, he quit before the end of the season and went home to recover in the fresh air of Mountain Park. His condition worsened. On 29 September, he was taken to Edmonton, where he was diagnosed with typhoid fever; he died the next day in the Misericordia Hospital. He was twenty-three years old.

After the 1924 tournament, Deacon White was never able to repeat his promotional successes of earlier years. He began to lose money endeavouring to field and promote new hockey and football teams. In 1932, his sports offerings battered by the Depression, his money all but gone, and his eyesight beginning to fail, White said goodbye to his many friends in Edmonton, boarded a train, and went home to live with his elderly mother near Chicago. Little more was heard of him in Edmonton until late in 1939.

> Throughout western Canada the news of the death of Deacon White will bring a touch of sadness today, but here in Edmonton his passing strikes much deeper. In a way you can say that it was the Deacon who launched this city into the big time—the man who showed what could be done with the proper organization and coaching.

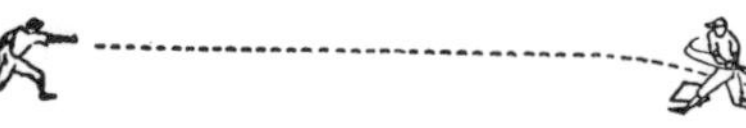

The glum-looking White (centre), who was prone to gambling later in his career, lost a lot of money when the CNR team from Mirror, Alberta upset the promoter's Outlaws, largely on the pitching of Cliff "Tiny" Turner, the player standing at left. Courtesy of the Edmonton Archives EA 524-14.

So wrote *Bulletin* columnist Jack Kelly on 7 November, after news of White's death in Chicago reached Edmonton. Sports fans were shocked. Kelly went on to predict that

> As long as the name "Eskimo" is associated with Edmonton sport, Deacon White will be remembered, for he was the one that seized on the name as one that typified this northern city.

History would prove Kelly wrong on that count. White himself was all but forgotten by a new generation of Edmonton sports fans in the 1950s, when the Eskimo name was again carried by both the city's football and baseball teams. It would be twenty-five years after his death before White's

associates and admirers, led by John Ducey, would gain some manner of lasting recognition for "the Deacon" in Edmonton's sporting history.

6

From player to umpire

ON A SUNNY SUNDAY AFTERNOON AT THE END OF AUGUST 1994, THE LATE RILEY MULLEN SAT IN A BOX SEAT BEHIND HOME PLATE IN JOHN DUCEY PARK. He was watching the last game that would ever be played in the sixty-first season of what had once been Renfrew Park, renamed for Ducey after his death in 1983. Mullen reached back some seventy-five years to reminisce about his early school days with John Ducey:

> By the time he was twelve, John had organized his first four-team league among the altar boys at St. Joseph's. Then he got us going against other church teams. After that, he was organizing baseball every spring for most of the rest of his life.

John Ducey began to play baseball with many of his fifth-grade classmates at Grandin School in 1919. Ducey is at the fourth desk in the second row from the right. Life-long friend and baseball colleague Riley Mullen sits two seats behind him. Courtesy of the Edmonton Archives EA 524-17.

Mullen began school with Ducey in the fall of 1914, in a small wooden schoolhouse called the Tenth Street School. A year later, the school was moved into a new, three-storey brick building. At the urging of its first principal, Mother Alice Mohoney, the school board agreed to name it after Bishop Grandin. Still in use today, Grandin School offered a full city block of playground space.

Baseball had been played at the old Tenth Street School as far back as 1907. Mullen, Ducey, and several others took up the game as soon as they were big enough to throw a baseball ninety feet. In the summer of 1919, they moved beyond the school confines to play against other school and church teams. Among these were the "South Side" boys on the Holy Trinity team, led by Stan Moher, who came to Edmonton with his family

Ducey at age ten. His mother made sure he was always well dressed, a trait that stuck with him for life. Courtesy of the Edmonton Archives EA 524-18.

in 1912. Joe Malone, who later gave up any thought of baseball for the priesthood, was on Moher's team. More than twenty teams played in three levels of church leagues by 1919; by 1921, there were more than forty such teams. Along with the Catholic churches, teams came from United, Baptist, Presbyterian, and other congregations and from several of the city's schools, with the entire operation under the administration of the YMCA.

Ducey, slight and shorter than most of his early team-mates, had been encouraged by his father's great love of baseball. But the spark that kindled his zealous, life-long love of the game was the family link to National League umpire Hank O'Day. The distant relative was young Ducey's own tie to professional baseball, although he would never meet O'Day, who

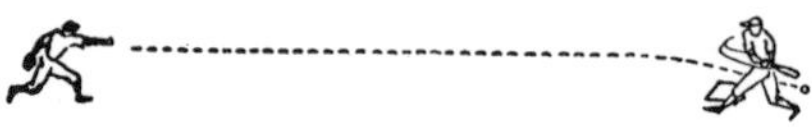

played, managed, and umpired in the National League from 1886 through 1926. When he was old enough to play team baseball, Ducey decided his future in the sport lay as a left-handed pitcher, which he already knew was a desirable baseball commodity. His sister, Mary Broderick, told of how he pampered his throwing arm:

> During the baseball season, he used to rub some kind of oil on his left arm at home in the evenings. He believed it would make his arm more flexible and turn him into a better pitcher. Then he'd wrap it overnight in an old woolen sweater, in the belief that the oil would soak into the arm.

In the winter, Ducey practised his batting swing in the living room, much to the mortification of his mother, who feared for the family china. By the time he turned twelve, Ducey was protesting the family's annual summer move to Alberta Beach because it took him away from his baseball team. He eventually won the argument and was allowed to spend the summer playing baseball on school lots, as well as hanging around Diamond Park, where Deacon White had just introduced his new Class B professional team to the city. He recalled,

> As a youngster I practically lived in old Diamond Park in 1920. In 1921, I realized a young fellow's dream when I was named batboy for the visiting clubs at Diamond Park.

His experience as batboy in 1921 and 1922 elevated Ducey to a position of unchallenged leadership among his youthful baseball confreres.

In the summer of 1922, he expanded their playing horizons. He organized, managed, pitched, and played first base for his altar boys' team in the new Catholic parish baseball league. Ducey and his pals made up their own schedule and played other church teams all over the city. He later wrote,

> Our transportation was by foot, bicycle and street car. One of our greatest supporters was a big, genial Irish priest, the beloved Father McKenna, who at that time was head of St. Joseph's Seminary. He was from the U.S. and had much affection for baseball. He would attend all our games, even the work outs. Often he would take the whole team for a treat of banana splits after we won a game, down at the old ice cream parlour, then on 109th Street. We played against church teams and by the time we were 14 years old we were even playing against intermediate teams which had men up to 20 years old. We had a good ball club and won a lot of those games.

Riley Mullen shared catching duties with Ed McHugh on that team. Even then, Ducey was a stickler for style:

> His attitude right from the start in those days was that everything about baseball had to be done with class. He insisted that if he was going to run the baseball team, everything had to be topnotch. John wanted the club to have uniforms, but they had to be professional quality, similar to what the New York Yankees were wearing—with the pin stripes. He went out and tried to raise the money but couldn't get enough.

Ducey prevailed on his mother to ask the president of the Women's Altar Society of St. Joachim's Church to put up the rest of the money to buy the team uniforms. She agreed, but the money, said Mullen, came with a catch:

> The woman had a son who had absolutely no athletic ability, but he was a nice kid. She said the Altar Society would help. However, there would have to be a compromise. Her son would have to play on the team and get a uniform. Poor John had to accept the compromise, knowing that the boy couldn't help the team. But he got the money and the team got its uniforms. They were to be unveiled at the annual sports day at St. Joseph's College.

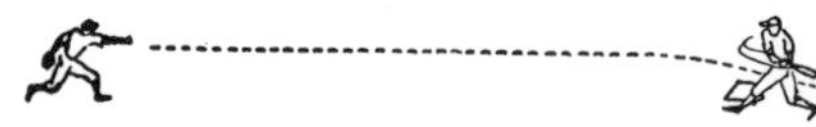

> As soon as John saw the opposition, he knew the team had no chance without some help. He wanted to get a kid named Harry Dawes into the lineup. He talked the problem over with a couple of his bigger team-mates and they hatched a plan. They somehow coaxed the poor misfit out into the bush behind centre field and they stripped his uniform off and gave it to Harry Dawes. The other boy had to go home in his underwear!
>
> When the mother heard the story from her son, she went right over to St. Joseph's and raised hell with Archbishop O'Leary himself. Well the Archbishop, who was quietly pleased with the initiative Ducey had shown in organizing the team, had to rule on the matter. John got his wrists slapped, but the team got to keep the uniforms.

The team expanded its play over the next few years. As they started to play for higher stakes, Mullen observed that Ducey looked further afield for talent:

> John wasn't above bringing in extra talent when it was needed. He brought in a couple of guys from the west end, "Hammer" Davis and Pal Powers among them. He recruited some kids for the St. Joseph's team who didn't even know how to make the sign of the cross, but that was all right with the rest of us.

Ducey left Grandin School and the church league behind when he went on to Separate High School in the fall of 1923. There he followed through with his intentions to take a "commercial" course, to give him some business skills to take with him after high school. To the disappointment of his parents, he had no desire to pursue any further education.

Henry Boulanger (front right) and his 1924 IOOF team. Third baseman Hugh John MacDonald (third from left) gave up baseball for the law and became a justice of the Supreme Court of Alberta. Courtesy of the Edmonton Archives EA 524-19.

After the collapse of Deacon White's Western International League in June 1922, Edmonton's baseball attention shifted to the intermediate and senior city leagues that played at Diamond Park. Local baseball was supported by men such as dry-cleaner Henry Boulanger, a dedicated baseball booster, and printer Reg Godson. In 1924, Godson sponsored and managed the Red Sox, while Boulanger managed the Foresters. In 1925, Boulanger invited seventeen-year-old Ducey to join his Yeoman team in the City Senior Baseball League at Diamond Park. Boulanger, impressed

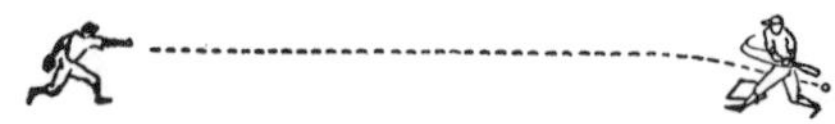

The 1926 Edmonton Elks pose at Boyle Street Park. Courtesy of the Edmonton Archives EA 524-16.

with Ducey's fielding ability, told the youth to put aside his ambition to be a left-handed pitcher and made him the team's first baseman. Happy just to make the team, Ducey was ready to play anywhere.

In the first reported mention of him, of a game played 3 July, the *Edmonton Journal* misspelled his name "Ducy." The record shows he singled off Central's pitcher, Robinson, batting in a run and then scoring on Paul Maher's double. However, the Centrals, led by Phil Horn and lawyer Clarence Campbell, won the game 17-11. They later went on to the league finals, eventually losing to the Radials, a team sponsored by the Edmonton Street Railway Company.

Boyle Street Park

That summer, the local senior teams moved between Diamond and Boyle Street parks, depending on the demand for the larger park: Diamond Park

was normally the site of inter-city, tournament, and exhibition games. Ducey's fellow players on those 1925 senior teams included Ed McHugh, Ken Duggan, Johnny Dorsey, Cam McKinnon, Paul Maher, Gub Peddis, Dr. Allan Hall, Hubert Thompson, Phil Horn, Clarence Campbell, Johnny McDonald, Dan Carrigan, and Norm McIntyre; he remained close to these men all his life. Edmonton's most noted umpire of the day, Frank Drayton, called balls and strikes from behind the plate in the senior league during that era.

Boyle Street diamond, at 97 Street and 104 Avenue, became the centre of juvenile and junior baseball about 1922. It was a popular spot, with bleacher seats for only about 1,100 of the 2,500 fans who regularly turned out for Sunday games. Chicken wire protected them from foul balls behind the plate. The playing field was dusty but close to the packed crowds.

Cecil "Tiger" Goldstick first saw Boyle Street when his family moved from Edson back to Edmonton, where he had been born. He began his life-long sports career in 1927 as a batboy for the senior league Cubs at Boyle Street:

> My father had a hardware store in Edson, but he came back to Edmonton in the mid-1920s when they made him the city's first rabbi. My Dad bought a house from Tom Ducey and that's how I eventually got to know John. I liked baseball but wasn't much of a player. So I started out as a batboy.
>
> In those days, there was a bit of a feud between the senior league and Diamond Park, so they played at Boyle Street. It wasn't much of a park, but at the time there was nowhere else to play. The right-field and left-field fences were very close, so if a ball was hit out of the park, it became an automatic two-base hit. The seniors got tired of the place and they eventually got an agreement that brought them back to Diamond Park.

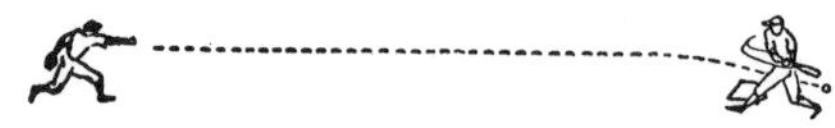

Dick Noon had moved from Provost, Alberta to Edmonton with his family at age three, in 1926. The family settled just three blocks away from Boyle Street, where Dick saw his first baseball game. He watched the game there until Boyle Street closed in 1936:

> An old ball player, Buck Eaton, lived down the street. So we'd follow him over to Boyle Street and watch them play there. That's how I got interested in baseball. The park was just in a city lot with the York Hotel right in centre field. On a Sunday there would be a crowd all the way around the outfield and the fellows would go around with a hat and take up a collection to help pay for the day.

At Boyle Street, Ducey turned out to be perhaps the best fielding first baseman of his day. Unlike Phil Horn, however, he was a notoriously poor hitter, as he was the first to admit:

> I was never active with the bat, unless it was around two o'clock. You played for fun in those days so I got away with just playing first base.

He did not escape unscathed, however:

> Down on Boyle Street one night, Hub Thompson wheeled a third strike past the hitter, which Eddie McHugh dropped momentarily. McHugh pounced on the ball and let it go with a terrific heave to first base. His throw took me across the inside of the foul line. As I was reaching for that ball, the runner hit me like Bud Williamson used to make those football tackles. I came up with a $60 shiner that stayed with me a week and took a lot of explaining, particularly at the Saturday night dance at Alberta Beach.

The *Bulletin* confirmed the assessment of Ducey's "good field, no hit" capabilities:

> For several years, "Lefty" was convinced that he would be the best first baseman in baseball. He had the style and even looked good striking out. But "Lefty" struck out so often, even a blind manager was forced to replace him!

Still, the left-handed first-baseman had his fans. They liked him for his colourful style, his smooth fielding, his on-the-field chit-chat, and his hustle. By now, he had cultivated the U.S. accent he had picked up in his summers around Diamond Park. It stayed with him all his life and was best described as a cross between Bronx and the Old South, bringing additional distinction to his persona and, for a while, the nickname of "Buffalo John."

When he failed to turn out for baseball in 1928, his absence sparked a newspaper comment that underscored his fan appeal:

> Speaking of baseball, many of the faithful who follow the games at Boyle Street are asking why John "Lefty" Ducey is not performing around first base for one of the senior teams. And it is a hard question to figure out.
>
> As a fielding first-sacker, the eccentric one is without a peer in these parts and for this reason, if no other, he should be capable of holding down a berth on some one of the clubs. "Lefty" has a goodly share of colour and, ride him as they may on occasions, the fact remains that most of the fans like to see him out there doing his stuff.

But the absence was only temporary and Ducey returned, playing with Norman Dodge's Imperials at Boyle Street until the end of the 1930 season. With the slugging Phil Horn holding down first base, Ducey was relegated to right field. By then, "the eccentric one" was twenty-two years old and needed to support himself, just as the Depression was making jobs scarce. He had tried a variety of sales jobs, but in 1930 his knowledge of sports served him well and he landed a permanent job as a sports

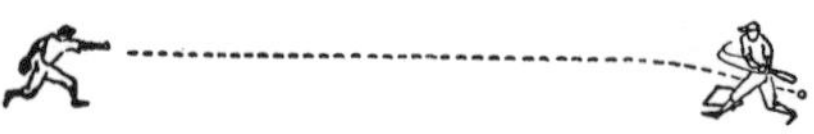

Covering sports for the Edmonton Bulletin, *Ducey and Bill Lewis sent out this seasonal card featuring highlights of Edmonton sports in 1932-33. Courtesy of the Edmonton Archives 45-1117.*

reporter with the *Bulletin*, working with sportswriter Bill Lewis. A keen hockey fan, he also picked up some small change for three winters as official timekeeper for the senior hockey league.

Ducey could consider himself fortunate to get such a job in 1930. Roughly twenty to twenty-five percent of Alberta's labour force was unemployed in the early 1930s, and thirteen percent of Edmonton's population received relief payments. In *Alberta: A New History*, Howard Palmer describes the 1930s in Alberta as "a period of crisis," with intense economic depression, slow population growth, class and political crisis, and labour and social violence. By 1933, the lowest point in the depression, bread lines and

soup kitchens had formed in the cities, and conflicts between unemployed workers and police were routine. Edmonton, with a population of 78,500, was promoting a beautification program, urging residents to spruce up their homes and gardens—even though 50,000 lots had been forfeited to the city because of unpaid taxes and the city owned some 275 tax-sale buildings.

While the "Golden Age of Sport" of the 1920s was at an end, much of the sports world still reflected an eerie sense of well-being. In May 1930, ex-Eskimo Babe Herman was leading the National League hitters, batting .437 (Herman would end the season at .393—the thirty-eighth highest in major-league history—but come second to the Giants' Bill Terry who hit .401), and the first night baseball game was played before 7,000 fans in Des Moines, Iowa. With a daily average circulation of 31,582, the *Edmonton Journal* had outpaced the *Edmonton Bulletin*. Moreover, it offered up-to-the-minute scores of the Edmonton Grads' international championship series against Chicago to any basketball fans who phoned its special telephone number. Those with radios could tune in to the *Journal* radio station, CJCA, for a play-by-play description of the game. The paper itself offered two full pages of sports coverage, with detailed reports on everything from British cricket, racing, boxing, and football, to Davis Cup tennis, America's Cup yacht racing, and big-league baseball.

Edmonton's new Highland Golf Course opened that May, while Boyle Street Park got new wire netting for the right-field bleachers to protect fans from line-drive home runs from the likes of Phil Horn. But local baseball had some problems. At both Diamond Park and Boyle Street Park, residents were complaining to City Hall about the noise caused by Sunday baseball crowds. A bylaws committee recommended curtailing Sunday sports at city facilities. That brought lawyer Clarence Campbell to speak before council on behalf of the Edmonton hockey association. As a result, council put the recommended bylaw aside for six months, hoping the issue would cool off. The senior baseball league wisely moved its Sunday games to the newly built Lakeview Resort at Cooking Lake for the remainder of the summer.

From one umpire to another

In the fall of 1930, Beans Reardon returned to his home near Los Angeles. He had just completed his fifth year as a major-league umpire by working in his first World Series. Reardon announced that he would stage an umpiring school in Los Angeles during the winter months. When John Ducey heard this news, he knew that if he was going to continue an active romance with baseball, it would not be as a player. This was his chance to do the next best thing: make the jump from player to umpire.

With the blessing of his father and the expressed concern of his mother, he scraped together enough money for the trip to California. In October 1930, he left Edmonton for Los Angeles. He was encouraged and accompanied part of the way by friend Paul Maher, who was heading for the Portland Buckeroos' hockey training camp. Maher had made the leap from Edmonton junior hockey to the Hollywood Millionaires the previous season; his contract was then sold to the Portland team. Professional hockey was popular in Los Angeles, as it was all up the coast, with major cities—including Victoria and Vancouver—linked by the Pacific Coast Hockey League. Paul Maher was one of several Edmonton players who began their professional careers in the PCHL in the early 1930s.

To Ducey, Los Angeles sounded glamorous—and a great alternative to an Edmonton winter. He was going to California, he told a colleague, because "I want to see some big time stuff, and besides, I hate winter underwear." Ducey's departure was noted in the "Sporting Periscope" column of the *Journal* with the suggestion that young Ducey would be both watched and missed:

> Prominent in sports circles of this city for a number of years, a smart enough baseball player, prominent hockey official and one of the most enthusiastic supporters any Edmonton rugby team ever had, Jack "Lefty" Ducey left Edmonton today en route to Los Angeles where he will enter the umpiring school which will be conducted by "Beans"

> Reardon.... "Lefty" had a place all his own here. There was no one more welcome to sport confabs. He added life to every meeting and following an extensive study of southern languages he had that air of the old southern gentleman—he even smoked the best Virginia brands.... Sportsmen of Edmonton, particularly baseball fans, will watch with interest Ducey's progress under Reardon.

Upon his arrival in Los Angeles, Ducey settled in the Hollywood area. He was a regular fan at Pacific Coast League hockey games and spent considerable time with two Edmonton brothers, Dan and Tom Carrigan. In the winter of 1930-31, they played starring roles for the Hollywood Millionaires. Dan was the team's leading scorer, while Tom served as goalie and coach. Another Edmontonian, Lindsay Carver, also played for the team. In a note to the *Journal*, Ducey wrote that the calibre of play wasn't that much better than the senior hockey in Edmonton: "With a couple of good subs, Ira Stuart's Edmonton Superiors could lick any team in the California professional circuit."

With his own knowledge of the game, Ducey mixed in well with the local hockey crowd, which soon led to a job as a hockey writer for the *Hollywood News*. This provided him financial support until the start of Reardon's umpiring school. In December, Ducey received a ringing endorsement for his writing in an unsolicited letter to the editor of the *News*:

> Please arrange to have your paper delivered to me at the above address. My reason for subscribing to your paper is your excellent hockey writeups. The writer, Jack Ducey, in my estimation, is the best hockey writer in Southern California. I am from Toronto. Ducey covers the games more like our newspapermen back home.

Unfortunately for Ducey, Reardon's umpiring classes failed to materialize after the New Year. Due to movie-making demands in the off-season, Reardon abandoned his plan to hold a school for aspiring arbiters. He had

become involved in Hollywood films while umpiring in the Pacific Coast League and continued with this off-season diversion for many years. The ruggedly handsome umpire appeared in bit parts of all but one of Mae West's movies during the years she was a major star. He also had bit parts with other stars of the 1930s, including Victor McLaglen and Gary Cooper. "Look after Beans," Mae West once ordered her production team, and they did.

The cancellation was a major disappointment for Ducey, who reminded Reardon he had come all the way from Edmonton to attend umpiring school. Reardon recalled Ducey well from his second year of umpiring at Diamond Park in 1921 and was flattered that the younger man had come so far to learn from him. They got to talking about umpire Hank O'Day, the distant relative Ducey had never met. Reardon told Ducey how O'Day had taken him under his wing while he was in the Pacific Coast League, coached him, and later recommended him to the National League. Reardon shared with O'Day a love of horse-racing and used to drive him across the border to the track at Tijuana on Sundays. There the two umpires could gamble on the horses without fear of sanction from Commissioner of Baseball Judge Kennesaw Mountain Landis. The link with O'Day, and Ducey's burning desire to become an umpire, convinced Reardon he should help the young man from Edmonton.

Reardon agreed to give Ducey private lessons over the winter, telling him to begin by memorizing the Baseball Rule Book. He put him through an intense grounding in the rules of the game and the mechanics of umpiring. He also schooled Ducey in his approach to professional umpiring, including lessons he had learned from the great Hank O'Day. Reardon had a reputation as a tough guy on the diamond. His several physical dust-ups in the minor leagues had taught him to be tough and firm, but he always claimed that he did not set out to provoke trouble. On the other hand, Ducey abhorred physical confrontation. He decided, however, that as an umpire, he too would be tough and firm, in the hope of avoiding physical violence. Taking a page from Reardon's book, when

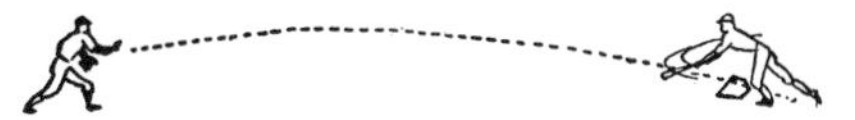

Ducey put on his umpiring togs, he also put on a tough-guy front. In that role, he never gave an inch to players, managers, or even league officials. Yet those were rough times and like Reardon, he too became involved in a few punching episodes on the diamond.

Reardon found the twenty-two-year-old neophyte a natural umpire, with the potential to be a good one. Along with a huge dose of enthusiasm, he had all the necessary skills, with plenty of showmanship thrown in for good measure. The tutor was pleased that Ducey, with a solid knowledge of the game for his age, worked hard and learned his lessons and baseball rules extremely well. Years later, Reardon said that had Ducey stayed an umpire, "he would have been in the majors today."

By late March the umpiring lessons were over, the hockey season was ending, and baseball's spring training was underway in California. Ducey just needed a bit of experience and he could go home. Reardon arranged for him to try out his new umpiring skills in a few spring-training games with Pacific Coast League teams. Then Reardon took him to offshore Catalina Island to visit the spring-training camp of the Chicago Cubs, managed by Rogers Hornsby. It was the thrill of a young lifetime, and Ducey related the experience in lengthy letters home to Bill Lewis, who ran them in his column in the *Bulletin*:

> ...the Cubs' every move was followed with hawk-like interest by Jack "Lefty" Ducey, well-known Edmonton ballplayer. As everyone knows who ever came in contact with "Lefty," he was what might be termed "baseball crazy" and never passed up a chance to discuss or read about his favourite topic. His knowledge of major-league ball stars was prodigious and it isn't hard to believe that he was the most interested and at the same time highly informed "fan" at these work outs.
>
> Ducey was probably the most colourful athlete who ever performed here at Boyle Street and he had a large following of fans who came just for the express purpose of drawing some entertainment from the antics of the smooth first baseman.

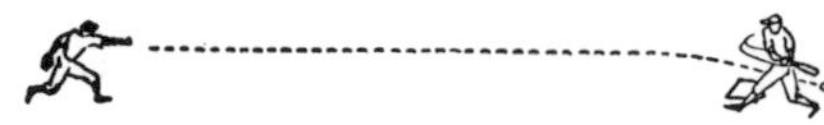

Ducey gained the one and only "diploma" from the Beans Reardon private school of umpiring in the spring of 1931. He was almost ready to return to Edmonton, with the hope of following in his mentor's footsteps. Reardon's teaching would launch him on an umpiring career that would last the next fifteen years. Those who knew the game well and saw Ducey umpire said he had the talent to make it to the big leagues. But the Depression, World War Two, and family obligations foiled any dreams Ducey had about following in the footsteps of Hank O'Day and Beans Reardon.

Ducey's Diamond Park debut

In May 1931, as the Pacific Coast League hockey playoffs got underway in California on artificial ice, a new baseball club was limbering up at Edmonton's Boyle Street Park. Calling themselves the "Professional Pucksters," the team included several National Hockey League hockey players and a sprinkling of local semi-pro players. They played exhibition games against the local senior teams and visiting clubs.

Webb King's Stockyard Bulls, Henry Boulanger's Imperials, Henry Loyer's South Siders, and the Young Liberals made up the senior amateur league that year. They played most of their games at Boyle Street. As they warmed up with a twin-game exhibition match before their 13 May opening game, *Bulletin* sportswriter Bill Lewis reported to readers that "the eccentric one" would soon be on his way from California:

> One of my operatives appeared last night with the information that the colorful Jawn "Lefty" Ducey, that likeable personage who has been missing for the past six months, may be expected to reach Edmonton from California in about a week's time. The left-hander is reported to have left Los Angeles and its sunshine and is somewhere along the route home. Also this operative informs that the former first-sacker may don a uniform and pitch for one of the senior amateur teams when he reaches the city. Whether this is right or not, I do not know. In a letter

to this reporter, he expressed a desire to do some umpiring here if he returned. And he wouldn't do badly at that, if he were given the chance.

By early June, there was no sign of Ducey, but baseball was in full swing in Edmonton. Not only were the seniors battling each other at Boyle Street, they had to share the park with a new "Big Four" amateur league made up of teams representing St. Albert, Riverdale, the Alberta Hotel, and the CNR. Meanwhile, down at Diamond Park, the Pucksters were taking on all comers from both leagues.

In mid-June, Lewis reported that Ducey was finally driving back from California with Dan Carrigan. He arrived home 19 June:

> With a heavy load of tan and a more pronounced southern drawl than ever, Jawn "Lefty" Ducey, Edmonton's most colorful sports personality, returned to the city late yesterday after an eight-month sojourn in Los Angeles... at Boyle Street he was given the big glad-hand by "the boys," who had missed him and his eccentricities more than a little during his stay in the south.

(Lewis was also given to referring to Ducey from time to time as "the Duce." However "Jawn," revived again in later years by writers such as Don Fleming, stuck with him long after "Lefty," his playing nickname, faded from the public prints.)

Despite his reputation on the local baseball scene and all the coverage by Lewis, Ducey was surprised to find he could not walk into Diamond Park or Boyle Street and start umpiring. He wanted to begin at the top in the city senior league, but the league already had its own people in place and stalled him:

> The city league were looking into left field on my plea to umpire. So I went to Dave Little, a great baseball booster and then president of the

> Intermediate League. Dave said, "Sure John, you go in this Sunday and work the doubleheader."

In late June, thousands of Edmonton ball fans were looking forward to the biggest day of the young baseball season. They would get to see two prime games by donating to a modest "silver collection." The first was a seven-inning Big Four intermediate league game between the CNR and St. Albert. But the main event was a special exhibition match. Local boy Leroy Goldsworthy would be on the mound, leading a team of hockey players against an all-star team from the city senior league, managed by Clayton Dolighan. It would be "the pitching tid-bit of the season," wrote Bill Lewis.

Goldsworthy, a talented all-around athlete and another of Ducey's close life-long friends, was then playing in the National Hockey League for the Detroit Falcons. "Goldie" had been born in Minnesota but moved to Alberta with his parents in 1909, at age three. He was an accomplished track and field star at Edmonton's Westmount High School as well as its star pitcher in Church League baseball. He excelled on the ice and jumped from Joe Driscoll's junior hockey Eskimos to Duke Keats' senior club in 1925. When the Western Canada Hockey league disbanded after the 1925-26 season, he was among several players sold to the NHL by the Patrick brothers. Goldsworthy gave up a chance at a professional baseball career and went on to play hockey with the Detroit Red Wings, Chicago Blackhawks, Boston Bruins, and Montreal Canadiens. He ended his career as a popular golf pro at Jasper Park Lodge and Vancouver's Point Grey club.

Goldsworthy's 1931 "Professional Pucksters" included hockey stars Eddie Shore, Paul Maher, Murray Murdoch, and team manager Roger Jenkins. Born in Wisconsin, Jenkins moved to Edmonton as a boy and went into professional hockey with the Edmonton Superiors in 1927, straight out of high school. He had moved up to the Toronto Maple Leafs by 1931 and went on to play seven seasons in the NHL, with the Leafs,

John "Lefty" Ducey at Edmonton's Boyle Street Park, shortly after beginning his umpiring career in the summer of 1931. Courtesy of the Edmonton Archives EA 524-20.

Bruins, Blackhawks, and Canadiens. At third base was Murray Murdoch, who was born in Ontario but grew up in Edgerton, Alberta, near Wainwright. He played baseball in Edmonton in the 1920s and managed the Edmonton Shastas to the Northern Alberta senior baseball championship in 1934. He made his career in hockey, however. After captaining the University of Manitoba to the Memorial Cup, he joined the New York Rangers in 1926. Murdoch played left wing for the first eleven years of the Rangers' existence, gaining a reputation as an "iron man" for playing in 600 consecutive games. He later coached Yale University's hockey team for twenty-seven years, ending his career as Yale's sports administrator.

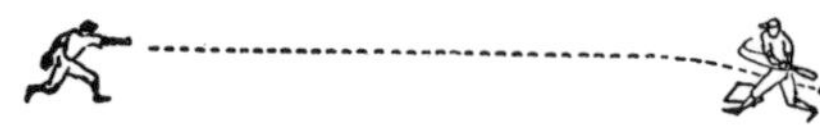

On 28 June 1931, several thousand baseball fans flocked to Diamond Park to see their local hockey heroes on the ball field. Ducey, the former batboy, now twenty-three years old, would make his inaugural appearance as the lone umpire before a packed house. Bill Lewis described Ducey as "possessed of as much color as an Indian blanket." At first, Ducey feared he wouldn't be able to make the assignment, because he didn't have his own "professional" umpiring outfit. He later recalled,

> I had to borrow equipment, but I went behind that plate for the first time and worked 19 innings alone, before 5,000 fans at Diamond Park. The next week I was in the senior league.

As Jack Kelly observed the next day in his sports column, it was a notable start for the new umpire:

> There are umpires—and then there is John "Lefty" Ducey, and if you haven't seen him in action you missed something. No fooling! Sunday afternoon at the double-header at Diamond Park, "Lefty" got going and the big crowd of fans that packed the grandstand and bleachers got a new slant on how the position of umpire should be played.
>
> Ducey wants speed, order and no back talk—and he gets them. Like the dynamic "Beans" Reardon, "Lefty" believes that a game is, to a large extent, just what the man with the indicator makes it, and the games which he handles will have plenty of snap in them or it won't be his fault. He handled 19 innings on Sunday without the assistance of a base umpire and whenever a runner started to slide into a sack, "Lefty" was there waiting for him, no matter where he had been when the play started.

The error-filled second game was a marathon match. Goldsworthy fanned nineteen batters, while teen-aged southpaw Duke Baer struck out twelve for the opposing side. Ducey put all he had learned from Beans

Reardon into his role and hustled the players through twelve innings in just two hours and fifteen minutes. But after three scoreless extra innings, Ducey had to declare the game an 8-8 draw because of the Sunday curfew. In his first umpiring job, he had come up against the *Lord's Day Act*. The Act not only prohibited charging an admission fee on Sunday for commercial events, but also banned the staging of commercial public entertainment after 6:00 p.m. on "the Lord's Day." The 1907 law contained a provision for the provinces to opt out of it, but Alberta had not. Instead, the province amended the act in 1913 to allow for a cash donation from attendees. This meant athletic promoters could ask for contributions to a "silver collection" at the entry gate. There was little they could do about the curfew provision. This law would nag Ducey throughout his career.

On that Sunday evening, however, Ducey was relieved to get the lengthy nineteen innings over without incident. His mother delayed his first Sunday dinner at home in eight months until he could slip away from the congratulations of friends and fans. She was simply glad he was home. His father beamed with pride that they now had an umpire in the family and quietly slipped him the money to buy his own umpire's outfit.

Dusty diamonds: Depression-era baseball

Ducey was elated that his new baseball career was officially underway. He continued to umpire for Dave Little's intermediate league but quickly turned his attention to the city senior league. To pressure them to hire him, he had a local sports paper run a one-column photo of him, dressed in his new umpiring garb. Under it was a short message: "John Ducey, Edmonton's Most Popular Umpire, Born Buffalo N.Y., age 23 years and single." He soon made a deal with the senior league and spent the rest of the summer umpiring for it at Diamond Park and for the intermediates at Boyle Street, attracting two sets of fans. There were those who liked his hustling game and those who could not stand him, with his Yankee

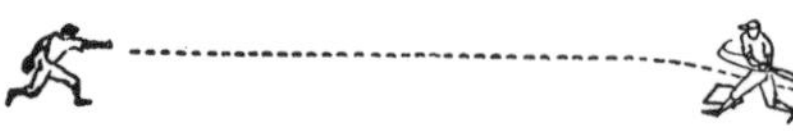

Ducey calls a close one at home plate as Tommy Scotwell slides home against Cam Smith in a senior game at Boyle Street Park in 1931. Located in what was then a residential district near 97 Street and 104 Avenue, the park was a busy centre for amateur baseball between 1925 and 1935. Courtesy of the Edmonton Archives EA 524-21.

accent and his "baw-tuh's" and "stee-rike tree's". The fans were never neutral when "Lefty" was behind the plate.

Umpiring paid good money in the early 1930s: $2.00 to $5.00 per game, depending on league resources. But there wasn't enough work to make a living from it. Still, the job paid Ducey enough to support an active social life. In those years, the Saturday night highlight during the summer months was the dances at Alberta Beach. The CNR ran a train service out to the dances, and Ducey was a popular attendee. To supplement his umpiring fees, he again prevailed on Bill Lewis to get him on as a sportswriter for the *Bulletin*; the reporting he had done the previous winter in Hollywood helped him get the job. After the 1931 season, Ducey's writing

In the midst of the Great Depression, Sunday crowds continued to fill Diamond Park in 1932, the last season for the old park. Umpiring solo, home plate arbiter Ducey can be seen at far left just after a close call at first base. Courtesy of the Edmonton Archives EA 524-25.

spurred Harry D. Ainlay, then president of the Edmonton Baseball Council, to commend him to the editor of the *Bulletin*:

> We feel that he has set a standard for other local sport reporters for this work and that such reporting in detail of our games did much to promote the success of the sport. His work has received many favorable comments on the part of the base-ball fans of the city.

Although the Depression put a damper on many activities, Edmonton remained a hotbed of baseball interest in 1932, and Ducey was delighted to have been thrust into the middle of it. Thanks to coverage on the sports pages, he quickly became a well-known local personality. His umpiring was even more colourful than his playing. The same fans who had cheered

In the early 1930s, while working as a sports reporter for the Edmonton Bulletin, *Ducey was a fashion plate off the field as well as on. Courtesy of the Edmonton Archives* EA 524-24.

or jeered him as a player turned out in sizable numbers to see him "calling 'em" behind the plate at Boyle Street and Diamond Park.

The personality traits he had developed in his early years stayed with him all his life. He was a warm, gregarious man with a genuine interest in people and a wide circle of friends both in and out of sport. Off the field, he was always smartly dressed, a bow tie from his umpire's uniform deco-

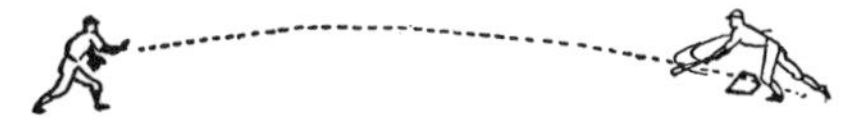

rating a three-piece suit, usually light grey. He was very clothes-conscious and remained fastidious about his dress all his life. A handsome man with black, curly hair, Ducey's round, boyish face offered a wide, toothy smile to all he met.

In the 1920s and early 1930s, local and visiting sports celebrities met and mingled with journalists in a tight geographic circle in downtown Edmonton. This included Joe Driscoll's hardware store, Johnson's Cafe in the Selkirk Hotel, the Shasta Cafe, Deacon White's pool hall (by then renamed "the Eskimo Pool Room"), and Mike's News-stand. All were within a baseball throw of the main crossroads of the city, at Jasper Avenue and 101st Street. Ducey spent most of his time as a sportswriter moving between those key locations and the *Bulletin* building, a few blocks further east on Jasper Avenue. During the years Jasper Avenue was the social centre of Edmonton, he could never walk more than a block along it in any direction without stopping to talk with someone he knew. With Ducey, the talk was always about baseball.

The senior league played most of its games at Boyle Street from 1926 through 1931. In 1932, the league was reorganized by three men who returned to the game in new administrative roles: Frank Hughes became league president, printer Henry Roche, vice-president, and lawyer Clarence S. Campbell, secretary. They agreed to take on league operations provided that they could move it out of the Boyle Street grounds, described as a "corner lot atmosphere," back to Diamond Park. Roche gained a sublet there from the Football Association, which was playing most of its matches at Renfrew Park. Ducey, a beginner who could not get an umpiring job a year earlier, won the assignment to umpire the opening senior league game at Diamond Park in May 1932. Said one report,

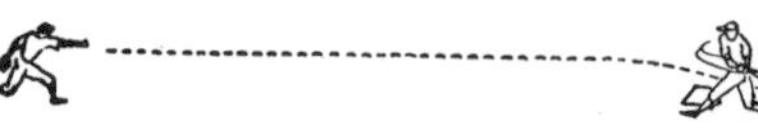

Ducey sports a three-piece umpire's suit in the early 1930s at Calgary's Mewata Park. Ducey umpired in Calgary throughout his career, frequently because of salary disputes in Edmonton; he was always better paid when he worked in the southern city. Courtesy of the Edmonton Archives EA 524-23.

> Ducey, the fiery and inimitable, will handle the umpiring. He too will make his season's bow at Diamond Park in style. He will be a perfect picture of what the well-dressed major-league umpire should look like.

Well dressed he was, certainly as far as his shoes were concerned. Unable to get made-to-order "regulation" umpire's shoes from New York in time for opening day, Ducey prevailed upon his mentor Reardon, who promptly shipped him a pair of his own shoes—reportedly those worn by Reardon in the 1931 World Series.

The 1932 senior baseball league was made up of the Arctics, Royals, Imperials, and Liberals, managed by Henry Loyer, Wilbur King, Norman

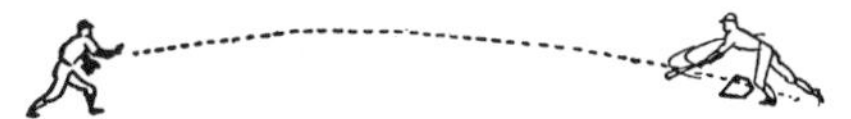

Dodge, and Hugh John MacDonald respectively. Frank Drayton, who had been Edmonton's leading umpire back in Ducey's early playing days, later took over management of the Edmonton Liberals from MacDonald, not long after the team had been renamed the Shastas. Drayton had broken into Edmonton baseball in 1915 with the Borden Park Bearcats, a team that came from nowhere to win the senior league title that year. MacDonald reluctantly put baseball aside to embark on a legal career which saw him become a supreme court justice in Alberta. Years later, "his Honour" often found time to slip away from the courthouse to catch an afternoon game at Renfrew Park, once Ducey took it over. Ducey kept a box seat reserved for his old friend "the Judge" and assigned young Allan Wachowich the task of ensuring the seat was cleaned before his arrival.

Wilbur "Webb" King, one of the most colourful figures in Edmonton senior baseball, was again at the helm of the Royals in 1932. His managerial career began when he took over the old North Edmonton team about 1925 and turned it into the Stockyard Bulls, representing one of northeast Edmonton's major industries. The Imperials, who became the Cubs a year later, were managed by Norman Dodge, who began his local baseball career in 1918 with an *Edmonton Journal* team. He played for Reg Godson's Red Sox in 1926 and later with the semi-pro Edmonton Selkirks. However, it was youthful Henry Loyer who would manage his South Side Arctics to the championship that summer of 1932. His club advanced to the Northern Alberta finals before losing to a team from the mining centre of Cadomin.

George Green was another gregarious baseball personality of the day. He was voted the most popular player in the senior league in 1932, largely due to his endless chatter, his spark-plug personality, and his fleetness of foot in the outfield and on the bases. A member of the South Side Arctics, he could also bat powerfully and hit .311 that year. One of his youthful admirers was Des O'Connor, who used to visit Green at his work in the old CPR station at 109 Street and Jasper Avenue on snowy winter evenings, long after Green's playing days were done.

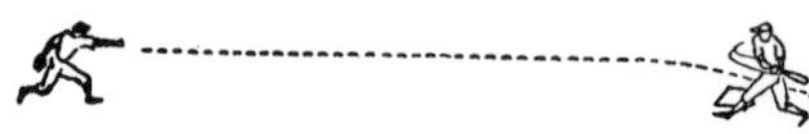

Green was one of the most colourful and popular ballplayers who ever appeared at Renfrew Park. At the end of an inning, he always had trouble getting back to the dugout. He would stop and talk with the fans all the way in from the outfield. One night somebody hollered at him, "George, why don't you get a horse?" So the next inning when he was coming in, he had the batboy slip his bicycle behind the bleachers and came peddling down the foul line on the bike, waving to the fans as he rode by.

Phil Horn, the big left-handed first baseman for the Imperials, was the base stealing leader in 1932, with twelve stolen bases in eleven games. Dave Fenton, the Arctics' third baseman, would win the batting championship with a mark of .356. At the other end of the hitting spectrum that year were two of Ducey's closest friends. Sportswriter and tennis sharp Stan Moher held the strike-out record, fanning eighteen times in thirty-two at-bats. Ed McHugh had been moved from catcher to the outfield. Both played for the Imperials, Moher hitting .154 and McHugh .158.

Hitting wasn't everything in those days. The important thing was *being* there, being on the team or in the supporting cast. Baseball was part of the Edmonton social scene in those years. A man who could pitch or hit could play. If he didn't have those skills, he could be a league secretary, an assistant coach, a ticket taker, or just a regular fan. What was important, especially on Sundays, was to *be* at the ball park. Male and female, dressed in their best suits and straw hats, thousands of baseball fans and Sunday socialites went to Boyle Street or Diamond Park, and later to Renfrew Park. There they would *be* a part of the afternoon festivities. For a few fun-filled hours each week, the struggle of the Depression—and later the grief of World War Two—was left outside the ball park gate. Inside, the fans cheered the players, booed the umpire, and put aside the cares of the real world.

Around the dusty diamonds of Boyle Street and Renfrew Park, they began roaring at the umpire as soon as he shouted out the batteries for the day's game. If it was Ducey, in those pre-public address days, he would roar back at them. "Aw shud-up!" he once bellowed at a particularly loud female critic.

The fans rooted fervently for their favourite players. The boys on the field responded by giving their very best, which sometimes wasn't very good. It was all great fun, though, and on a summer Sunday afternoon in Edmonton, the ball park was the place to *be*.

The senior league of 1932, under the day-to-day direction of Henry Roche, was a great success with Edmonton baseball fans. Every club in the league made money and despite the Depression, enough was left over to pay $2,000 in park rent to the Football Association. Ducey umpired the final game of the league playoffs before 7,400 fans, calling it "the largest crowd I ever saw at Diamond Park." Unfortunately, the season was marred by the loss of the injury-weakened Arctics in post-season play, as they bowed to the visiting Cadomin club in five games. Edmonton fans later gained a measure of revenge as they watched the Nacmine Athletics win the battle of the coal-mine teams at Diamond Park, taking the Alberta title from Cadomin in three straight games.

The high level of interest in the sport put Edmonton "on the baseball map" and resulted in two notable post-season visits by touring professional teams. The first was a two-game exhibition series between the Montreal Royals and the Toronto Leafs. The big names were Toronto's second-baseman Chuck Dressen and the Royals' classy first-baseman Oscar Roetteger. Dressen played with Cincinnati from 1926 through 1931 and returned to the majors the next season, ending his playing days with the New York Giants before starting a fifteen-year career as a big-league manager. Roetteger, who had played for Brooklyn in 1927, managed to get sixty at-bats with Connie Mack's Athletics in 1932 but never threatened to replace the great Jimmy Foxx. Ducey umpired both games, then after each hustled up McDougall Hill to the *Bulletin* offices to write his game

Umpire Ducey (far right) leaned into this group photo of Earl Mack's 1932 American League All-Stars and the Edmonton All-Stars at Diamond Park. Brooklyn's Babe Herman is third from left in the front row; Washington's Heinie Manush is seventh from left in back. Courtesy of the Edmonton Archives WA 45-1110.

report for the paper. The first game, described from the young umpire's point of view as "listless and indifferent," took one hour and thirty-five minutes to play. Ducey was a lot happier with the second game, over in one hour and fifteen minutes. He described it for *Bulletin* readers as a "hustling" game that gave the fans "a taste of real baseball that brought plenty of applause from the stands."

The closing highlight of Ducey's season was when Earle Mack's touring major-league All-Stars made their first appearance in Edmonton at Diamond Park in early October. It was an occasion for Ducey and local fans to renew friendships with Babe Herman and Heinie Manush, who, with the All-Stars, thrashed the local team 13-0. Ducey was thrilled to call balls and strikes on the two former-Eskimo stars, as well as the likes of Charlie Gehringer, Red Kress, and Bill Dickey. Herman and Manush told reporters that the young umpire reminded them of Beans Reardon as Ducey hustled the teams through a game of one hour and forty minutes. It had been slowed somewhat by the crowd-pleasing antics of baseball comedians Al Schacht and Nick Altrock, who gave the youthful arbiter a hard time.

In spite of the cool weather, the visit of the big-league stars to Edmonton was a major civic event. They were wined and dined, and several of them taken out by local fans to the surrounding countryside to do some duck hunting. Eric McNair of the Philadelphia Athletics caught a bad cold after a damp morning on the marshy outskirts of the city. But the next day, such had been the hospitality in Edmonton, he and Charlie Gehringer of the Detroit Tigers gladly accepted a request to make a bedside hospital visit to ailing Alf Bessey, a former Canadian football star with the old 1912 Edmonton Eskimos.

Bessey, a rabid baseball fan and a devoted follower of McNair's Athletics, was totally surprised by the visit, which had been engineered by a couple of old sporting friends, Hugh McGill and Hugh McGarvey. The visit cheered the sick Bessey as he talked baseball with the two young major-league stars. Ducey, who had become friends with McNair, accompanied the two ball players on the visit, reporting it for *Bulletin* readers. McNair played thirteen seasons in the American League, while Gehringer was in the midst of an eighteen-year career with the Tigers that would eventually lead him into the Hall of Fame.

Edmonton baseball fans, and Ducey in particular, were crestfallen when the next day's game was cancelled due to bad weather. Ducey had been looking forward to umpiring with the Philadelphia Athletics' great pitcher, Robert "Lefty" Grove, on the mound for three innings of that second game. As it turned out, the single game with the touring major-

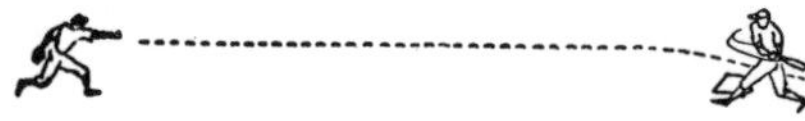

leaguers was one of the last baseball games of any note to be played at Diamond Park. In a bizarre twist, the success of the 1932 season would force the baseballers out of the old stadium that Deacon White had helped to build twenty-five years earlier.

7 Renfrew Park

RENFREW PARK WAS LOCATED A FEW BLOCKS SOUTHWEST OF DIAMOND PARK ON THE ROSS FLATS FOOTBALL GROUNDS.

The Edmonton and District Football Association had played soccer in both locations for years. In 1923, the Prince of Wales made a thirteen-day visit to Alberta to stay at his E-P ranch near Calgary. The Football Association wanted to mark the royal visit by inviting the Prince to the football grounds, but his planned trip to Edmonton never took place. The Scottish-dominated Association was disappointed but undaunted. In October of that year, it petitioned City Council to have the name of the soccer pitch changed to "Renfrew Park," in honour of the royal visit to Alberta.

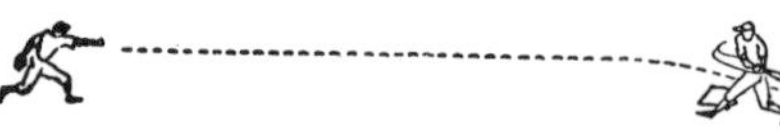

Renfrew Park, built on the site of a former soccer pitch to baseball specifications by Henry Roche and Clarence Campbell in 1933. It was renamed John Ducey Park in 1984 and torn down to make way for Telus Field in late August 1994. Courtesy of the Edmonton Archives EA 524-28.

A royal baseball visit

That event had been long forgotten some thirty years later, when Edmonton author Tony Cashman answered the question about the origin of the name Renfrew Park. He cited *Whittaker's Peerage*, which shows the barony of Renfrew is an ancient but little-known Scottish title dating back to 1398 and conferred on the Prince of Wales. On 16 October 1923, City Council had agreed that the Ross Flats Football Grounds be called Renfrew Park—marking a visit the future King of England and Duke of Windsor never made to Edmonton.

The irony is that Edward Prince of Wales had made his first and only visit to Edmonton in 1919, when one of his official functions was to attend a baseball game. On Saturday, 13 September, his biggest public appearance in a busy two-day schedule was at Diamond Park. The first game of an exhibition double-header between Deacon White's Veterans and the

His Royal Highness the Prince of Wales takes in a baseball game at Diamond Park in 1919, during a short visit to Edmonton. Players on the right were with the visiting Calgary Hustlers. The future King of England indirectly affected the later naming of Renfrew Baseball Park. Courtesy of the Edmonton Archives EA 160-1606.

Calgary Hustlers was halted when the young Prince arrived on schedule at 2:30 p.m. He took the pitcher's mound and made a ceremonial throw, autographed the ball, and formally presented it to the Edmonton Great War Veterans Association as a souvenir. He later endeared himself to fans by climbing out of the royal box and sprawling with other patrons seated on the ground alongside the playing field. John Ducey later said it was the day he made his own first visit to Diamond Park, at age eleven. Con Bissett gave the future king his baseball cap to wear as the prince threw out the first ball. A native of Manitoba who had been playing baseball in Edmonton since 1915, Bissett handled ten chances at third base that day

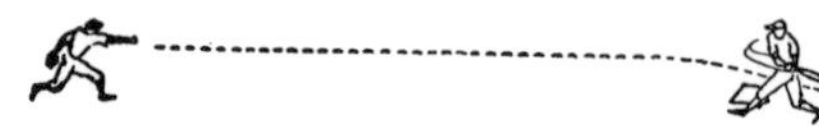

and later confessed his relief that he "didn't boot one" in front of the royal visitor. Four years later, the soccer pitch a few blocks away from Diamond Park became Renfrew Park.

Roche and Campbell rebuild Renfrew Park

As 1933 dawned, it became clear to Henry Roche that senior baseball was facing a new crisis. The footballers wanted more space than the Renfrew Park playing field offered. They had taken the $1,500 earned in baseball rent from Roche the previous season, paid off their debts, and moved back into Diamond Park, where they planned to level the fences and expand the facilities for football. They would not allow Roche back into Diamond Park that summer, but agreed that Roche could take over the Renfrew Park soccer pitch and play baseball there. The problem was, Renfrew was not designed for baseball and the 1933 season was near. Clarence Campbell described the situation in a brief to the City:

> Ways and means for financing the necessary alterations were fully canvassed, and the City Commissioners finally announced that the City itself was not in a position to undertake the project. Many conferences and league meetings were held in an effort to form a syndicate to build a new baseball park on the Renfrew Park site but they all failed and finally the Commissioners at one of the conferences proposed to Mr. Roche that he should undertake the venture himself, and assured him that the City would render every assistance which was within its power....

Roche obtained a five-year lease to rent the park for the assessed taxes, some $1,700 over the period, along with an option to purchase it for $5,000 if he had not recovered his investment in five years. In return, he put up $5,000 to build the baseball diamond and necessary facilities. Had it not been for Henry Roche, senior baseball in Edmonton might have

failed in 1933 and disappeared for the duration of the Depression and the War.

Roche put young lawyer (and sometime baseball player) Clarence S. Campbell in charge of building the new park. Campbell had come to Edmonton in 1920; he began his hockey career there as a referee in the 1929-30 season. At a baseball Oldtimers meeting in 1979, the then-president of the National Hockey League bragged about the Renfrew Park chapter of his life:

> I built Renfrew Park. Henry Roche, Frank Hughes, and I are responsible for Renfrew Park. I did most of my playing in old Diamond Park, but I designed Renfrew Park. I supervised the construction of Renfrew Park and I ran the place.

Diamond Park was then twenty-five years old, so Roche was happy to leave it behind. With Campbell, he turned Renfrew's former soccer grandstand into the third-base bleachers for the new baseball park. The old roof was installed on a new, wooden grandstand behind home plate. Paved walks, a paved entrance way, and a restroom for ladies were among the innovations. To build the crowds, Roche also gave the ladies their own day, with free admission to Thursday games. With the economy still mired in the Depression, Roche kept the admission prices at 1932 levels.

Renfrew had a larger playing field than Diamond Park. While the right-field fence was only 279 feet away from home plate (versus 282 feet at Diamond Park), the centre field fence was 451 feet distant (versus 433 feet). The left-field fence was pushed out to 319 feet, 19 feet further than at Diamond Park. In the 1950s, Renfrew's left-field fence would be pulled in some thirty feet, to give right-handed hitters a better chance to hit home runs. Near the end of its time, as recorded by Bill Kirwin in 1992, Renfrew's fences underwent several adjustments, until the left-field foul line was at 333 feet, centre field at 405 feet, and the right-field line at 315 feet.

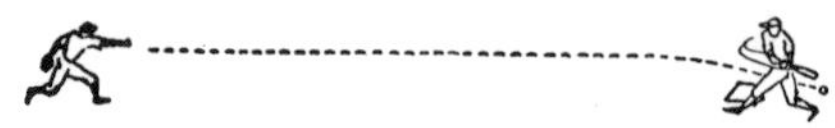

"Help us to make Renfrew Baseball Park the finest baseball headquarters in Western Canada," Roche appealed in a written message to local fans in the spring of 1933:

> A new season revives for all of us the memories of thrills we enjoyed in other years, whether as players or as spectators and we await with restless anticipation, the umpire's resonant call "play ball," which denotes the inauguration of the great summer pastime.

To top it off, Roche awarded a season's pass and a cheque for $15 to youthful Bunny Moir for suggesting the new name, "Renfrew Baseball Park," for what the local press was now calling western Canada's "palatial new baseball plant." The senior league schedule was expanded to twelve games per team. The Imperials became the Army & Navy Cubs, sponsored by the ever-generous Harry Cohen, while the Liberals were renamed the Shastas in honour of their new sponsor, the Shasta Cafe. Roche could not get the new park ready for league play until late May. But baseball would not wait.

On Sunday afternoon, 11 May, there was an exhibition game at Diamond Park between the Goldsworthy/Jenkins hockey stars and a Wetaskiwin team. It was probably the last baseball game played in Deacon White's old park. *Journal* writer Jack Kelly described the atmosphere as "baseball hunger evident in almost starvation proportions." Diamond Park was packed tight, with fans overflowing into right field. After the game, several hundred of them walked over to Renfrew to see the new facilities, which Kelly described as already bringing "a little faster tempo to the hearts of Edmonton's thousands of baseball fans."

Continuing to build interest for the opening of Renfrew Park, Kelly's column carried a photo of John Ducey and was laudatory in its praise of the young umpire:

> Announcement by President Henry Roche of the Edmonton Senior Baseball league that John "Lefty" Ducey would umpire the opening game of the season at the elegant new Renfrew Park on Wednesday afternoon tops off a baseball picture that the most fastidious can find little wrong with. Ducey is the last handful of spice required to put the show over with a bang.

Warming to his task, Kelly wrote,

> Ducey has showmanship plus, it is born right in him. There are plenty of umpires who know the rules, but they cannot awe the fans with the magnificent egoism of Ducey. In fact, he is sublime in this.... John "Lefty" Ducey has called his bad ones like any other umpire that ever donned a mask and protector and the fans have risen with blood in their eyes and bottles in their hands, only to sink back in pop-eyed astonishment at his next caper. You can't stay mad at a guy like him—no matter if you should.

Kelly also reminded league officials what a good catch they had in umpire Ducey:

> The port-sided-arbiter would probably be valued twice as highly in any other town. Calgary has been eager to get him there and Saskatoon has also been feeling out the chances of getting him away.

But in truth Ducey, who had umpired the season opener at Boyle Street Park two days earlier, was getting offers for his services from much further afield than Calgary and Saskatoon.

The opening of the "palatial new baseball plant" re-established the bitter rivalry between Henry Loyer's South Side Arctics and Webb King's Royals. It was a reminder that more than a river still separated the "South Side" from the rest of the city. The Victoria Day holiday of 24 May 1933 dawned sunny and warm, ensuring a capacity crowd of 3,500 would find their way down the hill to Renfrew Park that afternoon. Hoping to attract the affluent fans, local taxi firms advertised 50¢ rides to the new park from anywhere in the city. A few fans came by automobile, with special parking allocated for that purpose in the dusty field across the street. But most fans took the street car to 101 Street and Jasper Avenue, then walked down the hill past Diamond Park to Renfrew, where the flags and pennants were flying for opening day. For those fans who wanted an extra dose of baseball to get them in the mood, the Capitol Theatre was running *Elmer the Great*, a new Hollywood film with comedian Joe E. Brown. It featured thirty-five big-league stars, including Babe Herman, and a cameo role by umpire Beans Reardon.

At Renfrew, excitement mingled with the aroma of freshly fried onions, wafting up from the new concession stands below the first-base bleachers. The spacious wooden grandstand quickly filled with buzzing fans wanting to size up the players during pre-game practice. Adding to the drama was the new Army & Navy Store sign in right field, which promised "$5 worth of merchandise to any player who smacks a hit across our sign." With the fans in their seats well before the start of official ceremonies at 3:30 p.m., a small party of officials, including umpire Ducey, marched around the new diamond to home plate.

Alberta's attorney general J.F. Lymburn declared the park officially open and threw the first ball to the honourary batter, Mayor D.K. Knott.

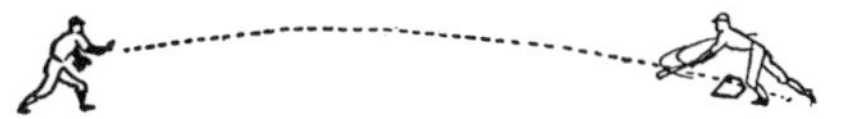

Then the real game started. Big Herman Loblick of the South Side Arctics began to throw a seven-hit shut-out at his mates of the previous season. The crowd roared as popular George Green got on base when Clayton Dolighan fumbled his high fly to centre field. Green then scored the first run at Renfrew Park when Pep Moon sent him home from second base with a sharp single, the first official hit in the new ball park. No one smacked a ball over the Army & Navy sign, but Lammie, Luna, and Williamson each hit triples, while Herman Loblick struck out nine Royals. With Ducey hustling the teams along, the Arctics triumphed 3-0 in a game that was over in ninety-five minutes. Renfrew's first season was off to a fine start.

The clubs would play each other regularly through a thirty-six-game schedule, divided into two halves. This promised to "make a keener race and give all slow starters an even chance in the second half, which will commence around Dominion Day," said League director Frank Hughes. Loyer's Arctics, with the likes of Loblick, Green, Moon, Fenton, and Luna, did battle with the Royals' Russ and Clayton Dolighan, Foreman, Eaton, and "Chief" Jimmy Rattlesnake; Shastas "Roxy" Rochue, Val Berg, Henry and Lindsay, scrapped with the Cubs, whose roster included Cap Speissmann, McCready, Horn, McHugh, Maher, Henderson, Gerlitz, and Robinson.

A new ball player from out of town was on hand that summer, but no one knew very much about him. Bill Lewis of the *Bulletin* made this early assessment:

> Unless I'm wetter than an April rainstorm, baseball fans hereabouts are going to be toasting a new hitting sensation in the Senior Amateur League during the approaching semester....
>
> The name is Pete McCready of the Cubs....Squat and sturdy, with the general lines of a piano-mover, this gent from out West of the Rockies hits the ball for distances such as we haven't seen in amateur ball here for years....How the outfielders will back into the fences

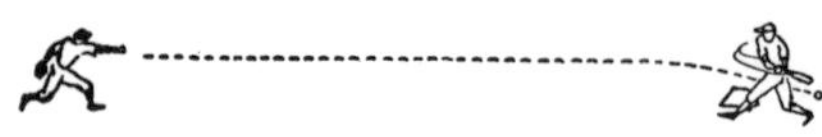

> when he goes to the plate to bat!...I saw him in two practices over the week-end and what he did to some of Norman Dodge's perfectly good baseballs was a whole lot of no good...for the balls. He may strike out swinging at times but he's likely to prove the best distance-hitter this city has had in a decade.

McCready, in the eyes of those who saw him, proved to be the best distance hitter ever seen at Renfrew Park for the next decade as well, although he did not play very long in Edmonton. Ten years later, George Mackintosh of the *Journal* was still writing about a line drive McCready had hit over the left-field fence, as well as a ball he hit over deep centre field on one bounce. Cecil Goldstick was one of those who watched McCready play at Renfrew Park:

> McCready was one of the four or five good ballplayers brought in by Harry Cohen who sponsored the Army & Navy Cubs. His real name was Stagg and he had run afoul of the law on the coast. So he changed his name and came to Edmonton. He was a colourful guy who, if he caught the third out, would run right in from centre field, past home plate and jump up on the grandstand screen like a monkey in the zoo.
>
> In later years he became an awful guy with the booze, but he was a great hitter who could have played in the Pacific Coast League. He later played one year up in the coal branch, then when the Second World War came along, he joined the Army and no one here ever heard of him again.

All that was known of McCready's past at the time was that he had come from Bellingham, Washington. Harry Cohen gave McCready, soon nicknamed "Pounding Pete," a job working at his Army & Navy store. Cohen often found his star player sleeping off the night before in a stock room. But on the field, McCready was all business.

Another of Renfrew Park's baseball builders was Frank Hughes, who operated a barber shop on 101 Street, just north of Jasper Avenue. Keenly interested in curling, hockey, and golf, Hughes' first love was baseball. In 1926, with Selkirk Hotel owner Bob McDonald, he took over sponsorship of the Selkirks in a three-team league at Diamond Park, which also included Central Garage and the Elks. When the senior league, then playing at Boyle Street, transferred its operations to Diamond Park in 1932, Frank Hughes was named president. As baseball moved to Renfrew Park, Hughes helped Henry Roche with administrative matters.

During an afternoon game at Renfrew in 1933, Ducey ran four players out of a game to settle down a large rhubarb. After the game, the first of a double-header, Hughes softly reprimanded Ducey for being too severe. Ducey spoke up in his own defence and thought the matter was settled when Hughes offered to drive him up the hill to the umpire's dressing room at the Selkirk Hotel for a respite. "Frank didn't say a word until we got into the room," Ducey later related. "Then all he said was 'that will cost you ten bucks'." It was Ducey's first and only fine. "Frank Hughes was a good president and a good man to work for," said Ducey, "even if I never did get that sawbuck back."

Edmonton historian Tony Cashman best captures the mood of those heady days at Renfrew Park and what the Sunday ball game meant in the city of 80,000 people:

> My grandfather never missed the ball game and wore his black suit because it was on Sunday. Jim Younie, the mathematics teacher, came at one o'clock and chose a seat in the sun, having calculated that by three o'clock, when the game started, the sun would travel 30 degrees to the west and put him in the shade of the grandstand roof.
>
> The large lady with the voice to match came early to get a place directly behind the plate, from which judgment seat she could get on the back of the young umpire, John "Lefty" Ducey.

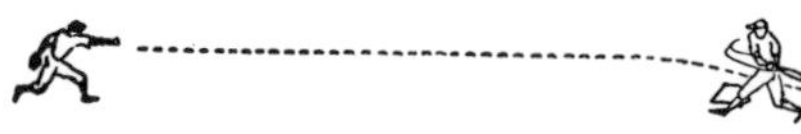

The ball game was played at Renfrew Park on Sunday afternoons of the mid-Thirties. Historic Diamond Park, sacred to the memory of Beans Reardon and Babe Herman and Raw-Meat Rogers, was on the brink of demolition. The glory of Boyle Street had dimmed. The centre of attention was Renfrew, which printer Henry Roche had converted from a soccer pitch to the finest ball park in the west. There were ball games at Renfrew during the week. They started at 6:15 p.m. because there were no lights. But THE ball game was played on Sunday afternoon.

The biggest Sunday afternoon game of 1933 took place on 20 August, when a huge crowd packed the new park in the sixth game of the senior league playoffs. Most fans expected to see McCready and the Cubs eliminate the South Side Arctics and take the city title. *Bulletin* writer John Oliver described the scene:

> Renfrew Park was gay and crowded as it had never been crowded before for the event. After a close conference, President Henry Roche and Secretary Clarence Campbell estimated the customers as totalling 5,500. In some places they were standing 20 deep around the sidelines. The fans were all set to see a new champion crowned or the old guard hold firm.
>
> Cheers rent the air as umpire Danny McLellan announced the batteries, conveying the information Loblick would pitch for South Side. Cubs batted first and as the giant Stony Plain agrarian ascended the hillock he got a great hand. Throughout the afternoon the big South Side hurler got himself into few jackpots from which he extricated himself without yielding the game.

The big duel was between Loblick and McCready. "Big Herm" managed to tame "Pounding Pete" with a strikeout, an intentional walk (which brought a loud "razz" from the crowd), and a weak grounder snapped up

Ducey (right), coach of the 1932 Arrow Busses, sponsored by Vic Horner. The junior club included future hockey stars Mac and Neil Colville, along with Morey and Walter Rimstad and Fred Lupul. Courtesy of the Edmonton Archives EA 524-26.

by Fenton at third base. Loblick also scored a run following his triple, one of three by his club. With McLellan behind the plate and Ducey on the bases, the game was over in an hour and forty minutes, the Arctics winning 3-2 to force a seventh and deciding game the following Tuesday evening. Loblick's heroics sent the 5,500 fans home from Renfrew in a festive mood. Meanwhile, up the hill, another 500 fans at Boyle Street Park watched as his brother Carl pitched the Young Liberals to an 8-4 win over Safeway Stores in the first game of the provincial junior finals. It had been a fine day for Edmonton's baseball fans, and a distinctly great day for the Loblick brothers.

The day of the final and deciding game, the league announced that Pete McCready had won the league batting championship with a .345 average, which included a league-leading five home runs. Close to 5,000 fans crowded their way into the ballpark for the 5:30 p.m. start. The south-side team had their young ace, Duke Baer, on the mound, against veteran

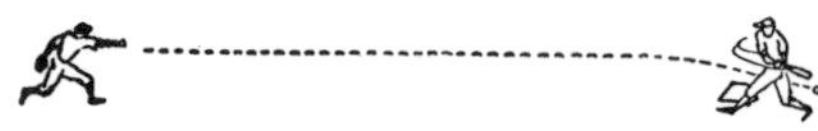

Bud "Cap" Speissmann. In the first inning, with one man out and Wilkie on with a single, McCready and Baer dueled for several pitches. Then "Pounding Pete" connected on a mighty swing and the ball soared toward the centre-field fence on a tremendous arc. As the crowd rose and cheered its flight, centre fielder George Green seemed baffled, stopping two or three times as he raced backward toward the fence. The ball flew over his head and reached the deepest portion of the centre-field fence on one bounce. McCready stood on third with a triple and the Army & Navy Cubs were out in front to stay as the Cubs took Edmonton's senior league baseball championship in Renfrew's opening year. Two weeks later, the Cubs went on to defeat Trochu three games to two to win the Alberta senior title.

Ducey saw a lot of the new ball park that first season, both as an umpire and as coach of Vic Horner's junior Arrow Busses. His club, which included Neil and Mac Colville, Fred Lupul, and Morrie Hawkey, finished first in the five-team league but lost in the playoffs to the Young Liberals. But by the time the 1933 season was over, umpire Ducey would be on the outside of Renfrew Park, looking in.

8

Baseball battles

RENFREW PARK PROVIDED A NEW FOCUS FOR BOTH FANS AND YOUNG BASEBALL PLAYERS IN SURROUNDING ALBERTA COMMUNITIES. Baseball interest flourished despite the depths of the Depression. Farmers, cattlemen, and market gardeners bringing stock to Edmonton tried to combine a visit to the capital with a stop-over for a Sunday ball game. Even for those who could not come to the city, baseball remained an important part of rural Alberta life.

Former Renfrew Park batboy Allan Wachowich was born in Edmonton but spent his early boyhood in a rural community before his family moved back to Edmonton in 1944. He recounts,

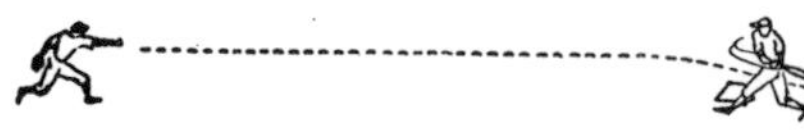

> Baseball is a family game. There's a spirit to the game and I think that within the spirit is a sense of pride that in turn unified these little communities. Everyone would cheer for the hometown's team.
>
> My Dad was a great baseball fan. He was a merchant and the sponsor of the Opal, Alberta baseball team. We used to have community picnics in the country on Sundays and baseball was the feature attraction. Often there would be a tournament, in fact you'd see a half-dozen of them over the summer. The community teams had uniforms and took a great deal of pride in themselves.

For Doug Darrah, born in 1921 in the hamlet of Islay, near Vermilion, and brought up in Viking, baseball was the best way to keep busy and have fun in a small town:

> On the prairies, in little country towns...during the Depression there was nothing else to do. We had maybe three baseballs and that's all. I've sewn up a lot of old baseballs in my day. We only had a few bats...we spliced a lot of bats so we could keep playing.
>
> You have to live in a small town to realize that if you don't play baseball, sneak into the pool room, start curling, and play some hockey, there's not much else to do. In the 1930s, everyone played baseball on the prairies because they never had enough players to make up all the teams. We would get players from all over, including imports, so we could play in the tournaments and make some money. Sports days were big, and first place meant maybe $20. You have to have lived in those days to believe it, because baseball was horns blaring and sweat and dust and dirt and no showers. Winning was the thing...it was hard-knocking baseball.

There was usually a dance after the ball tournament. Darrah and his teammates would attend, still dressed in their baseball uniforms, the dust and grime of a day's play adding to their aura as swaggering diamond warriors.

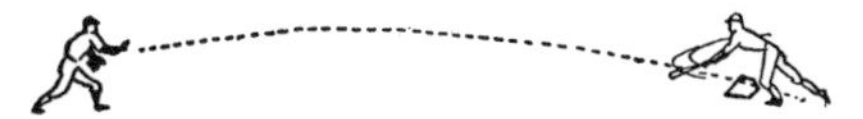

Darrah describes the summer fair at the Viking Fair grounds in the 1930s where baseball and other sports were played in the infield of the race track, with the races on at the same time:

> The track itself was dust and gopher holes. It was hard-nosed racing with big, tough horses. In the centre the baseball game was on and you'd suddenly hear the thunder of hooves and then clouds of dust. I'd look over and try to see how one of our family's horses, Old Torpedo, was making out.

In his late teens, Darrah travelled from Viking to Edmonton by bus to play junior baseball there just before the start of World War Two. He was a right-handed fastball pitcher, his control a bit on the wild side at times. After joining the armed forces, he played service ball in Calgary, eventually returning to play senior baseball at Renfrew Park in 1946.

Des O'Connor also came from a small town. Like many boys born in rural Alberta, he turned to baseball at an early age because it was the only competitive game available for youngsters during the hot summers of the early 1930s:

> I was born at Rochester, Alberta, a little village with one grain elevator.... I guess I grew up with a glove on my hand. I became the batboy for the Rochester team. We used to go to Alberta Beach for a big tournament there. I remember watching the Namao club...my eyes would just pop out, watching them chew tobacco when they were up at bat.... I was thirteen years old and had been a batboy for years and one night we were short a guy and I went out and played right field against a team from Athabasca.

Later in his teens, O'Connor would go into Edmonton to play junior baseball. After a day of practice and play, he would have to hitchhike the last several miles back home from the end of the North Edmonton street

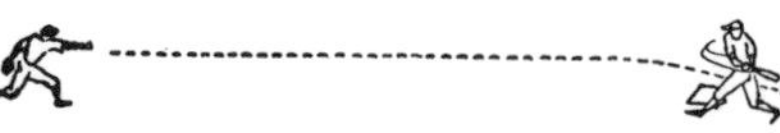

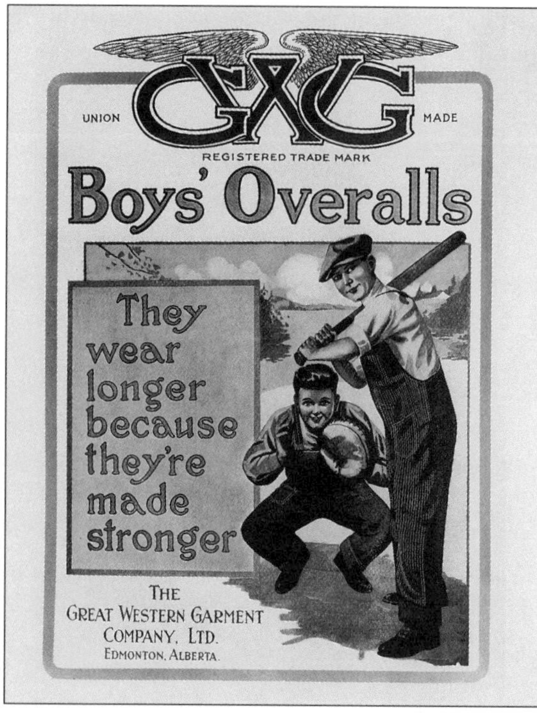

For most youngsters growing up on the prairies between the two great wars, baseball was "the summer game," as reflected in this advertisement for the Edmonton-based Great West Garment Company. Courtesy of the Glenbow Archives, Calgary, Canada, NC 6-5977.

car line. Some nights he didn't get a lift and would have to sleep over at Clyde. On the other hand, Darrah, a pitcher, often rode home in comfort. Playing for clothier Henry Singer's team in Edmonton, he would be slipped $5 by Singer after pitching a winning Sunday game. Most of the money went for his bus fare back to Viking. O'Connor played as a third baseman for both Calgary and Edmonton in the Alberta Big Four Intercity League, while Darrah pitched for Edmonton.

One of their opponents, Dick Noon, born in Provost, Alberta, spent his boyhood growing up near Edmonton's Boyle Street Park. He watched local stars like Ralph Morgan, Tommy Brant, Silver and Fred Lupul, and Buck Eaton play there and at Renfrew:

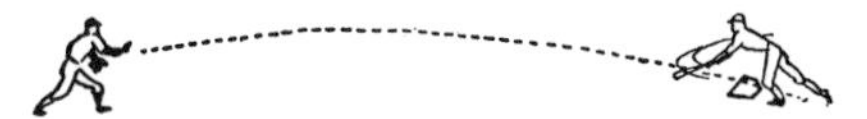

> After watching a ball game, I'd come back home and we'd play in the back yard. Our neighbour had a catcher's mitt and ball, so we'd borrow them. I'd pretend I was a pitcher and I'd give them the old wind-up, just like the big guys at Boyle Street. That's how I started out in baseball. I began playing out in north Edmonton about age thirteen or fourteen. This one particular day they were short a left fielder, so I went in.

Noon played junior and senior baseball in pre-war Edmonton, service ball during the war, and left field for Calgary Purity 99 in the Big Four league from 1947–50.

For most of the young Depression-era ballplayers, baseball was the central focus of their boyhood. Cliff Johnston, born in British Columbia, saw his first real baseball game in Seattle at age three:

> My mother later told stories about me playing out in the front yard at three or four years of age. I'd have the bases all lined up, I knew where they were supposed to be. I'd stand up at the plate and swing, then run down to first, then run down to second and slide in...come around third and then slide into home. I was never able to do that when I played semi-pro ball!

Johnston's father was a railroader for the CPR and had to move his family to Edmonton in 1930. That allowed Johnston to play all of his minor and junior baseball in Edmonton before joining the Eskimos of the Big Four league in 1947:

> As a boy in Edmonton I played for the West End Sluggers against the Riverdale Rats. Jack McGill and Harry Ornest were some of my teammates. We played around 116th Street and that area and we used to go down to the municipal golf course, which had a ball diamond at the

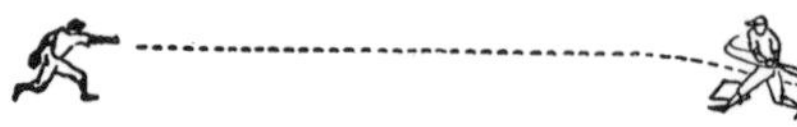

HOUSE OF DAVID

VS.

A. & N. CUBS

Featuring

GROVER CLEVELAND

ALEXANDER

One of the Immortals of Baseball, Hero of 1930 World's Series and Benton Harbor's First String Players

"The Most Colorful Team in Baseball"

"OLD PETE" ALEXANDER

ONE DAY ONLY—RENFREW PARK

MONDAY, JUNE 26, 6.30 P.M.

REGULAR ADMISSION PRICES

Come and See Their Famous Pepper Game

An advertisement for the 1933 appearance of the fabled Grover Cleveland Alexander who pitched at Renfrew Park with the House of David team. The next day, he returned and put on a private clinic for Ducey's junior team. Courtesy of the Edmonton Archives EA 524-27.

east end. Every Saturday there was a game, rain or shine. We'd play there one weekend and the next Saturday we would play with the Riverdale guys on what became the parking lot just north of Renfrew Park.

Everybody knew baseball well in those days, the fans knew it as well as the players. If you made a mistake, they let you know it. I played baseball because I loved the game. In fact "love" is a minor word when it comes to what I think about baseball. With me it was a passion.

After service in the Navy during World War Two, Johnston changed from a catcher to a hard-hitting outfielder in the Alberta Big Four League. Johnston's baseball career evolved from a boyhood dream, through those first neighbourhood and juvenile teams, to the point where he was good

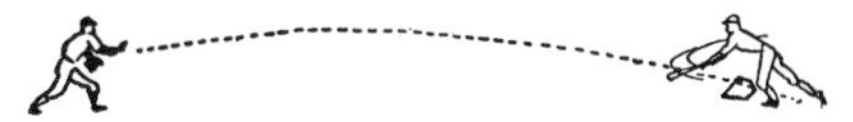

enough to play semi-pro baseball and fortunate enough to be in Edmonton where it thrived.

The new, up-to-date facilities opened at Renfrew Park also restored Edmonton as a destination for touring professional ball clubs. In June 1933, the bearded House of David All-Stars arrived for an exhibition game against a squad of all-stars from the senior league. The highlight of the House of David visit was a celebrity appearance by Grover Cleveland Alexander. Baseball fans knew him as the great right-hander who had won 373 games during his 20 years in the National League from 1911 to 1930. At Renfrew Park, the forty-six-year-old pitching immortal cruised through the opening two innings. The only exception he made was for Pete McCready, when he cut loose with all his speed to strike the slugger out. His bewhiskered team-mates from Benton Harbor, Michigan won 10-1. Ducey umpired behind the plate and received high praise from the visitors. There was even talk that he might join them as an umpire on their upcoming winter tour of Japan, but nothing came of it.

Alexander was an added "celebrity" and didn't need to grow a beard like regular House of David players. Ducey and Vic Horner later called on Alexander at his hotel, asking him if he would meet their young Arrow Bus team and give them a talk on baseball. A very obliging man, Alexander agreed and came to the park the next morning after the House of David had left for Calgary. Alexander gave the junior ball players a fifteen-minute talk on the ideas of sport in general and baseball in particular, then took the club's pitchers in hand and coached them in many of the finer points in pitching. "Avoid throwing the curve ball until you've reached full maturity," he told the celebrity-struck youngsters. "Speed, control, and a change of pace are the chief weapons of any good pitcher." With the clinic over, he joined his waiting wife, and the two drove off in their own car, down the gravel highway to Calgary.

Ducey was so charmed he sent a photograph of Alexander and the young players to *Baseball Magazine* where it was published along with his account of the visit:

> This kind gesture on Alex's part did more for baseball among the kids in Edmonton than can be imagined. Grover Cleveland Alexander will always be remembered by the youngsters of Edmonton as a wonderful old man who even though he is one of baseball's immortals, took time out to help the kids along and instill in them a real desire to be ballplayers.

Coaching the junior Arrow Busses was a pleasant sideline for Ducey, but although his club made the playoffs, umpiring remained his main job in 1933. Working at Renfrew and Boyle Street, he was also in demand at tournaments and exhibition games around central and southern Alberta, where the pay was much better. He finally had a salary squabble with Roche, who banished him from umpiring at home plate to the base paths for a lesser salary. In a huff, Ducey then quit the senior league for tournament baseball.

The senior provincial championship between the Army & Navy Cubs and Trochu Cubs drew a cloud over Ducey's 1933 season, when he became the first umpire to be thrown out of a game at Renfrew Park. Henry Roche had to leave the assignment of playoff umpires to the officials of the Alberta Baseball Association. Ducey, who had been freelancing around the province, was not one of those chosen for the big series. The umpiring was bad and after the second game, Trochu complained. Association officials stepped in and appointed Ducey as umpire-in-chief for the third and final game. Ducey's selection was okay with manager Henry Loyer of the Edmonton Cubs as well, but Roche's own league umpire, Danny McLennan, had been scheduled for that game. The Edmonton league president demanded that he be used or else, in Roche's terms, "there would be no ball game." Association officials got Roche to agree to let Ducey umpire on the bases but Ducey, his ego challenged, would have none of it.

Ducey arrived at Renfrew Park in his umpiring togs and had an immediate confrontation with Roche. The two argued on the field, in full view

of the fans. The feisty Ducey threatened to punch Roche, who then ordered the umpire ejected from the park under police escort. The crowd went wild. Ducey's season as an umpire at Renfrew Park was not only over, it also appeared he would not be invited back as long as Roche was running the park and the league. That didn't stop Ducey from going to his rule book and firing a final volley. He announced to the press that he had declared the third game of the series "no contest," based on the regulation that the umpire-in-chief shall have full authority to conduct the game for its duration and the fact that he had been the Alberta Baseball Association's designated umpire-in-chief. When that didn't work, he went back to managing his junior team.

In the fall of 1933, Ducey became a sales representative in the sporting goods section of Motor Car Supply Co. The 105 Street store ran advertisements stating that "the well-known sports enthusiast will be at your disposal on all sports equipment problems." He was glad to get a job with better hours than a sports reporter, and the *Bulletin* had decided he should not be reporting on games in which he umpired. Even Ducey couldn't argue against that decision.

The fight with Roche was an embarrassing chapter in Ducey's early umpiring career. Playing to the crowd but confident he was right, he allowed his trigger-like temper to get the best of him for a brief moment. He never talked about the blow-up after that. In truth, he admired the stern Henry Roche, who was a principled, religious man and a close friend of Tom Ducey. Relations between Ducey and Roche eventually mellowed, and in 1947, he prevailed on Roche to serve as the first president of the new Big Four Intercity Baseball League.

Despite staging and winning the provincial playoffs at Renfrew Park in its first year, Roche took in a third less money than at Diamond Park in 1932. Clarence Campbell wrote that the blame lay with the club managers, who spent more on player salaries because of increased competition. Ducey claimed it was because *he* had packed in the fans during his first full season as an umpire at Diamond Park. That was debatable, but

everyone was concerned about the decline in 1933 revenues. Roche made it clear he would not have Ducey back for Renfrew's second year unless he apologized for the playoff incident.

No apology was received, so Roche named other umpires for the 1934 season opener on 18 May, one of them being Henry Loyer, who had never umpired before. But the game was rained out, and a three-day delay proved long enough for Roche and Ducey to make amends. The battling umpire having finally apologized for his behavior of the year before, Ducey was named umpire-in-chief for the opening game.

Soon after his return to Renfrew Park, Ducey found himself on the same side as Roche in an argument during in a hectic game between the South Side Athletics and Cubs. Glen Wilkie, the Cubs' pitcher who was taken out at the end of the fifth inning, began riding Ducey from the bench. Ducey banished him from the game, but just as he left the field, the angry Wilkie ran into Henry Roche and became embroiled in an argument over his ejection. Ducey called time, hustled over, and insisted the local gendarmes escort Wilkie from the park, much to Roche's relief. By now, both crowd and players were in an uproarious mood. Al "Silver" Smith, coaching at third base, was ordered to the bench by Ducey. In the next inning, the Athletics sent in George Green to coach at first base; Ducey promptly "ran" him too, for stepping from his playing role into the coaching box. This irritated the high-strung Green to no end and set the stage for a friendly rivalry between Ducey and Green for years to come.

A day later, coaching the Arrow Busses at Renfrew Park, Ducey became the first to be banished from Renfrew in two non-playing roles: first as an umpire, then as a coach. Ducey quarreled with two separate rule interpretations by the umpiring brothers Herb and Bob Coxford. There were dozens of short, sharp clashes between Ducey and the Coxford brothers, until Herb, who finally had enough of Ducey's "know-it-all" attitude about the rules, threw him out of the game.

Ducey's team lost, so immediately after the game he filed a protest about the umpiring decisions. The league executive met and upheld his protest, ordering the game to be replayed later in the season at Boyle Street. Still, it bothered Ducey to embarrass two fellow umpires, so he issued a statement published by the *Journal*:

> It is no reflection on the two umpires that I take this stand. Both boys are out there, impartial and absolutely honest, giving their decisions to the best of their ability. It is simply a case of them having slipped up on the rules. I am perfectly satisfied that these two boys are absolutely giving their utmost to a job that is a tough one and not even appreciated at the best of times.

Ducey spoke with experience and some compassion for his fellow arbiters. He went on to umpire with both Coxfords over the next ten years and hired them himself when he took over Renfrew Park.

George Green's revenge came a few weeks later at Boyle Street Park. This time the roles were reversed. Ducey's junior team had made a steady run from back of the pack to challenge the Army & Navy Grits as the league's first-half champions. The deciding game was described as one of the most spectacular battles witnessed at Boyle Street that season—"red hot as far as action and vocal outbursts were concerned." Ducey's "Bussmen" rallied in the late innings and threatened to take the lead and the title. Throughout, his club continually protested the calls of the umpire, none other than George Green. "As though the affair was an oratorical contest instead of a ball game," Green threw Vic Horner out for disputing his calls, leaving Green's booming English voice against Ducey's southern drawl. This time Green won, throwing Ducey out of the game and out of Boyle Street Park. Thus, Ducey was the first non-player thrown out of *two* Edmonton ball parks, as an umpire, then as a coach in one, then as a coach in the other. The fans took great amusement at seeing Ducey on the receiving end for a change.

Umpiring in professional baseball

The growing numbers of fans now coming to both parks to see Ducey umpire were soon to be disappointed. He had already turned down an offer of $150 to umpire the Saskatoon Exhibition's week-long 1934 baseball tournament. He wanted more money than they had ever paid an umpire to handle the popular annual event.

Then an offer came, almost out of the blue, by telegram from the Class-D Northern League. In early July, after the officials agreed to his demand for transportation expenses as well as wages of $115 a month, he agreed to join the sprawling league. Armed with a certificate from optometrist Irving Kline that he had "perfect normal vision," Ducey boarded a train for Winnipeg to begin his new assignment. At age twenty-six, the job made him one of the youngest umpires then in professional baseball.

The Northern League was said to be better than its D-class designation. It included points like Superior, Wisconsin; Grand Forks and Fargo, North Dakota; and Crookston and Duluth, Minnesota. Winnipeg, Manitoba was the only Canadian team. It was an informal operation, as were many of the lower minor leagues in those days. League president Lute "Daniel" Boone also doubled as the playing manager of the Crookston team. Ducey's good friend Leroy Goldsworthy pitched in the league in both 1933 and 1934 and played a key role in getting Ducey the umpiring job.

Goldsworthy was a fastball pitcher who got his start in Edmonton's church leagues in 1923; he began playing junior ball in 1925. Over the summers, he made extra money pitching at tournaments, sometimes as often as two or three games a day. In 1928, he pitched a perfect game, no hits and no runs, at Diamond Park. When the Northern League was revived in 1933 after a twelve-year absence, Goldsworthy signed with the Winnipeg Maroons and led the league with twenty-two wins and six losses. The Philadelphia Athletics tried to buy his contract that fall, but the deal fell through. He then declined an offer to join the St. Louis

Cardinals organization. Goldsworthy pitched in the Northern League for three summers during his National Hockey League career, but decided his future was in hockey.

The life of an umpire in the Depression-era Northern League was a lonely one. If Ducey couldn't catch a train or a bus, he had to thumb a ride to get from city to city. Once, on an off day, he went over to Bismarck, North Dakota where a black pitcher named Satchel Paige was gaining a lot of attention with an integrated Bismarck team:

> What a workman he was. When he threw his fast one the ball looked about the size of an aspirin. It was easy to see why he was faster than Bob Feller ever got to be. I remember running into Herb Hester the next day. He was the booking agent for Earle Mack's American league all-stars, then touring that part of the country. Mack had guys like Jimmy Foxx on his club so it was no easy touch.
>
> I asked Herb why he didn't book his big leaguers into Bismarck. He didn't waste much time answering either. "Satchel Paige is over there and we don't want any part of him. We admit it too. That guy's the best there is, white or any other color."

By then, at age twenty-seven, Paige was at his early prime and had already played ten years of black baseball, the previous three seasons with the Pittsburg Crawfords. But the all-white major leagues wanted nothing to do with him. He was forty-two years old before the Cleveland Indians finally brought him into the big leagues in 1948, a year after Jackie Robinson had paved the way.

Ducey was lonely and homesick in his Northern League job, but he stuck it out for the two-month duration. He had some wild and woolly experiences, the most bizarre of which was umpiring his first game "under the lights." He found himself in Fargo when the team had an open date:

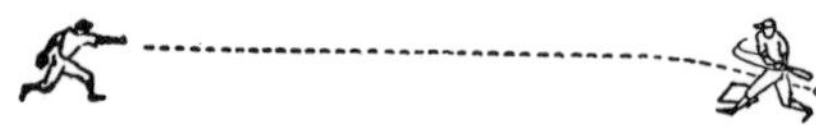

> They agreed to play a travelling ball club that called itself the Detroit Night Hawks, but they must have been from Painted Post. They carried their own lighting system. I had never even seen a night ball game before, but Jack Landry and I took on the job, with me behind the plate.

The touring Kansas City Monarchs, a black team, had begun playing with a similar lighting system in 1929. It allowed touring clubs to get in three and sometimes four exhibition games in a single day. But in 1934, it was a brand new experience for Ducey:

> First thing, when we get into the park you can't hear yourself think. The visitors had a tractor roaring on the sidelines, furnishing the power for the lights! They had a screen canopy over the plate to prevent fouls from going out of the park. Back of the grass diamond it was pitch dark. Picture me behind the plate with the catcher and the batsman. When the ball is fouled, we all duck! They rattled off that steel screen wire like bullets.

Things were no better in the outfield, which tailed off into the darkness. When a fly ball was hit out with men on base,

> the runners just put their heads down and ran, while the outfielder stood still, trying to hear where the ball had landed. The climax came when a right-hand hitter knocks one. The catcher believes he is in a world series game and bellows "foul." I can't see the ball. I call time and go out and speak to Landry.
>
> I say, "Jack, I don't see the ball, do you?" He shakes his head—"Lefty, I don't either, where the hell is it?" In the meantime, the locals, who were down 13-2, had checked in three runners—while the game was halted and of course while we saw figures running around in the shadows.

Washington Senator Heinie Manush, a former Edmonton Eskimo, cracks out a home run over Renfrew's right-field fence as a member of the visiting Earl Mack American League All-Stars in 1934. Courtesy of the Edmonton Archives A-96-15.

If that wasn't enough, Ducey was then to witness one of the strangest scenes of his entire umpiring career.

> Along about the eighth inning I could smell ham and eggs. I take a look around and over by that tractor the manager of the visiting team is cooking the boys supper! Right on the field!

It was too much for Ducey, who had quickly grown tired of small-town hotels, poor meals, and travelling dusty prairie roads. His assignment finished when league play ended, and he was happy to return to Edmonton with the hope of umpiring the provincial finals in the friendlier confines of Renfrew Park.

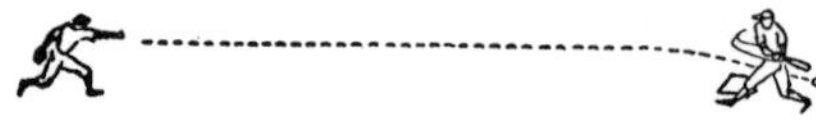

Ducey wound up the 1934 season in mid-October when Earle Mack's All-Stars returned to Edmonton for two exhibition games. Ducey was behind the plate as Heinie Manush, making his second all-star visit to Edmonton, smashed a towering home run over the right-field fence. Bill Lewis described the big Washington Senator outfielder as "the starriest of the starry troupe of visitors." The major-leaguers won 9–2 and 20–2 as they brought the curtain down on Renfrew's second season. Ducey was happy to be home.

9

Settling down

IN APRIL 1935, LUTE BOONE WROTE DUCEY, PRAISING HIS WORK THE PREVIOUS YEAR. At the same time, he told him the Northern League would not need his services for the coming season. The cost of transporting Ducey round-trip from Edmonton and his cross-border travel expenses were more than the league could pay:

> It is not necessary to have you come so far from home to do the work. Personally I want to compliment you on your work of last season. Any time you feel I can be of some assistance toward your going elsewhere, call on me.

Ducey was not overly disappointed and got Boone to write a second letter to the *Journal's* Ken McConnell, lauding his 1934 umpiring performance:

> He was a man of splendid habits and character, very proficient in his duties as an umpire. He controlled the game at all times and had the respect of the baseball players and managers.

As far as baseball was concerned, with the exception of brief umpiring assignments out of town, the balance of Ducey's career would be played out in Edmonton.

The "dish" behind the plate

Ducey now had a steady job at Motor Car Supply that allowed him time off for umpiring assignments. But the real reason for staying closer to home was that romance had bloomed in his off-diamond life. This was the year he married the young woman whom he had first spotted in the crowd at Diamond Park in August 1932:

> I was umpiring. I used to go back to the ball box every once in a while, not just to get new baseballs, but to check out the dolls in the stands. During one game I went back to the ball box and I saw her. She just hit me between the eyes. I made several trips back to the ball box that night.

It took a while before Ducey could track down the sun-tanned woman in the white suit he had seen at Diamond Park. Grace Mungall was a secretary in the Edmonton firm where Clarence Campbell toiled as a lawyer. Born in England, she was one of five children of a Scottish father and an English mother, Andrew and Jane Mungall. The family had emigrated from Newcastle to Edmonton in 1915 and briefly settled on Connors Road. Soon after the start of World War One, they moved to Rosedale,

near Drumheller, Alberta. Her father found work there as a coal miner, and her mother made ends meet by running a boarding house. In the early 1920s, the family moved back to Edmonton. Grace was an outstanding swimmer, and the only thing she liked about baseball was booing the umpire. And that was what she was doing when she caught Ducey's attention.

A few weeks later, Ducey learned from a mutual friend, hotelier Brant Matthews, that if he showed up at a Saturday night dance, he would find Grace there. He did, she related:

> We ran into each other at a dance one Saturday night. He just came over, introduced himself, and cut in, telling the boy I was with that he, John, was taking me home. And that was that.

She would never admit to being a baseball fan and called Ducey "baseball crazy" all his life. Despite baseball—and out-of-town umpiring trips—the romance persisted. With boyhood friend and former catcher Ed McHugh as best man, John married Grace at St. Joseph's Cathedral on 13 July 1935. She was his biggest fan for some fifty years.

As a new bride, Grace was not pleased when John explained that he had to leave for Saskatoon a week later to act as umpire-in-chief at the Saskatoon Exhibition baseball tournament. But it meant $125 plus expenses for a week's work, so he got to go. Soon after, when he proposed she accompany him to the west coast for a forty-game umpiring assignment with the Pacific Coast League, "and turn it into a real honeymoon," she put her foot down. As a result, he passed up the chance to follow in Reardon's footsteps and showcase his talents in the Coast league.

It was a watershed decision for Ducey. Few doubted he could have made it to the major leagues had he succeeded as a PCL umpire. The two eight-team major leagues were then an elite circle to crack as an umpire. He later explained his decision:

> There are twenty-six major-league umpires in the United States and unless an umpire is in the majors, his is a poor profession. In the minors an umpire lives in a suitcase. There is no end to their troubles, they travel constantly, and for family men as I am, travelling isn't exactly the best way to maintain a happily married life.

Despite external perceptions, in Ducey's mind "Gracie" always came first, with baseball merely a very close second. To make a home life with her, he decided to combine year-round employment with "independent" umpiring. While he never made much money at either, he made a living and he liked what he was doing.

Ducey spent the 1935 season umpiring at tournaments in Camrose, Wetaskiwin, Ponoka, and elsewhere, as well as in league and exhibition games at Renfrew Park. On one occasion, Ponoka was playing the Edmonton Shastas in a four-team semi-pro league and the visitors arrived at Renfrew Park with only nine players:

> Big, burly Virgil Neis was throwing for Jack Kelly's squad. About the third inning the ball was fouled off. I throw in an alternative ball and Virgil throws it back. "Give me a better one," he says. I say, "you'll use the one I gave you and like it." Virgil never says a word, takes his position on the rubber, goes through his motion and throws that baseball high and far over the back of the park.

Ducey called the pitch a ball and glowered at Neis.

> There I am, in the middle. I can't run the big lug, as Ponoka has only nine players and it would cause a forfeit game. Moreover, if I call the game, I don't get paid. I like to give the fans their money's worth, so I go out to the mound and give Virgil the big speech and he gives me "the neck" and the fans give me the big bird! I was burning at the time,

"When time stood still." In this photograph (c. 1935), a group of four intermediate clubs, their coaches, and fans gathered for a picture following a Sunday series at Edmonton's old Boyle Street Park. Courtesy of the Edmonton Archives EA 524-22.

but after the ball game, I appreciated the humour of Neis's play and Virgil never got any of the worst of it from me in the future.

Ducey was the first professionally trained umpire the fans at Renfrew Park had ever seen. He was a stickler for enforcement of the rules and professional conduct by players. In one game, he called George Green out when the batter had clearly beaten a throw to first base. Green's supporters erupted in confused fury. That evening, there were angry phone calls to the sports departments of both newspapers from fans demanding to know why Ducey called Green out. It was because Green had run well outside of the three-foot line on his way to first base.

Another time, Ducey got a good hand from the stands when he sent pitcher Herman Loblick of the Royals back to the bench to dress prop-

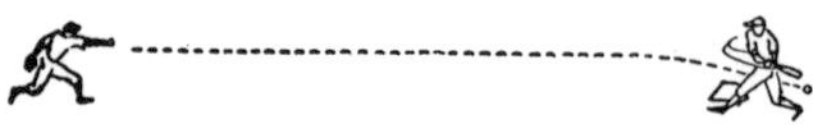

erly. He had come to the plate wearing his favourite blue sweater. Wrote an approving reporter,

> While this may have seemed a small item to some fans, it is this meticulous attention to detail that is putting the snap into the circuit and apparently making an unusual hit with customers.

At the next game, Loblick's entire team appeared on the field in sweaters to give Ducey the raspberry. The sports reporters covering the game agreed that it was a "bush league" display and from that point on, they were on Ducey's side as far as a professional diamond attitude was concerned. After that, all the Renfrew Park teams tried to dress and act like professionals.

Encroaching progress took over the grounds of the old Boyle Street diamond in 1935. Junior baseball moved to Renfrew Park but then declined for two seasons in the face of senior-league competition. On that diamond, "Chief" Jimmy Rattlesnake, a full-blood Cree from the Hobbema reserve, left Renfrew Park and the city senior league to join the Wetaskiwin team for the 1935 season. The tall, lanky left-hander led his new club back to Renfrew and the provincial finals against the Edmonton Shastas. But Buck Eaton proved more masterful on the mound, and the Edmonton club won the series three games to one as another season came to a close.

Grace presented Ducey with their first child in the spring of 1936: a son, Brant, named after Brant Matthews, their good family friend. John arrived at the hospital with an autographed baseball, hoping to launch the baby as a left-handed pitcher, but it did not turn out that way, causing the *Bulletin*'s Jack Deakin to observe a few months later,

Harry Cohen's 1937 Army & Navy Cardinals included such well-known local players as Dave Brockie, Tom Brant, and Ralph Morgan. Manager Walter "Phats" Rimstad is as right. Courtesy of the Edmonton Archives EA 524-29.

> John, I hear that despite your best efforts to make Brant, the Ducey junior, a southpaw, the youthful fella is still using his right hand to eat with, to talk back at you in a strange dialect and in fact to pick up objects that look like baseballs in his right hand. Boy, what a smack in the puss that must be!

Ducey continued to coach Vic Horner's Union Busses that year in the juvenile league and was pleased at the initial performance of a young, left-handed pitcher. Ed Belter had just turned fifteen when he won his first game at Renfrew Park, a 7-5 victory over the Riverdale Athletics. Reports on his four-hitter said, "He showed a fine curve ball together with a good fast ball."

In 1937, another new name popped up on the local sports pages. A young fellow named Cecil Goldstick began covering junior baseball for

the *Bulletin*. In the spring, he checked out Ducey's Union Bus team, forecasting that "Edmonton is going to see some first class homebrews in the near future." There were several outstanding young ball players on that Vic Horner-sponsored team, including Ed Belter, Harry Ornest, Cliff Johnston, Jack McGill, and Milt Trann, and Ducey coached them to the 1937 junior-league championship.

The 1937 senior crown was won by Ralph Morgan's Army & Navy Cardinals after a deluge of rain swamped Renfrew Park on 26 September. With the Cards leading 2-1 after four-and-a-half innings, sudden heavy rain caused umpire Ducey to call a thirty-minute delay while fans huddled for shelter in the grandstand under the old soccer-pitch roof. Some fans sought shelter in the press box, but not for long as it quickly filled with water. The grandstand roof sprang several leaks, while water up to a foot deep covered the area around home plate. It was one of the first of many soggy messages Ducey would get from the weather gods during his career at Renfrew Park. (Years later, Tony Cashman noted that Renfrew Park was built on the site of the second Fort Edmonton, established in 1803, and that ancient burial grounds were nearby; he surmised that ancient spirits still influenced what went on there.) Ducey called the game and the championship was awarded to the Cardinals. The few fans who remained had to wade through ankle-deep water to get out of the flooded exits as a curtain of rain brought down the 1937 baseball season.

Ducey left his job with Motor Car Supply that fall and moved a few blocks over to 107 Street, joining Herb Webb's Hardware as a representative for CCM sports equipment. The job gave him more leeway to travel to out-of-town umpiring work. Although dollars were scarce, the local sports scene remained very active. Many of the better athletes excelled at more than one sport. The Professional Pucksters put on a series of exhibition games at Renfrew Park to raise money for local charities. Five years after they started, a typical lineup still included Leroy Goldsworthy and Eddie Shore of the Boston Bruins, Roger Jenkins and Louis Trudel of the Chicago Blackhawks, and Earl Robertson, formerly of the old New York

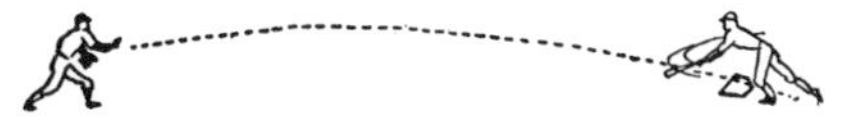

Americans. Now joining them were Neil and Mac Colville of the New York Rangers, and other professionals including Bill Carse, Walter Rimstad, and Cliff Kilburn. In one such match, Ducey joined in to play first base and do a bit of pitching. He thrilled the crowd with two hits in four at-bats. Clarence S. Campbell called the balls and strikes, while Ed McHugh umpired on the bases. Ducey's pitching efforts were without success, however, as the senior all-stars drubbed the hockey all-stars 16-3.

Later that year, Goldsworthy's team played a benefit game for Pete McCready, then the popular, hard-hitting centre fielder for the North Edmonton Belmonts. McCready had broken his arm when he was hit by a pitch, and his baseball pals wanted to raise some money for him. By then McCready's heavy drinking had taken its toll, and his best playing days were behind him. Still, a large crowd of loyal fans turned out to support the colourful slugger and threw $161.90 onto the Sunday silver collection tables. A highlight of the event was a foot-race around the bases between the two umpires, Ducey and George Green. Huffing and puffing, Ducey won only because Green spotted him a ninety-foot lead, starting from home plate while Ducey led off from first base.

Even Ducey occasionally changed sports, lacing up the skates to "umpire" exhibition hockey games. Once, refereeing an Oldtimers' game at the Arena, he kept up with the veterans until late in the third period, when every one of the players spilled over the benches and each threw a puck on the ice. Referee Ducey was faced with watching a dozen different games at once. He sensibly gave up.

In July of 1935, 1937, and 1938, Ducey was chief umpire at the Saskatoon Exhibition's annual baseball tournament. It was one of the prairies' most prestigious tourneys, established in 1922 by John C. Cairns to provide citizens with some good baseball entertainment after the old Western Canada League had prematurely folded. With the exception of 1924, the tournament ran continuously through 1969, an indicator of how seriously baseball was taken in Saskatoon and surrounding countryside. Ducey received warm praise for his performance from a local sports

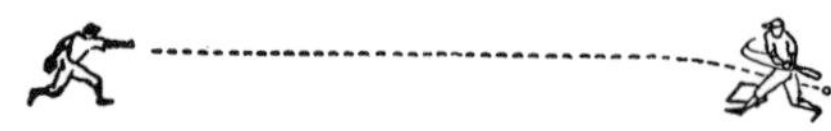

columnist after umpiring the final game in 1938, won by the Rosthern Wheat Kings over the Lanigan team 4-0:

> Then there is the "Man in the iron Mask," John Ducey of Edmonton, who combines the most efficient umpiring with a crowd appeal that cannot be under-estimated. John keeps every game under perfect control, calls 'em as he sees 'em and has players and fans liking it every moment, and if you think that's a cinch—try it some time.

Ducey's former Arrow Bus team moved up to the senior league in 1938, and it pleased him to be umpiring as they won the league championship, beating the Army & Navy Cardinals 5-4 in the final game of a seven-game series before 4,500 fans at Renfrew.

The umpire turns to the ice

Late in 1938, Ducey received an attractive offer to return to California, this time as the manager of the huge Pan Pacific ice arena in Hollywood. Professional hockey had lapsed in Hollywood but an artificial-ice boom had hit California. Arenas were filled with eager amateur skaters who paid 40¢ in the afternoon and 55¢ at night to skate. The Olympic success of Sonja Henie and her subsequent skating tours sparked the rise of travelling ice shows such as the Ice Follies and the Ice Capades, drawing huge crowds to arenas across the continent.

Ducey was enticed back to Hollywood by contacts made there in 1930-31. By the spring of 1939, when his first season was over, a quarter of a million skaters had paid to use the Pan Pacific rink. Skating lessons, rentals, and sharpening gave the arena an extremely lucrative season. And whenever a movie star laced on skates, Ducey himself was usually teaching. Charlie Chaplin, Norma Shearer, and Joan Crawford were some of the big Hollywood names who took to the Pan Pacific ice regularly while Ducey managed the rink.

The author, Brant Ducey, at age three, in the arms of Babe Herman at Gilmore Stadium, Hollywood, California, in April 1939. Herman was just beginning the first of six seasons with the PCL club after twelve years in the major leagues. From the John Ducey Collection.

The Hollywood stint also allowed him to renew acquaintances with a couple of old friends. Marion "Red" McCarthy, who would later become a skating star with the Ice Capades, was born in Edmonton and played sandlot baseball with school chums Ducey and Riley Mullen. Afflicted with Saint Vitus' Dance, he took up skating to restore his health. He became a Canadian skating champion, earning a position on the Canadian speed-skating team that went to the 1932 Olympics. By the late 1930s, McCarthy had turned to exhibition barrel-jumping and become world champion. He was famous throughout North America for his ability to jump fifteen wooden barrels, each two feet wide. But the jumping took a heavy toll on his body, finally forcing him to turn to figure skating.

The other Hollywood friend was Babe Herman, then in the twilight of his baseball career playing the first of six seasons for the Hollywood Stars of the Pacific Coast League. The Pan Pacific Arena was just a few blocks from the Gilmore Field ball park. Ducey would head over to the ball

park, son Brant in tow, to visit with Herman and take in an occasional afternoon ball game in the spring of 1939. In June, the success at the Pan Pacific brought Ducey an offer to go to San Diego to work at a new arena opening there, but by August, the deal was turning sour. With Grace expecting a second child in the fall, the couple decided to return to Edmonton. Ducey was soon back umpiring at Renfrew Park. In October, their daughter Duane was born.

Canada was enjoying its last summer of world peace in 1939, but there was little peace at Renfrew, where the baseball wars continued, usually with Ducey in the middle. In one game, outfielder Fred Lupul got in a shoving match with him and knocked the umpire's mask off in a dispute over a strike. Lupul was tossed out and Ducey wrote the league president demanding a stiffer penalty, but with no result. A few weeks later, young Eddie Belter was pitching a four-hitter against the Dodgers when two sudden hits and an error cost three Dodger runs. Disgusted, catcher Cliff Kilburn got in an argument with Ducey, then walked out of the catcher's box. Ducey tossed Kilburn out of the game, but the fiery catcher came roaring back, kicking him in the shins and popping the umpire a glancing blow on the face. Team-mates had to restrain Kilburn from any further damage. One of the loudest rhubarbs of the year was turned over to the league president's office. (Belter's fine pitching job was gone too, victim of a 4-0 loss.) Kilburn and Ducey continued to mutter at one another in the future but a restrained respect developed on both sides and they never had another major rhubarb. In a moment of reminiscence decades later, Kilburn recalled Ducey saying, "Don't you mess with me or you're gone again." Replied Kilburn, "I won't take any messing from you while I've got this bat in my hand."

As the baseball season came to a close, Ducey soon had another off-diamond offer, this time to manage the Winterland Gardens ice rink in San Francisco. He took it. A few months later, Grace and the children followed him by train to settle there for the winter. But the world was

quickly changing around them. Just as they were planning the trip to San Francisco, Canada entered World War Two. Ducey's mother, to whom he was devoted, was now bed-ridden with a serious illness. Still, sensing he might be on the verge of a good off-season career, he could not pass up the San Francisco job.

The winter of 1939-40 proved to be another good season for ice-skating in California. Beans Reardon came to town and, at Ducey's urging, dropped into the rink. Ducey got him on skates, and on the ice, for only the second time in his life. He also got lots of publicity in the sports pages with Reardon pictured hanging desperately onto the railing, dressed in a three-button suit and tie. Relieved to get off the ice, Reardon took Ducey for a few beers at a nearby tavern. The two baseball buffs spent the evening discussing old times in Edmonton and Reardon's starry career in the National League. Ducey talked of going to Hawaii that fall if plans for a skating arena in Honolulu materialized, but they never did. So in the spring of 1940, the skating season over, the family returned to wartime Edmonton.

By 1 May, six of the eight columns on the front page of the *Bulletin* were taken up with news of the war. Young men were volunteering for the army, air force, and navy in large numbers; after brief basic training, they were quickly shipped off to England, which was leading the Commonwealth's battle against the German invasion spreading through Europe. The Edmonton Chamber of Commerce announced it would cooperate with other boards of trade in the west to secure a larger measure of war contracts for western Canada. The demands of war quickly drew the city and the province out of the Depression as new economic and production demands took over, and all of this activity was magnified several times over when the United States was drawn into the war in December 1941. Edmonton, by virtue of its heretofore isolated location on the northwestern prairie, became a major staging point for the war in the Pacific theatre.

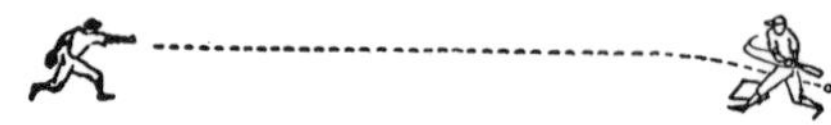

The spring of 1940 was far later than usual in Edmonton but sporting interest was just as keen. The Edmonton Grads and their coach J. Percy Page were preparing to disband after their spring games, bringing an end to twenty-five years of outstanding competition in women's basketball. Bob Feller had pitched modern baseball's first opening day no-hitter, with Cleveland's 1-0 victory over the Chicago White Sox. Two weeks later, James Otto (Tex) Carleton, a veteran major-leaguer who had spent the previous season in the minor leagues, pitched a second no-hitter as Brooklyn beat Cincinnati 3-0.

Renfrew Park offered some escape from the news of the war, mused Jack Kelly in the *Bulletin* on opening night:

> A bright, snappy league such as this promises to be will do folks a lot of good this season. I went down to the park last night with my head throbbing from war bulletins and flashes. Inside of five minutes, the old familiar howls from the grandstand wolves, umpire baiting and the game itself had routed the war shadows. Most of the fans probably had the same experience and left the park feeling a lot better than when they entered it.

For the record, the Dodgers trimmed the Arrows 6-2 in Renfrew Park's first wartime baseball game.

The four-team Central Alberta League was populated by former junior players who carried the hometown colours for Laurel Harney's Arrows and Ralph Morgan's Dodgers against Charlie Lewis' Ponoka Stampeders and Pete Ryan's Wetaskiwin Mustangs. Ducey arrived home on the last

Saturday in May, and the next day was back umpiring at Renfrew Park for the Central League. The *Journal* reported,

> John "Lefty" Ducey returned to action behind the plate on Sunday. The popular umpire was given a big hand from the large crowd as he was introduced. It was not merely a coincidence that the large Sunday crowd saw one of the best games to date in the Central League. Ducey kept the game going at a fast clip. There were no arguments and John simply abhors any stalling. Thus the players came in on the run and out on the double for ten of the best innings seen in the league to date.

Ducey also pitched in to help his friend Stan Moher start a new juvenile baseball league, putting on umpiring clinics and helping with the coaching. The *Bulletin*'s Kelly praised the effort as the kind which earlier developed the current crop of senior players:

> Back a few years ago a bunch of far-seeing ball fans organized a junior baseball league for the city. Vic Horner, Dave Little and John Ducey and a handful of others worked hard on this loop.... that work is paying off today. If it hadn't been done, we wouldn't have the framework of players here that made possible the present Central Alberta Baseball League and baseball would be dead and buried in these parts.

Kelly also made a pitch for encouraging youngsters to play baseball at an early age, a cause that Ducey also championed throughout his own career:

> Baseball is still our finest summer sport show. Once it gets into your system nothing will ever eliminate it. So far no one has devised a better way to spend a summer evening than by watching a good ball game. But to keep the game up to par here, we have to keep the kids playing it and to do that we have to give them a little help in getting organized.

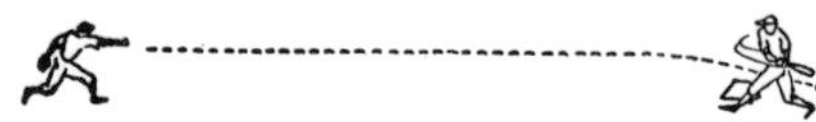

> Our schools have gone overboard for softball because it is the easiest and cheapest way to get the youngsters playing an organized game. Softball doesn't make a baseball player and never will, but it has just enough to satisfy a kid's normal urge to play ball. If you yourself prefer softball, or don't give a hoot one way or the other, you needn't bother about the foregoing, but if you get a thrill out of hearing the crack of a stinging three-bagger, of hearing a smoking pitch zip into a catcher's mitt, you'd better help sonny along the road you prefer—or he'll likely take the easy one.

Ducey's plans to return to sunnier climes for another winter of arena management had to be put off in the fall of 1940 as his mother's condition worsened. He had a near fatal experience himself, suffering a seriously ruptured appendix: he barely made it to the hospital. On 22 November, while he was still in the hospital, his mother died at the family home. Ducey was heartbroken when his doctor refused to allow him to attend her funeral. He stayed close to home and family that winter, working out of Herb Webb's Hardware and talking baseball. The loss moved him to become much closer to his father, Tom, who remained in Edmonton until he passed away in his ninetieth year, in 1962.

In March 1941, with Canada deeply engaged in the war effort, Henry Roche surrendered his lease on Renfrew Park, turning the operation back to the city in return for a $3,000 cheque. Including the capital he had invested to develop the baseball facility, he had probably lost close to $5,000 in the eight years he held the park. The city decided that henceforth it would lease the park on an annual basis to qualified baseball promoters. Many of the ball players had left for military service by the summer of 1941, but there

were still enough players for two senior clubs, the Arrows and Cal Pickles' Dodgers. Junior baseball returned to Renfrew Park and received great coverage on the sports pages: the *Bulletin*'s Jack Kelly served as league president and the *Journal*'s Stan Moher as secretary. It was a revival of sorts for junior baseball, which had flourished from 1932 at Boyle Street to 1937 at Renfrew and then almost died away as the crop of players graduated to senior ball.

That year, Henry Singer became the sponsor of the Henry Singer Clothiers, coached by Saul Ornest. Ducey managed the Cubs, and Morris Shields managed the Maple Leafs, whose lineup included a left-fielder named Dick Noon, then in his first year of junior baseball. Dick Speer headed the Canadians, who were starting young Des O'Connor at second base and flashy Albert Superstein in centre field. Another junior making his first Edmonton appearance that year was Doug Darrah of Viking, who came up against Ducey's Cubs in his first game. Darrah struck out thirteen of the twenty-three batters he faced over five innings, yielding only four hits; in a subsequent outing, he struck out seventeen. Over the summer, he pitched Singer's Clothiers to the league lead. But the Canadians met the Clothiers in the final series and, despite Darrah's strong pitching, beat Singer's team in three straight games.

The juniors shared Renfrew Park that summer—including Sundays—with a three-team senior league, made up of the Dodgers, the Arrows, and the Ponoka Stampeders. The ball park was packed for the last regular Sunday game as the Dodgers and Stampeders locked horns in what the *Journal*'s Ken McConnell described as "one of the season's best ball games." In the fifth inning, the Ponoka bench stormed onto the field to argue with Ducey over a called third strike with two out and the bases loaded. Ducey marched into left field to get away from the protesters, but the entire team followed him there in animated, angry fashion. The crowd was in an uproar as Ducey pulled out his watch and gave the Ponoka team sixty seconds to get back to the bench. When that failed, Ducey called a police officer and had one of the Ponoka officials escorted out of the park for foul language directed at an umpire. Peace eventually

returned to the diamond and a tight 4-3 win over Ponoka put the Dodgers into a playoff with the Arrows.

The provincial finals went to a seventh and championship game at a packed Renfrew Park on the evening of 11 September. Ralph Morgan, who had won the league batting crown, was on the mound for the Dodgers. The Arrows countered with their ace, Bill Lupul. By the sixth inning, the sky was turning dark and it appeared the game would soon be called due to darkness. In the bottom of the sixth, Morgan belted a drive over the head of left-fielder Freddy Lupul. As it rolled to the scoreboard, he raced around the bases with an inside-the-park home run, giving his club a 3-1 lead. In the top of the seventh, Mac Colville of the Arrows was picked off first base by Morgan. The call by Bob Coxford was heatedly disputed by the Arrows, and Arrow second-baseman Jack Carney began throwing baseballs onto the field, in the general direction of Coxford. That brought Ducey out from behind the plate. He promptly threw Carney out of the game and sent the angry Arrows back to their dugout. Morgan got the side out just as darkness fell, and Ducey was forced to call the game. The hard-fought 1941 championship went to the Dodgers.

Ken McConnell of the *Journal* liked the spirit shown by the underdog Dodgers and was optimistic about baseball's future:

> Best part of this series has been the interest shown by the fans. Baseball may not be coming back and reaching its old time appeal, but it is coming closer all the time to the position where it is Edmonton's favourite summer pastime. The crowds throughout the season have been good... in the playoff games they have been excellent. And this indicates that next year senior baseball will be even more successful.... Renewed interest in baseball indicates a return to better times.

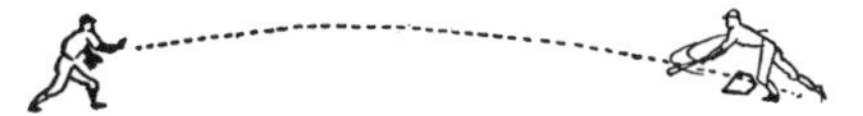

Eddie Shore

As the season of 1941 drew to a close, hockey great Eddie Shore made another of his periodic visits to Edmonton and was in the Renfrew Park stands as Ducey umpired the final playoff game. Shore was born in Fort Qu'Appelle, Saskatchewan in 1902 and broke into professional hockey with Regina in 1923-24. Years later, Duke Keats told the story of how he brought Shore to Edmonton the next season:

> I'd been worked over by some pretty good ones in my time, but there was this little guy from Regina who didn't play much, but when he did, he gave it to me good. I told my partner Ken McKenzie, "Get that little runt. I want him on our club." I offered Art Gagne and Bob Trapp for him.

The "little runt" was Eddie Shore, who would play in Edmonton for only one season. He had turned professional with the Regina Caps before Keats brought him to Edmonton. In 1926-27, he began a thirteen-year career with the Boston Bruins. Until Bobby Orr came along, Shore was unchallenged as the greatest NHL defenceman who ever played the game. He won the Hart Trophy four times and was an NHL all-star seven times. Shore was one of the original inductees to the Hockey Hall of Fame in 1943. He liked Edmonton, bought a nearby farm, and played baseball there in the summers. He and Ducey struck up a life-long friendship.

Shore was a tough, controversial man, full of contrasts. He is described as both the most loved and most loathed man in hockey. In 1940, he quit the Bruins in a feud with manager Art Ross and bought the Springfield Indians of the American Hockey League. He ran the club like a dictator

until 1967, finally selling the franchise after losing a stormy battle on player unionization. Still an active player in the summer of 1941, Shore was looking for help in his new role as club-owner. He asked Ducey to come to Springfield to manage the Eastern States Coliseum rink for him. Massachusetts seemed far away and Ducey, wife Grace, and his father discussed it for days. Ducey finally came to terms with Shore and accepted, arriving in Springfield in early September. There, Ducey was one step away from hockey's big league.

The first season with Shore was a busy, exciting, and sometimes zany experience. Ducey often found himself with Shore in smoke-filled hotel rooms in Boston and New York City, filled with hockey notables arguing with the wily Shore about player trades. At age thirty-eight, Shore still played defence for his team and his club dominated the league in the 1941-42 season. Shore kept his word and delegated absolute authority for the rink to Ducey. When the team was on the road, Ducey was booking the Ice Capades and the Ice Follies, supervising public skating at the Coliseum, and serving at no charge as business manager for an amateur hockey club. On the afternoon of 7 December, Ducey was in the Springfield Coliseum when a radio flash announced the Japanese attack on Pearl Harbor. The news made him cancel a local hockey game underway there, and things were never quite the same after that.

In February 1942, Beans Reardon arranged for Ducey to meet him at the annual dinner of the New York Baseball Writers Association. It was the most prestigious event of its kind in those days and attracted a thousand of baseball's top personalities and sportswriters. Reardon could not make it to New York but saw to it that Ducey had the time of his life, meeting with the "dean" of major-league umpires, Bill Klem. When Ducey was introduced as an umpire "from away up in Canada," Klem took him aside and talked to him about umpiring for some fifteen minutes. Klem ended the private audience by advising Ducey to put hockey aside and concentrate on umpiring:

> Young man, I am in the evening of my life, but my success as an umpire was because I am an umpire winter and summer. I have umpired for baseball and baseball only.

Ducey was dazzled as Klem parted with a final admonition: "Good luck, young man, and don't forget what I told you."

Ducey also met umpires Dolly Stark and Bill McGowan. He rubbed shoulders with such legendary baseball luminaries as Commissioner of Baseball Judge Kenesaw Mountain Landis, Babe Ruth, Bill Terry, Hank Greenberg, Joe DiMaggio, Mel Ott, Joe McCarthy, Frankie Frisch, George Weiss, Bob Quinn, Connie Mack, and Ford Frick, among others. It was "the most exciting night of my career," he would later say. The experience with Klem stuck with Ducey all his life, although he was never able to resume full-time umpiring.

Grace and the children joined Ducey at Springfield a few months later and were surprised to find themselves in the middle of air-raid drills. Suddenly the war, which had seemed so far away in Edmonton, appeared to be almost on their doorstep in Massachusetts. But the war didn't stop baseball, at least at the major-league level. In April, Ducey got to see his first big-league ball game when he visited Boston's Fenway Park on opening day of the 1942 season. He watched young Ted Williams connect for a home run against Connie Mack's Philadelphia Athletics as the Sox went on to a 5-1 win. The pitcher for the A's was Phil Marchildon, whom Ducey described as having "pitched a great game, despite the loss." Marchildon was a native of Penetanguishene, Ontario, in his third season with Mack's team. He and Ducey would cross paths again some forty years later.

After the hockey season, Ducey spent time umpiring regularly in a local Springfield industrial league and as a substitute in the Class-A Eastern League, which paid a rich $10 per game.

In Edmonton, U.S. consul John Randolph threw out the ceremonial first pitch as 3,000 fans watched the defending champion Dodgers,

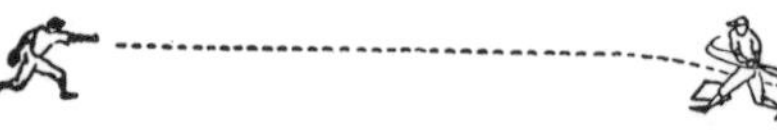

Many well-known Edmonton baseball names were in the lineup of Vic Horner's 1942 Arrows, champions of the Edmonton senior league. They included Mac Colville, Eddie Belter, Leo Ornest, Morris Hawkey, Doug Stevenson, Pete Danylowich, Phil Horn, Fred Lupul, Joe Shandro, and Colin Kilburn (batboy). Courtesy of the Edmonton Archives EA 524-30.

coached by George Green, take on Dick Speer's Arrows. Members of the league's third club, Aircraft Repair, were decked out in their new red and white uniforms to take part in the raising of the Union Jack to open the new season. Young Lefty Belter struck out eight for a decisive 11-2 win. Dick Noon moved up to senior ball, replacing Doug Stewart in left field after he joined the air force. Like Marchildon of the Athletics, Stewart would soon spend the balance of the war in a German prisoner-of-war camp. New to senior ball with Dick Noon was Albert Superstein, who started in right field. The two young outfielders were anchored by Dave Brockie in centre field. The Dodgers and Arrows battled for the lead, but Belter and Morrie Hawkey pitched the Arrows to victory in the 1942 playoffs.

Just as they were wrapping up the season at Renfrew Park, word came that 100 Albertans were among the 3,300 Canadian casualties suffered on the beach at Dieppe in France. By early fall, the war's effect was all-pervasive. In the U.S., gasoline rationing put an end to Ducey's visits to Fenway Park in Boston. Then the U.S. Army took over Shore's Eastern Coliseum for staging purposes, putting the Springfield Indians out of the league and Ducey out of work. He suddenly found himself and his family stuck in the eastern United States with no job and a mortgage on the first house he had ever owned.

Ducey, a family man approaching his mid-thirties, had been ruled out by the services and classified "4-F" because of "flat feet." Still, if he wanted to help with the war effort, a job would be found for him. He was hired as a plant guard with American Bosch Corporation and sworn in as a civilian auxiliary member to the U.S. military police. The job, which he would hold for the next fourteen months, required him "to protect war material, war premises and war utilities." It came complete with a policeman's uniform, badge, and holstered .45 pistol, which, fortunately, he never had to fire.

That winter, Shore had Ducey organize an amateur hockey team, the Springfield Warriors. They played on an outdoor rink, and it was no fun standing around an open rink during the Massachusetts winter. Shortly thereafter, Shore left to take over the Buffalo Bisons hockey franchise in the eastern division of the American Hockey League. The future began to look bleak for Ducey. A possible full-time umpiring job with the Eastern League the next summer looked like it might be a casualty as well, as most minor leagues were closing down for the balance of the war. In the

end, the Eastern League operated throughout the war, but the minor leagues declined from forty-one in 1941 to just ten in 1944.

The only cheering note was a visit from his father, who arrived just as the 1943 major-league season was starting. It was an excuse for the two to take in the opening game of the Boston Braves at Braves Field. They later went across to Fenway Park to watch the Red Sox beat the Yankees. Ducey was thrilled to see Bill McGowan, dean of the American League umpires, behind the plate. He noted on his program,

> McGowan has more color than all the other A.L. umpires put together. National League umpires are much more lively and colorful. The American League favors a dignified, conservative type.... In other words, no rhubarbs. McGowan should have been a National Leaguer.

His bias toward Reardon clearly showing, Ducey could have added that he took the National League approach all the way, including Reardon's use of the big, inflatable chest protector. After a brief tour of New York City, Tom Ducey left to visit relatives in Corry, Pennsylvania. Ducey was saddened to see his recently widowed father leave. Nor was he thrilled to carry a lunch bucket to guard duty at the Bosch plant. Facing a summer in Springfield with no baseball, Ducey then got a lucky break.

Still an American citizen, Ducey qualified for a job with a Utica, New York construction company, one of sixteen engaged by the U.S. government to build the Alaska Highway. The job was based in Edmonton. Ducey jumped at the chance, putting Grace and the children on a train for Edmonton in early May; he soon followed. Before long he was behind a desk as a freight expediter for Bechtel, Price & Callahan, helping organize massive freight movements northward with the U.S. Army Corps of Engineers. The job came through the help of his good friend Leroy Goldsworthy, also born an American citizen and now heading the expediting department for the contractors.

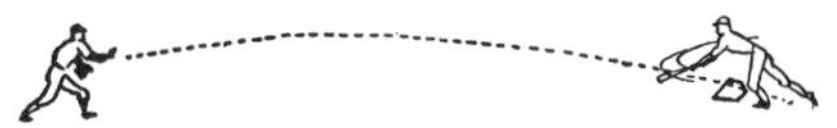

Ducey with long-time pal Leroy Goldsworthy (left), in May 1943, just after "Goldie" rescued him from wartime Massachusetts and got him a job in Edmonton where the two worked as freight expediters for the U.S. Army engineers. Courtesy of the Edmonton Archives EA 524-31.

Ducey's good fortune did not end with his new assignment. The war, which had taken baseball out of Springfield, had brought the game to Edmonton in a big way. The huge influx of U.S. personnel provided enough players for first one and then two U.S. Army teams. The Americans also brought more than enough baseball-hungry fans to keep Renfrew Park jam-packed for the rest of the war. At first, though, just what would occur was a bit of a mystery, noted Ken McConnell of the *Journal*:

> Bud Corcoran of the Dodgers is busy endeavoring to line up talent and it is whispered that the club looks pretty good.... Aircraft Repair may be the team to beat.... But the team that holds the most interest at the moment is the U.S. Army Air Force outfit. It would be nice to know

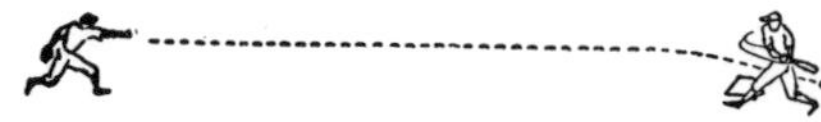

> more about them. Maybe it's the censor.... Maybe we are phoning the wrong numbers.... So far the U.S. club is rumored to be pretty fair, with a sprinkling of minor-leaguers.

McConnell's musings were soon answered, as a unique chapter of Edmonton's baseball history began to unfold.

10

The Yanks invade Renfrew

IN THE SUMMER OF 1943, DUCEY'S FATHER HELPED HIM FIND AND BUY THE GLENORA HOME WHERE HE WOULD RESIDE FOR THE REST OF HIS LIFE. It was an easy walk to the street car stop on 124 Street and then on down Jasper Avenue to his office on 112 Street... or downtown to 101 Street, where he could walk from the Selkirk Hotel down to Renfrew Park. Ducey did not own a car until 1948, when his Dad gave him his old war-built Willys. As a result, Ducey was a poor but not accident-prone driver, and he was always happy to turn the driving over to Grace.

In 1942, Edmonton's population was 97,000. By the next year it is estimated that this had been augmented by some 20,000 Americans. Many

were troops, air crews, and military support staff, but most were occupied with staging work for the Alaska Highway and the Canol Pipeline. Bechtel, Price & Callahan was involved in both of the huge construction projects. There had been only three senior baseball teams at Renfrew Park in 1942. Now the fans were buzzing about a new city senior league—"a league which figures to offer the best brand of ball Edmonton fans have seen in several years," predicted the *Journal*. The new league was made up of the U.S. Army Yanks, Vic Horner's Arrows, the Dodgers, and the Aircraft Repair Hornets.

Among the local boys playing as the season began were Ed Belter and Ken McAuley with the American-dominated Hornets. George Green, Dick Noon, Dick Tougas, Ralph Morgan, Tom Brant, Ken Samis, and Albert Superstein led the Dodgers, while Leroy Goldsworthy tried a comeback at second base. Only Fred Lupul and Morrie Hawkey remained from the Arrows' old guard. Depending on their military status, others joined the league later. The fans were delighted to welcome them back for another season. *Journal* sports editor George Mackintosh also had a welcome for Ducey:

> Regulars among the league's followers will get a bang out of seeing John (the Great) Ducey calling balls and strikes again. A notable absentee from Renfrew Park for a couple of years, Ducey returns to the scene of some of his biggest umpiring triumphs tomorrow. He'll probably have a lot of "the jockeys" giving him a ride about his eyesight, but he'll have as many agreeing with his decisions, and he'll handle the game the right way; you can depend on it that he'll be the boss out there.

On a warm, sunny 23 May, a Sunday afternoon crowd of 5,000 packed Renfrew. The fans spilled over into right field and were in high spirits as they settled down to watch two American batteries start the season off. The Edmonton Arrows had Hal Stafford of Vermont pitching to "Tex" Fowler of Dallas. The U.S. Army Yanks countered with Walter Misosky

Captain Frank Wrigglesworth (standing, right) and his U.S. Army Yanks became one of Renfrew Park's favourite teams during World War Two. One of two American military teams to play in a local four-team league, the Yanks usually beat any visiting U.S. service clubs. Courtesy of the Edmonton Archives EA 524-32.

from Pennsylvania and Andy Konopka from Milwaukee. The official ceremonies also had a distinctly American hue, with two fully uniformed U.S. majors and a lieutenant handling the ceremonial first pitch routine. The Stars and Stripes flew from the top of the packed first-base bleachers, and the military trappings added to the holiday mood of many in the big crowd, who roared right back when umpire Ducey roared "play ball!"

Along with a handful of Americans, coach Bill Downes' Arrows featured some local ball players: Harry Ornest at second base, Joe Shandro at shortstop, Pete Danylowich at third base, and Fred Lupul in the outfield. Captain Frank Wrigglesworth, playing second base, went with an all-U.S. army squad. Walter Misosky was too much for the Arrows, holding them to three hits, as his team won 9-3. But the overflow crowd went home happy. Baseball was back at Renfrew Park in a big way.

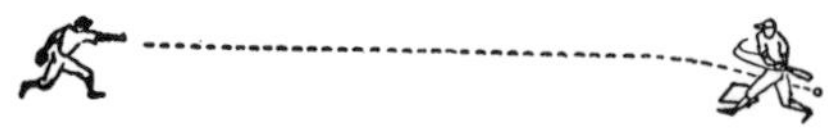

It wasn't long before Edmontonians had adopted the U.S. Army Yanks team as one of their own, as other U.S. military teams flew into Edmonton to play exhibition games. On 4 July, a record Sunday crowd of 8,700 fans put their silver on the collection tables and jammed into Renfrew Park for a double-header. The excess crowd was seated on the grass behind the first-base foul-line and behind ropes strung from right field to centre field. Ducey umpired behind the plate; Bob Coxford worked the bases. In his first start as a pitcher in the senior league, the Dodgers' Forrest Hunter struck out seven Arrows, allowing only three hits for a 3-2 win. In the second game, the Yanks blasted out fifteen hits to win 14-6 over a fatigued U.S. Army team, which had flown in from Great Falls, Montana that morning.

It was fun for the crowd too. Of considerable surprise to the local fans was a new custom the Americans brought to Renfrew Park:

> We could become befuddled though, around the seventh inning when the hundreds of American people now residing in the city stand up for their "seventh inning stretch." They like their baseball and attend regularly. They also have a great number of their kin to cheer as all teams have players from the United States in their lineups.

While the league played weekday games as well, Sunday at Renfrew Park was "the big day." By law, nothing but the churches was open on Sundays. Commercial entertainment, such as movie theatres and bowling alleys, was restricted by the *Lord's Day Act*; baseball admission was by silver collection. For a nickel or more in change, thrown onto the wooden tables at the entrance gate, a fan and his family could get into Renfrew Park. It was the best entertainment value in town, and it packed them in every Sunday. What was lost on gate receipts was almost made up by selling peanuts, hot dogs, and soda pop to the huge crowds.

Yet for all the people looking for a bargain on "silver Sundays," there was a greater number of loyal and generous fans who came out because

Renfrew Park remained *the* place to be on Sunday afternoons during the war. Observed one reporter,

> It was just like old home week. Into the park came Alex Watt and brother Gordon, home on leave from the Navy...Each has played plenty of hockey in these parts...Paul Maher, former Pacific Coast Hockey League star...The Martell brothers, Henry, Burns and Emil, the former fresh from a nifty 71 at the Highlands golf club tournament... remember how Emil could go and get 'em in centre field?...Ed McRae representing the long arm of the law, and Roy Gerlitz, ex-law enforcer...Mr. and Mrs. Barney Sanderson, red-hot baseball fans...Mr. and Mrs. Russell Love...Bill Lewis of the Fourth Estate...Syd Hamilton, star shortstop in the lush days...Young Jerry Dea, Maple Leaf juvenile hockey star and son of Howard of the old western Canada hockey circuit...Bob Causgrove, promising young ice star...Martin Collingwood, the big soccer man...Bob Donovan, who was managing hockey teams in Edmonton when many of the ball tossers on parade Sunday were just cutting their eye-teeth...George Snowden, manager of the E.A.C. junior hockey team...Bob Muter, municipal golfer...Hales Ross, the lumber tycoon...T.J. Ducey who was confident that the game would be well umpired...And also along was Frank and Mrs. Coulson, with many other members of the family, and many other good citizens....

The ball park was the place to see and be seen.

Baseball fans were also happy to help out with the war effort. One Saturday night in July, 3,000 turned out for a benefit game between the Canadian and U.S. all-star teams in support of the "Stamp Out the U-Boat" campaign. The *Journal* reported the campaign raised $1,000 through admissions and the purchase of War Savings Stamps at the park, "enough to buy nearly 12 depth charges to blast Nazi subs." The fans were happy as their boys defeated the Yanks 10-6, and one fan won the pool on the final

Wartime baseball was a popular attraction at Renfrew Park as a large influx of Americans swelled Edmonton's population. A capacity crowd lined the outfield fences as Ducey called balls and strikes on a Sunday afternoon in 1943. Courtesy of the Edmonton Archives EA 524-33.

score, taking home $185 in War Savings Stamps. A few weeks later, fans raised $1,000 for sailors on the destroyer *Athabasca*.

The two-nation crowds were good-natured and got along well. The larger the attendance, the more festive the mood. The only frustration came when concessionaires could not keep up with the demand for ice-cold soda pop on some of the warmer Sunday afternoons. Big Bill Matthews, Renfrew's loudest fan and Ducey's nemesis, was back too, leading a cheering section from the first-base bleachers, according to the *Journal*:

> He gave John "Lefty" Ducey a pretty fair "ride," and was up to some of his old tricks too. He recruited a gang of boys, promising them an ice cream cone if they joined him in giving Ducey the well-known Bronx cheer.

Matthews also made it his business to ensure both players and umpires were kept on their toes and urged to perform at top calibre. He enjoyed his greatest day of razzing over an event that got umpire Ducey national coverage on the Canadian Press wire and into sports pages in the United States that July.

Because there were limited facilities under the old wooden grandstand at Renfrew, the umpires customarily dressed for the game uptown in a basement room at the old Selkirk Hotel at Jasper Avenue and 101 Street. Then they would walk down the hill and over to the ball park where they put on their spiked shoes and equipment. While umpiring behind the plate with his partner Bob Coxford on the bases, Ducey suddenly called a halt to a game in the second inning, much to the confusion of the crowd. Unknown to them, he had split his blue serge pants, "in a section which threatened to cause him no little embarrassment." The always composed and immaculately garbed umpire had to sidle over to the field-level press box and ask the scribes if anyone had a safety pin. Of course no one did. Calling the managers over, Ducey had to canvass both teams before finding someone who had a pair of blue pants big enough to fit him. They were the street clothes of Hornets' shortstop Harry Jones.

"They covered up the umpire's nakedness," wrote George Mackintosh of the *Journal*, "but it was the first time this corner has seen Ducey when his face was red!" Said Ducey himself of the sartorial crisis after the game, "Boy, I knew I was in the bag. I attempted to side-saddle toward the grandstand with as much poise as possible." He described the trousers he borrowed from Jones as "...the morning type, having a purple tinge and wide stripes. Jimmy Walker would look like a hillbilly alongside my symphony of stripes and purple."

From the bleachers, Bill Matthews soon figured out Ducey's dilemma and rolled his own pant legs up above his knees, tied his green sweater around his middle like a kilt and put on a piping skit to mock the embarrassed umpire. Mackintosh wrote,

A U.S. Army news photographer (left) was usually on hand for Sunday games at Renfrew Park during World War Two. Courtesy of the Edmonton Archives EA 524-34.

> The fans roared at his antics, and the league owes him a vote of thanks for helping to make the customers forget about the hold-up in the game.

It was seldom dull on Sunday afternoons at Renfrew Park, especially when Ducey was behind the plate.

The season was a great success, much to the satisfaction of organizer Bill Harris and his supporters, who had gambled on wartime baseball and won. The Arrows defeated the Hornets three games to one to qualify for the final series against the Yanks. That battle drew 7,000 fans out to the park on the last Sunday in August as the Yanks took a quick two-game lead. The Arrows won the third game 4-3, beneficiaries of a contentious decision by Ducey, who called the game after seven innings due to

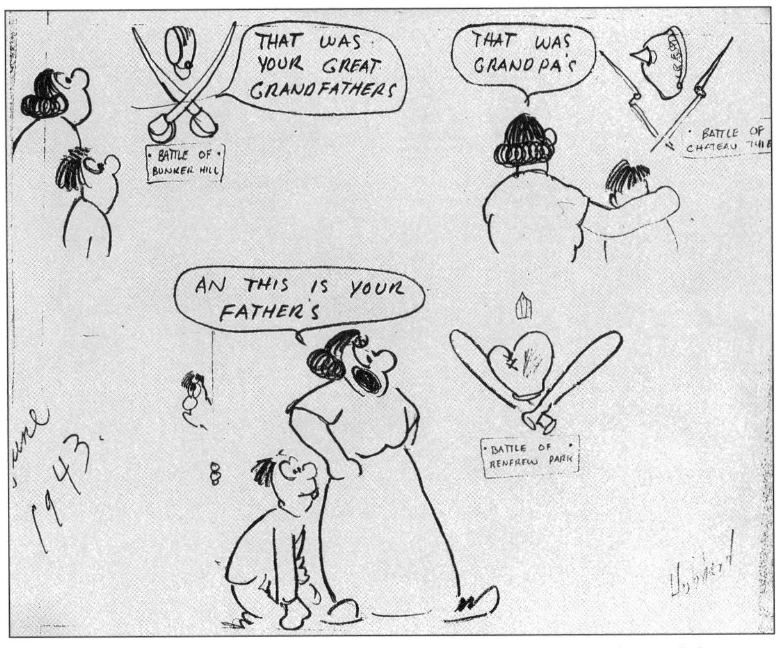

Ducey's diamond battles as an umpire at Renfrew Park were the subject of this cartoon in a 1943 U.S. services publications. Courtesy of the Edmonton Archives EA 524-36.

approaching darkness. The Yanks roared back to take the next game 16-5, then won the championship before 6,300 fans on Labour Day weekend with a 6-1 win. In the *Journal*, George Mackintosh concluded that the season had been a great success:

> The Yanks put color and attractiveness into the league all season long and helped in every way to create new interest in baseball around here. If they happen to be quartered here when another season rolls around, they can be sure of getting real support from Edmonton's baseball-loving fans.

Bob Coxford umpiring on the bases at Renfrew Park as a U.S. Army Yank beats out a close call at first base. Courtesy of the Edmonton Archives EA 524-35.

The next Sunday a crowd of 7,000 cheered "their Yanks" as they won the first of a best-of-five playoff series 7-6 against the visiting Calgary Navy team. The Calgary team had its supporters, though. Its roster included local favourites Doug Lane at first base, infielders Harry Ornest and Max Bentley, and catcher Hector MacDonald. The Yanks went on to take the series and the provincial championship three games to one. Some 23,000 fans packed the Edmonton park for the four games. "Edmonton is a real ball centre," reported the *Calgary Herald*, noting that "the work of John Ducey was one of the features of the series."

Baseball visitors to Edmonton, including major-league scout Jimmy Hamilton of the Chicago Cubs, were amazed at the size of the crowds and the quality of ball played at Renfrew Park during the war. Hamilton particularly liked the performance of pitchers Morris Hawkey, Maury Lavold, and Doug Darrah, as well as the play of Fred Lupul. He also had

praise for the "very good umpiring by a pair of men in blue [Ducey and Bob Coxford] who call them like big leaguers." A Calgary reporter speculated that Hamilton's visit might result in a move upward for Ducey:

> One thing the Chicago scout was impressed with was the efficient umpiring of John Ducey, so don't be surprised if the Edmonton arbiter advances into pro ball next season. Ducey is in a class by himself, and has been for a long time and the Edmonton league wouldn't be the same without him.

Ducey would indeed get an offer from professional baseball as a result of Hamilton's visit, but from a most unexpected source.

11

On the move again

IN FEBRUARY, DUCEY PREPARED FOR THE 1944 BASEBALL SEASON WITH A MAJOR WORRY ON HIS MIND. Shortages during the war had caused rationing on many civilian fronts: everything from butter to nylons was on a restricted list. Wartime shoppers had to save up and carefully dole out their food stamps and meat tokens to buy what previously had been freely available. The government also legislated the type of clothing to be manufactured and how many of pairs of shoes each person could purchase during a year.

It dismayed Ducey to learn that both blue serge cloth and umpires' spiked shoes were on the restricted list. His dilemma was described by Stan Moher in the *Journal*:

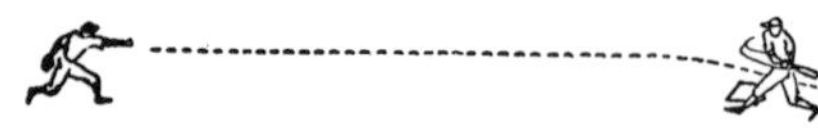

> Ducey has always prided himself on his appearance while carrying on his umpiring duties. Only blue serge would do in a suit and he had to have the correct shoes, the black tie, white shirt and peaked cap. This attitude on his part has gained him quite a reputation as a regular Adolphe Menjou of the diamond.... You can just imagine the state that John is in at the present time, when you learn that blue serge is out for the duration. And there will be no more umpires' shoes available.

Ducey appealed to the Edmonton Chamber of Commerce, which supported his cause with a letter to Ottawa. Within two weeks, he had a letter back from the Priorities Branch of the Federal Department of Munitions and Supply. It contained the good news that the Wartime Prices and Trade Board had issued a permit for his umpiring suit. Warren K. Cook Clothes of Toronto would make it to Ducey's specifications, with one minor hitch:

> All special features are being permitted with the exception of the pleats in the trousers. It is explained this addition is not permitted in the United States and since the countries are in accord, this exception is not thought advisable.

For the shoes, Ducey quickly turned to his former source and old friend, Beans Reardon. In a few weeks, one pair of used umpiring shoes, worn in the 1943 World Series, arrived in the mail at Ducey's home. A week later, the mail brought something else—this time a very big surprise.

The All American Girls League

Stan Moher got the scoop at the regular Saturday night, bring-your-own-bottle party at Ducey's house. The headline "Glamor Girls' League Wants John Ducey on Umpire Staff" greeted readers of the *Journal*'s Monday sports pages. Ducey had received a letter offering him a job from Ken

Sells, president of the All American Girls Professional Baseball League, which had been started the year before. The new league was bankrolled by William Wrigley, whose family also owned the Chicago Cubs. Jimmy Hamilton, the Cubs' scout who had been impressed by Ducey's umpiring at Renfrew the summer before, had recommended Ducey be hired to umpire in the new league.

Wrigley had put up $100,000 to start the league as a response to the need for recreation in towns occupied with large amounts of war defence work, much of which was being done by women. Associated with Wrigley were Branch Rickey, president of the Brooklyn Dodgers, and Paul Harper and Ken Sells of the Cubs. Wrigley's idea was to find the best women softball players on the continent and turn them into baseball players.

The offer Ducey received from Sells was attractive. Although his initial reaction was "now I've read everything," he had to give it some serious thought. With minor-league baseball all but shut down for the duration of the war in the United States, Wrigley and others felt that the All Girls League could be a box-office success in baseball-starved America. The league had begun with four teams: South Bend, Indiana; Kenosha and Racine, Wisconsin; and Rockford, Illinois. In 1944, Milwaukee and Toledo were granted franchises, and the promoters were eyeing an invasion of major-league cities when the war ended.

Real baseball was nothing new to an earlier generation of Edmonton women. In 1934, a four-team "city girls league" played at Boyle Street during the summer: Scona from the south side, the Eskimos, the Cubs, and the Eagle Toddies. Soon after, though, softball became the game of choice for women. Three Edmonton women softballers were among eight Canadians who successfully tried out for the All American Girls League in 1943. Kay Heim and Annabelle Thompson had played in the league the first season and were planning to return again in 1944. Heim was a catcher for the Kenosha team, while Thompson pitched for the champion Racine club. Thompson put off her wedding plans to travel to Chicago in 1943 for a tryout, after a successful softball career for Edmonton's

Walkrite team. She made the Racine team and was paid $90 a week to play. Travelling with her at the time was Helen Nicol, who had been an all-star pitcher for Harry Cohen's Army & Navy Pats. Nicol won a place on the South Bend Blue Sox in 1943 and went on to AGL stardom, pitching until 1952. She became the all-time AGL leader with 163 wins, setting the league record for strikeouts and games played. (Baseball historian Bill Humber lists fifty-three Canadian women who eventually played in the AGL, nine of them from Alberta.)

When the AGL began to look like a success, Wrigley told Ken Sells to go out and find more managers and umpires for the second season. In Edmonton, Stan Moher, now chasing a good story, reached Kay Heim at her home and described her as "enthusiastic" about the idea of Ducey umpiring in the AGL. "I think he'd do very well down there," she told Moher. "As a matter of fact they need someone just like him. I certainly hope he accepts." By now, Moher was having some fun at Ducey's expense. Working the story for all he could, Moher went on,

> Should Ducey grab at the bait and decide to head south again, he'll find umpiring for the femmes something of a brand new experience. Never averse to cursing it out with an irate balltosser who was of a mind to, "the Voice" will have to be more circumspect with the young ladies. He'll have to use nothing but honeyed words.

"Not that an umpire's life in the Glamor wheel is all old lace with nary a suggestion of arsenic," chided Moher. "Fact is, the silk uniformed performers get quite het up at times and are not above going after the arbiter with all finger nails bared and mayhem in their hearts."

That possible scene was enough for Grace, so the arbiter composed a diplomatic letter turning down the offer, "due to prior commitments." He probably did not at the time know that the AGL played softball, a fact that would have caused him to decline in any event. Both Edmonton's *Bulletin* and Calgary's *Albertan* took turns speculating on Ducey's pos-

sible move to the women's league. "They'd miss him and baseball in Edmonton would lose a lot of its color during the 1944 season should Ducey accept," speculated the Calgary paper.

Umpiring further afield

As it turned out, the new season saw Ducey umpiring more frequently in Calgary than in Edmonton. A dispute over umpiring fees between Ducey and the senior league broke in the Edmonton papers, and the story soon spread to Calgary. Despite the successes at Renfrew's box office in 1943, Bill Harris sent Ducey an offer of $7.50 per game, a cut from the $10.00 he had been paid the previous year. Ducey rejected the offer, failing even to reply at first. A concerned George Mackintosh broke the news to Edmonton sports fans:

> John "Lefty" Ducey, the peer of the west's umpiring fraternity, won't be out there on the diamond at Renfrew Park Sunday in his natty blue suit when the curtain goes up on the first offering of the city league season.
>
> That's a circumstance that will be regretted by a large number of fans. Over the years, Ducey has become something of a baseball institution—the Bill Klem of these parts. Even those who don't always see eye to eye with him are willing to admit that he runs a nice ball game and never fails to keep control when the going gets tough.... It will be unfortunate, this corner thinks, if some satisfactory agreement isn't reached that will bring Ducey back on the umpiring staff.

Ducey was rumoured to be holding out for $25 per game, which wasn't true. He simply wasn't going to umpire for less than the $10 he had received the year before. The hold-out continued and the league schedule went on without him. Ducey toured the north, umpiring army exhibition games along the Alaska Highway at Watson Lake and

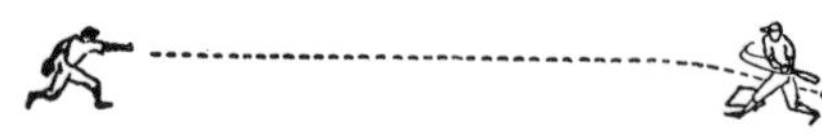

Ducey also had off-the-diamond battles relating to his umpiring wages and in 1944 went on a one-man strike until he was paid what he felt was proper. Courtesy of the Edmonton Archives EA 524-38.

Whitehorse. It was his first trip in an aircraft, a drafty, military DC-3, and landing and taking off in some locations gave Ducey a fear of flying that stayed with him all his life. Still, the trip was an adventure, and he would later repeat it. He had a great time talking baseball with the troops and was warmly welcomed by U.S. military personnel on his several northern umpiring stints.

In early July he went to Calgary to umpire a few games in the Foothills League and put on a clinic for that league's umpires. The *Albertan*'s Harry Scott termed it a rare treat for local baseball enthusiasts to see the Edmonton arbiter do his stuff. Neatly attired in a regular uniform of an umpire, Ducey looked the part the moment he took his position in the centre of the diamond to announce the batteries. And his work behind the bat was flawless.

To pressure the Edmonton league to re-hire Ducey, Hal Dean of the *Bulletin* simply re-ran Scott's entire *Albertan* column about the umpire. The *Journal* headline read "Ducey Umpires, But Out of Town":

> Umpire John Ducey returned to the diamond on Sunday. He didn't do his stuff at Renfrew Park but journeyed to Calgary for his initial start of the 1944 season.

Mackintosh and Stan Moher kept the pressure on. "Couldn't something yet be done to bring the parties involved to a round table discussion on the matter?" asked Moher. "Neither side seems willing to budge," wrote Mackintosh, "which this bureau thinks is unfortunate, for everybody concerned, fans, players and league."

The fans and even the players got into the dispute in the local papers. Dodgers' manager Bud Corcoran was authorized to speak on behalf of the team managers about the argument:

> We are primarily concerned with seeing to it that the players—who after all are putting on the show—are properly cared for. Expenses of a ball club are high. It is our belief that we are paying our umpires more than any other Canadian league of a similar type.

But Corcoran then strayed from the prepared script and put his foot in it, saying, "Frankly we need Ducey and we know it. But we don't need him

for any more money." Moher then revealed the league had decided that all umpires, regardless of experience, working either behind the plate or on the bases, would be paid $7.50 per game. "What does Ducey say?" Moher asked. Ducey replied, spelling out his umpiring credo:

> I am ready to return in an umpiring capacity for a fee consistent with the crowds being attracted by the league games. In the depression years I played ball in the matter. An umpire—particularly in the independent field—who has ability, hustle, and the capacity for keeping a tight rein at all times is worth something extra. The fans have the right to the best umpiring available. One would not expect the beginner to draw the wages of an old hand.... Nerve, judgement, thorough knowledge of the rules and correct interpretation of same, umpiring technique, these are the successful umpire's ticket. I feel that I have that ticket.

The league couldn't sustain the media barrage, and Ducey soon had a call from the senior league's Bill Harris. Yes, they would pay him what he wanted if he would just return to Renfrew. He did.

The 1944 version of the Edmonton City Baseball league was made up of the U.S. Army Yanks, the U.S. Signals, the Dodgers, the Arrows, and the Aircraft Repair Hornets; the Yanks and the Dodgers were favoured as the strongest of the teams. When the season ended, the power-laden Yanks again placed first, followed by the Dodgers, the Signals, and the Arrows. The Signals defeated the Dodgers in the playoffs, winning the final game 1-0 in front of 6,500 fans on the Labour Day weekend. But in the final series, the Signals were no match for the Yanks, who took the series four games to one, repeating as league champions.

Ducey returned to work for Eddie Shore a second time, managing the Buffalo hockey rink during the winter of 1944-45, but decided to return to Edmonton and baseball for good. Courtesy of the Edmonton Archives EA 524-37.

In mid-September, squadron leader Bill Hansen brought his Calgary Air Force Fliers into Edmonton to take on Wayne Adam's Yanks for the Alberta senior championships. But frigid weather hit the capital over the weekend and forced the teams to go to Calgary to play. Some 5,000 fans had filled the Calgary park to overflowing for the Sunday double-header with Calgary down by one game. Big John Carpenter, who had won the opening game 4-3 on Thursday, was back on the hill for the Fliers in game four. The 220-pound ex-policeman from Nelson, B.C. struck out eleven to win his second game against the Yanks and tie the series at two games each. That set the stage for the final, with Calgary's Stover facing the Yanks' Wilbur Ray. After ten innings, Stover and Ray were still pitching,

tied 4-4. In the top of the eleventh inning, Gino Valenti singled and stole second. He came home with what proved to be the winning run when Crumly cracked out a double. There were seven stolen bases in the game and it was one of the most exciting ever played in the annals of Edmonton and Calgary's inter-city rivalry—even if Edmonton had been represented by a team of American soldiers.

Ducey was not involved in the series. Earlier in September, he officially finished his stint with Bechtel, Price & Callahan and was transferred over to a similar civilian post with the U.S. Army. That allowed him to take a winter leave of absence and accept a position with Eddie Shore, assisting him with rink operations in Buffalo, New York, where Shore was running the Buffalo Bisons of the American Hockey League. Shore had also come into possession of the Baltimore Blades franchise and brought in Leroy Goldsworthy to manage that operation.

Ducey wanted one more try with the erratic Shore to see if he could make a career with him:

> After the Buffalo season ends next May I do not know what my plans will be. Eddie may wish me in Springfield immediately or he may not require me until the fall.

Because the situation looked rather uncertain, Ducey agreed that Grace and the children, both now in school, would remain at home in Edmonton until something permanent developed with Shore. Ducey, who had a game-day rink staff of 120, gained valuable administrative experience with Shore, and he always gave Shore credit for the learning opportunity. The two shuttled back and forth to Baltimore to help Goldsworthy, who found himself in a public relations quagmire. It had been created by Shore himself, who raised ticket prices and cut several members of the media off the "free pass" list. It took Goldsworthy the entire season to win back the goodwill of the writers and the fans with his own solid management performance.

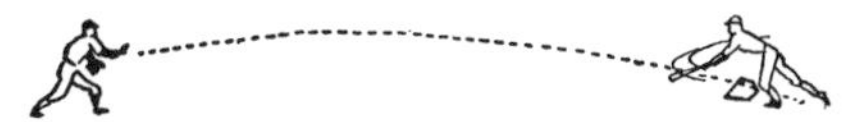

The dictatorial Shore brought on other problems in Buffalo, although they did not affect Ducey. But by spring he decided to pursue his future back home in Edmonton because he did not want to subject his family to another major move. Ducey was extremely devoted to the hard-nosed Shore and remained one of his most loyal defenders, a role few would play:

> I always had the greatest respect for Eddie. He treated me squarely. All he ever asked was to be honest with him and to do your best in your job. I never put any stock in his players' complaints that he was a tough boss. The truth is that players who got into trouble with him were in that situation simply because they tried to curve him. I was very close to Eddie in the three years I worked for him. I travelled with him, ate with him and played with him.
>
> He used to say, 'When we work, we work, when we play, we play." I was always grateful for the opportunity to work with him and believe me, I received a fine education in the administrative side of sport. It helped me no end when I went into the business side of baseball.

By the end of 1944, Edmonton's citizens had grown war-weary. The heady success of the Normandy invasion in June had soon given way to growing casualty lists in the daily papers as Canadian troops advanced through France, Holland, and Belgium at great sacrifice. Then with the spring of 1945 came hope. The tide of war turned, and the allied forces pressed on into Germany and toward Berlin. On 8 May, V-E Day brought an end to hostilities in Europe. In the Pacific theatre, U.S. forces were now winning the war island by island. Suddenly, it seemed the 1945 baseball season would be the final chance to watch the U.S. Army Yanks and

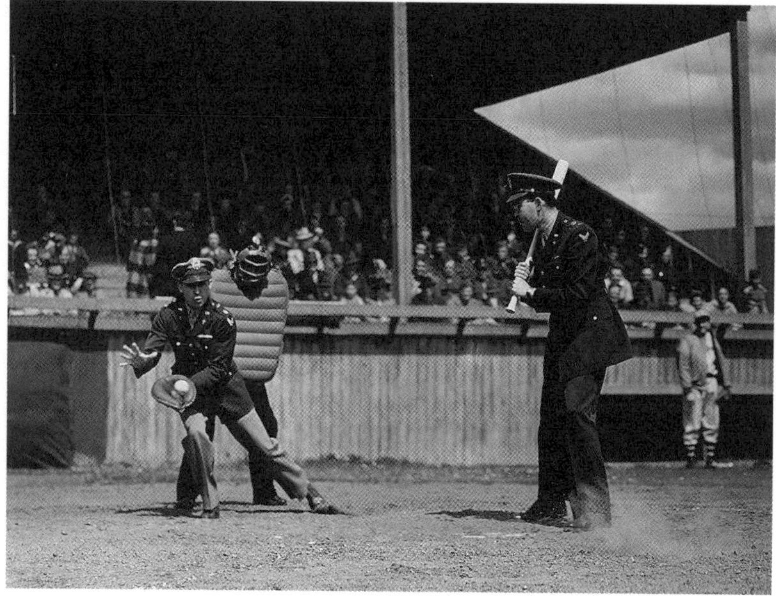

A special treat for Edmonton fans and umpire Ducey was the surprise appearance at the plate of U.S. Army sergeant Joe Louis, heavyweight boxing champion of the world, on 20 May 1945. Louis was making a tour of American military bases. Courtesy of the Provincial Archives of Alberta B1.542/1.

the Signals play at Renfrew Park. Continued cold spring weather kept the 19 May opening-night crowd down to 1,150 fans, who watched U.S. consul R. B. Streeper make the ceremonial first pitch to Alderman Fred Mitchell. The Arrows chased veteran Ralph Morgan from the hill with eight hits and eight runs in five innings. Playing his first game at Renfrew Park, new shortstop Frank Finn impressed the fans with a fine throwing arm and contributed a single and a stolen base. His team went on to dump the Dodgers 9-1 behind the pitching of Major Hal Stafford and Lefty Thomas.

The "real" opening day came the following Sunday afternoon, with the Yanks playing the Signals. It brought a big surprise for the 5,000 fans who jammed Renfrew on a slightly warmer day. Without prior announce-

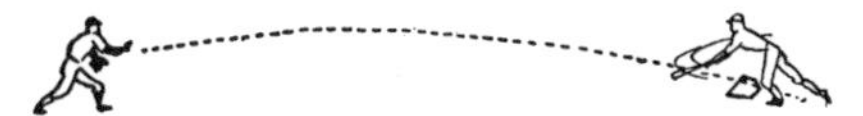

ment, the heavyweight champion of the world and boxing hero of every schoolboy was introduced on the field, wearing his U.S. army uniform. Sergeant Joe Louis, on a tour of U.S. forces, arrived at 2:00 p.m. and stayed for almost an hour, playing catch and posing for photographers. He then donned a catcher's mitt to receive the second ceremonial pitch of the weekend from U.S. Air Force Col. E. Stevens. Renfrew Park ballboy Ken "Emo" Awid, then a mascot for the Yanks, was on the field to see the great man himself and a bit surprised at his close-up view of the world champion:

> Joe Louis was a big guy. I remember he had a bumble bee on his nose and he didn't even know it was there!

Broadcaster Art Ward interviewed Louis on the field before game-time as the fans pressed against the wire netting of the grandstand for a closer look at one of democracy's greatest sports heroes. Stan Moher described the scene as youngsters started to converge toward "the Brown Bomber."

> Finally...the kids got to him. They couldn't get out on the playing field so they swarmed down—dozens of them—to the wire netting of the grandstand. Through the mesh they thrust bits of paper, envelopes, postcards...almost anything big enough for Joe's comparatively brief signature. He signed them all...and here and there he had a friendly word for some pop-eyed youngsters.

Cranked up by the sight of such a famous sports idol in their midst, the crowd rooted for the underdog that day. Their hopes were rewarded by the Signals' uncelebrated pitcher, Helmuth Brown. He tamed the Yanks by scattering ten hits through eight innings and led his team to a 7-4 upset. Louis watched from the Yanks' dugout, then left in the fifth inning to play a round of golf at Mayfair. The crowd stayed until the very end as the Yanks threatened with two runs in the bottom of the ninth but could

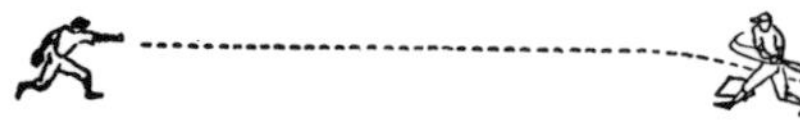

do no more. "It looks like a fine summer!" concluded George Mackintosh on an exuberant note.

On 29 May, there was another historic occasion at Renfrew Park as the Yanks again faced the Signals before a small Wednesday night crowd of 1,500 people. Herb Coxford was umpiring behind the plate with Fred Lupul on the bases. In the top of the third, the lead-off batter was Yanks pitcher Johnny Gray, batting against the Signals' George Yarrow. Gray took a mighty swing at a fastball and connected. The ball soared out toward the 410-foot mark in left-centre field. The entire crowd rose to its feet, cheering as the ball cleared the scoreboard and the sixteen-foot-high fence by some ten feet. It was later found sixty feet beyond the fence, so the mammoth swat had carried the ball some 470 feet. It was the first ball ever to be hit over the scoreboard at that distance. George Mackintosh, who had been following baseball in Edmonton for more than twenty years, termed it "probably the longest hit ever made in an Edmonton ballpark."

It was the first time the feat had been performed since the stockade below the hill was built, and it was something no regular at Renfrew had ever hoped to see. They'd have laid any kind of bet that it wouldn't happen. Everybody knows better now!

It was also the Yanks' first win of the new season, as Gray led his team to a 9-5 victory over the Signals.

By June 1945, Ducey was back home at his U.S. army job and negotiating for an umpiring post at Renfrew Park. He had a discussion with Dave Little, president of the Edmonton Baseball League, and proposed a fee of $10 per game as umpire-in-chief behind the plate, provided that, if base umpires were paid the same fee, he would rotate assignments between the bases and the plate. But if he was to work all games behind the plate for the same fee as the base umpires, he wanted an unspecified increase. To avoid the rhubarb which occurred the previous season, he put the details of his requirements in a confidential letter to Little and waited for a response.

The war years had caused a five-year break in Edmonton's junior baseball play. To help meet the need for a fresh crop of young ball players, Ducey volunteered to get a new junior baseball league up and running. Phil Horn, who served as league president, Paul Martell, Buck Eaton, Clarence Moher, and Cecil Goldstick, among others, organized a five-team league, and Ducey put on umpiring clinics. The group got the City of Edmonton to open a new diamond for the juniors in a field adjacent to the football facilities at Clarke Stadium. Groundskeeper Dick Gittens turned the park into a real gem. Along with Clayton Dolighan, Ducey pitched in to help coach the Edmonton Athletic Club team. The other teams in the league were the South Side Athletics, the Dodgers, the Arrows, and the Canadians.

Still waiting to hear from the senior league, Ducey received offers to umpire for the Vancouver Senior Baseball League, a semi-pro circuit, as well as the Foothills League in Calgary, which offered him $50 a week. He couldn't get the time off from his job to accept either offer. Meanwhile, down at Renfrew Park, Dave Little could not get his league colleagues to

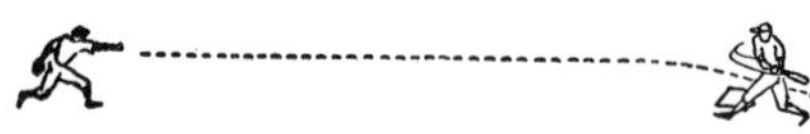

agree to Ducey's letter on umpiring fees for 1945. Some of them found the umpire too "dictatorial," and the season again opened without him. This time, the team managers issued a written statement which ended by saying that the league would have to watch its costs closely once the war ended and the American fans left town:

> We anticipate a drop in gate receipts and we would like to have on hand men who will work for a normal fee and not be in the hands of an umpiring monopoly.

One of the managers spread the story that Ducey was asking for $25 a game. That charge made its way into the *Journal* where George Mackintosh, who had been league president the year before, was quick to shoot it down as misinformation. In July, the one-man umpiring "monopoly," supported by his friends in the local media, won out. The ballclubs had grown unhappy with the existing umpiring talent. Dave Little announced that Ducey would umpire behind the plate at Renfrew for the balance of the season. The news was well received by local baseball fans.

By early July, the heavy-hitters on the Yanks moved the club into a first-place tie with the Signals. Burchfield, Hackney, Crumley, Valenti, Galvin, and Meyers continued to spray the ball around the park and over the fences. It didn't look like they needed any help, but for a brief time, the Yanks gave Edmonton fans a look at one of the most accomplished ball players ever to appear at Renfrew Park. Alex Kampouris, a stocky infielder, was on his way home from military service when he stopped off to join the Yanks near the end of the season. He had played in 702 games from 1934 to 1943 in the National League for Cincinnati, New York, and Brooklyn and had a .243 career average before joining the service. Then in late August, less than two weeks after the war with Japan ended, the Yanks locked up the lead and waited to play the winner of the Signals versus Arrows semi-final series.

The beginning of the end of wartime baseball at Renfrew Park. Managers Frank Wrigglesworth of the U.S. Army team and Calgary's Ray Nicklin with umpires Herb Coxford and Ducey. Players from the Yanks and Calgary Currie Barracks were already being mustered out of the services just as the 1945 provincial playoffs began. Courtesy of the Edmonton Archives EA 524-39.

Despite a gallant effort by Samis, Superstein, Finn, O'Connor, and Morrie Hawkey, the Arrows were edged in two close games, losing the series to the Signals three games to one. Appropriately, perhaps, the last playoff series of the wartime league was an all-American affair. Kampouris was around just long enough to help the Yanks take their third straight Edmonton title as they swept the out-classed Signals in four straight games.

Ducey accepted another umpiring tour of U.S. Army points along the Alaska Highway in early August. He was in Watson Lake on 10 August when the announcement came that the war with Japan was over. Within weeks, his U.S. Army job had ended as well. As the baseball season drew to a close at Renfrew, he realized he would again have to look for a per-

manent job. Before he did, he went to Calgary on business for ten days and managed to umpire four playoff games for the Foothills League.

He was struck by the support baseball was finding in Calgary, where the senior playoffs drew crowds of 2,500 to 3,000. Junior baseball was also thriving, with considerable young local talent in the southern city. As he reported his observations of the Calgary scene to George Mackintosh, a plan began to germinate in his mind about post-war baseball in Alberta:

> The calibre of ball is good in Calgary. Frankly I don't think any of the clubs have the power and class of the Yanks of our Renfrew park circuit. But then the Yanks are a superior ball club in these times, in this part of the country. Calgary's baseball is highly competitive and the fans seem prepared to overlook whatever shortcomings may be present in the playing end.

Besides, he noted, improvements were being made to Buffalo Stadium all the time and its grass infield was one of only two in the west (the other was in Vancouver).

Much of the excitement among Calgary baseball fans had been generated by the Currie Army Barracks club, which beat out a tough Purity 99 team in the playoffs. Their roster included Doug Lane and Dick Noon, flashy ex-Purity shortstop Woody Huckaby at third base, and hockey players Ken Stewart and Max and Reg Bentley. As the provincial playoffs started in mid-September, U.S. players were being moved home, while many Canadian men were being discharged from the services. Max Bentley went directly from the Calgary ball field to rejoin the Chicago Blackhawks of the National Hockey League in late September. As a result, playoff baseball in 1945 was not representative of earlier league play. A weather-delayed seven-game series between Currie Barracks and Edmonton's U.S. Army Yanks was cancelled with Calgary leading three games to two, when most of the American team was moved back to the States for discharge. Still, the *Albertan*'s Tom Moore reported that the

series had "caught popular sporting imagination like no other athletic event this season." Currie Barracks continued to play for a few more days, until members of its own club were discharged. Led by player-coach Charlie Lewis, the team was declared the champions of western Canada after an abbreviated two-game series with a team from the railway centre of Transcona, adjacent to Winnipeg. Ducey had umpired the series in Calgary as Calgary won the fist game 11-1. The next day, darkness forced him to call the second game in the tenth inning with the teams tied 3-3. It was the end of wartime baseball in Alberta.

The large influx of returning veterans came home proud of the role Canada had played in the war but fatigued over its length. They wanted to work, settle down, raise families, and lead normal lives. While many returned to the land and some sought homesteads, most of them came back to the larger cities like Edmonton and Calgary in the pursuit of work or government-aided higher education. One result was a house-building boom, which aided a healthy post-war economy.

To earn a living that winter, Ducey negotiated a job as director of public relations for Art Potter's Edmonton junior hockey league, the first such job created in western Canadian junior hockey circles. But all his free time was spent trying to hatch the scheme which had been brewing in his mind since the Americans left Renfrew Park. He was also acting as a part-time baseball scout for the Seattle Rainiers of the Pacific Coast League, but it was clear that he needed something more substantial. Signing a few Edmonton ballplayers to professional contracts and the junior hockey job would not provide enough to raise his family and pay the mortgage. He entered discussions around town about what directions baseball should take in post-war Edmonton. With the U.S. Army players

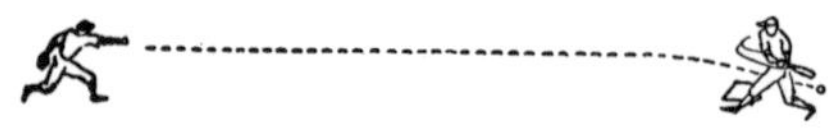

gone and the many American fans leaving town, he began working on a new senior baseball combination which he felt would keep local fans coming into Renfrew Park in 1946.

He enlisted the help of two diverse partners in a plan to gain control of Renfrew Park. One was a relatively new acquaintance, Capt. John Beatty, a native of Baltimore, Maryland, still stationed in Edmonton with the U.S. Army. The other was old schoolboy chum Riley Mullen, then coaching the Edmonton Flyers. Mullen was selected to enhance the trio's profile with Edmonton sports fans. With their help, Ducey began to lobby City Hall to get the park lease. They proposed to organize a semi-professional league of three or four teams and play an interlocking schedule with Calgary teams.

But there was opposition. Another group, composed of Wally Aldridge, Jack McLean, and Bill Bull, among others, was also after the lease. Their approach was to organize three teams made up of local players as a less formal, play-for-fun operation. Ducey, however, didn't believe Edmonton ball fans would go for that idea after the calibre of ball they had enjoyed during the war years. He proposed to import a handful of professional players from the States to play with the local players, adding some box-office appeal for the fans. He mounted his lobbying campaign in the local sports pages, stressing that he had already lined up a working agreement with the Seattle Rainiers to supply him with twelve to fifteen ball players. All of these, he claimed, had the potential to make the Pacific Coast League after some seasoning. None ever came to Edmonton.

In Skagway, Alaska, in the middle of one final mid-winter business trip for the U.S. Army, Ducey got the cheering news from his partners that City Hall had awarded them the ball park lease. After working behind the plate almost every year since Renfrew's opening thirteen seasons earlier, the umpire now had the keys to the ball park.

The Renfrew revival

Early in the winter of 1946, Edmonton's sports pages were suddenly filled with news about local baseball developments. A few weeks later, similar stories began to appear in Vancouver, Calgary, and Winnipeg as Ducey kindled talk of a revival of the old Western Canada League of the 1920s. He bolstered his Seattle baseball links and announced he had also lined up a working arrangement with the New York Yankees through scout Joe Devine, who had been the manager of the Calgary Bronks in the early 1920s. In April, Ducey and his partners formed a joint-stock company, The Edmonton Baseball League, Ltd. With John Beatty as secretary-treasurer and Ducey as president, the league would operate out of Ducey's house until they could afford a permanent office. In reality, it was run mainly out of Chris Diamond's Johnson's Cafe, the Selkirk Hotel, the Shasta Cafe, and Mike's News-stand, as well as the sports offices of the *Journal* and *Bulletin*.

Ducey, Beatty, and Mullen confirmed they would have a three-team, semi-pro league in Edmonton, made up of both local and imported American players. They proposed an interlocking schedule that had an Edmonton team playing in Calgary and a Calgary team playing in Edmonton each weekend. Then Ducey announced he was heading for Seattle and California to meet officials of the Seattle Rainiers and the New York Yankees.

As some thirty-five to forty local hopefuls arrived for tryouts at Renfrew Park on 1 May, reports of his progress soon reached Edmonton. Joe Devine and San Francisco Seals president Charles Graham got Ducey a story in the *San Francisco Chronicle* which read a bit like a Christmas wish list. The paper reported,

> Ducey has it within his powers to immediately employ three catchers, two shortstops, three pitchers and two left-handed outfielders. If you want a shot at the Canadian circuit, call Ducey at the Hotel Stewart.

It worked. Within a day, Ducey had sixty phone calls from hopeful ballplayers, thirty of whom he interviewed. With Devine, he signed six players, including Gino Valenti, who had been with the U.S. Army Yanks at Renfrew. By the time he got home, another half-dozen former wartime players had been added to the list.

With the American players on the way, Ducey realized he would have to find housing for them. So he ran an advertisement directed at baseball fans, asking, "Do you have a room or an apartment to rent?" The response wasn't bad, but to get all the players sheltered, he had to persuade his sister Mary and his father to room Tony Chula and Frank Gonzales at their house for the season.

To further media interest, Ducey claimed that, given his warm reception by organized baseball people on the west coast, a return of the Western Canada Baseball League by 1947 was a real possibility. That meant play between Edmonton, Calgary, Saskatoon, and Regina might start up again after a twenty-five-year absence. But he cautioned it would depend on how well the interlocking schedule worked out with Calgary in 1946.

Taking over a ball park under a neophyte management, securing ballplayers from both sides of the border, organizing teams, and trying to work out arrangements with the Calgary clubs within two months was an awesome task. With a little help from their friends, however, the three partners did it by the 22 May Opening Day. Don "Red" Ferguson was their first employee, signed on to manage the food and drink concessions. Fred Lupul agreed to act as chief umpire. *Journal* sports editor George Mackintosh agreed to serve as the league's new president. Dr. Gig Dobson said he'd volunteer to serve as doctor for the teams, something he did for the next thirteen years without charge. Cecil Goldstick said he'd do anything, from running the grounds-keeping crew to acting as trainer to the players. Harry Ornest, who had already secured a starting job at second base, said he'd take on management of the program, cushion, and souvenir concessions, thereby setting himself on the road to a lifetime career in vending and sports management.

An entire subculture of ball park denizens offered to work part-time for very little: ticket sellers and takers, pass-gate staff, concessionaires, and off-duty policemen. The Awid boys, who lived across the street from the ball park, returned as ballboys and with groundskeeper Bob Chapman, to unofficially run the park. From the professionals came more expensive talent, offered at little or no cost out of civic pride from the lawyers, Smith, Clement, Parlee & Whitaker; the auditors, Winspear, Hamilton and Anderson; and the Bank of Nova Scotia.

Still, it was no easy task to start a three-team league in post-war Edmonton. Even finding enough new baseballs was difficult. Help came from George Weiss, then general manager of the New York Yankees. He had George "Twinkletoes" Selkirk, then managing the New York Yankees' farm club in the International League, bring two dozen regulation baseballs across the border and mail them to Ducey from Toronto. Weiss refused Ducey's offer to pay for them and wished him good luck with the new endeavour.

With help from the bank, Ducey, Mullen, and Beatty managed to put together $20,000, "more money than we'd ever seen before in one place," quipped Mullen. Yet they needed help to buy home and road uniforms and equipment for each team. Team sponsors needed to be found to help with the start-up costs for three new baseball clubs. Ducey knew exactly who to call on, and the three men he picked all said yes to his request to sponsor a team. His close friend, hotelier Brant Matthews, was the first to step in, agreeing to sponsor the New Edmonton Hotel Eskimos. Harry Cohen said his store would underwrite the Army & Navy Cardinals. Haberdasher Cal Pickles enthusiastically took on the task of backing Cal's Cubs. Somehow, by 22 May, the preparations were complete. It was time to play ball.

12

Back to baseball

THE EDMONTON OF 1946 WAS VASTLY DIFFERENT FROM THE CITY OF 1939.

The population had increased from 90,400 to some 120,000, but the economic legacy of the war was far greater than these figures suggest. "The war," writes Howard Palmer in *Alberta: A New History*, "lifted Alberta out of its economic depression." Spurred by the large influx of Americans as well as by the Commonwealth and other air training programs located there, Edmonton suddenly had an aviation industry which linked it with the rest of the world and helped to open up the North. Wartime projects like the Alaska Highway and the Canol pipeline continued to spur growth in the North, to Edmonton's benefit. Returning veterans were eager to get back to work and educational pursuits. Women, who had held down many of the wartime jobs, had to go back to their homes, but their venture into the workforce would soon result in permanent social change.

The province itself was now under the political direction of Ernest C. Manning, who had become premier in 1943 upon the death of William Aberhart. Manning presided over a continuing transformation of Alberta's economy and society until 1968.

In May 1946, the *Edmonton Journal* reported that Quebec's Premier Maurice Duplessis had told a Dominion-Provincial conference that if an agreement was not forthcoming on certain principles of confederation, he was "going back home." Edmonton's bank clearings, city tax collections, land sales, and building permits all showed record-breaking advances for the first four months of 1946. It indicated, said the *Journal*, "the ever-expanding importance of Edmonton as an industrial and trading centre." In sports, Bob Feller had just pitched the second no-hitter of his career as Cleveland beat the Yankees 1-0. The outgoing hockey committee of the Edmonton Flyers recommended the re-appointment of Riley Mullen as manager-coach for the 1946-47 season.

That spring, Doug Darrah was temporarily living in stables at the Calgary Exhibition race track. He and his brother were racing horses brought down from their home at Viking:

> I had an appointment to see Sam Timmins and Harold Cundal about playing ball for Calgary. But one day, right at the race track, I got a call from John Ducey. "Hello Doug," he said in that clipped American accent. "You know you can't play ball in Calgary. We'll give you a better deal in Edmonton. We'll pay your way up here, get you a job, and pay you $385 a month." To me that was almost like a million dollars. I told my brother he was in charge of the horses, and I caught the next bus for Edmonton.
>
> John met me at the bus station and said, "C'mon, we'll go out and meet your new boss." It wasn't exactly what I expected but the job was on the bottling line out at Sick's Brewery in the west end. Ducey and the brewmaster, Mr. Herunter, were friends. I got a rooming house miles away, near the end of the streetcar line in the west end. They

> didn't serve any breakfast, so I'd get to the brewery and during the day the only nourishment I had was a "green" beer when the line went down. Then I'd have to get down to the ball park for practice by four o'clock. Often I'd be "glowing" pretty good and Ducey knew right away what the trouble was. "Okay Darrah, you get out and run in the outfield and don't you stop running until I tell ya."

Darrah's problem was solved when he took another job, but the incident illustrates the one sore-point about Ducey's scheme to mix American ballplayers with the Canadian boys. Most of the latter had to hold down full-time jobs to supplement their slim baseball salaries, while the American imports were paid more just for playing baseball. It continued to bother some Canadian players, but by the time they completed their years in the Big Four League, most agreed they had learned a lot more about playing baseball alongside the Americans. Said Des O'Connor,

> I played two years for the Calgary Buffaloes, and I learned more about baseball from Alex Uffleman and more about pitchers from Jimmy Gibson than I could have imagined. As kids we got very little if any coaching, but we learned how to play baseball in the Big Four league.

Ducey brought Bert Culver back as player-manager for the New Edmonton Hotel Eskimos along with Gino Valenti, the fleet centre-fielder who had starred for the Yanks the two previous seasons. Two other popular imports were outfielder Pete Tedeschi and shortstop Art Flores. Local players included Darrah, Belter, Price, and Stevenson. Johnny Galvin returned to play for the Army & Navy Cardinals, along with Bob Arieta. Their Canadian players included Ornest, Brockie, McGill, Latiff, Lane, Hawkey, Miller, Douziech, Seaman, and Buck Eaton. Eaton had begun his career at Boyle Street in 1929 on Ken McConnell's *Journal* team. A hairdresser in civilian life, he played service ball during the war. The 1946 season would be the old knuckle-baller's last in baseball.

Cal's Cubs, with John Beatty as their business manager, began the season under manager Ralph Morgan, who was later succeeded by Laurel Harney, another of Edmonton's two-sport hockey players. Harney began playing baseball in the late 1920s with Webb King's Stockyard Bulls. In 1927, he briefly joined the touring House of David ball club after they arrived in Edmonton with both of their catchers out with injuries. When Harney moved to the west coast in August 1946, Ducey imported third-baseman Arnold Martin as the Cubs' player-manager. Except for Martin, the Cubs were made up of local players, who included Albert Superstein, Stewart, Samis, O'Connor, Brant, Nick Masikewich, Bill Gadsby, Frank Finn, Jimmy Rattlesnake, and Lefty Thomas. It would be Rattlesnake's last year at Renfrew Park. He had been discovered and brought to Edmonton by Webb King in the mid-1930s. The "Chief" pitched for Wetaskiwin and Ponoka, as well as making intermittent appearances at Renfrew Park. In the spring of 1942, he organized an all-Indian ball team which briefly played in the Hobbema-Ponoka area. The tall, lanky left-hander pitched most of that season for Cal's Dodgers. In 1943, Harney took him to Vancouver, where he pitched briefly. A popular but uncomfortable success in a white-man's world, he had to battle personal lifestyle problems. When he came up from the Hobbema to pitch in Edmonton, his passions were "Sweet Marie" chocolate bars, steak, and beer. Because of the latter, he was never paid until after he had pitched.

The irrepressible George Green also decided to retire after twenty years as a player and joined Fred Lupul as an umpire. He was just as colourful behind the plate. Bob and Herb Coxford were the other umpiring team, although Ducey himself continued to umpire in league, playoff, and exhibition games whenever one of the other four was unavailable.

Edmonton fans quickly split into three partisan camps. Those who cheered for the underdog Cubs, made up of local boys, largely despised Ducey's own flashier Eskimos. The Esks, with a small nucleus of American players, had a large core of fans who stuck by them over the next five seasons. The balance supported the Cardinals and their roster of starry local players.

After taking over Renfrew Park in 1946, Ducey often shed his promoter's suit to umpire during regular senior league play, even though he was general manager of the Eskimos. Nonetheless, both the opposing Cardinals and the Cubs were happy to have him behind the plate. Courtesy of the Edmonton Archives EA 524-40.

The teams battled each other through the summer and provided entertaining, competitive baseball, about as good as semi-pro baseball ever got. The fans were also treated to some exhibition baseball. Saskatoon arrived in late July but was beaten by each of the three Edmonton clubs. Chicago Blackhawks star Max Bentley brought his Delisle Tigers into Renfrew in early August, but they were completely rained out. The Los Angeles Ligons, a black touring team, played a local all-star line-up a week later. The Ligons claimed they had won all but six of the eighty games they had played since spring training, but the Edmonton all-stars beat them 12-0 and 4-1.

The fans enjoyed it when the teams were divided up with the Americans playing against the local players. The promise of a lucky number draw for two dozen pairs of "free nylon stockings," a luxury still in scarce supply, drew in 4,000 fans for a benefit game on behalf of the Kiwanis Boys' Home. The Canadians beat the U.S. all-stars 9-6 on a fine pitching performance by Tommy Brant. Behind the plate, Ducey warmed up the crowd by engaging in a fierce argument with Albert Superstein. It ended with him throwing the fleet outfielder out of the game. Superstein was one of Renfrew Park's most colourful and talented players. Fans and players still remember his speeding runs and spectacular catches against Renfrew's right-centre field fence. Off the field, he and Ducey were often at odds over his salary demands. Superstein felt that if he made the club, he should be paid the same as the Americans, whether he had a local job or not. To make his point, Superstein often skipped road trips, but Ducey held his ground. Superstein eventually walked away from the league over the issue.

The two international squads went at it again in late August and with Tommy Brant pitching, the American players won the rubber match of the three exhibition games, 4-3. Renfrew Park had again become a popular place, and the mix of league and exhibition games with touring clubs drew in the fans. Soon Ducey began beating the drums for regular games with Calgary. It was something he had promised the City of Edmonton in return for the park lease. The idea of inter-city play had nothing to do with boosterism in 1946 but had everything to do with attracting paying fans to the ballpark. Ducey's frequent umpiring stints in Calgary over the years made him popular with the Calgary media. However, in the role of a promoter between the two rival cities, he quickly found himself striking out.

A challenge to Calgary

Purity 99's Harold Cundal and Calgary Buffalo general manager Sam Timmins were simply not interested. Their Foothills league was drawing good crowds to Buffalo Stadium. They wanted nothing to do with the expense of taking a team into Edmonton each weekend while hoping that Calgary fans would turn out for a regular weekly visit from an Edmonton team. Besides, it was Ducey's idea, and he had not talked to them about it. They said they had no space in their schedule for inter-city games.

After these failed attempts, Ducey enlisted the Edmonton media and a few sympathetic Calgary writers in a war of words to goad Cundal and Timmins into playing against Edmonton teams:

> You don't want to get your heads knocked off. That's what will happen if you take on any of our clubs...I think Calgary is losing its nerve. Things are popping, boys! It's the Western Canada League in 1947! Let's lay the groundwork for the return of organized baseball with some inter-city baseball.

Happy to have a Calgary platform, Ducey let loose:

> It's about time we got out of this kid's league and dress up for the show, give the fans what they want and come out of the petty larceny, 10 cent pop gun, chiseling, drug store baseball methods of operation. Let's get up town a little bit and show the fans that Edmonton and Calgary are ready for a good deal.

The public challenge worked. Ducey got a phone call from Harold Cundal, who was incensed over Ducey's suggestion that Calgary teams were afraid to play against Edmonton. "We will play any of your clubs, any time, any place," Cundal shot back. It was just what Ducey wanted to hear. They agreed each would bring a ball club into the other's park in an exhibition series in late July.

Ducey operated on the premise that the greater the conflict, the more fans would come to the ballpark. He was happy to warm up the rhetoric in the Calgary papers to create a better draw at the gate, whether in Calgary or Edmonton:

> We'll take the semi-pro out of that biscuit league, but I want extra police protection to send our Cardinals into Calgary for these two games and I will accord you the same protection when our Calgary clubs come to Edmonton. Our fans are now convinced that Calgary is choking up.

When Calgary writer Tom Moore suggested Edmonton needed Calgary teams to spice up its league attendance more than Calgary needed Edmonton, Ducey was happy to set him straight:

> I don't need your clubs here to put across baseball. We are doing all right, but our fans are eager to see Calgary scalps hanging in left field.

With the date finally set for the Army & Navy Cardinals to invade Buffalo Stadium, Ducey had an "unavoidable conflict" and was unable to go, sending Riley Mullen in his place. He hastened to assure Calgary fans he was not afraid to appear in front of them, after hurling insults at their ball club:

> I cannot possibly accompany the team on this trip, but hope to do so on the next trip, if your clubs have sufficient fortitude to play further games. The man does not breathe in Calgary who can intimidate Ducey once Ducey's spiked shoes hit the green in the Calgary park. You can take down that screen in front of that two-bit ball park in Calgary if I decide to umpire. I don't need it. I call 'em as they are.

Lloyd Hawkins, the Purity 99's business manager, fired right back:

> You better see to it that you guys and your Edmonton fans have plenty of [Chief of Police] Reg Jennings' blue coats on deck for Saturday when we start pushing your Edmonton clubs around. Not to protect

> our players but to protect any Edmontonians rash enough to incur the wrath of any of our boys.

The sportswriters in both cities were having a field day, and fan expectation began to rise, as the script had called for.

With Riley Mullen preparing to take the Cards to Calgary, Ducey got to what was, to him, the heart of the issue—that Alberta baseball needed inter-city play if it was to survive:

> Western Canada is ripe for a return to organized baseball, but how are we going to affect the changeover when the men heading the game in Calgary are content with their own little show? After all, hockey is promoted on an inter-city basis in Western Canada. There's no reason why a real attempt shouldn't be made to establish a diamond circuit along the same general lines. Maybe the wrong guys are in control in Calgary.

He would repeat this theme frequently over the next ten years.

The battle finally turned to the diamond. Led by playing manager Johnny Galvin, the Cardinals routed Purity 99 in the first game, 10-4; in the second, they were edged by Calgary 11-10 in the late innings. A week later, Purity 99 visited Renfrew and won both games of a split double-header. In the afternoon game, neither Doug Darrah nor Chief Jimmy Rattlesnake could hold Purity, who defeated the Cubs 12-4. Tony Maze, who drove in four runs while playing first base, pitched the nightcap, striking out fourteen and beating the Cardinals 5-2. Meanwhile, in Calgary, the Eskimos

Inter-city baseball returned to Alberta after a twenty-five-year absence when Harry Cohen's Army & Navy Cardinals defeated Calgary Purity 99 in 1946. The series set the stage for four seasons of entertaining rivalry, which began the following year with the formation of the Big Four semi-pro league. Courtesy of the Provincial Archives of Alberta A 7254.

split two games with the Calgary Bears, losing 5-4 then winning 7-5 behind the pitching of Lefty Belter. The reception was warm in both cities and the fans were noisy but not threatening—in fact, they loved it. Ducey's point was made. Seeing the fan response and the gate receipts, Cundal and Timmins agreed that when their seasons finished, the winners should play for the championship of Alberta senior baseball.

Edmonton fans were treated to a full diet of post-season baseball in the fall of 1946. When darkness forced a tie game, the Cards and Esks waged

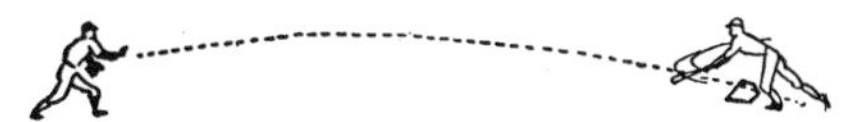

an eight-game playoff in late August and through the Labour Day weekend. Ducey turned the ball park operations over to Johnny Beatty and umpired both games of the Labour Day double-header with Fred Lupul. No one accused him of being partisan. In the first game, things got a bit out of hand when Harry Ornest tangled with Esk manager Bert Culver in a close play at second base and treated the crowd to a brief fist-fight. To the delight of the Cubs fans, the Cards beat Ducey's Eskimos in the lengthy series. The upset gave them the right to play Purity 99 for the Sick's Brewery Rainier Trophy, the emblem of the Alberta senior baseball championship.

Just as the Edmonton playoffs were ending, Johnny Galvin had to leave the Cards to return to his job at Purdue University. Young Harry Ornest was named acting manager for the provincial series. In Calgary, the Purity 99s wrapped up their final win over the Calgary Bears before a Labour Day crowd of 4,600, which had overflowed cramped Buffalo Stadium. Not wanting to miss the struggle he had done so much to promote, Ducey donned a uniform to serve as field manager of the Cardinals in Calgary. His appearance caused blood to boil in the stands. Some 2,600 fans began to vent steam at the now-despised Ducey and his Edmonton team. Morrie Hawkey was shelled early and Belter, added to the team for the injured Dick Latiff, came in with Calgary enjoying a 5-4 lead. "Belter never pitched a better game in his life," observed George Mackintosh, as the left-hander shut Purity out on one single with nine strike-outs over the next six innings. The Cards took the opener 10-5, then left Calgary fans muttering when they won the second game 3-2.

At Renfrew Park, Calgary found their footing and took the next two games. Now the Edmonton fans were shell-shocked. But Edmonton won the fifth game, which meant the championship would be decided in Calgary. Ducey was a bit more subdued as the clubs returned to Calgary to settle the matter.

Some 3,000 fans were at Buffalo Stadium for the sixth game. The Esks' Bill Whyte held Calgary to one run until relieved by Ed Belter in the

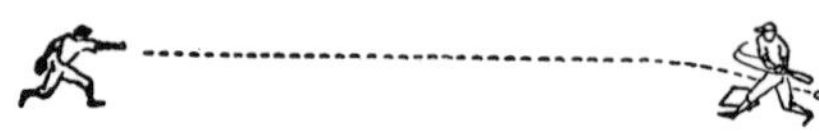

sixth. Promptly yielding a three-run homer, "Lefty" then settled down and shut Purity out the rest of the way. With Edmonton down by one, Harry Ornest ignited a four-run rally in the eighth inning, aided by Doug Lane, Pete Tedeschi, and Jerry Seaman. The 99s threatened to score in the bottom of the eighth, but Walt Gully died at third as a long fly to right field ended the inning—and what proved to be the game. Darkness then forced home-plate umpire Fred Lupul to call the game, causing a chorus of boos and giving Edmonton the championship. Both Ducey and Cundal decided then and there that they needed lights in their respective parks so darkness could never again interfere with an important game.

The Cardinals finished off the visit by splitting a two-game Sunday exhibition series at Buffalo Stadium the next day. In the second game, Albert Superstein's severe ankle sprain caused Ducey to juggle his lineup. With Edmonton leading 5-2, the thirty-eight-year-old former umpire elected to come in to play first base in the late innings. At the plate, Ducey faced big Alex Uffleman, who quickly got two strikes on him, much to the pleasure of the Calgary fans. Then Ducey connected, lashing a line drive over third base for a single. From first base, he began to heckle the Calgary pitcher, taking a lengthy lead. On a second attempt, Uffleman picked Ducey off first base by five feet. It was the official, humiliating end to Ducey's playing career. As he trotted dejectedly across the diamond in front of the pitcher, Ducey asked "Alex, why did you do that?"

"Well," said Alex, "I just had to, John, I just had to." Ducey's only consolation was that he ended the season—and his playing career—batting 1.000.

At a dinner hosted the following Monday evening by Harry Cohen of the Army & Navy Stores, Ducey told Mayor Harry Ainlay of the great things that lay in store for baseball in Edmonton if the City would install floodlights and a grass infield at Renfrew Park. Ducey also lobbied the mayor for renewal of the ball park lease. Riley Mullen had left the partnership by this time, to devote full time to his coaching post with the Edmonton Flyers. Word was going around that another group would try to wrest the park away from Beatty and Ducey over the winter. However the pair got Stan Moher's support in the *Journal*:

> there's no disputing the sincerity of their efforts to provide good baseball below the hill or of their plans for a bigger and better program a season hence. They rate another crack at it all, as any fair-minded individual will attest.

In the *Bulletin*, Hal Dean noted that despite Edmonton's better and larger park, Calgary's fans turned out in far greater numbers during the final series than did those in Edmonton:

> The baseball provided by Ducey and Beatty at Renfrew Park this year did not draw the support it merited. The weather during the early part of the season was bad, but there is no doubt an unjustified under-cover campaign also was directed against the league.

It was not long after these pointed remarks before the mayor and city council agreed that the two promoters should get another chance, allowing Ducey and Beatty to lay plans for what they felt would be a truly

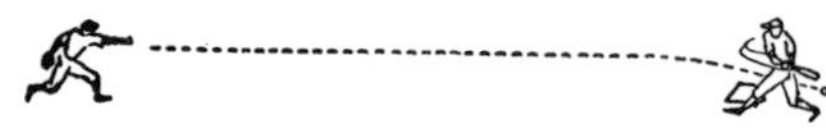

big season at Renfrew Park. But first they had some special visitors to accommodate.

With the war over, Earle Mack's touring major-league all-stars were making their first swing through western Canada in more than ten years. After negotiating a $1,500 guaranteed fee, Ducey booked them into Renfrew Park for 9 and 10 October. With a lot of advance publicity, attendance was expected to be good: Wednesday afternoon was a half-holiday in Edmonton, and most stores and offices were closed. But an Arctic cold front swept the city and a sparse crowd of 1,000 shivered through what is still remembered as one of the coldest ball games ever played at Renfrew Park. Still, even with a few snowflakes falling, the all-stars were happy to get the game in. Their two previous starts in North Dakota and Moose Jaw had both been snowed out. Despite good hitting from Doug Stewart and Ken Samis, the major-leaguers coasted to an easy 10-3 win.

The weather improved the next afternoon, but with most fans back at work, the crowds failed to turn out and the promoters took a financial bath. The only Edmonton winners were the hundred young boys from the Edmonton area who managed to attend the baseball school put on that morning by the major-leaguers, led by the great Cleveland Indian pitcher (and soon to be greater New York Yankee) Allie Reynolds. The game's highlight was a sterling pitching performance by Lefty Belter, who shut out the major-leaguers on one hit for three and two-thirds innings. Then the likes of Bob Swift, Jesse Flores, Jimmy Outlaw, and Doc Cramer teed off on Belter and the pitchers who followed him, for a 6-1 win. Both ball clubs thawed out that night at a dinner hosted by Ducey's sponsors at the Macdonald Hotel.

Hal Dean gave his assessment of the 1946 baseball offerings in the *Bulletin* the next day:

> From the standpoint of the game itself, the year now officially closed with the bringing of the major-leaguers, appears to have been highly successful. But while nobody seems to be complaining, it is suspected the financial returns to those primarily interested have not been commensurate with the quality of entertainment provided.
>
> Nevertheless, Messrs. Ducey and Beatty are justly entitled to be congratulated upon the manner in which they have conducted baseball affairs at Renfrew Park throughout the year. Speaking on behalf of the press, these two gentlemen have been very cooperative and courteous during the entire season. Should they seek to remain in the baseball picture in 1947, this corner would like to extend to them best wishes for greater success.

Despite disappointing attendance and generally poor weather throughout the 1946 season, Ducey considered his first season at Renfrew a success. He had to build a league, form the teams, and get the park running in a very short time, yet the fans had been treated to an entertaining season. One of his teams had defeated Calgary for the provincial title, which spurred him on to improve things for 1947. He began to pour an immense amount of energy into three objectives. The first was to set up a new league with Calgary and establish it on a solid foundation. In turn, this would require Edmonton to field two competitive teams to meet the always-strong Calgary opposition. His third goal was to get the City to upgrade Renfrew Park.

That fall Ducey met with promoters in Saskatoon, Regina, Calgary, and Lethbridge about reviving the old Western Canada League in 1948. He knew the first step would have to be an Edmonton-Calgary league in 1947. Ducey and Beatty went to Calgary in mid-January and had a good meeting with Timmins and Cundal. Ducey reported back in mellowed tones:

> There's no doubting the enthusiasm of the Calgarians for an inter-city league. Where a year ago they wanted no part of a deal that involved hitting the road for Edmonton, they are now all steamed up at the prospect.

A new league depended on both ball parks getting lights for night baseball. In Edmonton, Ducey put forward his case:

> Baseball, like hockey, football, the movies and so on, is primarily presented to the fans as entertainment. These other attractions are staggered at such times as make it convenient for followers to attend. That's what we have in mind for the baseball fan in these parts. Play the games in the evenings, starting at an hour when it's easy and convenient for the public to get to the park. Night baseball is the answer, the only answer.

Creating a new league

On Sunday, 16 March, with Henry Roche present, Ducey and Beatty, representing the Eskimos and the Cubs respectively, met secretly in Red Deer with Harold Cundal of Calgary Purity 99 and Sam Timmins of the Calgary Buffaloes. In an all-day meeting, they adopted a constitution and bylaws officially forming the Alberta Senior Amateur Baseball League, which was to be known as the Big Four Intercity Baseball League. Each club paid an entry fee of $25, along with its application. Roche and Dr.

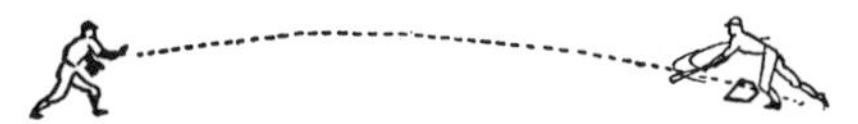

Dan Birch of Calgary were officially elected president and vice-president of the new league. With opening day set for mid-May, Edmonton and Calgary would be regular inter-city baseball rivals once again after a twenty-five-year truce.

As the winter drew to a close, Beatty and Ducey were showing Lew Fonseca's World Series highlights movie to audiences in Edmonton and around central Alberta. Beatty usually drew the rural assignments on these tours. On occasion, his Yankee drawl gathered little sympathy from farmers kept waiting when he struggled through snowdrifts, only to arrive late. Meanwhile, Ducey would travel almost anywhere in Alberta in support of minor baseball or to talk about what lay ahead at Renfrew Park for the coming season.

To Edmontonians growing weary of harsh winters, Ducey gave early promise of summer days to come with a steady flow of off-season coverage. It could be the tentative signing of an American ballplayer no one ever heard of again, or something more concrete, like his early March umpiring school for the Edmonton Recreation Commission, organized by its dedicated athletics supervisor, Jack Reilly. Offered Ducey,

> I believe the school will prove of very great benefit to baseball in this city. I have discussed various phases of the umpiring profession at various times with Beans Reardon, Bill Klem and Dolly Stark, and am anxious to pass along what I have picked up from these famous gentlemen.

For many a young man who bundled up on a cold winter night and crunched his way through the crisp snow down to the recreation commission's building on 100 Street and 103 Avenue, Ducey's umpiring classes held the promise that spring would eventually return to Edmonton.

13

The Big Four League

On 13 February 1947, just five weeks before Ducey and Roche met with their Calgary baseball counterparts to set up the Big Four League, Imperial Oil officially brought in its Leduc No. 1 well. It marked the start of the Alberta oil boom, which would transform the provincial economy, increase immigration, stimulate the growth of its cities, and add a distinctly American flavor to its culture. The period also saw an expansion of modern, paved highways and booming car sales as affluence and consumerism took hold. These were

Ducey and partner John Beattie (right) show off a soggy diamond to new league president Henry Roche, just before the start of the 1947 Big Four season. Roche had built and opened the park in 1933. Courtesy of the Edmonton Archives EA 524-41.

confident times, and the baseball organizers agreed that a Calgary-Edmonton league was just the ticket to draw fans into Buffalo Stadium and Renfrew Park.

Salary limits were formally set at $1,500 per month, excluding playing managers, but the teams found ways to pay more than that. American imports were paid for one-way travel and room-and-board expenses from the time of reporting until salaries commenced on opening day. Beyond that, the Americans had to take care of their own expenses. These matters were important to Ducey because he continued to stock his teams with a

nucleus of Americans. With umpires' fees set at $7.50 behind the plate and $5.00 on the bases, Henry Viney agreed to act as umpire in charge of all Calgary games for the season. Viney pointed out that a policeman should be in attendance at all games, and this detail was agreed to.

In mid-April 1947, the organizers announced the creation of the Big Four Intercity Baseball League. The 136-game schedule had each team playing 68 times. Ducey knew the league's credibility with the media, the public, and baseball circles would be enhanced by naming Henry Roche as its first president. Then in semi-retirement, the ex-printer had baseball roots reaching back to 1919, long before he developed and opened Renfrew Baseball Park in 1933. The vice-president, Dr. J.H. Birch of Calgary, was also a veteran baseball administrator. The popular Birch had been president of the old Western Canada League Calgary Bronks and was the man umpire Beans Reardon first reported to in 1920. Roche was a skillful promoter with a progressive attitude toward baseball marketing, as he soon made clear:

> Selling baseball is not unlike merchandising any other product. In this case we have to first attract the patrons to the parks and after that, make them want to come back. I think we have a splendid chance to do this.

In its formative years as a city, Edmonton had opted for a form of government combining an elected council with strong civic bureaucracies to ensure efficient planning and administration. City commissioners were appointed to carry out these operational chores and played the key role in the city's orderly growth and provision of services down through the decades. To get the agreement to do something required city council support. But to actually get it done required the approval and backing of the commissioners. Ducey recognized this division of powers early, which is perhaps one reason he was far more successful than his Calgary colleagues in securing regularly upgraded facilities for Renfrew Park. He stayed in constant contact with the city commissioners and his lobbying

soon bore fruit. On their recommendation, Edmonton city council approved a $25,000 lighting system to bring night baseball to Renfrew Park. It matched a new lighting system at Clarke Stadium, which to that time had little success in drawing football fans out on cold fall evenings. However, Ducey pointed out, as well as increasing baseball attendance, lights at Renfrew on warm summer nights would permit other events, such as concerts and boxing. Lights were only the first item on Ducey's long list of upgrades for the ball park. He also got the city to install grass sod and new drainage behind home plate and the infield foul lines, but he had his eye on an early installation of a grass infield at Renfrew.

With the 1946 provincial trophy in his possession, Harry Cohen of the Army & Navy Stores decided to step back from sponsorship, but he pledged his support as an advertiser in the scorecard and on Renfrew's fences. Cal Pickles felt inter-city baseball might be a bit beyond his means and also withdrew; the Edmonton Chevrolet Cubs were instead sponsored by Frank Wolfe's Edmonton Motors. Hotelier Brant Matthews again bankrolled the New Edmonton Hotel Eskimos, something he would continue for most of the next decade, Harold Cundal again represented Purity Oil's Purity 99s, and Sam Timmins ran the Buffalo Brewing Company's Calgary Buffaloes.

The U.S. soon ballplayers arrived. After a few days of "spring training," the best of the local talent was selected to form two competitive teams. The local boys were looking forward to playing in a league that would set them against their Calgary rivals. But disappointment followed for some. Des O'Connor, who had played the previous three seasons at Renfrew, had his heart set on making the Eskimos and felt he did during the tryout camp:

> Guys kept getting cut. Finally there were just three days left before the season opened. The regulars had made the team and all of them got uniforms except Des O'Connor. I went to Chuck Henderson and said, "Am I cut?"
>
> "No," he said, "you're not cut."

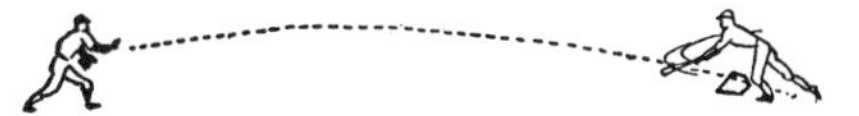

"But I ain't got a uniform." Finally Henderson said, "I asked for you on my club but Ducey says no, he's got some boys coming in."

"Well then I'm cut."

"No," he says, "you're not cut. Don't worry about it. We're going to Calgary for the weekend. Come and see me after Tuesday's game."

I did and he told me after the game, "I've asked for you again, but Ducey says no. But I've talked to the boys in Calgary and they could use some help. Here's Sam Timmins' phone number."

So I caught the midnight bus and was playing ball for Calgary the next night.

O'Connor played the next two seasons for Calgary and was a particular pest whenever the Buffaloes played Ducey's Eskimos. "I loved getting revenge—every player who was traded loved getting revenge," said O'Connor, who later grew close to Ducey in the Edmonton Oldtimers Baseball Association.

Dick Noon played his entire Big Four career in Calgary after Ducey apparently forgot him:

> During my discharge leave in 1946, I came back from Calgary to see my family in Edmonton. I went down and practised with the boys at Renfrew Park. John asked me if I would like to come back to Edmonton. I said, "I'd like to come back, but I have no job and no place to stay." I told him, "If you can get me a job and an apartment, sure I'll come."
>
> I don't know whether he forgot about it, it may have slipped his mind with everything else he had going, but he never got in touch with me. So I stayed in Calgary and played the balance of my career there.

Cliff Johnston was more fortunate, joining the Cubs as a left-fielder alongside Albert Superstein in centre field and Nick Masikewich in right. Johnston moved to the Eskimos in 1948:

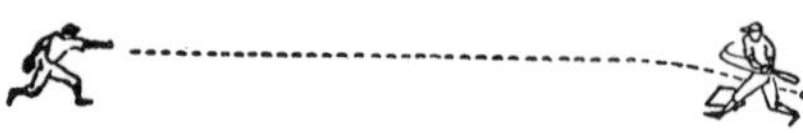

As a catcher, after six years in the Navy, I lost that little speed it took to catch the ball coming off the bat. John had others in 1946 who he wanted to play the position. So half way through 1946 he said, "Cliff, I can't afford to pay you and have you sitting on the bench." So I went out to Namao, where I had a lot of friends, and started playing in the outfield.

The next year I went down to Renfrew and signed on as a utility player, but it was my hitting which kept me in the ball game. It was baseball and I could have played for nothing, but everyone else was getting paid. I had to work all day and then come down and play. The American boys were getting about $200 more a month than we were. John was a tough guy to get a dollar out of, but he didn't have a lot of money to throw around.

Just as the 1947 season began, those who had been around when Renfrew Park opened in 1933 were saddened to learn of the death of the colourful Pete McCready. The 1930s import from the west coast had hit the first home run in the new park and became the darling of local fans until he left Edmonton to join the service at the start of the war. With McCready, something of the old era died too, but the Big Four League, staffed by many pre-war junior ballplayers, provided a continuing link with Depression-era baseball.

With tickets set at 50¢ for adults and 25¢ for children, Ducey was disappointed he could only draw 2,500 fans to Renfrew Park for his 16 May opening night. Yet fans and the sportswriters agreed that the brand of baseball looked pretty good. The Cubs turned Purity 99 back 3-2 in a strong battle between pitchers Lyell Rodgers and Tony Maze. Calgary got

Johnny Lupul (left) and Harry Ornest umpired the majority of games at Renfrew Park from 1947-52. Ornest began playing baseball in Edmonton during the mid-1930s and eventually became the owner of several professional sports teams in Canada and the U.S. Courtesy of the Edmonton Archives EA 600-4381C.

only three hits off Rodgers. Dick Noon batted in a run with a single, a reminder to Ducey and the hometown fans that he could play in the new league. Edmonton had its first "Big Four" win just one hour and forty-seven minutes after umpire Fred Lupul called "play ball." Meanwhile, the Eskimos had taken the bus down the dusty gravel highway to Calgary, where they exploded for eight runs in the sixth inning, edging the Buffaloes 9-8. Umpiring on the bases was Henry Viney, whose broad-

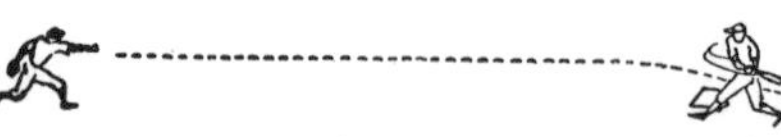

With the installation of floodlights at Renfrew Park in 1947, Ducey was able to show fans that for the first time, a baseball game could start in Edmonton at 8:00 p.m. Courtesy of the Edmonton Archives EA 524-42.

casting career would make him well known in the west. Viney often wore a railroader's cap as part of his umpiring garb—a shock to the fastidious Ducey, who would immediately file a protest to president Roche.

In mid-July, Ducey brought something new to Renfrew Park and western Canada: a baseball clinic sponsored by the Brooklyn Dodgers. Arranged with Dodger scout Howie Haak, the three-day school was open to all aspiring young ballplayers. More than one hundred of them came from Alberta, B.C., and Saskatchewan for tutoring by Haak and three of his Dodger colleagues. Local youngsters were impressed by the sight of the colourful big-league uniforms at Renfrew Park. Unfortunately, no future stars were discovered on this trip. For Haak, then northwest scout for Branch Rickey's Dodgers and later for the Pittsburgh Pirates, it was the

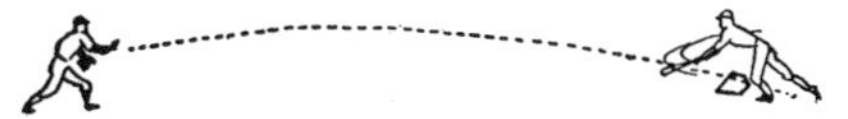

first of many official visits to Edmonton and the start of a long friendship with Ducey.

Night-time baseball comes to Alberta

Installation of the floodlights at Renfrew Park got regular photo coverage during the early summer. Eight eighty-foot steel towers were built to support lamps that provided 250,000 watts of illumination. It was claimed to be the largest installation of its kind on the continent, save for those at Boston's Fenway Park and Yankee Stadium in New York. Stan Moher described the towering lights as "...an innovation that would make the turnstiles click and 'illuminate' the way for Edmonton baseball to leave the sticks."

With the lights finally installed and tested, an advertising and media blitz was launched to promote night baseball, which officially came to Edmonton on 15 August 1947. There was excitement in the air that Friday evening as big Alex Uffleman brought his Calgary Buffaloes in to play the Eskimos. The anticipation made it feel as if the season was just starting. At 8:00 p.m. sharp, the lights were snapped on and the crowd responded with an audible gasp, followed by a hearty round of applause. Mayor Harry Ainlay made some appropriate remarks about how his city of 118,000 people was now just one step from major-league class, by virtue of the new lighting system.

Then umpire Fred Lupul got the game under way and for the majority of the players and most of the baseball fans, it was, as George Mackintosh of the *Journal* put it, "their baptism under the mazdas." It was a satisfying night for the more than 3,000 fans who filled the stands. Doug Stewart went three for four and drove Ralph Morgan in ahead of him with an inside-the-park home run, the first home run under the lights in Alberta. A 6-1 Eskimo victory sent most of the fans happily off into the suddenly darkened night. Ducey had quickly ordered the lights turned off to save on electricity. It was common practice in baseball but a bit disappointing

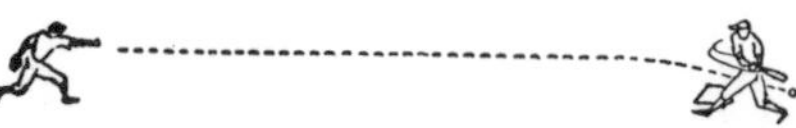

The first night baseball game to be played on the Canadian prairies under permanent lighting facilities took place at Renfrew Park on 15 August 1947. Courtesy of the Edmonton Archives EA 524-43.

to the fans who had wanted to linger under the lights that first night. While it had definitely been "top-coat" weather for the historic evening, down in Calgary, where lights would not be installed until the following May, the Cubs and Purity 99 were rained out.

For pitchers like Doug Darrah, night baseball offered a pleasant advantage:

> Baseball under the lights...what a thrill for a country boy. I loved playing under the lights. For a long while, the hitters couldn't see the fastball during night baseball and I was a fastball pitcher. I loved that.

Aerial view of Renfrew Park just after the floodlights were installed in 1947. With the small temporary bleachers in left field, some 5,500 people could be squeezed into the park. The left-field foul line was 319 feet from home plate, deep centre field 451 feet, and the right-field foul line 279 feet. Courtesy of the Edmonton Archives EA 600-371G.

The batters were not quite as thrilled. "I've just struck out twice," moaned Alex Uffleman, while Jack McGill had a more basic complaint: "It makes it a long time between meals."

Ducey and Beatty fulfilled their promise to City Hall to use the new lighting system to stage other events at the ball park. They teamed up with Edmonton band leader Lee Hepner and his orchestra to present four "Concerts Under the Stars" over the next month. Music from "Naughty Marietta" and "Concerto for Clarinet" wafted through an almost-empty ball park on Sunday evenings. "Stormy Weather" might have been more appropriate for the first concert. Rain forced an opening-night audience

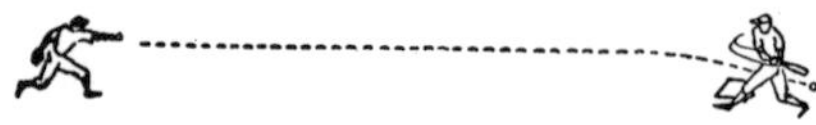

and the performers to take shelter under the covered grandstand. Then the roof began to leak and everyone went home.

Strengthening the Big Four League

The Eskimos chased the front-running Buffaloes for most of the summer. Late in the season, as all four clubs made up rain-outs and ties, the Eskimos swept four games from the Cubs and squeezed into first place. Purity took the third and final playoff spot and quickly knocked off the Buffaloes. The first Big Four championship series pitted Calgary against Edmonton.

Purity and the Eskimos played before capacity crowds in Edmonton over the Labour Day weekend. Sunday's game drew 5,500, but the Monday evening game, with 5,000 paying fans in attendance, was said to have been the largest weekday crowd ever to watch a ball game at Renfrew. In Calgary, a jam-packed crowd of 3,500 attended their first playoff game. The inspired Purity team, which played behind the Buffaloes and Eskimos the entire season, beat the Eskimos in six games to take the first Big Four championship. It had been a fine first season for both cities, and the fans provided solid support for the inter-city rivalry. Despite chilly weather, Beatty and Ducey managed to turn over revenues of $4,300 to the city treasury. From the playoffs, Purity and the Eskimos both received just over $3,000 for their club treasuries. Renfrew's 68 Big Four league games drew 101,000 paying customers in its first season.

With a successful first year behind him, Ducey turned to his dream of an expanded professional league for 1948. He travelled to Saskatoon and Regina to sound out local organizers on the idea. Lethbridge and Moose Jaw were again mentioned as potential participants in a new Western Canada League. In late August, he also hosted the first of many visits from senior Brooklyn Dodgers scout Bob Clements, enticed to Edmonton by Howie Haak, the Dodgers' northwest scout. While Clements made it clear that "my business is not to organize leagues," Ducey used the two

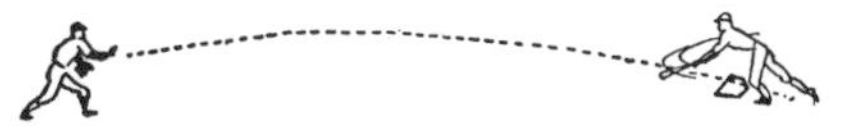

Rivalry between the Big Four League Chevrolet Cubs and the New Edmonton Hotel Eskimos was fierce. Line-drive hitter Cliff Johnston (above, left) switched to the Eskimos in 1948, joining Bill Price (left), the Esks' classy second baseman. Colourful centre-fielder Albert Superstein (above, right) rejected a later invitation from Ducey to play for the Eskimos. Courtesy of the Edmonton Archives EA 600-225B, EA 600-74A, EA 600-210.

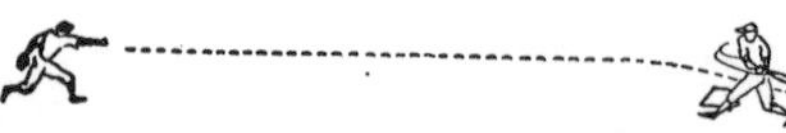

Post-season action on a Sunday afternoon at Renfrew Park in 1947. An all-star Edmonton team played against a visiting Vancouver team. Edmonton's Doug Stewart sprints for home as Fred Lupul gets ready to call the play. Courtesy of the Edmonton Archives EA 600-398B.

scouts' presence to remind sportswriters that a major-league affiliation was a first step to bringing organized baseball back to Edmonton.

While seeking approval for new bleachers along third base, Ducey and Beatty told city officials that a full season under the lights, along with the improved seating, could result in a doubling of revenues in 1948. City council approved an $8,800 expenditure for the new bleachers, to be ready for the next season. The unforgettable World Series of 1947 between the Dodgers and the Yankees (which would have Dodger fans saying, "Wait until next year") was ending just as Alberta's noted golf course greens-keeping family, the Brinkworths, arrived at Renfrew Park to install the new infield sod. "The grass will cut down interference due to weather," Ducey prophesied. It certainly helped, and the "Kelly green" sod, along

with the new lights, moved Renfrew Park's look out of the 1930s and into the modern, post-war era. No one could argue with Ducey's claim that it was now the most advanced baseball facility west of Toronto—no one except Ducey himself, when he was asking Edmonton city council to fund further improvements.

Attempts to expand the league east to Saskatchewan and south to Lethbridge failed, leaving Ducey and Beatty to work on strengthening the Big Four league for 1948. They met with Cundal and Timmins twice that fall. Both sides agreed to stick with the formula that let each team combine local talent with a handful of imported American players. Ducey continued to predict that organized baseball for Edmonton was not far off:

> The Big Four league is the fore-runner of the return to the prairies of organized baseball. In the meantime, we intend to provide the best baseball possible for our loyal fans.

In February 1948, Ducey and Beatty opened permanent downtown offices in the basement of the McLeod Building, "a place meant for the use of all who are interested in baseball," said Ducey. It was also a place where he and Beatty could entertain and chew the fat with the likes of George Macintosh of the *Journal*, Gordon Williamson of CFRN, Russ Sheppard of CJCA, Art Ward of CKUA, and Stan Moher, then in the process of becoming sports editor of the *Bulletin*. A few weeks later, a new arrival took over the *Journal* baseball beat. Don Fleming had worked for papers in his hometown of Nelson and in Trail, B.C. before joining the air force. He was stationed briefly in Edmonton during the war and saw a couple of games at Renfrew Park. As soon as he arrived, Mackintosh took him to the new office to meet Ducey; the two hit it off immediately. Ducey's own experience as a sportswriter had taught him the value of good media relations; his media friends—and they were his friends—were vital to keeping his product in the public eye. Ducey worked hard to pro-

vide them with the information they required and maintained personal ties with several of them. Moher was an intimate family friend from boyhood. Fleming and Ducey, who shared many renowned after-hours drinking bouts, remained close collaborators for some thirty-five years.

In March, Cundal and Timmins returned to Edmonton for more meetings with league officials. Cundal boasted his Purity team would again be the best of the pack in 1948, disclosing that his two pitching aces, John Carpenter and Joe Kanik, had re-signed. Timmins reported that Jimmy Gibson would again manage the Buffaloes. It was agreed to expand the schedule to an ambitious 150 games. Opening date was set for 14 May. Ducey announced he would go to California in early April and search for talent at the spring try-out camps of the Brooklyn Dodgers and the New York Yankees. Joining him were Morinville baseball promoter Alvie Steffis and Eskimo catcher Ken Samis. Steffis, who owned a big car, was the designated driver, while the veteran Samis, nearing the end of a long playing career, had designs on a managerial job at Renfrew. The trip was a northern baseball fan's dream junket. Ducey mailed letters back to the media at almost every stop, drawing continuing sports coverage back in snowy Edmonton.

Stan Moher reported that Ducey communiqués were "persistent and have run to bulk." Both Edmonton papers ran pictures of the three travellers posing with Dodger scouts at San Bernadino. It was reported that Ducey umpired four games and also put on a clinic on baseball rules interpretation for the minor-league hopefuls. He then wrote of a visit with Beans Reardon, who now had a thriving off-season beer distribution business in Los Angeles. Edmonton papers reported Ducey had renewed acquaintances with former major-league pitching ace Lefty Grove, while Samis suited up and caught some batting practice at the Yankee training camp.

In reality, the trip was more than just fun. Ducey had the Dodgers' Bob Clements, the Yankees' Joe Devine and Beans Reardon looking for talent for both Edmonton clubs. On his list was at least one and preferably two playing managers. Attempts to sign two earlier candidates had

Ducey's close relationship with Brooklyn Dodger scouts Don Lindberg (centre) and Bob Clements (right) resulted in several Dodger try-out camps being held at Renfrew Park. Courtesy of the Edmonton Archives EA 524-44.

failed. Then thanks to the Yankees, Ducey got lucky. He signed a twenty-six-year-old catcher named Walter Edward Morris, who played for Beaumont of the Texas league in 1947. Morris had been assigned to play for Victoria in the Western International League, but had refused to report, hoping to gain voluntary retirement status. After some convincing, he agreed to go to Edmonton as player-manager for the Eskimos.

Eddie Morris comes to Edmonton

"Eddie" Morris was a blond-haired, "aw shucks" kind of a guy, solid and strong, with a warm personality and a great sense of humour. Ducey found rental housing for Morris, his wife Jane, and their two young children in a west-end house next to his own; the two men quickly became good

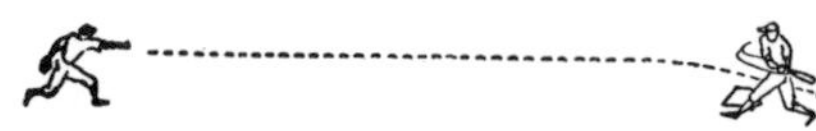

friends. The media and all but the most rabid Cub fans loved Eddie Morris. He brought humour and entertainment to the diamond—usually at the expense of umpire Johnny Lupul. Morris would argue to the limit with an umpire and then fall back, just in time to avoid banishment from the game—at least, most of the time. He chewed tobacco as had never before been seen at Renfrew Park. But he backed up his colourful diamond antics by being a good catcher, a solid hitter, and a popular manager with his players. Don Fleming had the job of trying to explain Morris to his readers:

> The fans either loved or hated Eddie Morris, there was no in-between. His arguments with the Lupul brothers were classics. Morris was a good ball player, an adequate hitter and a good catcher. He was a fiery guy who could get the team going.

Cliff Johnston had been traded from the Cubs to the Eskimos just as the season started and thus watched Morris from both sides of the diamond. Morris made him feel welcome:

> At the start, after I made a bad play, Morris broke the ice by saying, "I wasn't sure if Cliff came over to play with us or whether he was sent to infiltrate our ranks." In an argument, he would go nose to nose and start spewing tobacco at the umpire, getting it all over his shirt. One time he protested a game over an ineligible player in the game—which was him! Another time, when the first base bag came undone, he picked up the bag and tried to steal second. When they tried to catch him in the run-down, they had no bag to tag at first base.
>
> Once he gave me the steal sign, which he had set as grabbing his crotch. He'd sit against the bat at home plate, pull out his big handkerchief, blow his nose, and then hitch up his crotch. All the players' wives thought he was a dirty old man. I had to get my wife to explain it to them.

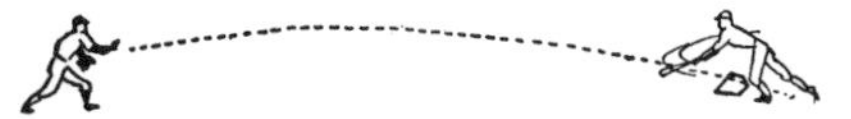

During the trip,. Ducey re-signed Frank Gonzales of the Esks and Tony Chula of the Cubs. He also signed catcher Gus Buono, infielder Ray Enjaian, outfielder Roy Canepa, and four others who in the end did not report. This nucleus of imports would change somewhat, but it was enough to round out the local players and provide two contending clubs for the 1948 season. Purity was chased by the Eskimos and Buffaloes for the first month of the schedule, but the Cubs were mired in the cellar. Their fortunes appeared brighter with the arrival of Enjaian and Buono from San Francisco State College in mid-June. In his first game, Enjaian electrified the Edmonton crowd with an inside-the-park grand-slam home run against John Carpenter of Purity. To add insult to injury, the ball stopped just below the Purity 99 sign at Renfrew's right-centre field fence. The Cubs beat the league leaders 7-0 and swept the weekend series. However, that was the high point of their season.

Most of the local players from the Edmonton clubs in 1947 were back again. They gave away nothing to their American team-mates and competitors. Their presence gave the Big Four clubs something organized baseball has always failed to deliver: continuity. They helped make the Big Four teams the most popular of Ducey's teams ever to play at Renfrew Park. Edmonton fans even had their favourites on the Calgary clubs, as well as their favoured targets. Alex Uffleman, Walt Gully, Woody Huckaby, John Carpenter, Ken Stewart, Babe Work, Ernie Choukalos, Tony Maze, George Petrunia, Jimmy Gibson, Jack Stover, and the two ex-Edmonton players, O'Connor and Noon, were soon well known to Edmonton fans. A few were admired, but most were cast as villains by the Renfrew Park regulars. Yet while the fans had their favourite players from both cities, the rivalry between Edmonton and Calgary packed them into the grandstand and bleachers each weekend, to root, root, root for the home teams.

Coming home to play against Edmonton was always stimulating for Dick Noon, who had been traded at the start of the 1947 season from the Buffaloes to Purity 99:

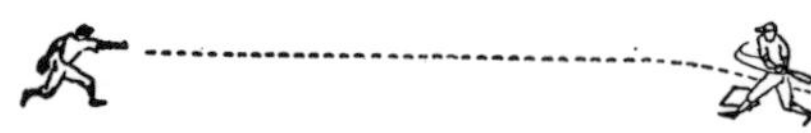

When you have to come back to your hometown and play against their team, you just try a little harder. You want to show them that maybe a mistake was made when they didn't bring you back. There was no animosity but you certainly tried harder to show them you were a good ball player.

Calgary was not the ball town that Edmonton was. Edmonton was always a ball town. What made Edmonton a better ball town? There was only one person who made the difference and that was John Ducey. He started everything.

Inter-city battles

On 20 June, Purity 99 gave Ducey and the Eskimos a shock, trouncing the listless Edmonton club 18-1 in Calgary. The game marked the appearance in the Big Four league of a young third baseman, just seventeen years old. As the *Calgary Herald* reported the next day, Glen Gorbous, born in Rosedale, near Drumheller, was still attending high school in Vulcan, Alberta:

> Glen Gorbous, Vulcan baseball star who still has to reach his 18th birthday, and is back in Vulcan today writing high school exams, provided the highlight of the Sunday afternoon stampede when the 99'ers walloped the Esks 18-1.
>
> The Calgary team had taken command early and Gorbous played his part with a two-run homer in the fourth inning. He also provided another two-run homer in the sixth, when the 99'ers went for six runs on five hits.

The slender youth, who turned eighteen on 8 July, was more than just a rookie flash. He ended the 1948 season batting .319, in ninth place on the hitters list. But it was not merely his batting prowess that drew attention. The future major-leaguer's rifle arm from third base excited observers,

including Ducey and Dodger scout Howie Haak. Haak signed the youngster to a professional contract for $500, directing him to report to a Dodger farm team the next spring. Ducey told Gorbous he was wasting his time in the infield—that he'd be better off in the outfield, according to a report by Don Fleming:

> In this Haak concurred, though he indicated that Glen might be given a serious trial on the eminence, as John Carpenter likes to put it. The lean youngster seems headed for greater things, and it's not that it isn't his due.

Cliff Johnston recalled Gorbous was once put in to pitch to show off his arm. The Edmonton batters feared for their lives in the event a fastball went wild, but fortunately, none did. Yet when Gorbous reported to the Dodgers in 1949, his file said he was a third baseman, so they kept him at that position. The next time Ducey and the Big Four league saw him was in 1950, in a Calgary uniform.

In August 1948, Ducey cranked the inter-city rivalry up a notch, giving Calgary's Harold Cundal something to shout about. When Henry Roche could not find a second umpire to work with John Lupul during summer vacation period, Ducey offered to stand in, if it was okay with Purity 99 manager Lefty Wilson. Wilson agreed, and Roche left town for a weekend at the lake. Ducey worked the Eskimos' 8-1 Saturday win with no complaints from the Calgary team. Cundal, listening to the radio broadcast in Calgary, almost fell out of his chair, enraged to hear Ducey was actually umpiring the game. How could that have happened with the Eskimos and his team in a dead heat and playing for the league lead? Despite frantic efforts, he could not get anyone to answer the telephone at

Renfrew Park. After the game, he finally reached Wilson at the club's hotel, ordering him to take his team off the field if Ducey umpired on Sunday.

The next afternoon, as was his habit, Ducey spent some time watching intently as the incoming crowds deposited their silver donations on the wooden tables at the main gate. Then he ducked under the grandstand and was about to emerge on the field in his umpiring suit when Wilson gave him the bad news from Cundal. Ducey exploded, and the two argued nose-to-nose for some five minutes. He made it clear to Wilson that as a duly-appointed umpire, he could forfeit the game to Edmonton if the Calgary club followed orders and walked off the field; at the same time, he knew that with a large Sunday crowd in the stands, he could not afford to force the situation and risk the anger of a big crowd wanting their money back—particularly when they had no ticket stubs! So he bellowed one more time at Wilson about "that lace-pants Cundal," and withdrew, leaving Lupul to umpire alone until help was later found.

There were several other scraps between the Edmonton and Calgary managements, the latter once suggesting the Calgary teams would quit the league. Yet the front-office opponents held together, spurred on more by competition than cooperation. As the season ended, Purity overtook the Eskimos by two games, gaining a bye in the playoffs. The Cubs, now under manager Laurel Harney, made a valiant effort but again finished last.

One of the sore points between the two cities was the size of Buffalo Stadium. It was hard-pressed to handle more than 3,500 people. Short fences made it a hitters' paradise, the reason, claimed some Edmonton players, that Calgary clubs had such healthy batting averages. Renfrew's larger outfield also made it more difficult for an Edmonton batter to win a hat or other article of clothing by hitting a home run over the distant Val Berg's or Cal's Men's Shop signs. Down in Calgary, the hitters regularly collected shirts for *every* home run hit out of the ball park. Purity outfielder Archie Wilder collected six shirts in a week and a half. This caused Tom Moore of the *Albertan* to comment on how the local sluggers might further improve their wardrobes:

> the shirts being rather nifty affairs, the barter rate should work out at about two shirts for one pair of slacks, 10 shirts for a suit, eight more for a topcoat and about 20 for one of those ensembles which include a suit, shirt, tie, socks, belt and shoes. Calgary's Buffaloes and "Puritans" may not qualify as the best baseball players in the world, but unless Buffalo Park fences are built higher, they are all soon going to be the best dressed.

Like many sports followers around the globe, Edmonton baseball fans lost a hero just as their own playoffs were about to begin. On Tuesday, 17 August, the *Journal* brought word that the legendary Babe Ruth had succumbed to throat cancer the evening before in New York. It was awful news. Ducey arranged a tribute to Ruth as the Esks and Buffaloes opened their seven-game semi-final series. It was the only quiet time of the evening. Before the night was over, the ballpark would see one of the stormiest games in its history.

The game got off to a chippy start. Calgary began by protesting the use of two Edmonton umpires for the playoff game when they saw Johnny Lupul behind the plate and Riley Mullen on the bases. Ducey had to remind them their representatives agreed to the set-up the week before. Only in the final series would there be an umpire from each city. In the fifth inning, Johnny Lupul called a second strike on Calgary batter Babe Work. That brought manager Jimmy Gibson steaming out of the dugout. Gibson, a left-fielder, was the league's top hitter with a .373 average and his team's leader in all respects. A heated argument followed, with Lupul pulling his watch on Gibson and telling him to "shut up and get back to the dugout." Gibson ignored the order and continued to harangue the

much smaller Lupul, who then threw him out of the game. The enraged Gibson called in base runner Des O'Connor from first base, along with his two coaches and led his entire baffled team off the field.

In a hurried conference between Henry Roche, Sam Timmins, and Ducey, Roche ruled that because of Gibson's actions, the game was forfeited to the Eskimos. Disappointed but concerned about the fans, Timmins agreed that the Calgary team would return to play on an exhibition basis. He then rushed out to try to talk his departing club back into the ball park. Don Fleming followed him out and recorded some of the debate:

> "You gotta think of the fans, Jim," Timmins pleaded. "You just can't do this to all those people in there. They've paid their four bits and they're entitled to their full change."
>
> "Yeah, but we don't have to stay there and get robbed blind," ranted Gibson. "Look, after Lupul called that one on Work, I asked him what was the big idea. Know what he said? Well, it was this: 'Sure I'm missing 'em, so what?' So I called him a crook and a cheat; so he tosses me out."
>
> "Well, all right, but we gotta go in there and take our licking, even if it's 100-0," ordered Timmins. "We have to show our sportsmanship. You can't just walk out like this. C'mon Jim...and [catcher] Carl [Mori], you too."

Base runner Des O'Connor was in the middle of the melee:

> It was very unfortunate. After the call, there was a big rhubarb and then Gibson hauled us off the field. Finally it was decided we were going back onto the field. In the meantime, Lupul had pulled the watch on us. We don't discover until we are out on the field that the game has been forfeited. What was the use of playing then? We just laid off and it quickly turned into a farce. Gibson soon knew he had made a terrible mistake.

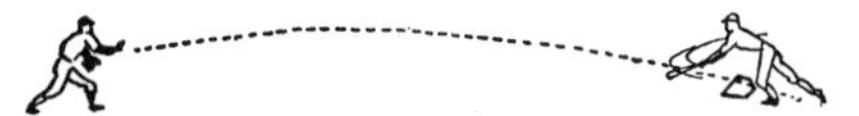

Timmins donned a uniform in place of the banished Gibson and led the Buffaloes back onto the field, to a chorus of boos from the fans, who had grown highly irritated. When it was announced the game would resume on an exhibition basis, the fans began streaming for the exits, many of them stopping to tell Ducey they wanted their money back. Some members of the crowd began to get ugly, but by then police reinforcements were on the way. Ducey calmed the angrier crowd members when he apologized and announced he would refund admissions for those who wanted their money back. Meanwhile, on the field, Timmins could do little to get his men to play competitive ball with nothing at stake. Two innings later, the game had turned into such a debacle that Ducey and Roche convinced Timmins there was no use going further. The "exhibition match" was called off. The event caused a major rift just as relations between Ducey and Timmins were taking a turn for the better. Ducey, fearing a setback to the league he had worked so hard to create, resolved he would never again allow Calgary to come into his park and subject Edmonton fans to such an amateurish display.

The Eskimos breezed to a second win behind the three-hit pitching of Eddie Belter and the series moved to Calgary. With Gibson out of the way, the Morris men were confident it would be an easy sweep. However, both games were close and the Eskimo contingent was shocked when each was decided by a home-run clout by bespectacled Greg McLellan, the Buffalo centre-fielder. In the first, his solo homer broke a 6-6 tie in the bottom of the thirteenth inning. In the second, a three-run homer broke a 3-3 tie in the bottom of the ninth inning, and the ecstatic fans poured onto the field to congratulate him. Eskimo eyebrows were raised when Calgary umpire Henry Viney patted McLellan on the back as he rounded third base in victory.

But that was all the celebrating the Buffalo fans could do as the Eskimos wrapped up the series with a sixth-game win. The Edmonton team then travelled to Calgary to meet the Purity 99s, hoping to avenge their loss of the championship the year before. The two evenly matched

Manager Eddie Morris (centre), surrounded by his victorious 1948 Eskimos after defeating the Calgary Buffaloes for their only Big Four league championship. Fronted by trainer "Tiger" Goldstick, the team included popular local players Jerry Seaman, Vern Callihan, Eddie Belter, Cliff Johnston, Dave Brockie, Ralph Morgan, Bill Price, Doug Darrah, Jack McGill, and Forest Hunter. Courtesy of the Edmonton Archives EA 600-1355.

clubs drew overflow crowds in Calgary and split the first two games, 10-1 for Edmonton and 8-7 for Calgary. When they returned to Edmonton, 4,406 Monday night fans (the largest crowd since the playoffs of the year before) packed Renfrew but went home disappointed. Calgary's John Carpenter, now a pre-med student, bested Eddie Belter as Purity 99 turned the Eskimos back 9-3. Edmonton fans sucked in their collective breath with their club down two games to one.

Solid Edmonton pitching proved to be the difference in the next three games. Jerry Seaman, who had beaten Buffalo on a four-hitter to move the Eskimos into the finals, threw a two-hit shut-out against Purity. Clarence

Mellbye, the McMinnville, Oregon school teacher who had joined the Esks after the season began, redeemed an earlier loss in the finals and gave the Esks a 3-2 lead in games. The two clubs went back to Calgary for the sixth game, and 3,500 fans squeezed into Buffalo Stadium, hoping to see their team even the series. But Doug Darrah, "the Viking Vindicator," who had won the first series game on four hits, scattered nine this time, holding Purity to three runs and giving the Eskimos their first Big Four league championship. Home plate umpire Riley Mullen had to suppress a satisfied smile as he walked off the Calgary field, while Henry Roche presented the President's Cup to a beaming Eddie Morris.

Morris had an outstanding series, as did most of the Edmonton players. Both the veterans and the younger team members had played their very best for him. The team voted Morris the series' most valuable player. At the victory dinner, no one was more pleased than host and sponsor Brant Matthews, who gave generous cash awards for key performances along with mementos to all present. Morris also got a special award—a fresh pack of chewing tobacco and several stalks of rhubarb, something for the fans to remember him by. President Roche predicted, "some day we shall look back and say again that it was you boys who paved the way for the return of organized baseball on the prairies." Mayor Ainlay praised the Eskimos as "a real civic asset." He also singled out Beatty and Ducey for the fine brand of baseball they had provided to Edmonton citizens. After that, Ducey never had a problem renewing the park lease. Renfrew would be his as long as he wanted it.

14

The Rajah of Renfrew

DUCEY WAS PLEASED WITH THE 1948 SEASON. His Eskimos brought the Alberta senior baseball championship back to Edmonton. The playoffs also capped a successful season at the gate, with added revenues of $4,610 for the Eskimos, $3,842 for Purity, and $1,805 for the Buffaloes. He proudly announced that the 72 league games, 6 playoffs, and 2 exhibition matches had drawn 115,000 fans into Renfrew—a record for the park's 16-year history and a solid achievement for a city of only 118,000. Of the 104 cities in Class-C organized baseball in 1948, Edmonton out-drew all but 12. At the Class-B level, only sixteen of sixty-eight cities bettered Renfrew's attendance.

Ducey claimed the performance at the gate and the calibre of baseball offered proved Edmonton could hold its own in the minor leagues—if it could find a league. For a while there was talk of bringing in Lethbridge and Drumheller and applying for professional status; however, potential

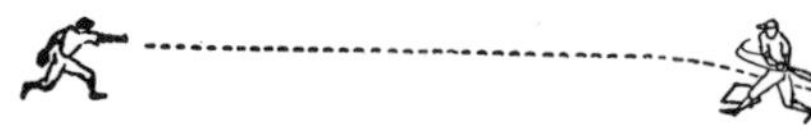

backers soon faded away. Disappointed but undaunted, Ducey turned his focus back to the Big Four league for the 1949 season. In November, salary limits were set at $2000 monthly, exclusive of the player-manager, but increased to $2500 in January.

A prime task was to find new management for the top of the league. Both Henry Roche and vice-president J.H. Birch retired in October 1948, after guiding the league through its first two years. Roche, who was semi-retired, cited "pressure of business" as his reason for stepping down, but the antagonism of the Calgary media also influenced his decision. Stan Moher said relations had been acrimonious near the end:

> Mr. Roche experienced his headaches while handling the affairs of the circuit through its first two seasons. Principally there was the traditional Edmonton-Calgary rivalry with which to cope...at times relations between team representatives, particularly, deteriorated to lower levels.
>
> It's no secret that the John Ducey-Sam Timmins feud, whatever its implications in the beginning (it was generally looked upon as good clean fun to start) had taken a more sombre meaning near the end of the 1948 season.

Some in Calgary accused Roche of being "too close to Ducey," claiming that as a result "Edmonton teams get all the best of it when he hands down a decision." Roche's suspension of Jimmy Gibson for pulling his team off the field in the 1948 playoffs caused a furour in the Calgary media, even though he was only suspended for the series. Ducey and other knowledgeable baseball officials felt Gibson should have been barred from the league "for life." Near the end of the 7 October meeting, Ducey made a passionate tribute to Roche's tenure, saying that "regardless of decisions that had gone against any club in the league, the president had made such decisions honestly, sincerely and with the interests of the league as a whole paramount." He ended by pointedly stating

Roche's administration of the league "far surpassed any few imaginative [sic] grievances that the four clubs might have felt had gone against them." Both Cundal and Timmins of Calgary endorsed the statement, which was recorded in the minutes.

Ducey, Cundal, and Timmins had no trouble agreeing that Calgary's W.R. "Sam" Irwin and Edmonton's Ken Duggan would replace Roche and Birch. Both were former ballplayers: Irwin played in Saskatchewan before serving as vice-president of Calgary's Foothills league in 1946, while Duggan played at both Boyle Street and Diamond Park in the 1920s and early 1930s. He and Ducey had been team-mates on Henry Boulanger's Yeomen in 1925.

The league also took a chance on the Alberta weather, expanding the season from seventy-two to ninety-six games for each team by extending play a further two weeks into September. For Edmonton, this also meant day-night doubleheaders on Saturdays. To avoid a repeat of what was called "the Gibson incident," the league ruled that any manager who pulled his club from the field during a game would be suspended for life. The rule was not retroactive, so Gibson was again named to manage the Buffaloes a month after the 1949 season began.

Playing in the Big Four league

Player signings and the question of Eddie Morris' return dominated baseball news in the early winter of 1949. Jerry Seaman, the league's leading pitcher in 1948, signed with the Eskimos again. Soon after, Ducey announced that, after a tough negotiating session, he had re-signed "Lefty" Belter. The news came in a phone call to Don Fleming late at night from the new oil town of Devon, where Ducey had been showing the 1948 World Series movie. Fleming reported that "Ducey would not reveal the amount of coin required to bring Belter to heel."

> Let us just say that we had a pleasant conference and that both parties are satisfied with the terms of the contract. I predict that "Edwin" will have one of his greatest seasons ever this year.

Belter had been pitching off and on for Ducey since 1936, at the age of fifteen, when Ducey coached Vic Horner's Union Bus team to the junior-league title. His peers called him "the man with the original rubber arm." He had a good fastball and a complete repertoire of "junk." Originally described by sportswriters as "slender," later as "portly," Belter was the pitcher called upon most often during a season. He pitched around 150 innings a season and could return to the mound with little rest. He was the workhorse of the Big Four League Eskimos with a won-lost record of 39-28 in regular season games. However, Belter's won-lost average was bettered by team-mate Jerry Seaman, who was 33-10 in Big Four league play. Seaman pitched only two games in 1947 and was used mainly as a utility infielder that year, hitting .261 in 195 at-bats. Bill Price, the classy young second baseman, surprised just about everyone by signing for his fourth season with the Eskimos. He had been in the middle of a tampering charge a year earlier when Sam Timmins tried to sign him and was caught in the act by Ducey, further straining relations between the two.

Eddie Morris, who had spent most of his adult life in ball parks, vacillated between baseball and a job with the Los Angeles police force. When the job fell through, he opted to return to organized ball and signed to play with Twin Falls, Idaho, in the Pioneer League. A disappointed Ducey announced that Morris would not be back in 1949. He then negotiated with ex-U.S. Army Yank Columbus Burchfield to return to Edmonton as his player-manager. After the war, Ducey had recommended the slugging Burchfield to the New York Yankees, who signed him to a professional contract. Just as Burchfield was about to accept Ducey's 1949 offer, his wife had to be hospitalized at their home in Texas. Disappointed at losing another colourful prospect, Ducey signed local veteran Ralph Morgan to manage the Eskimos.

Even Cecil "Tiger" Goldstick withdrew temporarily from the diamond, claiming his duties on the city's playgrounds in the service of the Recreation Commission required full-time attention. It was part of the annual spring ritual between Tiger and Ducey, closely chronicled by Don Fleming:

> Summer is coming. Goldstick has already resigned as Ducey's trainer. This'll go on all season. He's one quit ahead of schedule already.

"Either quit or quit quitting," a frustrated Edmonton Flyer coach Bud Poile once told the inimitable Goldstick when he went through the same ritual with the hockey club. But Ducey wanted Goldstick around and got him to agree to the less-demanding role of overseer in the new press box atop the grandstand.

While Ducey struggled to find a manager, the Cubs brought in a nucleus of good Canadian players to rebuild the club into a contending team. The architect of the Cubs' resurrection was Ducey's pal Leroy Goldsworthy, acting for sponsor Frank Wolfe. Goldie still had contacts in Winnipeg from his Northern League days in the 1930s. He signed Les Edwards, a tall, right-handed pitcher, as playing manager. A native of St. Boniface, Manitoba, Edwards had played "AA" baseball with the Memphis Chicks after the war. Several others followed Edwards. Reg Clarkson began the season at shortstop but moved to second base with the arrival of Jack Hobson. Clarkson was a gifted athlete who later played football for the Edmonton Eskimos and the Calgary Stampeders. At first base was another Manitoban, Hobie Clark, the first black player signed by either Edmonton club. However, Clark played only four games for the Cubs, breaking his collarbone while chasing a foul ball. He was replaced by big Jim Ryan, another Manitoba import.

Before the season started, Des O'Connor moved back to Edmonton to run his father's store. Ducey hesitated to approach him, for fear of being accused of tampering by Calgary. When he finally obtained league clear-

These three Chevrolet Cubs were part of a calculated charge to wrest the league title from the Eskimos in 1949. Pitcher-manager Les Edwards (above, left), first baseman Jim Ryan (above, right), and third baseman Des O'Connor (left) helped their team clinch the pennant and then take the playoffs from the Eskimos. Courtesy of the Edmonton Archives EA 600-2723C, EA 600-2723E, EA 600-2723B.

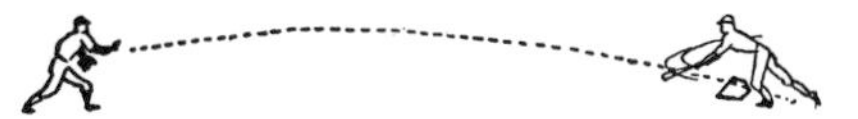

ance, he took O'Connor to lunch and offered him a position with the Eskimos. After being forced by Ducey to go to Calgary to play baseball in 1947, O'Connor was delighted to turn the offer down. Years later, when he had reached the qualifying age of fifty, O'Connor joined Ducey's Oldtimers Baseball Association and the two became close colleagues. As he filled out that part of the membership form which asked "Greatest thrill in baseball?", O'Connor teasingly wrote that among them was "getting a free lunch from John Ducey" and then being in a position to turn him down. He was one of the very few who did.

With Morris, Gonzales, and Peroni opting to play ball in the U.S. in 1949, Ducey burned up the telephone lines looking for additional American talent. His prayers were answered when Eddie Morris called a week into the season to say he had been released by Twin Falls and was ready to return to Edmonton as a catcher. "Get on the next plane and I'll pick you up at the airport," barked Ducey, whose two catchers were already suffering sore hands. Then Ducey announced the signing of a big, hard-hitting first baseman from the University of Washington. Scouts had tipped him off on Ted Tappe, who had just completed his junior year and appeared destined for a great career.

Two of the biggest names among both clubs remained unsigned. There were rumours that the Esks would trade outfielder Jack McGill for the Cubs' Albert Superstein. Ducey said of McGill, "His demands are too steep for us to entertain. It's up to him if he wants to play any ball this summer." The two never came to terms, and McGill did not play in 1949. Meanwhile, Ducey and Superstein continued to feud. "He's more bother than he's worth. He'll never play for my ball club," vowed Ducey. As the Cubs pulled away from the Eskimos in June, Ducey redoubled his efforts to get the speedy centre-fielder into his camp. By mid-June, Superstein had his release from the Cubs and Ducey reversed his field to announce the event in Don Fleming's column:

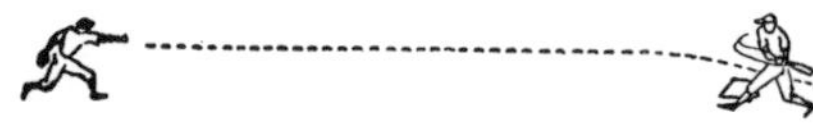

> I take great pleasure in revealing the signing of Mr. Albert Superstein. He is the greatest outfielder in the history of the league. And what a drawing card!

However, Superstein played only one game for the Eskimos as the two never agreed on final terms.

By 30 June, the Eskimos caught up with the Cubs and tied them for first place. Clarkson was literally carrying the Cubs and batting .370, while second in home runs and leading the league in triples, doubles, and stolen bases. He was chased by Cliff Johnston, the line-drive hitter enjoying his best year ever, batting .353 and leading in RBIs. Brockie, Morris, and Price added to the Eskimo attack, all hitting well above .300. The two clubs battled each other all summer, but near the end of August, the Esks began to fade. Des O'Connor attributed most of the Cubs' success to Clarkson:

> Clarkson was the key. He led the club in everything. I never saw an athlete like him. He'd hit a single into centre field and slow down after he rounded first base. As the fielder relaxed and let his arms down after the catch, Clarkson would suddenly speed up and get right into second base, ahead of the delayed throw. He would have played major-league baseball if his arm hadn't gone dead on him.

By Labour Day weekend, the Cubs swept the final two-game series and the Esks ended five-and-a-half games back. Purity was seventeen games out in third place, with the hapless Buffaloes another seventeen behind them. To shake his club up, Sam Timmins fired four veteran players: manager Jimmy Gibson, catcher Carl Mori, and pitchers Tony Maze and Bob Garrett. Gibson and Mori were hitting .326 and .312 respectively, and the Buffaloes were a spent force after they left. The Eskimos had to battle Purity 99 once again to defend their championship.

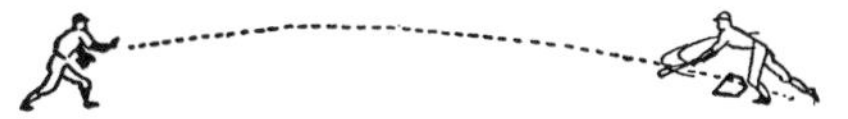

The inter-city rivals split the first two games at Renfrew as well as the next two games in Calgary. In the third game at Buffalo Stadium, Ted Tappe slammed out his second and third home runs of the series as Edmonton came from behind to win 9-3. Back at Renfrew, Calgary won 4-2, forcing a seventh and deciding game. The upstart Purity team shocked Eskimo fans, scoring two quick runs in the first inning. Stung by the possibility the season could be over, the Eskimos roared back for seven runs in their half of the inning. Then the skies opened and rain delayed the game for twenty-five minutes. Fearing a rain-out, Ducey charged out and directed efforts to dry the infield. When play resumed, the Esks added four runs to Purity's one. Calgary was eliminated from the playoffs, 11-3.

Ducey was chagrined when youthful promoter Al Oeming picked 14 September to open his fall wrestling season, the same night as the start of the final baseball series. The likes of the Cardiff Giant and other assorted "rasslers" drew a sell-out crowd of close to 3,000 at the old Stockyard Pavilion. Over at Ducey's pristine diamond, only 2,100 ball fans turned out. Cubs' manager Les Edwards was on the mound for the opening game and fashioned a brilliant five-hitter. The Eskimo hurlers threw wildly, allowing Des O'Connor to gain a further measure of personal revenge with four stolen bases as the Cubs won, 8-4.

A four-hit performance by Morrie Hawkey gave the Cubs an easy win the next night. Cub pitchers had found they could collar Ted Tappe with high fastballs and threw him nothing else. The big slugger was held to only two hits during the series, while the usually reliable Cliff Johnston and Billy Price also failed to come through. The listless Eskimos dropped the third game and were again facing elimination. Despite the threat of stormy skies, 5,200 fans packed the Renfrew stands Sunday, overflowing down right field. Most expected to see the Cubs thrash the Eskimos in four games. But the Esks finally got a strong performance from one of their starters as fastballer Bob Peterson won a hard-fought duel against

Vern Callihan, 4-3. A fly-ball in the eighth inning drove in the Esks' winning run, allowing them to play another day.

A far smaller crowd was in attendance on a frigid Monday night as Les Edwards again took the hill, this time against Eskimo ace Jerry Seaman. The starry Clarkson was held to a single Texas Leaguer, but Ryan, O'Connor, and Robertshaw came through with three hits each. Seaman was driven from the mound in the fifth as Belter relieved him with the score 7-1. Eskimo fans were treated to one last thrill from Ted Tappe when Edwards mistakenly threw him a low inside pitch that he lined over the right-field fence for a three-run homer. It was only Tappe's second hit of the series and his last appearance at Renfrew Park. The Cubs drove the final stake into Eskimo hearts with four unanswered runs in the top of the ninth to win 12-4. The Big Four championship was theirs at last. Ducey watched the end of the rout from the press box in uncharacteristic silence as the jubilant Cubs led manager Edwards off the field and threw him into the showers. "We need to do some housecleaning," was all he growled to Don Fleming as the park lights were turned off for the last time in 1949.

The Rajah rebuilds Renfrew

Ducey tried to buy Renfrew Park that fall, believing it the best way to bring stability to his operation, which was still on a short-term lease. City council, however, turned down the idea, saying the ball park was zoned as park area and could not be sold. The rejection was fortunate for Ducey in view of what would occur the next year. Commissioner John Hodgson, who liked Ducey very much, told council that while the promoter had returned $12,000 to the city in rents since 1946, improvements he had gained from the city had cost $20,000. In a tone of friendly frustration, Hodgson outlined his dealings with Ducey:

> Mr. Ducey is a most expensive man to deal with. There is no limit to his demands. In the past three years we've had to spend $9,000 more

on the park than we've gotten back. His present plans fill two sheets of foolscap.

Despite these comments, Hodgson supported Ducey's efforts to upgrade the park, but naturally put his duty to the city first. Hodgson earned some sympathy for Ducey when he advised city council that Ducey's personal return from baseball in 1948 was only $2,400, or wages averaging $200 per month, much less than he was paying most of his ball players. That was "well within reason in view of the great asset he was to the city," observed some aldermen. They liked the direction Ducey was taking and advised him to keep negotiating with the commissioners. "If you find them too tough, come back to us," quipped Alderman Bisset.

Ducey then tried to get a thirty-year lease but struck out on that idea too. He next told commissioners that "if protected by a long term lease," he'd make Renfrew "the best baseball park in western Canada." In the end, he had to settle for a five-year lease, with an option for a second five years. Instead of paying eight-percent rent on revenues to the city, it was agreed he would spend an equal amount on capital improvements to the park. He told council he had some immediate projects in mind, including a new fence, renovations to the dressing rooms, and improved restroom facilities. He foresaw construction of a new grandstand in another three years, raising the seating capacity to 10,000.

By this time, the playing facilities at the park, now seventeen years old, had been upgraded sufficiently that field conditions were acknowledged to be as good as anywhere in Canada. Along with the lighting system, Ducey had prevailed on his civic landlords to install an electric scoreboard, a grass infield, improved drainage, and for the first time, sunken dugouts for the players. While amenities for teams, fans, and media lagged well behind, new bleachers were put in place and a press box was finally built on top of the wooden grandstand. This allowed the "Fourth Estaters" to escape the mosquito-infested dugout under the grandstand. The umpires finally got their own room beneath the stands with direct

access to and from the field, ending the need to make those long walks up the hill to the Selkirk Hotel to change back into street clothes.

In December, Ducey said that facilities in most western Canada ball parks, including his own, were still not adequate for organized baseball. Underlining his point, high winds blew down eighty feet of Renfrew's rickety fence, making it necessary to build a new one early in the spring. Parks in Regina and Saskatoon needed both lights and a grass infield. Calgary's Buffalo Stadium needed more capacity. If these needs were met, said Ducey, organized baseball could be a reality on the prairies by 1951. Timmins and Cundal were saying much the same thing.

After lights and grass infields were installed in Regina and Saskatoon in 1950, Ducey began saying that if a new, covered grandstand seating 7,000 people could be built at Renfrew, professional baseball would definitely return to Edmonton. One possibility he suggested was a line-up with Montana clubs in the Class-C Pioneer League, although he preferred an alignment with Calgary and Saskatchewan cities. Calgary continued to be a problem for Ducey, however. The 1949 Buffaloes fielded a woeful team, keeping fans in both cities away in droves. The longer season in 1949 also proved to be too much baseball for players and fans alike.

Don Fleming kept trying hard to pin a nickname on Ducey and by 1950 had tried out "the Voice," "the baron of Renfrew," and "the laird of Renfrew." None stuck. In April he came up with "the Renfrew Rajah," which he then refined to "the Rajah of Renfrew Park." Later, he would embellish it as "the rabid Rajah of Renfrew Rounders," needling Ducey about the probability that his "great American game" originated in England. The charge never failed to get Ducey's Irish up. Stan Moher used "John (The Great) Ducey," "the diamond Mahatma," and "Diamond John," none of which caught on. Successive writers would use Fleming's "Rajah of Renfrew," but among most people of his day, Ducey was known as "Edmonton's Mr. Baseball."

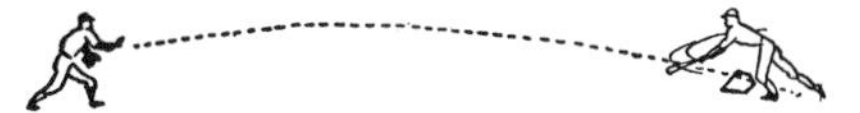

Sportswriters and Edmonton baseball fans acknowledged Ducey's love of baseball and were proud of the recognition it brought their city. Stan Moher tried to explain its depth:

> You have to understand that with Ducey, baseball is not merely a game. It comes close to being an obsession. He doesn't speak just of baseball, in so many words. He wouldn't be caught dead calling it anything less than "the great game of baseball."

Changing times

Edmonton entered the 1950s as a growing, confident, modern city. Several factors contributed to its progress, including a maturing post-war economy, the Alberta oil boom, northern development, and a post-war wave of immigration. Alberta's population grew from 803,000 in 1946 to 939,000 by 1951. In early May 1950, Alberta's industry minister A.J. Hooke officially welcomed Northwest Airlines and Western Airlines to Edmonton's Municipal Airport, stating, "the planes of two major American airlines now link the city with the world's globe-girdling air networks." The Redwater field, with 406 producing oil wells, had surpassed the older Leduc field with its 396 oil wells. The CPR heralded the introduction of "the Stampeder" and "the Eskimo," its two speed specials offering luxurious four-and-a half-hour rail service between Edmonton and Calgary. Indeed, the two cities experienced football frenzy after the Stampeders' 1948 Grey Cup victory and the Edmonton Eskimos' 1949 revival under coach Annis Stukus. For the first time in history, 17,388 fans watched Sunday baseball in Toronto as the International League Maple Leafs lost a double-header to Jersey City. The occasion attracted National League president Ford Frick to Toronto, where he predicted major-league expansion, observing "Montreal is a major league city right now and Toronto, now with Sunday ball, is getting there."

General manager Ken Samis watches as slugging centre-fielder Barry Robertshaw re-signs his 1950 contract with Cal's Dodgers. Successors to the Cubs, the Dodgers went on to defeat Ducey's Eskimos for the second year in a row, much to his frustration. Courtesy of the Edmonton Archives EA 600-4076.

Things weren't quite as optimistic down at Renfrew Park. In early February 1950, sponsor Frank Wolfe dropped a bombshell. He announced that his championship Chevrolet Cubs were withdrawing from the league. Running a semi-pro sports team was just too expensive for a purely local retail concern, Wolfe said. The practice of importing American players concerned him and a handful of others. Getting some U.S. players a job to top up their baseball salaries, as well as finding them housing, was too much, said Wolfe. The imports were still a sore point in some quarters.

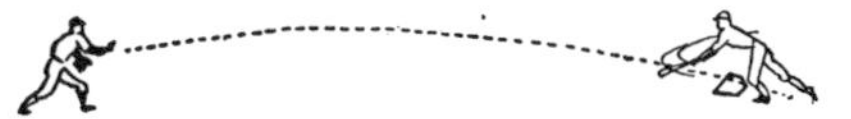

Extremely disappointed, Ducey initially said little about Wolfe's withdrawal. For a while it looked as if the Cubs franchise would be picked up by the oil-well supply firm of Sparling-Davis, but they backed off the $5,000 bond sponsors were required to post. Shortly after, Ducey prevailed on Cal Pickles to return as the sponsor of the Cub team. Ken Samis joined Pickles as a partner to both manage and handle the club's business operations. Pickles announced that the team would be known as Cal's Cubs, but changed the name to the Dodgers before the season began. Ducey then revealed that Eddie Morris would be back as his manager. The always-upbeat Morris came to Edmonton for the contract signing on a frigid February day, and the two put on a media reception so that Morris could do some clowning around. They both took a shot at the demise of the Cubs, and Ducey made the surprising statement that the Cubs' management "knew as far back as November that they were going to pull out." It was all he would ever say about the incident, but there were those who said Wolfe pulled out because Ducey was getting all the credit and all the publicity.

Integration of black ballplayers into the major leagues had continued at a slow pace after Jackie Robinson joined the Brooklyn Dodgers in 1947. For a while, the situation was no better in the minor leagues. However, in 1949, the minor leagues finally made some significant progress. Early in 1950, taking his lead from organized baseball, Ducey announced that he had signed his first black ball player, Marshall Johnson. The twenty-one-year-old outfielder had played with U.S. army teams in Alaska and was recommended by ex-U.S. Army Yank manager Capt. Frank Wrigglesworth. Johnson was due to be released from service in Alaska in early May. To reflect the influence of the new oil-boom on the city, Ducey and Matthews

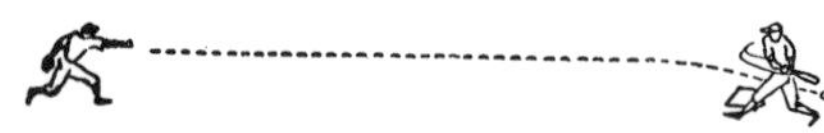

tried changing the name of their club to the Oilers. But the name did not stick, and by opening day the club was again the Eskimos.

Another new addition to the Eskimos that year was young Allan Wachowich, a park ballboy the previous year. For him, joining the ball club was a dream come true:

> I was in grade nine and I wrote John Ducey a letter, having heard that was what the batboy had done the previous year. It was not a contest, simply a letter that was well composed. I wrote it over Christmas and got a reply in January.
>
> One day I read in Stan Moher's column that I was the new batboy for the Eskimos. I met with John at his office and he went over the duties. I would go down to the park in the afternoon to shine the shoes, hang up the uniforms with the numbers facing outward, and make sure everything was in good shape.
>
> One of the things John insisted upon was that the uniforms and the shoes be clean. When it came to the style of the game, he wanted everything to be a replica of the major leagues. Same thing in the dugout...the bats had to be lined up...there could be no mess. Mind you, it was tough to keep that clubhouse and the dugouts clean, they were so old.

Samis and Ducey agreed to a trade that saw first baseman Jack McGill return to the Eskimos for a left-handed pitcher to be named later. McGill would be in the lineup on opening day. Before the season started, the Eskimos already looked ready to snatch the crown back from their local rivals. Even without Edwards and Clarkson, the two stars of 1949, Samis and Pickles were quietly assembling a solid club. Jim Ryan arrived back from fighting the Winnipeg floods just in time for opening day. The former Winnipeg Maroon first-baseman was signed as playing manager.

With the Korean War heating up, Americans were facing the military draft. John Beatty, who had originally filled the club treasurer's role, was called back into the U.S. Army early in 1950. Beatty said he would retain

his shares but management of the Edmonton Baseball Club was being turned over to his partner. Ducey was now alone, except for his key assistant, Brian O'Hanlon, who had joined him in 1949 and became accountant and office manager. It was O'Hanlon who had to keep reminding Ducey that they were not making any money:

> I never saw John feeling down about the financial situation. To me he would indicate that I shouldn't worry, it was going to be all right. I would be chewing my nails wondering where the next dollars were coming from. If we had a cold night and a pretty scant crowd, the dollars were pretty slim. I'd think, "Cripes, many nights like this and what are we going to do?" But I never saw John dismayed over finances. He could be dismayed with the ballplayers, but he never seemed to worry about the finances.

Ducey cranked up baseball interest in early April with extensive coverage on his visit to bring the 1949 World Series film to sports enthusiasts at Port Radium, N.W.T. At that time of year, the remote location was a hotbed of curling. But it was reported that after he orated on "the great game of baseball," he brought the house down when he "applied his Irish tenor to a solo rendition of 'Take Me Out to the Ball Game.'" Back in Edmonton, he told reporters that "baseball has now officially reached the shadow of the Arctic Circle." Then it was a quick round of exams for his annual umpires' school with the Recreation Commission, supervision of the signs being painted on Renfrew's new fence, inspection of the construction of the sunken dugouts and the press box atop the grandstand, and the signing of a handful of younger players from Edmonton's junior ranks. The Rajah was now ready for Opening Day at "the park below the hill." Wrote Stan Moher,

> for him, not even Christmas Eve, as he remembers it from his boyhood days, holds the same thrill, provides the same excitement as those last few hours before the cry of "play ball" ushers in a new season.

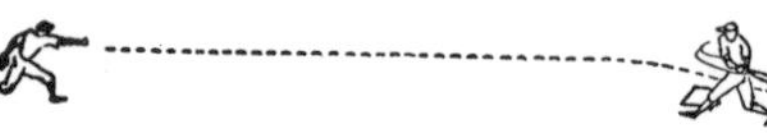

"The boys of summer." Happy to be back for "spring training" in 1950 for what would be the fourth and final season of the Big Four League were Mike McInerny, Don Bailey, and Des O'Connor of Cal's Dodgers. Courtesy of the Edmonton Archives EA 600-4269B.

The Big Four's last season

On a chilly Tuesday evening in mid-May, 2,500 fans paid 65¢ for general admission and $1 for box seats as the fourth edition of the Big Four League opened at Renfrew Park. With the game underway, Ducey loaded up with coffee and hot dogs and made the long climb up to the grandstand roof and over to the new press box. For anyone with the least sense of vertigo, such as Ducey, the walk across the rounded roof to the press box was frightening, especially if the wind was blowing. But looking after the media was important to him. That evening, *Bulletin* sportswriter Dick Beddoes listed a number of opening night firsts on the field, adding,

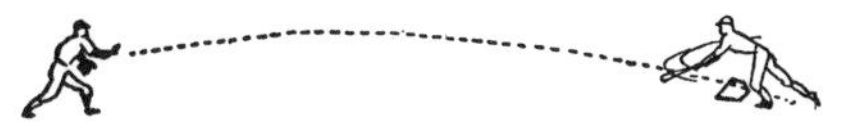

my own is Mr. Ducey himself. And my reason is simple enough: He was kind enough to risk his life climbing the hazardous steps to the new press box, transporting a pail of coffee and hot dogs to the working sportswriters. In this regard, the first hot dog to be consumed in the recently constructed press box was eaten by Mr. Gordon Williamson, the CFRN radio announcer. But he barely beat out Mr. George Dobie, a hungry young man who toils for British United Press.

On the field, Des O'Connor smashed out a double for the first hit and was driven in to score the first run of the new season. Eddie Morris had the first triple and the first of several run-ins with umpire Johnny Lupul over close calls at first base. The Dodgers' Jim Ryan drilled a 360-foot home run over the head of left-fielder Marshall Johnson and the newly shortened left-field fence. Morrie Hawkey and the Esks' Jerry Seaman battled each other through nine innings, each giving up eight hits. O'Connor broke a 4-4 tie in the tenth inning, scoring Ross Kortgard with the winning run as the Dodgers picked up where they had left off the previous season. To the south, the Calgary clubs could draw only 1,100 to Buffalo Stadium to see Purity edge the Buffaloes 5-4 in sixteen innings.

By the end of May, the Dodgers had won eleven of twelve games and the Eskimos were five games behind, causing Ducey some desperation. To bolster his fading Esks, he said that hard-hitting first baseman Ted Tappe might return if he could not conclude a bonus signing with a major-league club. Tappe, playing at Washington State, did not return, signing with Cincinnati a month later. Edmonton fans were pleased to learn in mid-September that he had cracked out a home run in his first major-league at-bat. But Tappe never had much of a chance at Cincinnati, being completely overshadowed by the great Ted Kluszewski, who owned the Reds' first-base job for ten straight years. After his signing, Tappe spent most of the year in the minors, as he would the next four years. He moved to the Chicago Cubs in 1955 but never lived up to expectations, getting only fifty-eight major-league at-bats, yet he managed to hit five home runs.

Was Bob Lillis "the greatest?"

Ducey made an exciting find when he signed Bob Lillis, a smooth-fielding nineteen-year-old California college shortstop who could also hit with power. The Brooklyn Dodgers arranged for Ducey to bring him to Edmonton, thus protecting his college eligibility. Led by Lillis, who was soon hitting .400, the addition of a handful of other American imports saw the Esks overtake the fast-starting Dodgers by late June.

The Rajah stirred up controversy among local fans when he ran an advertisement for a series with the Calgary Buffaloes. It called Lillis the "greatest ballplayer ever to perform at Renfrew Park." Letters taking issue with the claim poured in to the *Journal* and the *Bulletin*. The fans had equal praise for several other Renfrew players, many of them home-town boys. Stan Moher, whose *Bulletin* carried the advertisement, took as much criticism as Ducey did, to the latter's relief. In his own defence, Moher identified *his* choice as the best to ever play at Renfrew:

> In my book, the late Pete McCready still rates as the greatest player ever at Renfrew for any length of time. I can't forget how he covered ground in the outfield, the great arm he had, his base running feats, some of the whopping homers he belted over the OLD left field fence, down in the corner too. But don't get me wrong about Lillis. He's a piperoo and has a chance for a great future, particularly if he doesn't go on being the subject of ads that "deal" in superlatives.

Moher's parting shot was not lost on Ducey, and it was the last time he would ever make such a claim about an individual player. Before the argument could go any further, Ducey announced that Lillis had been invited to a try-out with the Cleveland Indians. General manager Hank Greenberg wanted Lillis to play shortstop for the Indians' Triple-A farm club at San Diego. This brought a speedy offer from the shocked Brooklyn Dodgers, and Lillis left Edmonton for try-outs with both teams on 28

June. While he was treated well in Cleveland, he decided against the Triple-A contract, preferring to finish his college education in the fall. Lillis then passed on the invitation to go to Brooklyn and returned to Edmonton. Manager Morris was truly relieved that his starry shortstop was back; Ducey was jubilant.

Glen Gorbous returns

Ducey felt less than comfortable about the return of two "renegade" players from organized baseball that June. They were Gus Buono, who had come up from California to join the Cubs as a catcher in 1948, and Purity's Glen Gorbous, now playing in the outfield. Both were assigned to the Brooklyn Dodgers' farm club at Medford, Oregon in the Far West League in 1949. But in 1950, unhappy at being sent to the Dodgers' team at Bisbee-Douglas, Arizona, the two had simply walked out on their club and on organized baseball. They got off a team bus one night and phoned Purity's Lefty Wilson to ask if they could play for Calgary. He said yes and Purity signed them on their arrival. According to Dick Noon, that was when Gorbous moved to the outfield:

> Glen went to coach Walt Gully and said he'd like to play the outfield. There was no problem with that as far as Walt was concerned, so he put him in centre field. He had a great arm. He couldn't bounce the ball on a throw into home plate. He kept it in the air dead on line. The catcher didn't know if it was coming in two inches off the ground or six inches off the ground, but he knew it would be air-borne all the way.

Gorbous ended the season batting .374, second to Lillis, who won the title by hitting .409, the highest average ever attained in the Big Four league. The two tied for most home runs at ten. Things did not go as well for Gus Buono. He could not push Bing Weaver out of the catcher's job and spent most of the season on the bench. Although he was later offered con-

Doc Talley, manager of the House of David touring club, signs an autograph in Edmonton in 1950. The bearded barnstormers from Michigan were frequent favourites in western Canada for almost thirty years. Courtesy of the Edmonton Archives EA 524-46.

tracts in organized ball, Buono's career was derailed by military service when the Korean conflict broke out.

There was talk that Gorbous would be permanently suspended, but by July 1950, Brooklyn scout Don Lindberg expressed hope in Edmonton that the trouble could be ironed out. On the strength of his throwing arm and his lusty batting average with Calgary, Gorbous was invited back by the Dodgers the year after his defection. After three seasons in Pueblo of the Western League, he was traded to Cincinnati and was in the Reds' lineup briefly in 1955. He was soon traded to Philadelphia and finished his short major-league career there in 1956, except for two at-bats in 1957. He appeared in only 115 major-league games, batting .238. Gorbous

gained a measure of ever-lasting fame for throwing a baseball farther than anyone else in the game. On 1 August 1957, while playing in the minor leagues at Omaha, he took part in a throwing exhibition and made the longest throw ever recorded in organized baseball, 445 feet, 10 inches. More than forty years later, his achievement is still listed in the *Guinness Book of Records*.

After Gorbous joined Cincinnati, he was sometimes reported as the first native-born Albertan to play big-league baseball. He was actually the third. Vince Barton was born in Edmonton 1 February 1908 but moved to the U.S. as a boy. An outfielder, he played in 102 games for the Chicago Cubs in 1931 and 1932, batting .233. Charlie Mead, born in Vermilion 9 April 1921, was a wartime utility player who appeared in eighty-seven games for the New York Giants in 1943-45. Also an outfielder, his major-league batting average was .245. He left the Giants in 1946 and jumped to Vera Cruz of the outlawed Mexican League. He later returned to organized baseball and Edmonton fans saw him play for Calgary in 1953 and Yakima in 1954 in the Western International League.

Baseball burn-out

By mid-August 1950, even with Gorbous hitting a healthy .373, Purity was last in the league, struggling to catch the Buffaloes. To Ducey, it all looked perfect. With only three games left to play, the first-place Eskimos seemed destined to regain the league championship. On 17 August, the Eskimos and Dodgers faced off for their final league encounter. If the Dodgers won, the two clubs would be in a tie for first place. Both Calgary teams were at least ten games behind the Dodgers.

The evening had a festive air as the Recreation Commission baseball school showcased its future "greats" on the Renfrew diamond. Among the "young" Esks and Dodgers in a short pre-game warm-up that night were Len Lunde, Ken Heffel, Al Wachowich, Orest Kinasewich, Neil and Ken Samis Jr., and Neil Hardy. Wachowich, in his one playing appearance

before a real crowd at Renfrew, displayed his talent for his "big club" Eskimos. He hit a single to drive in the winning run in the final inning of the exhibition tilt.

It was two veteran aces, Morrie Hawkey against Jerry Seaman, in the main event. Bob Lillis hit a prodigious 3-run homer over the 10-foot fence at the 330-foot marker in left field. Renfrew regulars said only Pete McCready had done that before. Cliff Johnston hit three for three, and the 12-8 win put the Eskimos a full two games ahead of the faltering Dodgers.

After the game, Ducey announced that Jack McGill had been fired for failing to return with the team after the last road trip. Another of Edmonton's all-round athletes, McGill was a free spirit who feuded with Ducey over the years. Driving his own car to a Calgary series late in the season, he stayed for the opening of a thoroughbred race meet. Taking his lead from major-league baseball, anything with a remote connection to gambling was anathema to Ducey, and this fear triggered the firing. Horse racing was the sport Jack McGill truly loved, while the ex-Boston Bruin merely excelled in such athletic pursuits as hockey, baseball, and golf.

The next night, the Eskimos clinched first place as they ended Purity 99's playoff hopes by a lopsided score of 14-1. After the park had been closed, a smouldering fire erupted into flames in the old wooden grandstand. For ballboy Ken "Emo" Awid, it was like awakening to a bad dream:

> We lived right across the street from the ball park. Every night after a game, I'd go home, and because of the kids who were smoking in that old grandstand, I'd tell my Mom, "Boy, that place is going to burn down some night." One night after I'd gone to sleep, my Mom was shaking me, "Get up, get out of bed, the ball park is on fire." I woke up and looked out the window and that place was just a mass of flames.

It was a night Dick Noon never forgot. The Purity team came to Edmonton needing to sweep the series with the Eskimos to make the playoffs.

Downcast at losing the first game, they returned to the hotel to change and have a late dinner:

> We were a little dejected. As we were going down for dinner the woman in the elevator said, "The ball park's on fire!" I jokingly said, "Yeah, we know, I set it on fire because we can't get in the playoffs. But there's no sense worrying about it."
>
> So we went to the dining room and while we were eating, someone came over and said, "Renfrew Park is on fire." I said, "Oh no!" We left the hotel, went down 101st Street, looked down the hill and sure enough, the ball park was in flames. The big lamp standards were leaning away from the heat. I always felt pretty bad about telling that elevator operator I had set it on fire. Fortunately I was never accused of arson.

The entire grandstand was destroyed. Only the office near the main entrance was saved, although firemen managed to protect the bleachers. Ducey was in Calgary attending a league meeting which lasted until 10:30 p.m. Roused from a deep sleep in the middle of the night, he had to rush back to Edmonton. He found a weary and begrimed Brian O'Hanlon at the park, sifting through still-smoking rubble, pulling out files, and searching for equipment. The team dressing rooms were gone and, other than the business office, little was left under the grandstand. One of the lamp standards had been structurally damaged. With the season almost over and a big playoff game coming up between the two home teams, the heart had been burned out of Renfrew Park.

Eskimo batboy Al Wachowich had no spikes to shine the morning after the fire—nor dressing room in which to shine them. Gone as well were the team's equipment and two sets of uniforms. Only the bats were saved. The Dodgers, on the road in Calgary, had sent their home uniforms to the cleaners. Before leaving for Calgary, Ducey had also intended to send the Eskimos' road uniforms to the cleaners that fateful Friday but

forgot to do so. Umpire Harry Ornest, who had only recently taken advantage of the umpires' new dressing room, reported that he and John Lupul lost $400 worth of clothes and equipment in the fire.

With Herculean effort, city work crews cleared most of the rubble away by noon Sunday. Then, wearing the Dodgers' home uniforms and scrounging shoes and gloves where they could, the Eskimos swept an afternoon double-header from Purity 99. With that, the season concluded, the Esks five games up on the Dodgers, who were falling to the Buffaloes in Calgary. While it did not seem serious, Lillis had injured his leg sliding into second base in the final game and was ordered to go for x-rays. The semi-final series between the Dodgers and the Buffaloes was delayed a few days while city work crews hastily erected bleachers behind home plate. Temporary arrangements were made for dressing facilities and a press box. By Tuesday, the park was ready for play to resume. Although they played some shaky baseball, the Dodgers got strong pitching from Hawkey and good hitting from O'Connor, defeating Calgary four games to two. The Eskimos, appearing to be the pre-ordained champions, put on a listless exhibition tune-up down in Lacombe, where they scored only one run in a double-header against a team that included several ex-Big Four players.

The Big Four league winds down

Despite the fire, Edmonton fans were excited about the prospect of another final series between the two home clubs. Des O'Connor believed his club could beat the mighty Eskimos again:

> The Eskimos had the superior team. People used to come into the store and ask me, "Well Des, how are you going to do against the Eskimos?"
>
> I had one piece of knowledge which I didn't tell them about. Ducey had never strengthened his pitching staff. I told my team-mates, "We can beat them." They started laughing their heads off.

But O'Connor got the last laugh. Instead of the veteran Hawkey, Samis and Ryan elected to throw the Eskimos a surprise by starting Al Purvis. He scattered twelve hits, and when the dust cleared, the Dodgers had upset the Eskimos to take the first game 15-4. It could be fate, mused Don Fleming:

> "There'll be no more of this," Eddie Morris said gruffly after last night's sorry show against the unpredictable Dodgers.... May be in the cards for Dodgers to win for the second straight year. Must be a team of destiny, for how else can you explain their continuing success despite pronounced deficiencies afield?

Ducey had a sinking feeling that, despite all the talent on his club, things were starting to go very wrong. By 1950, he had decided that as a general manager, he had no place in the dressing room laying down the law to a team of experienced semi-pro ballplayers. Ralph Morgan told a story of an earlier Ducey, who had once breached the clubhouse door to give the players a piece of his mind about their fading performance:

> What a guy that Ducey. He comes into the clubhouse ranting and raving about his players not hitting one day. He bellowed at the gang, asked them if they remembered so-and-so. Somebody said "Yeah, but he's dead."
>
> "Yeah," Ducey blistered back, "do you guys think you're any different?"

On this occasion, Ducey avoided the clubhouse, calling Morris into his office and telling him something had to be done to shake up the team. The next night, Morris juggled his lineup and ordered Belter not to throw the Cub sluggers any more fastballs, only "junk." The strategy worked, as Belter kept them quiet the rest of the game, striking out twelve to beat the Dodgers 7-4 and tie the series. The Cubs pulled another pitching surprise

in the third game. Young Eric Wigeland got the call to face the potent Esks and pitched the game of his life. He gave up only three hits in the first seven innings, then scattered another three, for an easy 18-2 drubbing of the favoured Eskimos. His mates shelled three Eskimo pitchers for a total of eighteen hits, to lead the series again. Ducey was livid at the Eskimos' performance.

In the clubhouse, batboy Allan Wachowich now had a clear impression that some of the members of the Eskimos were simply not trying their best during the series:

> The Eskimos had been in first place for most of the season. With the exception of Bob Lillis, a few of the American players let Ducey and Morris down a bit. It was the end of the season, they had won the pennant and after the fire, they were getting homesick. They simply wanted to get out of Edmonton. The cold weather made it worse.
>
> The local veterans did their best, Seaman, Brockie and Belter, but couldn't make the difference. The Cubs didn't have the same level of talent, but they had a lot of scrappy players like Des O'Connor, Mike McInerney, and Eric Wigeland.

The next night, the Dodgers won again as Vern Callihan held the Eskimos to seven hits and two runs. The vaunted Eskimos were never in the game after the first inning. Said Don Fleming,

> the only Eskimo warming up was General Manager Jawn Ducey... under the collar. Ducey is obviously nettled over his Esks pulling the same playoff folderoo as they did a year ago.

Ducey was also taking a loss at the gate. Cool fall evenings and the lack of a covered grandstand put a damper on the finals. Only an average of 1,500 shivering fans attended each game.

Ducey and acting mayor Alderman Dick Hanna congratulate Cal Pickles after his Dodgers won the last Big Four championship in 1950. A puzzled Ken Samis looks on. Courtesy of the Edmonton Archives EA 524-45.

Ducey and the Eskimo supporters were tense as umpire Harry Ornest called "play ball" on the evening of 7 September. Morris had his two best pitchers ready and started Belter on the mound. The fans were pleased to see the colourful Doug Lane return after a two-year hiatus to play first base in place of Bradish, who had left for university. But there would be no joy for the Eskimos that night. The Dodgers had another pitching surprise. Young Eddie Kapp, a rookie from Alberta's Coal Branch, scattered eight hits among the listless Eskimos. The Dodgers quickly scored eight runs. A lackluster Belter gave way to Jerry Seaman. The Eskimos scored six runs but their rickety infield collapsed, yielding eight errors. That woeful performance made it easy for Dodgers to win the game and the championship by a decisive 12-6 score.

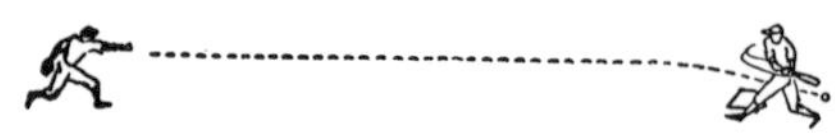

Although Lillis led the league with a .409 average and tied Glen Gorbous for the home-run lead, the season that seemed so bright for the Eskimos was in tatters. Marshall Johnson, the young left-fielder of whom much was expected, had been lost early in the season with a broken leg. With four of their key players ailing, the usually strong pitching of Seaman and Belter was not enough to stem the Dodger tide. Catcher Ross Kortgard and outfielder Bernie Andersen both hit .500 for the series. With the home-run power of Jim Ryan and a record five walks in five at-bats in the final game by Dodger outfielder Doug Stewart, it was all too much for the talent-laden but frustrated Eskimos. Ducey had to admit the Dodgers out-hustled his Eskimos, who "choked in the clutch" for the second straight year.

As Cal Pickles, Ken Samis, and Jim Ryan received the President's Trophy from Sam Irwin, an era appeared to be ending. In the Eskimo locker room, the lively Eddie Morris said he would not be back, electing to leave baseball for a steady job. Batboy Wachowich learned a lesson about the game of life from Morris, who had been playing baseball since 1936:

> He was a washed-up ball player in many ways, but he knew what baseball was all about. He knew the good and the bad side...he recognized the shortcomings of simply being a baseball player. At the end of the season, he was teasing me because I had to go back to school. He laughed about it and then I realized it was kind of a pathetic joke, because Eddie had no education at all and the only thing he knew anything about was baseball. I suddenly understood that he didn't have anything other than baseball in his working life. That realization

> taught me that as crazy as I was about the game, I would have to do more with my life than just be associated with baseball.

Wachowich packed away what was left of the bats and balls and said good-bye to his Eskimo heroes. The Korean War cast a shadow on the future of the Big Four league. Ducey predicted Edmonton and Calgary would operate local leagues in 1951 as a stop-gap measure and return to organized baseball in a year or two, bringing in other prairie cities. One of Edmonton's most popular and productive baseball chapters, based on an entertaining rivalry with Calgary, was at an end. The American imports went home for good, while the local boys pondered where they might play ball in 1951. Aging Renfrew Park, bereft of a grandstand, stood empty and quiet. Its Rajah, now without a business partner, was not quite certain what direction to take next season.

The Eskimo loss and the destruction of the grandstand were major setbacks for Ducey, but they did not deter him. One of his enduring qualities was his eternal optimism. There was never a time he came home, even after a tough day, that he was not whistling a happy tune. The whistle announced his presence as he came through the front door and frequently gave way to a song in his melodious tenor—the only time the American accent took on a decidedly Irish tone. Those who knew him agreed that no matter the circumstances he faced, he was a genuinely happy man. Observed Brian O'Hanlon,

> Sometimes he'd frustrate the devil out of me because he would be so optimistic and I would be trying to get the tough financial realities across. But the problems didn't make any difference with him. With

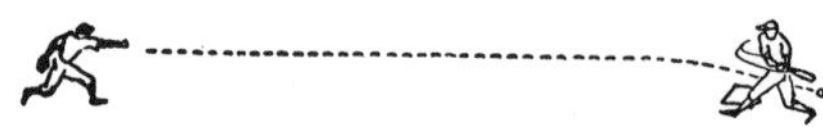

> him, it was the baseball that was important, not the finances. He would talk baseball anytime, at the drop of a hat. Baseball was his whole life, on the surface, in any event.

Ducey's optimism was a natural part of his character, but much of it was due to working at what he loved best, toiling in the service of baseball. Despite meagre financial rewards, he enjoyed the booming excitement of post-war Edmonton. He firmly believed that growing prosperity would soon bring organized baseball back to the city, then promoting itself as "the crossroads of the north."

The fire allowed Ducey to speed up his plan to replace the wooden grandstand with a badly needed modern facility. He put in a bid for a fast start on new concrete stands to a sympathetic city council. But Commissioner Dudley Menzies responded bluntly, saying space and financial reasons would not permit it. "You are talking real money when you talk a steel and concrete grandstand for 7,000 persons," he said. Speaking at the victory dinner for Cal's Dodgers, acting mayor Dick Hanna said that "baseball has a selling job to do," because money for a new grandstand would have to go before the voters as a money bylaw in November. It did, and Ducey was only temporarily dismayed when voters turned down a proposal to authorize a $50,000 borrowing toward a new concrete facility.

The determined promoter then convinced his friends at City Hall to write a new ten-year lease to enable the grandstand and other improvements to be financed out of baseball revenues over that period. He negotiated a $1 per year rental for the first five years, and an eight-percent rental on revenues for the second five. The rental would go to upgrade the park, as would all earnings over expenses in the first five years. The matter seemed settled, but without a solid league, two seasons would pass before the temporary bleachers gave way to a concrete grandstand.

The minutes of the last official league meeting in Calgary on 17 November are terse. It was agreed that Ducey and either Timmins or Cundal would meet the next day with delegates from Medicine Hat and

Lethbridge about the possibility of forming a new, four-city league for 1951. Nothing came of that meeting, and by late fall Ducey had to admit that the Big Four Intercity Baseball League was officially at an end. It was over not just because the Korean War made the supply of U.S. players uncertain. Feuding between Ducey and his Calgary peers had turned bitter, and they were not in a mood to "play ball" with him any longer. He had been harsh on Cundal and Timmins over the years because of a number of incidents that he termed "bush league." Still, he could not question their own love of baseball and the effort they had put into the game in Calgary. Their downfall was an inability to bring about an expansion to tiny Buffalo Stadium, referred to by Ducey as "that band-box." The old park could not accommodate the Calgary fans wanting to watch baseball and its outfield was far too small. Ducey, on the other hand, benefitted from good relations with City Hall and commissioners who wanted Edmonton to have proper baseball facilities.

The very element that gave the league continuity—"home-town boys"—was also blamed by some for causing fan indifference at seeing "the same old faces." At the same time, Edmonton sports fans had begun a major romance with their new football club. The Edmonton Eskimos had been revived in 1949 under the field leadership of popular Annis Stukus and were back in the Canadian Football League, doing regular battle with their nemesis, the Calgary Stampeders. The team had organized properly, gaining widespread financial backing from the business community and public participation with the introduction of an extremely popular "Touchdown Club," which allowed fans to meet the players and get in on the latest football happenings.

There was nothing like it for Edmonton's baseball fans, although Ducey had introduced a "Knothole Gang" for youngsters and provided them with their own bleacher seating in centre field. But compared to the CFL, semi-pro baseball in western Canada lacked a mechanism to create continued fan loyalty and a sense of community involvement. Despite the extended season in 1950—and with box seats at $1 and general admission

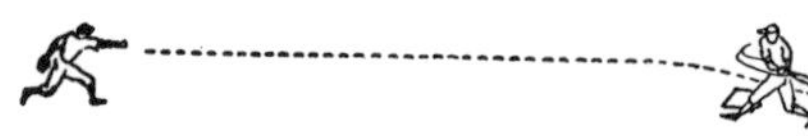

only 65¢—Edmonton baseball attendance had fallen some 29,000 off the previous year to 86,000. Ducey estimated the fire caused some 30,000 fewer fans to attend the 1950 playoffs. The season also cost him $6,900 of personal funds, lent to cover losses by his baseball company as well the Dodgers ball club.

Yet the Big Four league had enjoyed a good run. Many Renfrew Park fans remember it as the most colourful and entertaining baseball that Ducey staged in his thirteen seasons in charge of the park. The rivalry with Calgary, a good brand of baseball, and improved facilities had helped make the transition from wartime to the booming 1950s. Still, the end was a surprise in view of the promise with which the final season had begun. Would Edmonton ever see the Big Four's like again? Would future line-ups contain the familiar names which Dick Beddoes had exuberantly penned in verse to start the 1950 season?

"Jonathan Ducey's Band"

Oh, Johnson goes bang and Morris goes bang
And the pitchers blaze away.
Johnston wields a mighty bat,
And Karlson at shortstop plays.
Oh, the Eskimo fans sit in the stands,
And the cheering is something grand.
A credit to old Edmonton-town is
Jonathan Ducey's band.
Next week they will commence upon a
very swell affair;
It's the annual Big Four pennant race,
three others will be there.
They'll be the local Dodgers,
Calgary Puritys and Calgary Buffs,
They will come from near and far,

But none of them will be too rough
For Jonathan Ducey's stars.

Oh, Johnson goes bang and Morris goes bang,
And Seaman blazes away.
Brockie pumps his big brown bat
And Clark on third does play,
Oh, the Eskimo fan, he roots and hoots,
And the yelling is simply grand,
A credit to this dusty town is
Jonathan Ducey's band.

15

Pinch-hitting

DUCEY STILL BELIEVED HIS DREAM OF BRINGING ORGANIZED BASEBALL BACK TO EDMONTON WAS WITHIN HIS GRASP: IT DEPENDED ON CREATING A SOLID LEAGUE MADE UP OF THE RIGHT CITIES, INCLUDING CALGARY. In early January 1951, he met with men from Calgary, Medicine Hat, and Lethbridge to discuss organizing a Class-C league. All four cities had posted a $3,000 good-faith deposit and Ducey had Clement J. Schwener of Boston, Mass., a renowned baseball scheduling specialist, draw up three proposed schedules for discussion at the meeting. But unsettled international conditions and the fear of a heavy

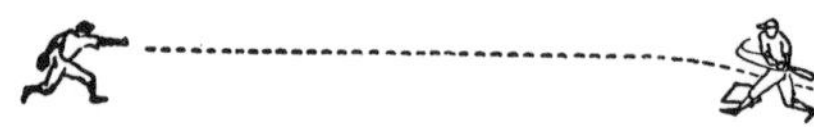

U.S. military draft, which might cause a shortage of American ballplayers, led the group to shelve plans of an all-Alberta league for 1951.

On 20 January 1951, Edmontonians were shocked to read the *Bulletin*'s headline announcing, "The *Edmonton Bulletin* Ends Publication Today," ninety-one years after its founding by Frank Oliver. Rising costs of materials and labour, restricted newsprint supply, and lack of funds to finance an overdue physical expansion were blamed. Ducey was saddened to see his former employer fold but particularly dismayed at the loss of its talented sportswriters, who included Dick Beddoes, Bill Lewis, and Stan Moher. Beddoes and Lewis would move along with several colleagues to Vancouver, but Moher became the Edmonton sportswriter for the *Albertan*, assuring Edmonton baseball excellent coverage in Calgary.

In February, Ducey purchased John Beatty's fifty-percent interest in the Edmonton Senior Baseball Club. Beatty was back on active U.S. military duty, based in Florida. He had married a Canadian woman, but it was now obvious that he was not coming back to Canada. Calgary showed little interest in a new league, so Ducey was forced to make temporary arrangements. Despite questions about the upcoming season, he remained optimistic:

> The future possibilities of this organization are good. The past five years of effort and groundwork will now begin to produce, considering the future in store for this city because of the steady increase of population and the vast wealth of natural resources surrounding Edmonton.

Edmonton had been enjoying its unprecedented oil-boom since 1947, the same year the Big Four League had begun. Acknowledging the dominance of the industry, Ducey again announced he was dropping the Eskimo name in favour of "the Oilers":

> It is our method of paying tribute to a city destined to become an important metropolis on the North American continent. It is our

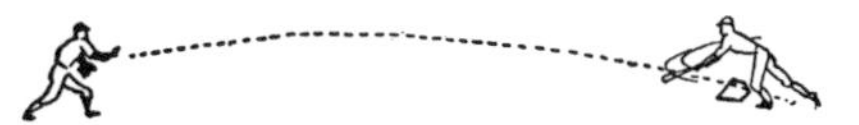

> tribute to the many and varied concerns engaged in the development of black gold, to their initiative in placing Edmonton "up town" on the "Hit Parade" of North America's vital and important cities.

He denied the name change had anything to do with the fact that the re-incarnated Edmonton football club had taken on its original Eskimos name and now dominated the sports pages. Sensitive to fan preference for new talent, he made an agreement with Ken Samis that his role would be to operate the park and bring teams in for exhibition games and the odd tournament. The former catcher would independently manage the Oilers and their business affairs; Samis and team would work on a cooperative basis and share the season's profits.

Tournament baseball

Samis had a good selection of players to choose from. His initial pitching staff included Eddie Belter, Hal Forss, Dick Lowe, Al Purvis, Jerry Seaman, and John Carpenter, who had toiled for Purity in the Big Four League. They were soon joined by submarine pitcher Cy Thorseth. Footballer Frank Morris and Bill Gadsby, who had just finished his fifth NHL season as a Chicago Blackhawks defenceman, shared duties in right field. Gadsby, a Calgary native, would go on to play twenty years in the NHL, finishing his career with Detroit; he was named to the Hockey Hall of Fame in 1970. He ended the tradition of the many NHL players appearing regularly in an Edmonton baseball uniform during the summer months.

Ducey had flirted with tournament baseball in 1950, umpiring with Harry Ornest at the first Lacombe tournament and also at Lloydminster. When observers claimed the quality of play provided by teams such as Delisle, Sceptre, Indian Head, and Medicine Hat's "California Mohawks" was far better than the Big Four League, Ducey quickly responded to the challenge. He brought the Mohawks in for an exhibition game and the

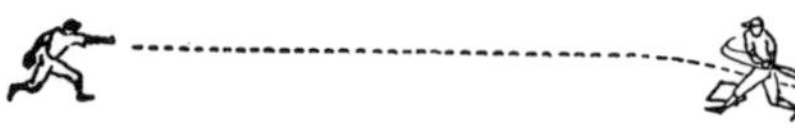

1950 Eskimos thrashed them 9-3, ending any claim that the Big Four League offered an inferior brand of baseball. In 1951, his only alternative was to give tournament baseball a try.

Incessant rain at Renfrew Park delayed the season opener with Max Bentley's Delisle Gems two nights in a row, a seeming repeat for the hockey-renowned Bentley brothers, Max, Reg, and Doug. They had made a 1946 visit to Edmonton and rain kept them in their hotel for four straight days. This time, the clubs got in two games on Saturday with the Oilers winning 11-5 and 9-6, largely on the strength of their talented pitching staff. On Sunday, the sun came out and 4,500 fans streamed into Renfrew, filling the bleachers to capacity. The warm afternoon was a pleasant reminder of old times. Working for a penny for every bottle sold, concessionaires hustled through the stands to meet thirsty demands for more "ice-cold" Coca Cola and Orange Crush. Making the day more satisfying, the Oilers beat Delisle 3-2, behind the strong pitching of Dick Lowe and Al Purvis.

The Oilers seemed well suited for tournament baseball, which was once again sweeping the Canadian prairies. They could hold their own with the many touring Canadian clubs: the Bentleys' Delisle Gems; Jim Ryan's Swift Current nine; oilman Red Nixon's Sceptre squad; Les Edwards' Penticton team; and assorted others teams from Saskatoon, Regina, Moose Jaw, Kamloops, and Trail. They even did well against the California Mohawks, a group of talented young U.S. collegians playing out of Medicine Hat. The Oilers also beat the renowned House of David All-Stars and won all twelve of their games with three visiting U.S. Air Force clubs. But the Oilers could not win in tournament play and make big money.

The two toughest clubs touring the prairies in 1951 were the Indian Head Rockets, an all-black team assembled in Florida that played out of the small Saskatchewan town for the second year, and Sceptre, which dominated tournament baseball on the prairies the previous season, winning some $17,000 in prize money. By early June, Indian Head had won twenty-seven out of thirty-one games since spring training. Its roster

included Big Jim Williams, a former player in the Negro Major Leagues of the 1930s. Sceptre had the venerable Chet Brewer, one of the all-time black greats who had been pitching since 1925 and had the third highest number of Negro Major League wins—eighty-eight—most of them for the Kansas City Monarchs. Those NML wins rank him behind Satchel Paige (124) and Raymond Brown (101) of the Homestead Grays.

In early June 1951, three large tournaments lay within easy driving distance of Edmonton: Lloydminster, Lacombe, and Camrose. These tournaments offered sizable prize money, which drew a number of talented barnstorming teams to the area. Ducey booked them all into Renfrew Park to play the Oilers. Tournament baseball was a bit of a financial gamble. A team could be hot for a week, enter a tournament and lose one game, and it was out of the running for the prize money. That was the main problem with the Oilers, as Des O'Connor later observed:

> We had an all-star club and should have made a lot of money from tournament games. But every time we went to a tournament, we seemed to lose the first game to a team we could normally beat eight out of ten times, like Kamloops, for example.

Most tournaments were two-day affairs, with games played at 9:00 a.m., noon, 3:00 p.m., and 6:00 p.m. To save on expenses, teams would leave home at 6:00 a.m. to arrive in time for the 9:00 opening round. The schedules were punishing: tournaments were grouped closely together to attract the best touring teams; they were in turn bracketed with exhibition games elsewhere in the area. For example, Sceptre played at Edmonton on Monday, 5 June. Both clubs played Tuesday and Wednesday in the Lloydminster tournament and met again at Renfrew Park on Thursday night. They then played Friday and Saturday in the Lacombe tournament. Edmonton hosted the Indian Head Rockets at Renfrew the following Sunday and Monday, then played in the Camrose tournament on Tuesday and Wednesday.

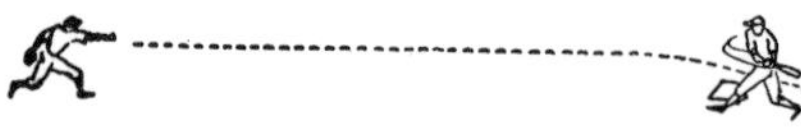

The tournaments were usually sponsored by local service clubs, such as the Lacombe Lions. Lacombe would manage to keep the most successful of the three tournaments alive for more than thirty years; in fact, by the late 1970s, Lacombe had the only diamond oasis left in baseball-barren central Alberta. But that possibility seemed improbable in busy June 1951. The North Battleford Beavers beat Alvie Steffis' Morinville club 11-1, to win the first tournament at Lloydminster. The Morinville club included ex-Edmonton players Ralph Morgan, Dave Brockie, and Leo Douziech, as well as Al Brightman, then the coach of Seattle University, who played for the Cleveland Indians briefly in 1943.

Ducey watched at Lacombe as the Oilers were ousted again, this time by Morinville, 7-6, with Brightman bashing out two home runs. A few hours earlier, Ducey had been tremendously impressed as he watched an unknown nineteen-year-old rookie from Ponoka upset the vaunted Sceptre team 4-3. Ralph Vold, pitching for the Central Alberta All-Stars, beat the fabled Chet Brewer, scattering ten hits until relieved with one out in the ninth inning. That game started Vold on a career in professional baseball. Vancouver broadcaster Bill Good Sr. had been lured to Lacombe to cover the tournament and was most impressed with Vold, who later told how he signed his first contract:

> Bill Good went back to Vancouver and told a scout for the Dodgers, Bill Sivilich, that he had seen a young kid who throws pretty hard. Bill flew out and I let my manager and mentor, Charlie Lewis, do the negotiating. I would have signed for fifteen cents but they started out at $1,000 and Charlie got it up to $3,000 on the understanding that they would take me to a training camp they were holding at Billings, Montana within a few weeks. That was how it all started.

But Lewis' Central Alberta All-Stars were soon eliminated. The Morinville team made it to the finals at Lacombe, but once more ran out of gas,

losing 11-1 as they had at Lloydminster, this time to Medicine Hat's California Mohawks.

The Oilers had only slightly better success in the Camrose tournament a few days later, getting to the semi-finals only to lose to Jim Ryan's Swift Current team. They fared far better with most of their opponents in the exhibition series staged at Renfrew Park that month, the only exceptions being Sceptre and the vaunted Indian Head Rockets. Oddly enough, neither of those teams was able to win any of the three major tournaments in northern Alberta that summer. In Edmonton on 10 June, the Rockets attracted a Sunday crowd of 5,000 spectators, drawn there largely to watch "Peanut" Davis, their highly touted pitcher.

A right-handed knuckle-ball artist, Davis toured with Jackie Robinson's All-Stars the previous season, winning nine straight games. The "Nut" had also played for the Indianapolis Clowns and the Ashville, North Carolina Blues. Among the victims of his exhibition wins were Bob Feller, Dizzy Dean, and Satchel Paige. To oppose the vaunted Davis, Ken Samis selected the quiet, reliable fastballer Jerry Seaman, a former Eskimo.

After hitting a home run, the Sceptres' starting pitcher, Danny Jenkins, gave way to Peanut Davis early in the third inning. By the fifth inning, Edmonton fans were buzzing as Seaman held the Rockets to a 1-1 tie with a masterful performance. Then a freak error changed everything.

Seaman ran into trouble with two out, giving up a single to Peanut Davis, then walking two to load the bases. With the count at 2-2, Seaman came in with a sweeping curve ball which the batter swung at but missed as it hit the dirt. Catcher Grant Warwick seemed to trap the ball cleanly against the ground. With a sigh of relief, he rolled it toward the mound and headed for the dugout. Most of his club automatically began to follow him. Meanwhile, the Rockets' manager, Jim Williams, alertly had his runners racing around the bases. By the time centre-fielder Barry Robertshaw realized what was happening and picked up the ball at the

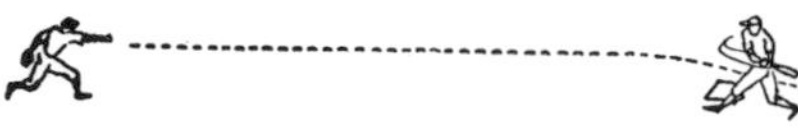

pitching mound, three runs had scored and the batter was perched on third base. After a trapped third strike with two out, the batter must either be tagged or thrown out at first base. However, in this case, with the bases loaded, Warwick only needed to step on home plate to force out the third-base runner. He did not and Sceptre went on to tally five unearned runs that inning, taking a heartbreaker 7-4.

Seaman gained some satisfaction a week later in an outstanding duel against Wayne Stevenson of Jim Ryan's Swift Current Indians. Both pitchers gave up only two hits, but Seaman was the luckier, scoring the game's only run himself in what Don Fleming described as "the best pitching duel of several seasons at the local ballyard." Only 900 fans came to the Friday evening battle, while across town 5,000 spectators attended Canada's first Triple-A stock car races at the exhibition grounds.

Despite a sunny 1 July weekend, just 1,200 fans were at Renfrew Friday and Saturday to watch the Oilers win two of three games from the renowned House of David team, making their final visit to Edmonton. Dick Lowe beat the bearded baseballers 4-3, then submarine pitcher Cy Thorseth turned them back 6-1. Don Fleming was disgusted at the lack of fan support:

> Is Edmonton really a baseball town? This is a question that Jawn Ducey and his colleagues would do well to determine beyond any shred of a doubt before they get in too deep.
>
> Ducey has shown implicit faith in this oil-booming city, and he has the support of experts in their line. High officials of big league organizations are on record as observing this is fertile territory for organized ball when the time comes that players are in sufficient supply.
>
> Il Duce has done his part. He is the right man for baseball promotion here. He is a fanatic of the game. He has done wonders in dressing up the game here, placing it in a setting unsurpassed in Western Canada, except by the new park Bob Brown has just opened up in Vancouver. But could he be coming to a dead end? Certain current

events are pointing that way. So far he and the Oilers are wading deep in red ink.

Fleming added that while "Ducey himself hasn't worn his wailing togs out in the open," manager Ken Samis was really "fed up" with the lack of support. The Samis players, who agreed to play for a split of the profits, had earned literally nothing six weeks into the busy season. While the clubs split the profits sixty/forty percent on a win-lose basis, there was often little left to share after expenses. With seats at 65¢, the 1,200 fans at each House of David game paid in $780 in admissions. Because the visitors had to be guaranteed $500 per game to come to Edmonton, little profit was left for the home players after expenses were paid. It was a situation similar to Renfrew's first season, when the 1933 club managers almost rebelled against Henry Roche over a lack of earnings.

There was no rebellion against Ducey, however, and the Oilers soldiered on. In early August, there was hope for a payday when oilman Red Nixon of Sceptre, Saskatchewan announced he would stage a $7,300 tournament at Renfrew Park. But after what had been mostly a hot, dry summer, the rains returned just as Nixon's week of tournament baseball was to begin. The clubs were rained out two days in a row and the diamond turned into a sea of mud. To get a semi-final winner, Ducey had cars driven around the base paths for an hour, packing down the infield which was then burned dry with gasoline.

Just as Medicine Hat's California Mohawks squared off against Saskatchewan's Eston Ramblers in the final contest, the rain came back, forcing a cancellation in the fifth inning. Brick Swegle, whose Mohawks held a 6-0 lead at that stage, technically could have claimed a victory and the $2,500 first prize. Swegle felt so badly for Nixon and the 2,000 Edmonton fans who turned out under threatening skies, he agreed to start all over again the next night to play another nine-inning contest. The game never took place because of continuing rain. If the rainy woes of early August were not enough, Nixon returned on the Labour Day

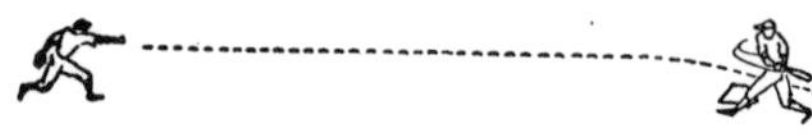

weekend to play an exhibition series between his Sceptre club and Swegle's Mohawks at Renfrew. This time he was totally rained out and left Edmonton baseball's soggy scene forever.

Nixon's tournament had one positive result for Edmonton sports fans. At second base for the Regina Caps in the first game against Edmonton was Rollie Miles, a twenty-four-year-old athlete from Washington, D.C. Miles had begun playing baseball at age fifteen and had played some professional ball after the war. Des O'Connor recalls his first appearance in Edmonton vividly:

> The Caps had a fantastic infield. We stood on the sidelines like spellbound kids and watched them during their infield practice. Grant Warwick said, "They're just a good-field, no-hit club. I've got to throw someone out early in the game."
>
> Rollie Miles was their leading base stealer and Warwick threw him out in the first inning and again later in the game. They beat us 3-2 but it was the most exciting game I've ever played in.

Up in the press box, Don Fleming was equally impressed:

> Miles was an outstanding second baseman and a good hitter. After the game I mentioned him to Regina's owner, Cliff Ehrle. He said, "Yeah, and he's some kind of a football player. Came out of one of those small colleges and nobody knows anything about him."
>
> I called up Annis Stukus who had the second-year version of the Eskimo football team at the time and said, "I've got a football player for you." Rollie turned out to be a great star in the CFL and I gained a reputation as a great talent scout.

Miles briefly returned to the Renfrew diamond in 1952 when Ducey hired him as an umpire, but by then the flashy running back was well on his way to being one of the CFL's most outstanding performers.

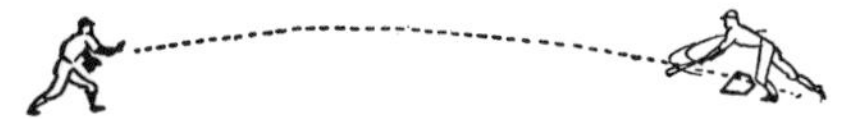

Despite weather problems, Ducey continued his promotions, staging exhibition games through August and the early part of September. He arranged a final series between the Oilers and the Great Falls Electrics, who had just become champions of the Pioneer League. He had long been interested in linking up with the Class-C league and felt such a series would be a good test, both on the field and at the gate. The three-game series was to begin Monday, 24 September, and Samis put his money-hungry club through weekend drills in preparation, expressing confidence that he could at least win one game. However, Samis never got his win and Ducey never got his test on the field and at the gate. It rained for four straight days and the Electrics finally left town. Ducey shut the park down for the season.

Don Fleming pondered the state of the Rajah's mental health:

> How come the guy doesn't pitch in the towel? How many bad breaks can one man get? Will it be the gas pipe or the High Level Bridge [for Ducey]?

As if the miserable season had not been bad enough, Ducey then learned of the tragic death of his old friend, Yankee scout Joe Devine. Devine had died of complications following an auto accident while travelling in Idaho. The veteran baseball scout had recognized and developed an enormous amount of star talent for the Yankees over the years, including the DiMaggio brothers and Joe Gordon. He had also worked closely with Ducey to help him get the Big Four League up and running in 1947. The two went all the way back to 1921-22, when Ducey served as Devine's batboy when his Calgary Bronks visited old Diamond Park.

There had been some long-distance discussion about the possibilities of Edmonton and Calgary joining the Western International League following the 1951 season, but nothing came of it. The season had been a financial disaster for both the promoter and the players, largely because of the weather and the guarantees needed to get some of the touring teams booked into Renfrew Park. With no income to slice up by the end of the season, the Oilers' profit-sharing plan had gone for naught.

A pleasant pause

In 1952, with no inter-city league to play in, Ducey again had to improvise. This time he structured a four-team local league. The briefly retired Brant Matthews came back in as a sponsor. Having recently purchased the Drake Hotel in the suburb of Beverly, Matthews backed the Beverly Hotel Drakes, managed by Jerry Seaman. Harry Cohen also returned to sponsor the Army & Navy Merchants, fielding a relatively strong team managed by Jim Ryan. Maurice Carter, a newcomer to the Edmonton baseball scene, bankrolled the Carter Motors Pontiacs, managed by Doug Stewart. The fourth team, the Leduc Oilers, languished in the league cellar all season and were described by a nauseated Don Fleming as "the weakest team to appear in Renfrew Park in years."

As if the fire of 1950 had not been enough, a flood threatened Renfrew Park in June 1952, forcing Brian O'Hanlon and the staff to hurriedly move office and concession stand contents to higher ground. However neither fire nor flood deterred Ducey from several trips to other cities that summer, in search of a new inter-city league for 1953.

While the play at Renfrew was not up to Big Four League calibre, the local boys could still play some good ball and the fans turned out in the usual numbers, an average of about 1,500 per game. The Drakes pulled ahead of the Pontiacs and won the league and the right to a bye as the Merchants took on the Pontiacs in the semi-finals. A shirtsleeve crowd of 4,200 fans took advantage of the Sunday silver collection to watch the

Pontiacs take the fifth game 11-8 and win the right to play the Drakes. Jerry Seaman's Drakes made short work of the Pontiacs, losing only the third game and taking the final series in five. They won the last 11-4 on 8 September, as young Dutch Lakeman struck out nine before a respectable Sunday afternoon crowd of 3,900. Ducey watched as the last fans filed out in the lengthening shadows of the fall sunshine. The Rajah was content that for most of one summer at least, he had gotten a break from the weather.

16

Organized baseball returns

DUCEY MADE VISITS TO MONTANA, SASKATCHEWAN, AND THE WEST COAST IN PURSUIT OF ORGANIZED BASEBALL. In Montana, joined by Calgary's Timmins and Cundal, he met with officials of the Class-C Pioneer League about a two-team Alberta linkup. Next was the west coast, where Ducey explored what even he conceded to be a long-shot, an alignment in the sprawling, Class-A Western International League (WIL). The WIL had operated continuously since 1937 and included Vancouver and Victoria for most of that time. Well established, few of its American members looked on Edmonton and Calgary with any great interest. In 1952, Ducey played a waiting game, believing that the WIL would eventually ask Edmonton and Calgary to join them:

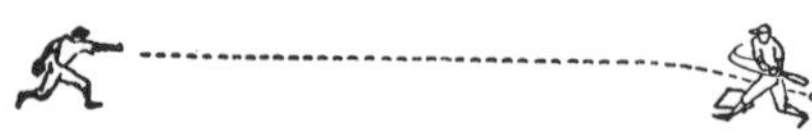

The first meeting of the Edmonton business leaders who put up the money to bring professional baseball back to the city in 1953-54. It was about the only time all the shareholders were smiling, as the club suffered heavy financial losses. Courtesy of the Edmonton Archives EA 524-47.

> I know they want Edmonton and Calgary in. However they seem to be getting a little panicky. We're not interested with Lewiston and Salem in the league. The distances would be a killer.

Building a professional franchise

Calgary's Timmins had earlier claimed he was on the verge of getting a WIL franchise and wanted Edmonton to join him. In the late fall, Ducey met with factions within the WIL, particularly Vancouver, that wanted the Alberta cities in. They offered much larger markets than most of the existing clubs and their close proximity made Edmonton and Calgary an attractive combination.

A WIL franchise was reported to cost $50,000 and the league was in need of some stronger clubs. Ducey pulled together a group of nineteen Edmonton business leaders (later expanded to thirty-five), who each agreed to put up between $1,000 and $2,500. The Edmonton Baseball Club was capitalized at $125,000, and $65,000 was raised with the initial private offering. It was the first time since the early days of Deacon White and Frank Gray that an Edmonton baseball team had received widespread backing from the business community, a reflection of renewed boosterism in the booming oil city. The directors, led by Brant Matthews and Cecil Ross, had answered Ducey's call in late 1952 to put up the money to bring organized baseball back to Edmonton. The original group also included Hales Ross, Harry Maddison, Ken Samis, Al Ernst, Clifford Lee, Fred Jenner, Ken Lawson, Robert McDonald, Fraser Duncan, Winslow Hamilton, George Golden, Dr. H. McLennan, J.L. (Whitey) Wilson, Dr. Rupert Clare, Cal Pickles, John L. MacDonald, and Russ Scorer. Many were Ducey's old and good friends, but several were simply Edmonton boosters who wanted their city to be represented in organized baseball. Their money would allow the club to buy players and make a franchise payment. Brant Matthews was named president. Still looking for a new concrete grandstand and a roof for Renfrew Park, Ducey managed to get city commissioner John Hodgson named the club's honourary president.

Ducey set his own conditions for entering the WIL, and they irritated Vancouver's veteran baseball administrator R.P. "Bob" Brown. "They need us in," said Ducey, who felt he could reduce the stiff entry fee and yet demand some special conditions, such as letting Edmonton and Calgary open the season on the road in the more southern cities. He was still talking about joining the Pioneer League, whose Montana cities offered lower travel costs. The talk caused the usually quiet Brown to blow up:

> Where does Ducey get off making suggestions like that? That's the first time I've ever heard of a fellow trying to get into a league and laying down conditions like he's proposed.

Ducey and Norman "Buster" Lacey of Calgary hand over their $25,000 franchise cheques to WIL officials Robert Abel and R.P. "Bob" Brown of Vancouver as the two Alberta cities prepare to re-enter organized baseball late in 1952. A.B. Cox of Victoria is at right. Courtesy of the Edmonton Archives EA 524-48.

Ducey respected the venerable Brown and courteously replied that he had taken his remarks the wrong way. He said he only meant that the best financial situation would determine where Edmonton would go in pursuit of organized baseball:

> I wasn't trying to tell them anything. Rather I was just making it clear what the situation would have to be before we could ever entertain the idea of applying for memberships.

Ducey soon got Brown calmed down and tempers returned to normal. Brown in turn assured him he knew Edmonton was a good baseball town and that the WIL wanted both Alberta cities in the league.

In October 1952, with shareholder money in their pockets, Ducey and Timmins went to the WIL fall meeting in Seattle. To the surprise of many observers they made a deal, each paying $25,000 for a franchise. After a formal vote at Yakima in November, Edmonton and Calgary were officially welcomed as the ninth and tenth cities in the Class-A Western International League. The backers had pulled it off: professional baseball would return to both Alberta cities for the first time in thirty years.

A 144-game split season was agreed to. Salary limits, exclusive of the manager, were to be $5,700 a month but were later set at $6,300. In Calgary, Sam Timmins stepped aside and Norman "Buster" Lacey was named club president. Harold Cundal stayed on as a director.

Ducey had finally realized his long-held dream: he was now a member of organized baseball. The club directors agreed he would be paid $5,000 a year to serve as general manager. He was finally a part of that far-off world he had faithfully read about since his boyhood days, in his weekly copy of Spink's "baseball bible," *The Sporting News*. Edmonton's franchise activities were therein reported for all the baseball world to read, as were its player acquisitions and league play. For someone who had always been on the outside looking in, Ducey's links to organized baseball were impressive. Now, however, he was "in," his fans were "in," and his town, Edmonton, was "in."

Those were heady times in late 1952, and the Rajah of Renfrew was in his element. He busily talked up the improved class of baseball Edmonton fans would see with the arrival of the WIL as he arranged with the city to expand seating up to 6,000 at Renfrew Park. After a long day at the office, he would sit with the telephone glued to his ear late into the night at home. Calls came in from his many baseball friends, and he in turn was calling the U.S. in search of playing talent. Then he was off to meetings in Seattle, Vancouver, and Phoenix. On the eve of his departure for Phoenix and the major-minor league meetings, *Journal* writer Jim Brooke termed him "as buoyant as a life raft":

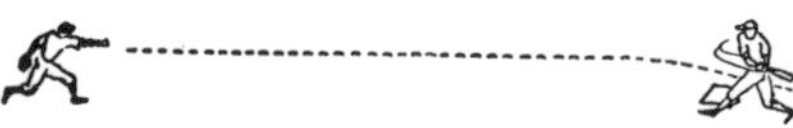

Former National League umpire Beans Reardon (centre) recommended Bob Sturgeon as manager of Ducey's Class-A WIL Eskimos. The ex-major leaguer acted as Edmonton's player-manager in 1953 and 1954. Courtesy of the Edmonton Archives EA 524-49.

> John Ducey left with his head held high and unquenchable faith in Edmonton's future as a professional baseball town. "Now that we are in organized ball at last," he said Thursday, edging his words around a torpedo-shaped cigar, "nothing will stop us."

At Phoenix, he rubbed shoulders with Branch Rickey of the Pirates and George Weiss and Casey Stengel of the Yankees, as well as meeting with old friends like Babe Herman and Beans Reardon. They gave him advice and quickly introduced him to a widening circle of major-league contacts.

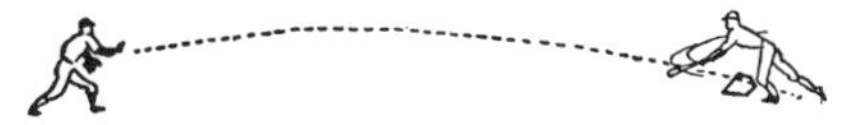

Ducey's new Eskimos

Herman and Reardon also provided Ducey with a list of candidates for the player-manager job. Because Edmonton did not have a working agreement with a major-league team, it was vital that he find the right manager. He needed a man with good baseball connections and the ability to groom younger players. Near the end of the Phoenix meetings, his old mentor Beans Reardon recommended that man. He was Bob Sturgeon, a thirty-two-year-old former major-league second-baseman. Sturgeon's playing career had been interrupted by World War Two, but he had played for the Chicago Cubs and Boston Braves. Ducey, a frequent cigar smoker himself, took to the stogie-smoking Sturgeon immediately. The curly-haired, Long Beach, California resident was a warm, outgoing, handsome man with a wide, friendly smile; he just loved to talk baseball. Ducey provided a brief description for the home-town fans:

> Bobby is a clean-cut fellow with a likable personality. He has always been known as a hard competitor. He has a wide acquaintance in baseball, which should be helpful.

Bob Sturgeon's selection as manager kindled the excitement of Edmonton fans. In his inimitable style, Dick Beddoes summed up Sturgeon's lengthy baseball experience in a Christmas greeting: "Hey John, this Sturgeon's no virgin." Sturgeon's one footnote to fame during his brief major-league career was chronicled by Dennis Bingham in *The Ballplayers*, edited by Mike Shatzkin:

> While playing shortstop against the Dodgers (in 1947), he passed up a double-play opportunity to throw the relay at Jackie Robinson, striking him in the chest with the throw. About six weeks later, Robinson reached first base and ran on the first pitch. Not sliding, Robinson

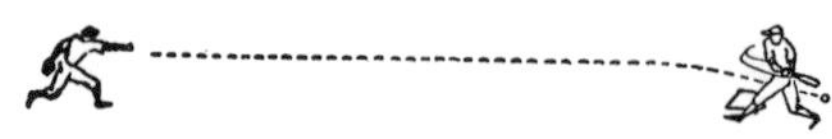

threw a block at Sturgeon and knocked him half-way into left field. Sturgeon suffered two broken ribs.

Tony Robello, then west coast scout for the St. Louis Browns, found several players for Edmonton. He arranged for Ducey to buy the contract of veteran right-handed pitcher Leon Day from the Browns, who had just shipped him off to Toronto for the 1953 season. The announcement of the signing said Day had been dubbed "the Satchel Paige of the Eastern league" the previous year, where he had a 13–8 record with Scranton. Other than that, little notice was taken of Day, who held out for a while, finally joining the club late in April.

It was no surprise early in 1953 when the club announced its new name, the Edmonton Eskimos, favoured by half the fans who responded to a "name the ball club" contest. Among "also rans" were the Gushers, Drillers, Derricks, Canucks, Alcans, Cariboos, Northern Lights, Capitals, and Ice Bergs. It never dawned on Ducey himself to suggest the Rainmakers. He cheerily predicted the club could draw 200,000 "if the weather is right and the club is in contention." He would be off by more than 100,000. A cold, wet spring and an August mosquito-plague combined to hold paid attendance to 92,758. It was both good and bad news that Edmonton led the league in attendance, which was far below the record 155,000 fans who had come through Renfrew's gates in 1949. The WIL had forty-four rain-outs in the first half of the season.

But all of that seemed remote when a tanned Bob Sturgeon arrived in sub-zero Edmonton early in March for his first look at his new locale. He announced the team would do its spring training at Compton, California. Ducey followed that up with a long list of additional player signings. Then he revealed that Cecil Goldstick had made an agreement with the Edmonton Flyers hockey club, which would allow the popular Tiger to leave his hockey duties before the playoffs started and join the Eskimos as trainer in time for baseball's spring training.

Trainer Cecil "Tiger" Goldstick, Bob Sturgeon, and Ducey confer at the Eskimos spring training camp at Compton, California in 1953. Courtesy of the Edmonton Archives EA 524-50.

The temperature soared to 88°F soon after Ducey and Goldstick got to camp in late March. Local sportswriters could not resist such headlines as "Eskimos in the Tropics." In fact, the first practice had to be cut short due to the intense heat. A week later, the fledgling club played and won its first spring-training game. A delighted Ducey found John Grady, who had pitched for Deacon White's 1910 Edmonton Eskimos, residing in California. He had the elder Grady throw out the first ball for the new Eskimos. By mid-April, they began working their way north with a series of exhibition games. At Kennewick, Washington, they won their first WIL game, 5-4 against Tri-Cities. By 12 May, they were in Edmonton and ready for opening night.

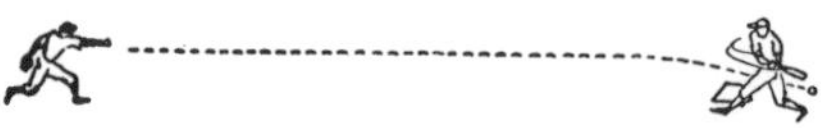

Pitcher John Conant is congratulated by Eskimo team-mates after another of his twenty-four wins in the 1953 WIL. Grounds crew member Brant Ducey is at left. Courtesy of the Edmonton Archives EA 524-52.

Renfrew Park was once again teeming with excitement, and fans continued to stream in right up to the moment league president Bob Brown threw out the first pitch. Ducey was pictured next to him, looking on with the ever-present cigar stuck in his mouth. Don Fleming of the *Journal* described the scene:

> Jawn Ducey had his best bib and tucker on for this one. It was a dream come true, getting Edmonton back into organized baseball again and into the Western International fray, in particular.

> Il Duce was bustling about, making certain there would be no last-minute hitches...ensuring the big new scoreboard was in working order, likewise the P.A....hustling out another turnstile to speed the admission of the hundreds of patrons milling outside the gates...all the while finding time to take bows as fans congratulated him on getting organized baseball for them.

Fleming also noted that the temperature at game time was 52°F but felt colder due to a chilly breeze. "The bleacher bugs didn't mind, though. It was a festive occasion."

The weather was as cool as some of the Eskimo players had ever experienced, particularly starting pitcher John Conant, who hailed from Tennessee. Trainer Goldstick tried to reassure him: "It's supposed to get warmer tomorrow."

"A lot of good that does me tonight," Conant fired back. But he took to the cool weather and pitched a full nine-inning game. Conant's wife later jokingly knit him a woollen cover for his private parts, and the novel handicraft was much celebrated in the club house by his team-mates.

Baseball fans welcomed their new ball club with a record turn-out for the WIL. Every seat was full as 5,112 fans watched what for most of them was their first professional ball game. Shortstop Whitey Thompson, whose ability would soon replace the memory of Bob Lillis, thrilled fans by smashing a home run. A batch of doubles by pitcher Conant, outfielders Vern Campbell and Andy Skurski, and young Don Herman, son of the great Babe, helped give Edmonton a slim but satisfying 5-4 win.

That first Eskimo lineup was pretty much the heart of the club for the rest of the year. Amiable Andy Skurski in centre field, hard-hitting Clint Weaver in left, and steady Vern Campbell in right made up the outfield. The weak-hitting Don Herman at first, capable Sturgeon at second, sparkling Thompson at shortstop, and compact Sammy Kenelos at third made up the infield. The catcher was the slugging Dick Morgan, backed up by Dan Prentice. The pitching staff was surprisingly good for a first-year

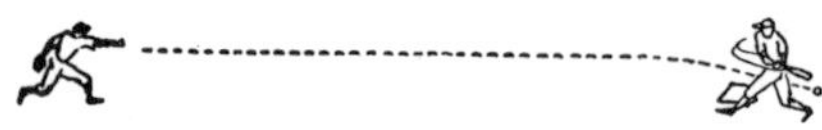

club. Led by league-leader John Conant, with twenty-four wins, the lineup included crafty veteran Ray McNulty, a sometimes surprising Jack Widner, the consistent Larry Manier, wild fastballer Pat Utley (a youthful Yankee bonus pick), a capable Don Tisnerat, and the quiet Leon Day, who joined the team in Edmonton. They were coached by George Caster, who had spent twelve years in the majors and appeared in two World Series.

Edmonton had a crowd-pleasing ball club, and the Esks gave fans a thrill, winning ten of eleven ball games late in the first half but falling just short, a game and a half behind the winning Salem Senators. First-half attendance was a disappointing 51,784, an average of 1,500 per game. The temporary bleachers, seating 900, probably hurt attendance as much as the cool, wet weather. Calgary could muster only 800 fans per game to watch the baseball Stampeders in the confines of tiny Buffalo Stadium.

Edmonton made a run for the top again but slid to fifth place as the second half ended. Injuries took their toll, capped when Sturgeon broke his arm in a collision at second base late in the season. While many of the injuries were enough to take players out of the lineup, trainer Goldstick was not impressed by the staying power of the professional ballplayers. Most were cry-babies about their health, compared to his hockey players who played through pain. Tiger used a lot of "Atomic Balm" liniment on sore arms that first year.

Problems of professional baseball

Throughout the season, it was never certain if the league would hold together. Minor-league baseball was in decline, and many of the WIL clubs had financial problems, partly due to travel costs but also due to lack of interest. The Salem Senators, of Oregon's capital city, some 1,100 miles away from Edmonton, drew only 500 fans per game. Few of them were interested in coming out to see teams from far-away places like Calgary, Edmonton, and Victoria. Calgary had major problems. Plagued

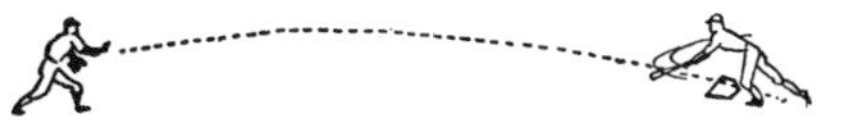

by apathetic fans and a park well below league standards, the team was soon $45,000 in debt. The facilities were so bad that Ducey publicly broke rank, joining Salem's Hugh Luby to say that unless something was done to improve the situation, Calgary should be dropped from the league in 1954. That did not increase his popularity in the southern city, which was given an ultimatum by the league to improve park facilities or face a $2,500 fine.

Edmonton's directors were relatively satisfied with the Eskimos' on-field performance but still unsure about the WIL. Net income of $72,000 had been exceeded by expenses of more than $110,000. Brant Matthews wrote the directors to say another $30,000 infusion would be needed to field the 1954 team. At the final wind-up dinner, Eskimo's vice-president Cecil Ross promised Edmonton would be back in professional baseball in 1954; it was a question of which league. Ducey made no secret that he preferred a more compact league composed of Edmonton, Calgary, Lethbridge, Vancouver, Victoria, Spokane, Tacoma, and possibly a Montana city. But after cutting back league office expenses— including eliminating a full-time president's office—the WIL directors decided to go with the same team alignment in 1954.

Ducey and his directors remained concerned about overall finances. In late October, Brant Matthews wrote to Mayor Hawrelak and the city commissioners to petition for a new, permanent grandstand to ensure the club's financial future. Matthews pointed out that the professional franchise had been financed by the directors with no public appeal for funds or assistance of any kind. He told the city that he and Cecil Ross would pledge to underwrite professional baseball in Edmonton for the next two seasons if a modern grandstand was built. He then gave a glimpse of what motivated the club's directors:

> The personnel of the shareholders is cosmopolitan; drawn from varied professions and occupations, quite representative of the city generally.... Those who subscribed for shares did so at a "calculated financial

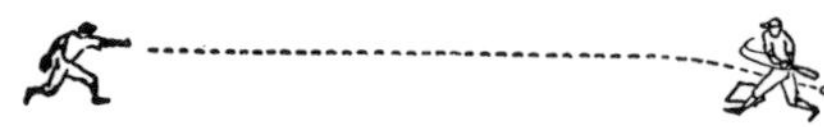

> risk" and were not motivated by the desire or hope of pecuniary gain, but only to assist in bringing to Edmonton a class of baseball which would merit the approbation of the sporting public. The results fully justify their confidence.

Matthews pointed out that the eight percent paid to the City on admissions and a further eight percent paid on earnings had returned $7,200 to the civic treasury; this kind of continued performance would pay off the costs of a new grandstand in twenty years. The city agreed with Matthews' optimism and began planning for the new facility.

Meanwhile, Ducey looked for ways to trim operating costs. Fans were promised two free passes for every foul ball returned. He announced that the contracts of two of his most popular and talented players, catcher Dick Morgan and outfielder Clint Weaver, had been sold to the New York Yankees so the two could move up to Triple-A teams the next season. Pitchers Leroy Johnson and Don Tisnerat were given their outright release so they could pursue other offers. Reluctantly, Ducey also released George Caster because the team budget could no longer afford the luxury of carrying a non-playing coach.

Leon Day

Leon Day, a dapper but quiet man who seemed older than his twenty-nine years, was given his outright release. He had joined the Eskimos reluctantly, appearing mainly in relief during May. He was also used as a pinch-hitter and relief player. Day had only an average season as a pitcher, appearing in twenty-three games, with five wins, five losses, and ten saves. In total, he played in forty-four games for the Eskimos, hitting .229 in seventy at-bats. To Edmonton fans, he appeared just another pro ball player on his way down through the ranks. But he was far from that.

Day had joined the Negro Major Leagues in 1934 at age seventeen, making his true age thirty-six when he reached Edmonton. Playing in the

Pitcher Leon Day is congratulated after another WIL win by shortstop Bob "Whitey" Thompson, as manager Bob Sturgeon (centre) joins them. Day's previous exploits in the Negro Major Leagues were little known to Eskimo fans but resulted in his entry to the Baseball Hall of Fame in 1995. Courtesy of the Edmonton Archives EA 524-53.

Negro leagues for most of his career, Day only entered organized baseball with Toronto in 1951. When Ducey bought his contract, he was classed as a "limited service player," one with less than three years' service in organized ball. Day could both pitch and hit and enjoyed his best years with the Brooklyn Eagles, who became the Newark Eagles in 1937. Except for 1938, and active military service in 1944 and 1945 (when he recorded some memorable post-war pitching performances in Europe), he played for Newark through 1946, starring in all-star games and the Negro Leagues' world series. Day beat Satchel Paige on at least three occasions and in

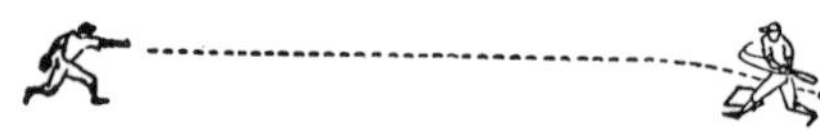

1942 set the NML single-game strikeout record with eighteen, one better than Paige was able to achieve in his career. The great Monte Irvin later minced no words in describing Leon Day in his prime: "He was like Bob Gibson. In fact I think he was a better pitcher than Bob Gibson." Some thirty-five years later, former team-mate Max Manning described him as "the complete athlete":

> Leon Day, that's my man! Good fast ball, good curve ball, good control. Leon was a complete athlete. He could bunt, he could run, he could play outfield, he could pitch. He was fast, he could field his position. I've seen him make plays—a bouncing ball hit to his right, go over and catch it. Do things the average pitcher couldn't do.
>
> The guy really deserves to be in Cooperstown. It bothers me because these guys get older and die out. It just seems a shame that at least some of these ball players don't even get a chance to be voted on.

Consistent with the shadow world to which black players were consigned by baseball's ruling class and the white-dominated media until after World War Two, none of Day's early heroics were ever revealed to Edmonton fans. He played out his year and was released. He ended his career in Canada, playing the next two seasons in Winnipeg in 1950 and 1951, where he had played before, and then at Brandon, Manitoba. Few in Edmonton ever heard of him again. Then, some forty-two years later, in August 1995, Max Manning's assessment came true. Leon Day was inducted into the Baseball Hall of Fame at Cooperstown for his accomplishments in the Negro Major Leagues. He learned of the honour just six days before his death, in March 1995. Day joined Heinie Manush as only the second Edmonton Eskimo graduate to gain entry to the Cooperstown Hall.

17

Renfrew reminiscences

"I'LL NEVER FORGET WALKING INTO THE GRANDSTAND AT RENFREW PARK FOR THE FIRST TIME AND LOOKING AT THE BEAUTIFUL GRASS. I had never seen anything as stunning in all my life. My eyes opened wide and took it all in. I turned to my brother and said, 'Boy, I'd give five bucks if someone would go out there at five in the morning and hit grounders to me.' It was a thrill to see it for the first time."

Des O'Connor was about twelve years old when he first saw the ballpark. Buck Eaton, then pitching in the senior league, had taken the boys there while they were on a visit to Edmonton with their mother. O'Connor's

romance with the ballpark lasted throughout his life and he played there, first as a junior, then in senior baseball, for several seasons. He even used it as the location to propose to his wife. He took her to the park on the pretense that there had been another fire. Then, in front of the ball park, he gave her an engagement ring.

Doug Darrah was a teen-aged pitcher by the time he first saw Renfrew Park. It was the pitcher's mound that got his attention:

> Renfrew Park. "Oh man," I thought. "Real grass, a grandstand, and a raised pitcher's mound. What a dream."

The Renfrew Park routine

For some of us, the ballpark was not just a field of play, not just a gathering place for the sporting crowd. It was our place of employment for several months each year.

Few people see a ballpark early in the day. Summer mornings found the park at its very best, empty of people and free of noise. I joined the groundskeeping staff, as a member of the clean-up detail, late in August 1951 and worked there through the 1955 season. We were proud of our jobs and spent our own money to order flashy baseball jackets with "Renfrew" emblazoned across them. We would arrive about 8:30 a.m. to begin a work day that would end near midnight on game days when we closed the park. Because Renfrew was in the river valley, the rays from the morning sun were just beginning to warm the park when we arrived for work. The tranquillity and the huge expanse of brilliant green grass—always "Kelly green" to my Dad—impressed me most. The fence shielded our view of the surrounding neighbourhoods and cut off the noise of passing automobiles. In the early 1950s, there were no high-rise buildings on the surrounding hills. Looking beyond the centre-field fence, all you could see were the smokestacks of the city power plant and beyond them, the tree-lined river valley and the sky. Looking north from centre field,

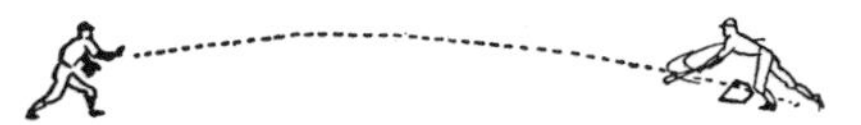

beyond the bleachers and the grandstand area, you could see what there was of the Edmonton skyline of those days. Dominating it were the Hotel Macdonald and the *Edmonton Journal* building. Since the 1960s, those two buildings have been lost upon Edmonton's modern concrete skyline.

Within the confines of the ball park, my eye was drawn to the spacious playing field, well more than a city block square. Coming from a home with a small yard, it seemed huge to me. Only the colour of the paint and the advertising on the outfield fences interrupted this pristine scene. From Cal Pickles' Men's Wear came the message, "Hit a homer through this hole and win a suit." John's Hat Shop offered, "A hat for a homer over this sign." Other signs from those years included The Nut House, Harry Cohen's Army & Navy Stores, Val Berg's Men's Wear, and Bill Hawrelak's Orange Crush sign. Inside those fences, it seemed as if you were miles from anywhere, rather than a ten-minute walk from the city centre.

The three or four of us on the early shift would start the day with clean-up detail. First was the cleaning of the area in front of the ball park, littered with paper from the previous day's game. Ducey wanted it clean before he arrived, usually between 9:30 and 10:00 a.m., after he made a stop or two downtown. We would then turn our attention to cleaning up the area inside the ball park, particularly around the concession stands and the main entrance. The clubhouses were left for the batboys and club trainers.

Upon his arrival, my Dad would have a look around, just to make sure we were "hustling." He would rarely interfere with special orders unless the weather was threatening. We knew our jobs and did them best when left alone. The biggest clean-up job of the day—and the one we tried to finish before noon—was the bleachers and grandstand. In those days, we had only brooms to sweep out the detritus from the previous day's game. By the time it got to the bottom of the stands, it seemed like a ton of soft drink cups, hot dog wrappers, and paper. Worst of all were the peanut shells. A few years after I left, technology introduced electrically powered

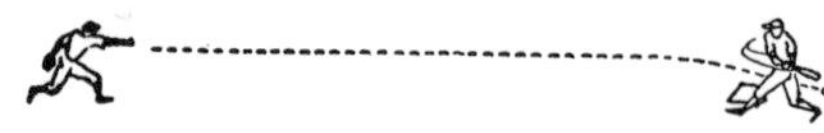

blowers, which now allow a single person to clean a huge seating facility in a fraction of the time it took several of us using brooms.

Just before noon, the senior man in the crew would begin working on the infield, which to me was the best job of all. On a dry day, this work began by "dragging" the dirt portion of the infield with the Cushman motor scooter. It pulled a series of mats behind it to break down the lumps of earth and generally smooth over the dirt surface. Following that task, one of us would thoroughly comb through the dirt, looking for clumps or small rocks that would occasionally come to the surface. Complaints from an angry shortstop after a ball had taken a bad hop the night before often spurred us on in this job. Then we watered the dirt area of the infield to keep the dust down. We cut the infield grass twice a week.

Work crews from the City Parks Department would usually come in once a week with a large industrial mower to cut the outfield grass. At first, they could not cut the grass cleanly in the corners, and in earlier days, more than one fair ball had been lost in the long grass against the fence. During one Big Four League game, Dick Noon lost a ball in the left-field corner and the batter got an inside-the-park home run. "That ball could still be there in the grass for all I know," Noon reminisced years later.

We usually had the field ready for practice by mid-day. After lunch, we would occupy ourselves with routine maintenance work and further clean-up chores. During the day, a variety of people would arrive. The small office staff usually arrived soon after we started, then a cheery Ducey himself would appear. The American ball players would often come in before noon to pick up their mail. Suppliers would bring in the concession items, towels for the rest rooms and clubhouses, and whatever else was on the order list. By early afternoon, the trainers and batboys were at work in the clubhouse, preparing for the pre-game arrival of the players. Manager Bob Sturgeon was usually the first to arrive. After a visit with Ducey to discuss player performance and game strategy, he would stop and talk with us about the field and the playing conditions for that evening.

In the days of the Western International League, the professional players from both clubs would arrive in the early afternoon. Some could sit and talk about baseball for hours. Coaches, managers, and veterans were the best talkers of all. Others would quickly and quietly get to work, either preparing their equipment, getting a rubdown in the trainer's room, or running "wind sprints" out on the field. By 3:00 p.m. on a game day, we were ready to wheel the batting cage out from behind the third-base bleachers and into position behind home plate. Then team practice would get underway. This was the second best part of the day because, with our work caught up, we could take to the outfield and shag fly balls alongside the players. The home team could get in as much field practice as needed, if the players wanted to start early. However, they had to move aside for the visitors, who would usually take the field at 6:00 p.m. for their batting practice. Truly dedicated fans would arrive early to watch batting practice, a tradition that continues even today.

By 7:00 p.m., we had wheeled the batting cage away, back to its spot behind the bleachers, and infield practice would begin. Each team had twenty minutes. By now, the balance of the serious fans would be in their seats to watch this ritual. At 7:40 p.m., the field again belonged to the grounds crew. We quickly re-dragged the infield, installed clean new bases, and raked over the areas around the pitcher's mound and home plate. Then came the task of re-applying the chalk marks to delineate the batters' boxes and the foul lines to first and third base. By this time, the murmur of the crowd had grown to a low roar, punctuated by the shouts of program sellers and concessionaires. There was a chorus of boos as the umpires appeared on the field. The local umpires, particularly Harry Ornest and Johnny Lupul, attracted the greatest levels of good-natured derision.

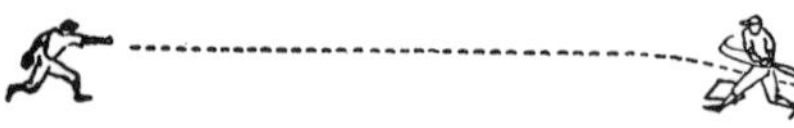

Umpires of the 1950s

As a young teen-ager in the mid-1930s. Ornest used to play catch on the boulevard with neighbour John Ducey when the two lived on 115 Street. Ornest began his baseball career playing for Ducey's Arrow Busses in 1937 and finished as the captain and second baseman of the 1946 championship Army & Navy Cardinals. He was a fiery competitor who argued loudly and would not back down from a fight. These traits carried over into his umpiring career and made him a colourful arbiter. Ornest umpired professionally in the minor leagues in 1947 and 1948. After returning to Edmonton, he umpired at Renfrew Park for several years while building a vending business that eventually took him into professional sports ownership.

As an umpire, Harry Ornest had "colour" and "hustle." Like Ducey, with whom he often worked tournaments, he was either loved or hated on the diamond. The fans and the players were never neutral about Harry. Johnny Lupul, on the other hand, had followed his big brother Fred, a former player, into umpiring. Fred had always said that the most difficult thing in his baseball career was making the change from a player to an umpire. Unlike George Green, neither Lupul was very popular as an umpire. John Lupul was a much smaller man than his older brother. Despite his size, he stood his ground in an argument. While he could become flustered, he was seldom intimidated by the players, except for Eddie Morris. With Morris, it was not physical but mental intimidation that plagued Lupul. Morris loved to bait him and always got the best of him, to the delight of the fans. When Lupul could stand no more, he would use his authority and thumb Morris out of the game. As a manager, Eddie Morris watched many ball games from the stands.

There was very little nonsense with the professional umpires employed by the Western International League, who, with a few exceptions, were anonymous to the Edmonton fans. Two who stood out from that group were Mel Steiner and Emmett Ashford. Steiner was a trim, tanned, friendly

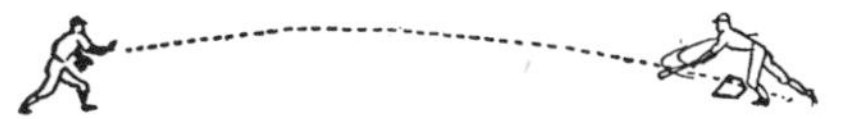

man who competently umpired several Renfrew Park assignments. Ashford was the first black man to umpire in the WIL, and it fell to him to break the colour barrier in his vocation throughout his career. He was as good as any we saw umpire at Renfrew Park in the 1950s. He was criticized as a "showboat" and did not quarrel with the accusation at the time. As they had when Ducey was umpiring, some fans would come out just to see Ashford umpire because of his entertaining style. After his single WIL season in 1953, Ashford spent twelve years in the Pacific Coast League, rising to the post of umpire-in-chief. In 1966, he became the first black umpire in the majors when Dewey Soriano sold his contract to the American League.

Two years later, while on vacation in Maine, my Dad and I had a pleasant reunion with Emmett Ashford after a ball game at Boston's Fenway Park. He was delighted to reminisce about his year in the sprawling WIL, laughing that it was the season he travelled more than any other in his twenty-two-year umpiring career. That season his salary totalled $1,134, while his travel expenses were $1,945. Ashford toned down his routine when he got to the American League, but he remained a colourful and competent arbiter until he retired after the 1970 World Series.

For those of us working as grounds crew at Renfrew Park, being around the professional ball players was both stimulating and educational. Pitching coach George Caster was a big, fun-loving Irishman, always looking for an extra advantage over the opposition. George, who had pitched in 376 major-league games from 1934 to 1946, showed us how to build Renfrew's first elevated pitching mound for the home-team bullpen. Of course, he would not let us build one for the visitors!

One night, pitcher Jack Widner was warming up on that mound, behind first base, when he was hit in the back of the skull by a line-drive foul ball. He was knocked unconscious and taken to the hospital for x-rays. Fortunately, he was not seriously injured. It was simply confirmation to his team-mates that Widner, the team comedian, really did have a thick skull! Nevertheless, "Jolly Jack" enjoyed two fine seasons as an Eskimo pitcher.

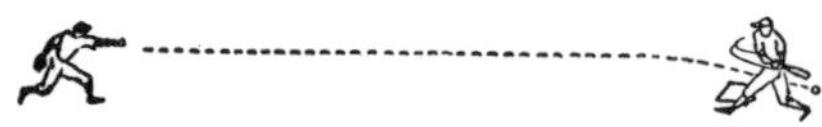

Watching expenses

The weather continued to be the biggest problem with the extended seasons demanded by professional baseball. Some nights in the early spring saw frost on the bleachers before the game was over. But rain was the biggest problem. We were often on the telephone to the weather office to get updates on incoming rain. After spending a small fortune in gasoline to burn the rain off soggy infields, we groundskeepers were treated to a huge, $2,500 canvas tarpaulin to protect the base paths and home plate area against rain. After having to remove it when it got wet and muddy, we wished we were back burning gas. One night, it became so heavy with wet mud that we did not have enough staff to pull it back on. The game was rained out.

Pouring tractor gas on wet infield mud so a game could be played was primitive, fun, and dangerous. We would transfer tax-free, purple tractor gas out of forty-five-gallon drums and into watering cans. Then we doused the wet spots liberally and threw a match to them. Hot flames would sear us as we tried to rake the burning mud and huge clouds of black smoke billowed across the field. As game time neared and the fans filed into the park, the pyrotechnics became a pre-game entertainment feature. I do not know how we escaped serious injury in this process, but we often came close. The worst incident we had was when one of my buddies had the bottoms of his pants burned off in front of several hundred cheering fans. I later got my Dad to invest in an industrial-type flame thrower, designed for burning weeds. I thought it would do the trick, just the way the U.S. marines used to burn out those pill boxes on Iwo Jima in World War Two. However, a tank of gas would dry a spot only about three feet square. We went back to the tractor gas and watering cans!

These additional expenses bothered Ducey, who was losing money every season and had to watch his costs closely. Once, after an exhausting week of working on rain-delayed games, I asked him if my grounds crew could get our first raise. Although we were high-school students, we had been working for sixty cents an hour for more than two seasons. It was a tense few days around the ball park and at home while I waited for an answer. He knew we really deserved more money but he hated being asked for it. Finally he approached me one afternoon as we readied the field. "Okay," he bellowed so all could hear:

> I'm raising you guys from sixty to seventy-five cents an hour. But don't forget, you're just going to have to pay more income tax!

Many years later, my Dad jokingly gave me a copy of my 1953 tax return. It showed I had earned $693 over a five-month period, well under the personal exemption of $1,000 in those days.

The price of baseballs, then about $47 a dozen, was a constant concern for Ducey. He always wanted his club to be professionally outfitted, so only the official big-league baseball ball, usually Spalding, would do. When the temporary bleachers were in place after the fire, we were losing a small fortune in baseballs as foul tips soared out of the park and onto the street. As groundskeepers, we would often spend a few innings out there, helping "Emo" Awid's ballboys recover baseballs. I was on the street after the start of a game one night when my Dad rushed out the front gate after a foul ball. A big guy I'd never seen before got the ball and was about to take off with it. Ducey, who would never threaten even a fly on a wall, and standing a head shorter than this guy, grabbed his jacket and lifted him off the ground and onto the hood of a car. "That baseball cost me $4.00 and I want it back... now," he roared. The big guy meekly handed it over and apologized. I stood there in disbelief and with a new sense of admiration for my father.

Ballboy Ken "Emo" Awid was a red-haired, freckle-faced youngster with a Huckleberry Finn look. He was popular with all the ball players, particularly Eddie Morris, who could easily relate to young kids around a ball park. As a youngster, Awid had been the team mascot for the U.S. Army Yanks and eventually followed his older brothers into the job of head ballboy. All from the Rossdale Flats neighbourhood, they were a tough, intimidating bunch who prided themselves on their ability to retrieve baseballs, as Awid recounts:

> It was fun in those days. I still have people coming up to me and saying, "You guys were the fastest I've ever seen. You should have been in the Olympics."
>
> If a ball went over the back fence and someone took off with it, we'd race him for blocks, just to get a stupid ball. We never lost a ball in that situation because after three or four guys came after a young kid, he was too scared to try to keep the ball.

The Rajah's Renfrew

Awid was a victim of the infamous Ducey memory. It went from being excellent in recalling anything about baseball and most people's names, to simply awful in other instances. Ducey kept won-lost records and batting averages in his head, but had to rely on a system of scrawled paper notes to keep track of anything not baseball-related. When he could not remember a first name or had never heard it, he either made one up or referred to his addressee as "Johnny." In Awid's case, it was somewhat more puzzling:

> One day John just started calling me "Emo" and that was it. I don't know why. Even to this day, everyone, including one of my older brothers, calls me Emo. The name stuck but I really don't know where he got it but I became known as Emo to everyone.

Des O'Connor suffered a similar fate: Ducey called him "Dennis" for years after his playing days ended. O'Connor suspects it was because he used the name when he first met Ducey, the day he acted as a substitute catcher for his brother in one game, on Ducey's 1941 junior team.

Although he was loquacious and was sought as a popular and entertaining public speaker, Ducey occasionally had trouble with the more sophisticated levels of the English language. Just before the opening of the 1950 season, he had proudly taken the press and radio representatives on a tour of the new press box atop the old grandstand roof, when Don Fleming said, "It looks just fine, John but how are you going to handle decorum up here?" Replied Ducey, "There'll be absolutely NO decorum in this press box, Don. If you want to drink, you'll have to drink BEFORE you come to the ball park."

Fleming and his colleagues were happy to escape the cramped confines of the old press dugout underneath the grandstand:

> Down in that dugout the pitching mound obscured a lot of things. We were also vulnerable to the players. I panned Jack McGill once in the paper for "hot-dogging" it. Before the next game, he came over and rattled the screen with his bat and threatened to knock my teeth down my throat. However, the mosquitoes were the worst part of it. We were forever indebted to John when he finally got us out of there and up on the roof where we could see what was happening.

To solve the "decorum" problem, Ducey got Tiger Goldstick to act as press-box custodian that year. It was a job Goldstick took on with pride and continued to do once the new grandstand roof was installed in 1954.

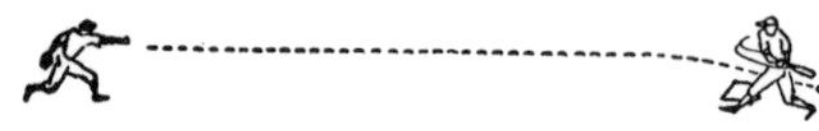

Goldstick took a lot of good-natured ribbing from the media but usually gave as good as he got. But Don Fleming tells the story of Tiger once getting more than he bargained for:

> On Sundays John would have a big tub of beer on ice for us up there. But there were no restroom facilities and if you were scoring the game, you couldn't dash away, so we used the empty beer bottles. One Sunday afternoon "Tiger" came back into the press box from a tour of the stands. He was prancing up and down and criticizing the Eskimos' pitcher, who, he said was "walking the ball park."
>
> "They'd better pull him," said Tiger to anyone who'd listen. He set his beer down and continued to pace back and forth, muttering about the game being lost. Then he picked up the wrong beer bottle, took a swallow, and without losing his stride said, "How come this beer's so warm?"

Media memories

Ducey always made sure the media were well looked after at the ball park because he knew from experience what their job was. They were also the people who showcased his product, so he always did his best to help them. However, he had to tread a fine line to ensure that he did not get too chummy and interfere with them while they were working. Occasionally, Don Fleming recalled, they had to draw the line for him:

> John was great for the game in all respects. The presentation of the game was very important to him. He was a stickler for proper dress. He could be a little tough with the players, but basically he idolized them. He could get upset with them once in awhile, but he'd soon forget it. They were his boys. In the later years, he had a walkie-talkie and he used to call us up in the press box and say that someone had questioned whether a play had been properly scored as a hit or an error, for

> example. I'd say, "John, you stay down there and count the house and I'll score the game from up here."

Don Fleming was one of Edmonton's most accomplished baseball writers and brought a lot of inside knowledge to his popular and informative column, "The Sports Mill." Working as official league scorer at Renfrew Park added greatly to his baseball repertoire, although his passion remained the coverage of thoroughbred racing. Fleming had an uncanny knack for sniffing out a party and once he got there, it usually lasted all night, often with Ducey at his side. Ducey had less "staying-power," so it usually fell to Fleming to get Ducey home and in the door in the wee hours of the morning. Dick Noon tells a story of how a party with Don Fleming ended up with the replay of a ball game back at Renfrew Park early one morning:

> It was after the second game of a playoff between Purity and the Eskimos, and John Carpenter had pitched and won the game. So we had a celebration. The party carried on and we got pretty loaded. Don wanted a play-by-play record of how we won the ball game. So he, Kenny Stewart, John Carpenter, and I ended up getting a cab, driving down to the ball park, climbing over the fence and going out on the field. Don is in the stands, acting as official scorekeeper. Kenny is behind the plate and John Carpenter is on the mound, providing a play-by-play account of how he's winning the ball game. All of this takes place in pitch-black darkness about two o'clock in the morning! Needless to say, the story never appeared in Fleming's column.

Ducey remained close to Fleming after he was out of baseball, continuing to supply him with a steady flow of both past and current baseball trivia for his column.

The *Journal*'s George Mackintosh, who spent forty-one years covering sports in Edmonton before he retired in 1953, was the "dean" of the press

and radio crew and one of the last remaining links between Diamond Park and Renfrew Park. Improvements in the *Journal's* sports pages can be measured from the time he became sports editor in 1917. Along with former colleagues Ken McConnell and Jack Kelly, who later transferred to the *Bulletin*, Mackintosh had been there when Ducey broke in as an umpire in 1931 at Diamond Park. He had also witnessed the opening of Renfrew Park in 1933.

Many of the Renfrew regulars, like Bill Lewis, McConnell, Dick Beddoes, and Jim Brooke, went on to notable careers in other cities. Stan Moher remained in Edmonton after the *Bulletin* closed down and continued to write a popular sports column for the *Albertan*. Moher was a gifted writer and a keen observer of the sporting scene. "You could not find a better guy for a competitor," said Fleming of Moher. He would go about his work quietly, usually sitting in each team's dugout for about a half-hour before a ball-game, talking with the players and managers to come up with excellent background material.

Among the radio crew were such men as Art Ward, Gordon Williamson, Al Shaver, Russ Sheppard, Walt Rutherford, Joe Carbury, and later, Don Chevrier, several of whom served as public-address announcers at Renfrew. Chevrier loved baseball. As a high-school student in the 1950s, he would sneak into Renfrew Park to watch batting practice by climbing over the fence behind the third-base bleachers. It was my job to throw him out, which I would do. But before the game started, he had sneaked back in again. I decided it was not my job to eject him a second time so as a student, he always saw the ball games for free.

Al McCann, Ernie Afaghanis, Glen Bjarnsson, and Bryan Hall could often be found in the press box in the 1950s. These men also worked in television after it arrived in Edmonton about 1954, but there was no live television coverage of baseball from the park in the 1950s.

CKUA's Art Ward was one of the earliest play-by-play announcers to work at the park, and Ducey was one of his greatest admirers. It was not economically feasible to send broadcasters on the road with the home team, so Ward would create and re-create game broadcasts. With him in the broadcast booth was Alex Caldwell of CNR Telegraphs, who would tap out play-by-play in Morse code and send it to other cities for re-creation and local broadcast. Caldwell would also join Ward in the studio to re-create some of the WIL Eskimos' road games. A small and humourous Scot with a great love of sport, Caldwell later became western superintendent of CN Telecommunications.

When time stood still

Another contingent of ballpark regulars were the front gate staff, under the direction of business manager Brian O'Hanlon. While they manned the pass gate, sold, and took tickets to weekday and Saturday games, one of their key assignments was to staff the big wooden tables for the Sunday silver collections. The kindest and quietest of men would turn into hard-nosed intimidators toward those who tried to bring in several friends under the guise of "family," all for one silver coin. Lending them an air of authority was "Big Tiny," the cop. "Tiny" was a corpulent 200-plus pounds and stood over six feet tall in his City of Edmonton police uniform. Despite his rotund figure and cherubic face, he would stand strategically behind the tables, trying to fix an official glare on those who brazenly contributed to bringing down the Sunday collection to an average of thirty-six cents per fan. Said O'Hanlon of those experiences,

> It was sometimes difficult to get money out of certain people and there were several who upset John. People would come in and they'd flip in a nickel and he would make a comment. Sometimes people would take exception to that and you'd think there was going to be an altercation, but it never came to anything more than a few hostile words.

The small contributions on the part of some Sunday fans always frustrated Ducey. One afternoon he happened to be in the press box when Cliff

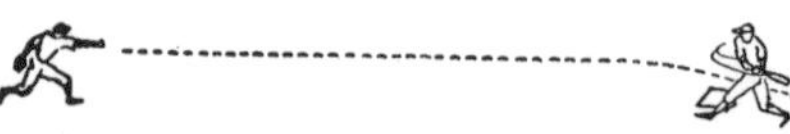

Ducey with members of his first "Knothole Gang," at Renfrew Park in 1953. Courtesy of the Edmonton Archives EA 524-51.

Johnston made a running, outstretched catch of a foul ball into the first-base seats. Ducey grabbed the public address microphone and announced, "Ladies and gentlemen, you've just seen a $10 catch and you only paid 17 cents!"

No ball game would be truly enjoyable without the concession staff. They were a small army of youngsters in red jackets who sold food and drink through the stands. Only soft drinks and coffee were available, no beer. The centre of operations was originally near the main entrance, under the first-base bleachers. The smell of coffee and fried onions would waft up into the stands, resulting in that particular area being the best-paying spot for the concessionaires. The kids, who came from all parts of the city for the prized job of selling peanuts, hot dogs, and soft drinks, got a commission of one penny per item. It was big money for a youngster in those days, and a good game could put a couple of well-earned dollars in one's pocket. Ray Bedard was one of the older sellers and a natural sales person. On warm Sunday afternoons, he could make a small fortune selling ice cream bars as he urged fans to "Buy a 'Revel' and give your tongue a sleigh ride."

However, it was the fans who made baseball possible, and a loyal contingent of them followed baseball at Renfrew through the Depression and World War Two and into Edmonton's post-war boom days. People like Rod Morrison, Mamie McNabb, Bill Matthews, and a good-natured woman known only as "Hilda," famed for her fog-horn voice, attended regularly. They were there not just because they loved baseball, but because Renfrew Park was *the* place to be and *the* place to see one another. While Edmonton was turning into a big city, the ball park remained their community centre. They all had favourite seats, usually in the first-base or third-base bleachers. They were knowledgeable and appreciative baseball fans, and most would cheer either side for a good play—even Calgary on occasion. Frank McCleavy, the band leader at the Hotel Macdonald, used to go to games with his wife, Ernestine, but she was such a rabid anti-Eskimo fan that he would never sit with her at the park. Mamie McNabb used to ride Jimmy Gibson, the Buffalo manager, unmercifully. It got so bad, according to Des O'Connor, that Gibson decided he had to do something about her incessant needling:

> One night, Gibson said, "I'm going over and meet that woman." So he went up in the stands before the game and talked with her for about fifteen minutes. He came back to the dugout and said, "My God, I just met the most wonderful woman. What a baseball fan she is! She is simply just a loyal Edmonton fan and that's all there is to it."

Just the same, she never stopped pestering Gibson and his Buffaloes.

Throughout the 1930s, '40s and '50s, all of those people—players, ball park staff, reporters, and fans—put aside their real-life cares for a few hours and lost themselves in the struggle on the diamond. As the city grew up and the world changed around them, they briefly tuned it all out. They kidded and competed with each other while turning rapt attention on the battle between the foul lines. Once the umpire hollered "Play ball!", they forgot their worries and united in a common and sociable passion. For a few hours, time stood still.

18

Striking out

PLAYING MANAGER BOB STURGEON'S .237 BATTING AVERAGE WAS A BIT OF A DISAPPOINTMENT IN 1953; HOWEVER, HE HAD SET A NEW WIL FIELDING RECORD WITH A .989 AVERAGE. Some wanted Ducey to search for a better-hitting manager, but after looking at other options, he was personally pleased to re-sign Sturgeon as manager. As 1954 began, Edmonton city council agreed with the commissioners' recommendation to build a new 2,000-seat concrete grandstand at Renfrew Park at a cost of $120,000. It was part of a civic package which also included new seating facilities for football fans at Clarke Stadium. A roof was a possible option for Renfrew,

California oranges were part of the attraction at the Lindsay, California Olive Bowl as the 1954 Eskimos opened spring training. Outfielder Bobby Brown of Toronto (standing, right) was the only one of these four players to make the Edmonton team. Courtesy of the Edmonton Archives EA 524-54.

perhaps in 1955. The new grandstand would increase the park's seating capacity to 6,153 and would be paid back under the existing lease at a rental of $8,000 per year. Ducey would finally have seating facilities to match the standards of the playing field. Then he went back to council and lobbied for a roof to cover the grandstand.

By the end of February, $20,000 was added to the plans for the roof and tenders were soon called. Ducey was grateful, agreeing to an annual rent increase from $8,000 to $9,500 to pay for the roof. The Rajah of

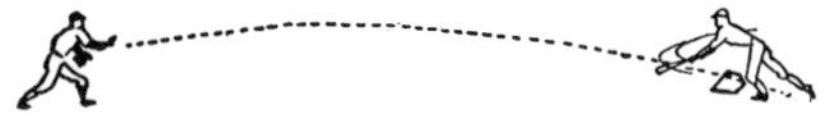

Renfrew reminded his Edmonton audience that the city was getting a good bargain:

> Organized baseball is a tremendous asset to a city and an attractive park goes with good baseball. Encouragement given by city council to baseball in Edmonton has resulted in our city having a park second only to Vancouver in the WIL....since the fire it has been an uphill battle to bring our people what they desired—organized professional baseball.

In March 1954, Ducey headed for spring training at Lindsay, California, this time without his trainer and sidekick, Cecil Goldstick. "Tiger" could not absent himself from his job with the Flyers for a second year of hockey playoffs and felt it best to tender his resignation. George Windwick, Goldstick's assistant the previous year, took his place. Ducey, Sturgeon, and the early sophomore version of the WIL Eskimos converged on the Lindsay Olive Bowl, set in California's San Joaquin Valley and the centre of the state's olive-producing region. A flood of spring-training stories again warmed the sports pages of the *Journal* as local fans awaited winter's departure and the Eskimos' return.

The problems begin

Calgary was training at Porterville, ten miles away. Manager Gene Lillard soon had to suspend the Stampeders' spring-training camp when money ran out and he could not reach club president Lacey or any of his staff. After an emergency league meeting, it was announced that both Lacey and financing had been found. With a guarantee in place, Calgary's team went back to the diamond, but the problem revealed how tenuous the league situation was. Ducey and Sturgeon struggled to field a team as strong as the previous year. For a while, it looked as if catcher Dick

Morgan would return, but after failing to catch on in Triple-A ball, he had to sit the year out with a bad throwing arm. Skurski, Thompson, and a sometimes-healthy Bob Sturgeon initially provided hitting power down the middle, along with utility player Dan Prentice. Catcher Tom Self gave way to the veteran Roy Partee in mid-season. From 1943 to 1948, Partee had spent four seasons with the Boston Red Sox and one with the St. Louis Browns. The 1954 Esks had no consistent sluggers to replace the hard-hitting Morgan and outfielder Clint Weaver. However, Edmonton fans saw some twenty past and future major-leaguers on 1953-54 WIL rosters. Among the latter were Chuck Essegian of Salem and "Pumpsie" Green of Wenatchee (see Appendix Two).

Ducey tried to introduce some Canadian talent to the club, signing young pitchers Pete Boisvert, a rookie from Trail, B.C., and Don Kirk, a native of Carstairs, Alberta. However, they could not hold a place on the roster. A surprise arrival as the club headed north was Torontonian Bobby Brown, a 5'8" outfielder who had compiled an impressive slugging record in three years of Class-C baseball in the U.S. Moreover, he was the son of Bob Brown, Sr., who had pitched for the 1920 Eskimos and who suggested Ducey give his son a tryout. The younger Brown never lived up to the twenty-eight homers he smashed the year before in Phoenix, but he managed to stick with the Esks as a utility outfielder. A more successful Canadian was pitcher Art Worth of Victoria, B.C., who had played for Spokane the previous year and also had an earlier stint at first base with the Big Four Calgary Buffaloes.

The 1954 Eskimos began their second season on 29 April before 1,342 chilled fans at Salem, Oregon, the smallest opening crowd there since 1940. Opening day weather was bad everywhere except Vancouver. The Esks lost the first two games of the season, then as they won in Kennewick, Washington a few nights later, they learned the League had lost Calgary. On 2 May, the league seized the Calgary club for non-performance. It had failed to provide its players with meal and travel money. After a week

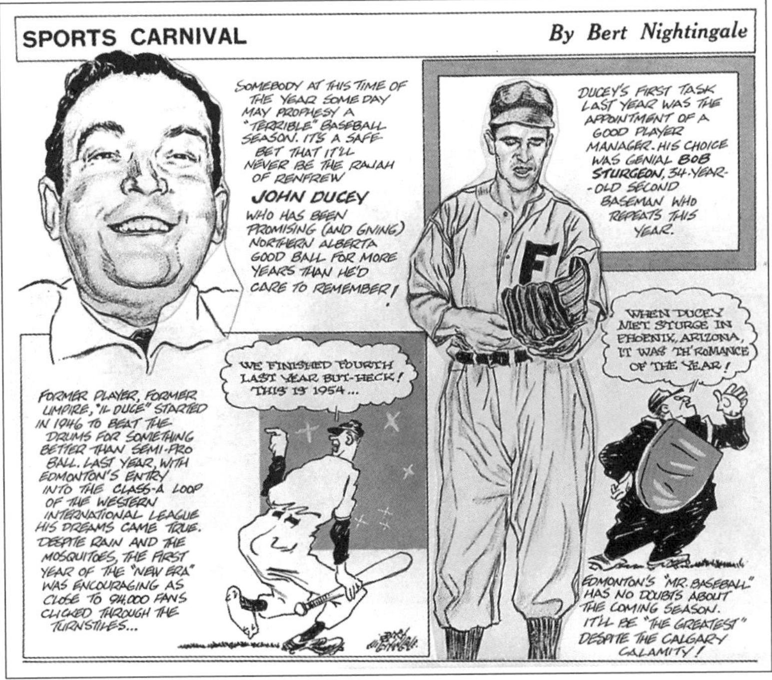

The "Rajah of Renfrew" and his 1953-54 Eskimos as featured by cartoonist Bert Nightengale of the Edmonton Journal. *Courtesy of the Edmonton Archives EA 524-55.*

of wrangling and meetings, local promoters, led by Buster Lacey, raised $35,000 and Calgary was back in—for a short while.

Sturgeon and his Eskimos returned to Edmonton after enjoying sunny, warm weather most of the way. In fact, catcher Tom Self arrived with a badly sunburned left arm from driving with his car window rolled down. They found Renfrew Park soaked under a week of steady rain. The field was a sea of mud. Inclement weather delayed the grandstand completion as well. Rain then washed out the entire opening series with Calgary.

Worried about a repeat of 1953, Ducey feared that the weather gods did not want baseball to be played in Edmonton before mid-May. Sturgeon was convinced of it. So they went off to sunnier Calgary. A Sunday split-doubleheader and a silver collection brought out a record crowd of 7,500.

On Tuesday, 18 May, with the new concrete grandstand complete except for a roof, Renfrew was finally dry enough to play ball. Mayor Bill Hawrelak threw out the first pitch as 3,546 fans both cheered and jeered the controversial civic leader. Hawrelak was an Edmonton booster from the old school and a tireless worker on behalf of the city. A soft-drink bottler, he had been one of Ducey's advertisers well before his election as mayor in 1951, and the two got along well. Hawrelak was a big proponent of civic and recreational facilities and fully supported Ducey's efforts to bring back professional baseball and give it the proper physical plant. The Mayor got the Eskimos off on the right foot as they scored six runs in the first two innings. But they failed to score on several more chances and fan enthusiasm sagged in the ninth as Wenatchee went ahead 7-6 and stole the opener.

Despite initially poor weather, Ducey remained positive and by early June was forecasting 135,000 customers in 1954, with yearly attendance growing to 300,000 in another four years. Don Fleming quoted the optimistic impresario:

> I've maintained all along that our city is one of the greatest potential baseball centres on the continent and I haven't changed my opinion.

The city was growing fast, added Ducey, saying he felt that if Los Angeles and San Francisco were to gain major-league franchises, then Edmonton and Calgary would eventually end up in a Triple-A, northern version of the Pacific Coast League. "I've made a good many other forecasts that have been borne out over the years and I'm equally certain of this one," said the Rajah. His forecast turned out to be correct but was almost thirty years late.

Calgary and Spokane fold

Among the regular pitchers, Conant reached fifteen wins while McNulty, Widner, and Manier, pitching out of the bullpen, also had strong repeat performances. The Eskimos briefly held on to second place but could not improve on their third-place standing as Vancouver won the first half of the schedule. In Calgary, general manager Lacey held things together for another month, but in mid-June the league suffered a double jolt. Both Calgary and Spokane folded, forcing the league into an eight-team format. Ducey, already subsidizing the travel costs of visiting U.S. clubs by $600 per trip, maintained Calgary's departure would not affect Edmonton.

Ducey blamed Calgary financial losses on "indifferent operation, lack of proper playing facilities and poor press and radio relations." Publicly, he claimed Calgary's withdrawal would not affect his club, expressing optimism about Edmonton's future. In truth, he knew that without Calgary he had a big problem. He took care to be gracious toward the Calgary fans, saying that with the right facilities, they would support professional baseball. Privately he hoped someone else would soon revive baseball there, once better playing facilities were in place.

With Calgary gone, there was talk in the other cities of ousting Edmonton. Ducey moved quickly to quell such an idea:

> The league cannot disenfranchise a club in good standing. If any such attempt was tried, the league directors would find themselves in the civil courts. They wouldn't want this to happen and we wouldn't either. We're very optimistic about our own future. We're on solid ground. We have a heavy investment, but we know we can get it back. Edmonton has great potential.

Six weeks later, the league was rocked again as the Victoria Tyees closed down. Once again the schedule had to be quickly redrawn, with each of

The 1954 Western International League Eskimos was the city's last professional baseball team until the Pacific Coast League Trappers came to Renfrew Park in 1981. Courtesy of the Edmonton Archives EA 524-56.

the remaining clubs contributing a few players to a team dubbed "the All-Stars," cobbled together to replace the Victoria spot in the schedule. Ducey once more had to deny rumours the league would dump his club at season's end. Despite a streak of eight wins in nine starts in mid-August, the Esks were edged out of first place by league-leading Lewiston with a week to go in the second half. They ended the season with sixty-two wins and sixty-three losses, well behind their 1953 performance of seventy-nine and sixty-one. Vancouver eliminated Lewiston in four playoff games. However, WIL attendance, at its highest in the late 1940s, had declined from 717,315 in 1953 to 475,716 in 1954. Edmonton was down 25,000 to 67,746, yet still second best in the faltering league.

Right after Labour Day, with the league's future under a cloud, the Sturgeons, Skurskies, McNulties, and Conants were gone again. This time

it was for good. There was no talk of "next year." Distance and weather had again conspired to bring another chapter in Edmonton's baseball history to a disappointing end. Tri-City and Lewiston announced that they would press for dropping both Edmonton and Vancouver from the league in 1955 at the upcoming league meeting. Distance and the lack of viable Sunday baseball in either Canadian city were given as key reasons. This caused Ducey "to do a violent burn," according to Fleming. The Rajah issued a clear response:

> We're not taking any notice of that kind of talk. We'll have no truck with the prophets of doom. We've heard them cry all year long and we're fed up with them.

At the league directors' meeting in Seattle, the other teams could not get Ducey and Brant Matthews to withdraw. When the matter came to a vote, Vancouver and Wenatchee sided with Edmonton. Without a required four-fifths majority, the motion to oust Edmonton was defeated. Then back-room politics prevailed. The five U.S. teams, including Wenatchee, simply withdrew from the league, leaving Edmonton and Vancouver in baseball limbo. Vancouver already had its eye on a Pacific Coast League franchise but without Calgary, Edmonton had no place to go.

It was another bitter pill for Ducey to swallow, yet he was already reviewing his options. As he left Seattle, he said there would be "an early effort to form an independent league that eventually will develop into a western Canada circuit of professional status." Inwardly wounded by his club's ousting from organized baseball, the Rajah publicly vowed that he was not ready to give up on Renfrew and its fans.

19

The Western Canada League

ALTHOUGH TELEVISION HAD COME TO EDMONTON WHILE THE ESKIMOS WERE IN THE WIL, PROGRAMMING WAS NOT PERVASIVE ENOUGH IN 1953-54 TO HAVE MUCH INFLUENCE ON LOCAL BASEBALL

ATTENDANCE. In the mid-1950s, an NBC television feed from Spokane brought the "Game of the Week" into Edmonton on Saturday afternoons. While Edmonton topped WIL attendance over the two-year period, poor weather and league instability had the biggest impact on fan support at Renfrew Park. Still, there was reason to expect

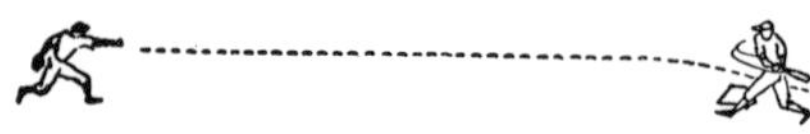

that baseball would do well in the Edmonton of 1955. Boosted by rapid expansion of the refining and petrochemicals industries, the city was booming again. Widely based distribution and service industries were growing, while the rural economy benefitted from new technology in the agricultural sector. Edmonton's population had reached 200,000 and Mayor Hawrelak, in the midst of his first nine years in office, was actively boosting the city and completion of the Yellowhead Highway. Everything seemed in place for baseball to share in the popularity enjoyed by the football Eskimos, who brought their first Grey Cup to Edmonton in 1953.

Cleaning up and moving on

Ducey first had to distance his franchise from the fiscal damage of the Western International League experience. In late October 1954, he tabled financial reports to the directors of the WIL Eskimos. After the $38,000 loss in 1953, the club had lost $44,700 the second year. However 1954's true loss was more than $65,000 because Brant Matthews and Cecil Ross had co-sponsored a loan of $22,500 to sustain club operations. Salaries and travel took $65,000 of some $102,000 in expenses. Ducey briefed the directors on the windup of the WIL and told them about an invitation to a meeting of the Saskatchewan Baseball League.

Semi-pro baseball was drawing well in Saskatchewan. The Saskatoon Gems topped 110,000 in 1954, far better than Edmonton's rain-soaked WIL attendance of only 64,746. Ducey felt that if he could get a league linking Edmonton and Calgary with several Saskatchewan cities, his club could share in the prosperity spreading across the prairies. It was decided that Edmonton should explore the situation. Ducey, Matthews, and Ken Samis went to Saskatoon and made a pitch to five of the six clubs that had made up Saskatchewan's independent baseball league. Ducey told them that a Class-C professional league had much to offer:

> Class-C clubs have an excellent opportunity of obtaining working agreements with major and Triple-A clubs. There are plenty of good young ballplayers to be assigned and those are the boys we want. One of the downfalls in our Western International League was the number of veterans, men who have played three or more seasons in organized ball. Our league had to have a limit of 12 to a team. It was simply too much because the big league clubs wouldn't send boys into our circuit because they had to compete against much older men. We want the younger fellows, the boys who are working hard to get to the big leagues.

Ducey then made a pitch for organized baseball:

> I've worked for years with semi-pro and independent teams and I know the headaches that can develop. You'll find that organized baseball won't be much more expensive, either. There are salary limits, player limits and you'd be surprised how much cheaper we can buy equipment. Of course, food and hotel and transportation are the same in any league.

However, Saskatchewan administrators were nervous about stepping into organized baseball. They were concerned about its rigid structure and its start-up costs, particularly when Ducey estimated the latter to be in the range of $20,000. Except for Regina's Denny Evenson, who did not field a team in 1954, they felt they did not have the contacts to field professional teams on such short notice. They spent three hours questioning Ducey, who laid out the pros and cons of organized baseball as impartially as he could, but in the end decided to spend another year in independent baseball and then consider a professional league.

Ducey had an alternative plan, suggested by Lee McPhail of the New York Yankees. Knowing Ducey to be a solid operator, McPhail told him

that if he went to an independent league, he could get cooperation to tap into the supply of talented U.S. college undergraduate ballplayers. Providing they could retain their college amateur status—supposedly by doing a little work around the ball park to supplement amateur baseball expenses—major-league scouts and officials would be happy to see them playing regularly in a well-run Canadian league. In reality, they earned around $300 per month to play, plus travel expenses, and did no work of any kind.

Ducey tabled the alternative proposal for consideration and returned home to await an answer. By mid-December, he had an agreement with Saskatoon and North Battleford to form the independent Western Canada Baseball League (WCBL). They quickly invited Regina, Moose Jaw, Brandon, Winnipeg, and Calgary to join them. Calgary would be the key to success, said Ducey:

> We need Calgary, regardless of what set-up we decide on. That city has a great potential and we hope that baseball enthusiasts there will soon embark on a crusade that will restore Calgary to its former glory in this sport.

When Regina and Moose Jaw joined, Ducey and Brant Matthews announced they were going to Calgary to investigate its potential to field a club in 1955. This caused a small stir when the media learned that none of the previous Calgary owners knew about the visit. But their withdrawal from the WIL in 1954 tainted them in the eyes of organized baseball, and Ducey would have nothing more to do with them. The men he did talk to were Gordon Littke and Harold Cohen. In the end, they could not secure a reasonable rental agreement for Buffalo Stadium. Once again, Ducey lacked a Calgary team to draw the fans into Renfrew Park.

He spent a couple of hours with the Calgary media, briefing them on the recent setup of the new Western Canada league. Observed Henry Viney,

> What Calgary baseball needs is Edmonton's John Ducey. Here in Calgary baseball needs more than just financial backing. They need someone who, like John, will talk baseball morning, noon and night, a man who will sell the game to the latent-type baseball fan that resides in this Stampede City. They need a fellow who can get along with press and radio, one who knows how to dress up both the ball game and the park in which it is played. Yes, if Calgary had Edmonton's contribution to baseball (Mr. Baseball himself here in Alberta—John Ducey) this city could once again hold its head high when talk of baseball was in the air.

This was a good tribute from the "enemy camp." But try as he did, Ducey could never again make the Calgary connection he felt necessary for organized baseball's return to Edmonton. In hindsight, the failure to get Calgary into the WCBL in 1955 would later result in the end of regular inter-city baseball in Edmonton for some twenty years.

In mid-February, Lloydminster became a surprise entry after the Calgarians opted out. The border city rounded out the new six-team league. It would start 8 June with clubs limited to fifteen imported players and a monthly payroll of $4,000. Ducey predicted the league could get Class-C professional status in 1956:

> Class C is all we would want out here, then pick up full working agreements with major-league clubs and we'd have a nice cozy little circuit.

However at times, the WCBL was anything but "a nice cozy little circuit," as several of the Saskatchewan franchises struggled to stay afloat. After the

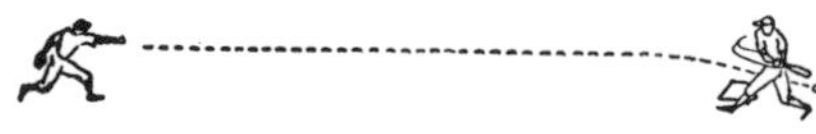

1955 season, first North Battleford, then Moose Jaw, talked of withdrawing for financial reasons, but they stayed in. The league remained stable in 1956 and 1957, but then began to unravel. In 1958, North Battleford and Lloydminster decided to merge their clubs and operate as one. This meant another team had to be found, and eventually the Oilers of Williston, North Dakota were enticed into the league, causing significantly higher travelling costs for Edmonton.

Baseball and business

After the losses in the Western International League of 1953 and 1954, Ducey had to wipe the slate clean and begin with a new financial base. He estimated $15,000 cash would be needed to get a club up and running in the proposed Western Canada League. Brant Matthews agreed to advance half of that amount, provided that the other directors made up the balance. Brian O'Hanlon described how this process worked:

> When we were short of money, John would basically go to Brant Matthews and he would often go to the other directors, such as Cecil Ross, and get them to match what he put up. Cec had the money but had he been approached directly by John I'm not sure he would have, but when John went to Brant and got him to negotiate with Cec and these other fellows, he got the money.

Ducey drew up an operating budget of $57,000 for the 1955 club, roughly half of the 1954 WIL expenses. As part of a proposal to the other directors, Cecil Ross and Brant Matthews agreed to write off their loans to the club of some $45,000.

A key part of the proposal was a public stock offering. The club would offer 2,000 preferred shares in the amount of $20 to the public. Fans could buy them in blocks of 1 to 125 and receive a general admission pass to all home games, a value of $25. Ducey laid the proposal out to the directors in a letter calling them to a meeting, ending on an ominous note:

> Now gentlemen, this is not the time for cajolery, or persuasion, for this letter is neither an ultimatum nor an appeal. It is a simple statement of facts to inform you that if you wish to protect your original investment; have membership in a league in which we wish to utilize our beautiful ball park; and continue to have baseball in Edmonton, then you will attend the directors meeting.... If you do not attend, then it can be reasonably assumed that you are no longer interested. In which case, there will be but one end. Inevitable.

The directors agreed with the overall plan and a public offering announcement was set for mid-February.

In December, still waiting to hear back from the proposal made to the Saskatchewan clubs, Ducey went off to the major-minor league meetings in Houston, Texas. He technically still had a professional baseball club until 1 February, but no league in which to play. He was there to sell the contracts of those players still on his roster and get some badly needed cash for his organization.

Ducey tried to put a good face on the fact that some of his players were moving up to Class AA but it was a sad, disappointing process to have to deal his professional club away player by player. While outwardly optimistic about the future, he suffered from the thought that after all his efforts to become a part of it, organized baseball, in the form of the Western International League, had deserted him.

A four-column advertisement in the *Journal* in February 1955 announced the preferred share offering to Edmonton baseball fans. It would move the club from private to public ownership and in so doing,

> stimulate greater interest by expanding the baseball atmosphere... and give sport-minded citizens an opportunity to join the baseball organization and take part in molding the destiny of baseball in this city.

The announcement said that "the proposal should be especially attractive to those in the lower income brackets." In the end, however, only 310 shares were subscribed, a disappointing reaction but perhaps understandable in the light of the heavy losses suffered by the club in the previous two years.

Undaunted by this seeming public rejection, Ducey carried on in typically optimistic fashion. The other directors, wishing to demonstrate that baseball still had the support of the business community, easily agreed to put up the additional $7,500 for start-up costs. Late WIL player contract sales brought in a few thousand more dollars, fence advertising drew another $3,300, and exclusive radio broadcast rights for the 1955 season were sold to station CJCA for $1,650. But revenues were never high enough for the Eskimos to meet expenses of $50,000 to $60,000.

It was not just average levels of fan support that kept revenues down. To accommodate the arrival and departure of the U.S. college ballplayers, the seasons were made far too short to earn a profit. In search of a winning team, Ducey also spent too much money bringing in and shipping home Americans. He should have used more local talent, but by then it was difficult to find local semi-pro talent to play at a Class-C level. The 1955 Eskimos had a loss of $18,400 on revenues of $38,500. Revenues moved up to $47,200 in 1956 and the loss dropped to $3,300. The championship season of 1957 would be a good one at the gate, drawing 80,000 for Edmonton's 33 home games, an average of about 2,500 fans per game. When the books were balanced, however, the club would have a loss of $7,200 on revenues of $52,000. Things would improve in 1958 when the loss dipped to $2,200 on revenues of $46,000. The final year, 1959, saw a loss of $5,700.

The 1958 season was typical, although it followed the high of 1957's Global World Series. Losing the semi-finals in 1958 cost the club badly needed playoff revenues. The shortened schedule, travel costs to Williston, a mundane performance for most of the season, and the constant shuttling of U.S. players in the attempt to field a winning team all contributed to another year of red ink for the Eskimos. Attendance for a mere 24 league games and 4 playoff matches amounted to 32,295 or just under 1,900 a game, well under the lengthier 1957 season. Ducey was disappointed in the results and the mounting deficit, but he put on an optimistic front:

> Naturally we are disappointed that we didn't do better, but in the overall picture, we are not too badly off. The fans have been going along with us very well in our eternal striving toward a return to organized baseball, which I am sure is not far off. In return, I think all will agree we have been giving them a fine brand of semi-pro ball.
>
> Edmonton has always had potential for an excellent baseball town. Representatives of many major-league organizations have come for a look at us and have gone home with enthusiastic reports. With an attractive geographical alignment, I am convinced we could look forward to great seasons sooner than some people may think.

Thinking positively

The WCBL financial problems lay ahead unseen when Ducey embarked on the 1955 season with great enthusiasm. Don Fleming described him as "that eternal optimist, going his best lick again." In mid-April, Fleming recounted a visit from Ducey, who was beating the drums for his summer game:

> Il Duce is traditionally given only to superlatives to describe the entertainment product he will shortly have on display, and this spring is no

> exception. And ever prominent in his morning-glory routine is assurance that he has enlisted the weatherman on his side.... Ducey waddled into our office at the weekend, with an armful of statistics, promising the brightest, warmest, most baseball-like summer of our time is at hand. That same optimism has been kindled in the great Ducey breast each year at this time, and even in the face of a series of disappointments in the past few seasons, Jawn hangs tough.

The Rajah, he wrote, was also equipped with the latest signs for a good summer "that the nature-lovers had read up at Rocky Mountain House" and the predictions were favourable:

> Baseball will be richly rewarded for its patience. It's been a rough wait the last three or four years, but you can depend on it this time. This will signify a new era of prosperity in our game across our great prairie wheat lands.
>
> Why, take a look at Renfrew Park this very day. Our beautiful stadium has never been in better shape. We could open our gates today to a new season. What a change from last year at this time, when a cold April greatly delayed construction of the new grandstand. Everything is spic and span right now and the grass is rapidly becoming Kelly-green.

Then the weather gods reminded Ducey they were still in command. Two weeks after his optimistic mid-April forecast, Edmonton and Renfrew Park were blanketed under an eighteen-inch snowfall. The month ended as one of the wettest on record.

Ducey's struggle with the weather continued throughout his years in the WCBL, but he never let costly rain-outs get him down. During the very soggy 1958 season, the sudden withdrawal of the Regina Braves saw Renfrew Park idle on three of the sunniest days of the summer. This caused the *Journal*'s Hal Pawson to ponder Ducey's strange relationship with the weather gods:

> A perfectly good and reliable weather machine exists right here in Edmonton. The worst thing to be said about it is that it sometimes sings Irish ballads at unpredictable, early morning hours. Still, little—if anything—in our world is perfect, including this machine's voice at those hours. This marvelous machine even has a name, and curly hair, too. Over at the Dominion Weather Office it is somewhat skeptically referred to as the "Renfrew Rain Maker." Down at the ball park it is known as uncle Jawn Ducey. By either tag there is no questioning its uncanny control as to whether the city will have good or bad weather.

Pawson went on to explain that whenever Ducey needed or was predicting good weather, he got rain and when the team was out of town, the weather was usually beautiful in Edmonton.

In 1955, however, Ducey kept his hopes up and promoted his new product at every opportunity, despite the weather. He was rewarded with a better month in May, and once the season began, rain-outs would not pose a problem. More than 3,500 enjoyed a perfect June evening as alderman Rupert Clare, subbing for Mayor Hawrelak, threw out the first ceremonial ball. Manager Carlson chose to go with experience, selecting Ed Belter as his starter, which was just fine with the fans. Fleming noted that Belter, a painter by profession, had spent the afternoon painting a sign on the left-field fence. It did not hurt his pitching, as Belter fashioned a five-hit, 3-2 victory over Lloydminster. To Fleming, Belter still looked good on the mound:

> Maybe his Sunday pitches have lost a little bit of the steam that made him one of the winningest pitchers in Edmonton history, but the venerable southpaw still has plenty left to get him over the rough spots.

It was to be the last Renfrew Park opener for Belter, who had begun his career with Ducey's 1936 Union Bus team.

By mid-July 1955, average game attendance was well beyond that of the previous two WIL seasons. The Eskimos contended for first place with Saskatoon throughout the short fifty-game season and went on to defeat the Gems for the championship. Edmonton drew 49,433 paying customers for 25 home games. While the league was not at the talent level of the WIL, Ducey saw that his team got full marks for effort and hustle, and the fans seemed to appreciate the potential of the young players.

Adding to WCBL interest was that the league champions would be Canada's entry into the Global World Series, an international tournament of independent baseball leagues held in the United States. To promote the upcoming event, most of the six WCBL clubs had lucky draws to award an all-expense-paid trip to the series for one local fan. Ducey did it a bit differently. He announced that Edmonton's draw would take place among the loyal supporters who had bought preferred stock in the ball club.

The 1955 Global World Series was to be played in Milwaukee, which expected 100,000 visitors for the event. There would be $40,000 in prize money for the contending clubs. More importantly, Milwaukee would be crawling with major-league scouts—the ideal place to showcase a team. Edmonton, having won first place handily, beat Saskatoon to win the seventh game of the league finals. Ducey and company prepared to head for Milwaukee. But it was not to be.

League rules required that any club going on to the Series had to be augmented by five players from other teams to ensure the strongest possible representation. This meant one Eskimo had to be dropped from the team to make way for the reinforcements. Four of the American players rebelled, refusing to go along with the arrangement if a team member had to be dropped. Canadian baseball commissioner Jimmy Robison then agreed Edmonton could go, if it took two players from other teams, which the Eskimos agreed to do. However the next day he reversed his decision, putting the final say in the hands of league directors. In a vote

by telegraph, they ruled that Edmonton did indeed have to drop one player and accept five others. Brant Matthews tried to solve the quandary by offering to personally pay that player's way to Milwaukee, but this too was rejected by the rebellious foursome.

The matter became an administrative nightmare that went on around the clock through two full nights. Under a full media watch, the Eskimos and their chartered bus stood by at Renfrew, ready to depart for Milwaukee. An embarrassed Ducey had to take the heat for not keeping his players in line. With two players unable to go to Milwaukee for other reasons and the four U.S. players refusing to go, Ducey was suddenly down to 11 players. He gave the league their names and stood ready to receive extra players from Saskatoon. But the league disqualified Edmonton and named runner-up Saskatoon to represent the WCBL at the series instead. Edmonton was out. The flavour of a championship season suddenly turned sour. Hal Pawson, *Journal* sports editor, put the blame on the four who had defied league rules, saying they had made Edmonton "the laughing stock of Canadian baseball circles."

It was a bitter pill for Ducey to swallow and to make it worse, Saskatoon's Ralph Mabee said it was just another example of Edmonton's inability to get along in the league, suggesting that perhaps the WCBL would be better off without Edmonton. Don Fleming predicted lightning would strike twice, that the Saskatchewan teams would turn their backs on Edmonton the next year, and the Eskimos would again be left without a league. However, at the November league meeting, Edmonton management was exonerated and the blame placed on the four players involved. On a motion by Ducey, the league threw out the five player addition rule. Then they announced that the WCBL, Edmonton included, would be in business again in 1956. To show that all was forgiven, they named Ducey as acting president until a successor was found for the retiring Cliff Henderson.

Managing managers

Prior to the start of the 1955 season, Ducey announced the signing of manager Roy Carlson, a thirty-year-old native of Elma, Washington, who was coaching high school baseball in Portland, Oregon. Several of Ducey's major-league contacts recommended Carlson as the right man to handle young baseball talent. Carlson asked for his release in mid-season to accept a job teaching the high-school children of U.S. service personnel in Germany. "We won't stand in his way but we're sorry to see him go," said Ducey. He did not add that the departure would improve the club budget because Carlson, hired as a playing manager, suffered both arm and eye problems early in the season and had virtually retired from the lineup. The choice of Jim Ryan to succeed him was popular with Edmonton fans, but Ryan stepped back from the job when the 1955 season ended.

That meant that in addition to a shopping list for player talent for the 1956 season, Ducey also had to search for a new manager. In the winter days of February, he again got baseball back on the sports pages. During a swing down the west coast to search for talent, he predicted that before long Edmonton would be in a Class-A coast league alignment. He was supported by former WIL colleague Dewey Soriano, by then general manager of the PCL's Seattle Rainiers. Ducey's visit with Soriano was his first chance to congratulate him for being named the top executive in minor-league baseball the previous season by *The Sporting News*. Soriano agreed that Edmonton would be invited into a coast league alignment as soon as Calgary and Spokane were ready to re-enter organized baseball. Ducey soon announced that he had signed fourteen college ballplayers but as was often the case, few of the signings translated into regular spots in the lineup by the time league play began. A second attempt to sign Al Brightman of Seattle University as his manager fell through at the last minute in early April, forcing Ducey to redouble his efforts.

Wayne Tucker is welcomed to Edmonton by Ducey in April 1956 as the new manager of the Western Canada League Eskimos. Then in its second year, the six-team semi-professional league was made up largely of U.S. college ballplayers. Courtesy of the Edmonton Archives EA 524-57.

His search ended when he signed thirty-three-year-old Wayne Tucker, baseball coach at Utah's Brigham Young University. A former New York Yankee farmhand, Tucker, like Bob Sturgeon before him, would both manage and play second base. He was just the kind of man Ducey wanted to look after young ballplayers. Tucker had been signed to a bonus contract by Yankees scout Joe Devine in 1943 and had played Triple-A ball under both Casey Stengel and George "Twinkletoes" Selkirk. He later managed in the Yankee farm system for eight seasons before taking over as coach for Brigham Young University. Tucker recalled his introduction to Edmonton:

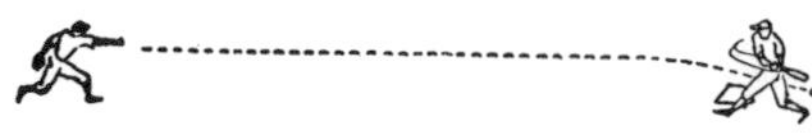

> Tony Robello and Lee McPhail, the Yankee farm director, told me about John Ducey and what he was doing in Edmonton. They wanted me to handle a bunch of promising college kids in the hope we could convince them to eventually sign with the Yankees. John called me and invited me up to a sportsmen's dinner in Edmonton where Leo Durocher was the guest speaker.
>
> I had played in Montreal and Toronto but had never been to Western Canada before. I was very impressed with Edmonton and the people I met initially, including Brant Matthews and Cecil Ross. John toured me through Renfrew Park and it didn't take us long to come to terms.

Ducey and Tucker enjoyed three good seasons together, bringing in a number of very talented young ballplayers, several of whom would go on to play in the majors.

The Players

There was some question whether fans who failed to support the Class-A offerings at Renfrew would turn out to watch U.S. college players fronting for the likes of North Battleford and Moose Jaw. It was dubbed "the Great Experiment" by Stan Moher in the *Albertan*. But Moher agreed that with lower costs and a strong contender in Edmonton, the league would do well at the gate. Edmonton fans responded well to the hustling young players, who played a lively brand of baseball.

Many of the local players who had starred in Edmonton from 1947 to 1952 had retired or were pursuing careers by the time the Eskimos joined the WCBL. The signings of first baseman Jim Ryan and catcher Stan Kulka put a local brand on the Eskimos' first WCBL entry. They were soon followed by infielder Len Karlson and several pitchers, including the ageless Eddie Belter, Jerry Seaman, John Doucette of Donnelly, Alberta, and young Murray "Zeke" Dea, who pitched for Gonzaga University in Spokane. Dea did not last the season, but the others were later joined by

Wayne Tucker usually called on Ralph Vold to pitch the clutch games. The Ponoka-based right-hander twice left organized baseball to star with the Eskimos through four seasons. Courtesy of the Edmonton Archives EA 524-62.

Vern Callihan and Hal Forss. Two Victoria natives from the University of Oregon varsity team added more Canadian content: outfielder Norm Forbes and second baseman Jimmy Johnson. The more numerous U.S. imports were juggled for a while to find a winning combination.

At the end of the 1955 season, Belter, Seaman, Karlson, and Kulka announced they were hanging up their spikes, so Ducey and Tucker got to work to build a strong contending club. From Utah, Tucker brought pitcher Owen Skousen and outfielder Gary LaComb. The biggest source of talent came from a new link forged with Rod Dedeaux, the noted

coach of the University of Southern California ball club, a college baseball powerhouse. Ducey had met Dedeaux in 1953 when his WIL Eskimos played three spring-training games with Dedeaux's USC club. Five starting players came from USC: pitcher Dale Zeigler, first-baseman Ken Guffey, shortstop Eddie Bertotti, third-baseman Bob Gerst, and catcher Tom Shollin. They were the first of many talented USC players Rod Dedeaux would send to Edmonton over the next several seasons.

Pitchers Don Kirk, who played for Saskatoon in 1955, and John Doucette, along with aspiring Edmonton catcher Ken Heffel, were the initial Canadian talent. Jim Ryan was not certain whether his work would allow him to play full-time, but he signed with the club. But the biggest addition was a hockey-playing cattle rancher from Ponoka, Ralph Vold. At age twenty-four, he had just been released after playing five years of professional baseball for the Dodgers organization, reaching as high as Class AA. He returned to his home just as the annual Lacombe baseball tournament was beginning:

> I was going to pitch again for the Central Alberta All-Stars. John Ducey heard about that and he phoned me and said, "Ralph, could you possibly come up and have a visit with me?" I did and met with him and Brant Matthews. They wanted me to sign with their club. I told them that I thought I was going to quit baseball and stay on the farm. We got into a long talk and then John said, "Would you consider playing home games?" I said I guess I would, but no road trips. Then he offered me more money just for home games than I had been getting full-time in professional baseball.

The largest acquisition headlines were reserved for the signing of Cecil "Tiger" Goldstick. Ducey lured him back to the Eskimo fold when George Windwick's day job prevented him from doing any further travelling with the ball club. The media loved to play up an ongoing, friendly feud between Goldstick and Ducey and were delighted to have him back. The

Journal reported that Ducey had announced Goldstick's return "after a stormy conference in which Goldstick walked out four times." It was not long before Don Fleming had Goldstick taking a run at Ducey:

> That Ducey is a real phoney. You can use that too because I'm not afraid of him. I've got a contract for the whole year. But guess where I saw him last night? Watching a softball game down at Kinsmen Park.

Softball was anathema to Ducey, and throughout his career he described it disdainfully as "a physical condition." (In their younger days, Ducey once admonished his sister, "Mary, don't you ever mention the word 'softball' in the same breath as the sacred name of baseball.") The taunt provided a great excuse for Fleming to needle Ducey, and the fun went on for years. Fleming and other writers also concocted a feud between Ducey and Clare Hollingsworth, who ran the softball league at Kingsway Park. Ducey enjoyed the media razzing about softball, but he was serious about the concern he often expressed about Edmonton schools allowing softball to creep onto their playgrounds at the expense of baseball.

A face from the past turned up among the WCBL opposition in 1956. The now-aging Eddie Morris signed as a catcher for the Lloydminster Meridians, and his presence in the 9 June opening lineup at Renfrew Park attracted a lot of former Morris fans and Morris-baiters. At the opening, Ducey turned from politicians to the fans, honouring the first two people to have bought tickets to Renfrew Park back in 1933. Longtime fans Mamie McNabb and Rod Morrison were both presented with season's tickets and then handled the official first-pitch ceremonies. They made credible observations about the best to ever play at Renfrew Park, Mrs. McNabb reaching back into the 1930s for her favourite:

> It was everybody's hero, that tough little guy at the plate, Pete McCready. All the fans loved Pete and his crazy antics, regardless of which team they were pulling for.

She selected Jack Starky as her Boyle Street favourite. Rod Morrison, who had lived in Edmonton since 1910, had a more contemporary choice:

> No question about my favourite. He's Whitey Thompson, the Eskimos' shortstop when we were in the Western International League a few years back. What a great glove man he was. As good a fielder as any I've ever seen.

The team Tucker and Ducey crafted for 1957 was undoubtedly the most talented ever seen in post-war Edmonton. Its nucleus came from Rod Dedeaux's USC Trojans. Ducey was relieved to learn Dale Zeigler would be back: Dedeaux said the big fastballer, who struck out twenty-one opponents in a college match, was delaying professional offers until he finished his education. Also returning were Ken Guffey, Larry Elliot, Bob Gerst, and Tom Shollin. Shollin, who hit .346 and led the WCBL in home runs the previous year, was also being chased by scouts. At the time, these fellows all received more early attention in the *Journal* than did the late signing of another USC student, Ron Fairly, then unknown to Edmonton fans.

Centre-fielder Ron Fairly had tremendous athletic skills and was being chased by several bonus-wielding scouts who claimed he was close to signing. Dedeaux convinced the nineteen-year-old redhead and his father to put the scouts off. He advised that a summer in Edmonton, under Tucker's wing and Ducey's watchful eye, was the ideal place for the talented youngster to protect his college eligibility while he further developed his baseball skills. Tucker knew all about Fairly's potential and had prevailed upon Dedeaux to send him to Edmonton for the summer.

Local fans were pleased about the signings of two Canadians in 1957, one of them the re-signing of Ralph Vold. Ducey gave him a $150 per month expense allowance to pay for a hired man to handle his cattle work in Ponoka, so Vold signed to play full-time. Ducey also made a rare deal with rival Slim Thorpe of the Meridians to buy the contract of outfielder

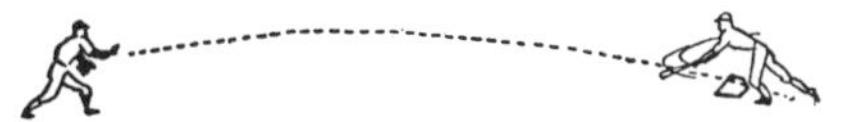

Don Stewart for $200. The native of Black Diamond, Alberta wished to relocate to Edmonton for business reasons. Ducey had wanted to get the hard-hitting Stewart for some time but feared being accused of tampering with another club's player. Stewart had played with Cal's Dodgers in 1950, then signed a professional contract with the Brooklyn Dodgers. He rose to Class-A before returning to semi-pro baseball in Canada. He managed the Lloydminster Meridians in 1955 and was a key member of the club that defeated the Eskimos in 1956.

Country cousins: Edmonton versus Lloydminster

If the Eskimos had one nagging problem, it was the constant struggle with the only other Alberta team in the WCBL, the Lloydminster Meridians. Baseball was a passion in the border city, then with a population well under 5,000; the prairie team drew in fans from surrounding rural centres in both Alberta and Saskatchewan. Lloydminster was the tough country team with dirt on their uniforms from dusty Meridian Field. Many of their players were grizzled veterans from minor-league baseball, in contrast to Ducey's clean-cut Yankee college boys from the big city. Those differences were apparent right from the start, but in 1956 the lowly Meridians took the Eskimos' measure.

Edmonton had dominated the league in 1955, but had trouble with Lloydminster on and off the field. Ducey and Walter "Slim" Thorpe carried on a running battle which had begun with Ducey's criticism of Thorpe's baseball dress the year before. It pained Ducey to see Lloydminster's general manager on the field before the game, his Hermanesque figure draped in an over-sized uniform and club jacket, wearing running shoes instead of baseball cleats. One night, the sight of the sneaker-clad Thorpe coaching at third base in Renfrew Park caused Ducey to explode. Mindful of the need to present a "class product," he asked league officials to remove Thorpe from the diamond whenever he did not dress "professionally."

Off the field, Ducey and Tucker both dressed as if they had stepped out of *Esquire* magazine, no matter what they were doing around the ball park. The two also imposed a strict dress and conduct code for their players, to ensure the young Eskimos presented a clean-cut, professional image. Here are some the rules they set out and enforced for the Edmonton players:

- Absolutely clean inner sox every day, shoes shined every day, both at a cost of $2.50 per day (to the batboy).
- Keep a tidy locker. Always hang up suits and wet stuff. Do not hang up caps on nails.
- Pitchers must wear coats or jackets when leaving clubhouse in the evening. Protect your arm and your health. It is your meal ticket.
- No baseball jackets or college lettermen sweaters on road trips or in hotels.
- No shorts on field or bare backs after gates are opened.
- Absolutely no hot dogs, peanuts or the like in dugout. No smoking in dugout, or on field or leaving game to go to clubhouse.
- Be business-like and professional in your ball playing actions.
- Keep respect of fans and players alike. Be gentlemen, please.!!

The slick Edmontonians were too much for Slim Thorpe:

> Ducey was able to push us around last year because we were poor country cousins. We'll have a real club this time and I think a lot of Ducey's big talk right now will be reason for plenty of embarrassment later on. We've waited patiently to get the laugh on the guys at Renfrew.

In 1956, the wily Lloydminster auctioneer assembled a gritty, respectable team that proved to be the bane of the Eskimos all season and into the playoffs. Tucker could seem to do no better against Thorpe than could Ducey:

> Lloydminster became an obsession with me and the players. We wanted to beat them so badly that we beat ourselves. "Slim" managed to get under my skin. Now I have to give him credit for antagonizing us to such an extent. He was the man who kept baseball going in Lloydminster and when we weren't playing against one another, we got along very well.

Lloydminster won eight of twelve league games against Edmonton in 1956. Pitcher-manager Stan Karpinski, who had played Class-A ball, was flanked by his pitching cousin John Karpinski. Their baseball savvy could usually spur the Lloydminster team on to best the talented but youthful Eskimos.

Despite struggling against Lloydminster, the Eskimos breezed through the latter half of the second season and prepared to meet the Meridians in the playoffs. Ducey was so confident of ultimate victory that he ordered new uniforms for his club, with "Canada" lettered across the front so the club would look their best for the Milwaukee trip. He was ready to seize the spoils that had been so unexpectedly taken from his grasp the year before. As the playoffs began, Thorpe unveiled a new acquisition, twenty-year-old Ron Perranoski, who had won ten and lost only one game in the South Dakota league before joining Lloydminster at the end of the season. The Meridians won the first game at Renfrew, with Stan Karpinski defeating Vold and the Eskimos 8-7. Then Perranoski dazzled the Eskimos, winning the second game 7-2. Perranoski became a Los Angeles Dodger in 1961, pitching in the majors for thirteen years, only to go on to an even longer career as the Dodgers' pitching coach.

Down two games to none, Edmonton finally got their first win. The next night, Stan Karpinski pitched an entire game and stole home in the fourth. The game ended as a 5-5 tie, called due to darkness in the ninth inning. League president George Vogan then ruled that because Lloydminster had no lights, the final two games would be played at Renfrew. This irritated the Lloydminster fans no end, who then turned their razzing from Ducey

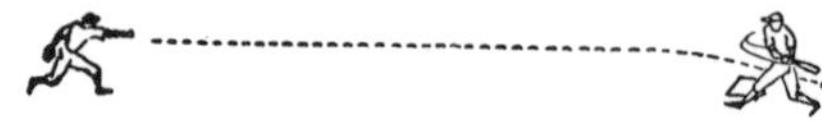

to Vogan. Home park advantage did not help the Eskimos. They fell victim to a fantastic performance by "iron man" Karpinski, who pitched his second full game in two nights and personally booted the Eskimos out of the playoffs. Ducey was left holding a set of new uniforms for the next season.

The Global World Series of 1957

As Ducey and Wayne Tucker worked with Rod Dedeaux in the off-season to build a strong club for 1957, scout Tony Robello helped them forge closer links with the New York Yankees. Robello told general manager Lee McPhail that "the Edmonton project was a good set-up, one of the best operated clubs in baseball." That view was endorsed by others, and Ducey became the first official delegate from an independent baseball league ever invited to the minor-league meetings, held late in 1956 at Jacksonville, Florida. There he met with John Quinn of the Milwaukee Brewers and McPhail of the Yankees. The latter agreed that the Yankees would stage a three-day baseball school at Renfrew Park in late May for young prospects from western Canada. It was the first major-league try-out camp at Renfrew in three years, cheering news to Edmonton baseball fans in the grip of sub-zero December weather.

In early January, the WCBL seemed to be in major-league trouble. Moose Jaw announced the Mallards were withdrawing for financial reasons. Days later, the champion North Battleford Beavers said they would also withdraw. Baseball was taking too much of their principals' business time. By the end of January, however, both clubs were back in. Then word came that the Global World Series would be moved to Detroit and held a week later, giving the WCBL more time to finish its playoffs. The 1957 season suddenly looked much brighter.

Popular Wayne Tucker returned to Edmonton in early May to help promote the coming baseball season. Tucker had ended the 1956 season batting .371 and again planned to take a regular turn at second base. On his arrival, he was optimistic but cautious about the Eskimo's chances in 1957:

> Don't get me too far out on a limb, but if any of those other clubs think they can head us off this year, they may find it a tall order. Several of our players will be back and a lot of them have excellent chances of going far in professional baseball and actually this season could decide plenty concerning their own prospects.

Ducey and Tucker hit the Edmonton banquet circuit, then spoke in Lloydminster, where Ducey and Slim Thorpe crossed good-natured swords about the 1956 playoffs and the coming year.

Ralph Vold was due to pitch the 7 June opener against the arch-rival Meridians. After the driest May in years, the weekend series was rained out, forcing the Eskimos to open the season with a single game in Lloydminster. Vold struck out eight, as the Esks gained some measure of revenge against Thorpe's defending champions with a 9-1 win. However, Don Fleming's dispatches were all about the young red-head in centre field. Tucker was also enthusiastic:

> The Edmonton fans will just love Fairly when they see him in action. Desire, guts, ability, Fairly's got it all. He's one of those rare boys who come along so seldom that you know can't miss. Talk about swinging a bat. When he comes around he just explodes. He made a wonderful catch and he's got a rifle arm. Yep, he'll do.

Fairly had hit a screaming line-drive homer into a gusting wind over the right-field fence, 340 feet away, scoring three runs. The 1,600 fans, one of the largest crowds ever packed into tiny Meridian field, were equally impressed. When the Esks returned home for their first game at Renfrew, Fairly had three home runs in three games and was hitting a lofty .667.

But despite their talent, the 1957 season was anything but easy for the Eskimos. On opening night, the crowd of 3,250 was shocked into silence when Bob Gerst was seriously injured. In the eighth inning, he was hit in the head by a vicious fastball from North Battleford's Benny Griggs. It

shattered his batting helmet, which probably saved his life. The injury and a lengthy convalescence ended the talented Gerst's playing career. (Gerst recovered at home and returned to USC to complete his schooling; he became a successful lawyer whose specialties included baseball arbitration at the major-league level.) An inning later, Don Stewart's hitting potential was also lost for the season after a ninth-inning walk. In his haste to get back to first base on an attempted pick-off play, he suffered a badly fractured ankle. That game set the tone for further physical problems among the Eskimos. Near the end of the season, Tucker threw out his shoulder in a double play and was out through the playoffs. Then Tom Shollin fell victim to the German measles. Just as he returned, Mike Blewett was temporarily shelved with scarlet fever.

As the season drew to a close, the ailing Eskimos could not catch the Moose Jaw Mallards. They remained four games ahead, carried by league-leading hitter Len Tucker, batting .414 with eighteen home runs. Fairly was hitting .388 with ten round-trippers. Zeigler led the Eskimo pitchers with a 10-3 record. Vold had run into trouble and was 5-8, while Blaine Sylvester was 9-5. Tucker was concerned about the wildness of several of his young pitchers. By 31 August, they had given up 345 bases on balls and hit 35 enemy batters.

The season ended much the way it had started. The Eskimos were rained out of two of their last three games in Lloydminster and of their final home game in Edmonton. Yet after a shaky mid-season, during which their pitchers had been uncommonly wild, the Eskimos had won twelve of their last thirteen games to clinch second place—and they had won them all without Fairly, who had to return to Los Angeles to write supplemental examinations at USC. Tucker had shown his youngsters the way, batting just over .400 until he was sidelined.

In the semi-finals, Edmonton got out to a quick lead, winning the first two games against Saskatoon. It looked as if the series would be over before Fairly returned. Then the Gems came back to win the next two games. Ducey was getting that sinking feeling again. But this time, his

men came through. Larry Elliot, used more in the outfield than on the mound, and Ralph Vold combined to win a 3-2 thriller. New York Giants scout Herman Franks, who was attending the series, liked the looks of Vold and said he would invite him to spring training:

> You know, there are plenty of relief pitchers up at the top who don't get the ball over nearly as well as Vold can. He's only 26. He's still got a chance of going somewhere.

A Labour Day crowd of 3,402 livened up Renfrew that afternoon, roaring their approval as Blaine Sylvester shut out Saskatoon for seven innings. Guffey hit four for five, and the just-returned Fairly cracked a one-run double as the Eskimos closed the lid on Saskatoon 8-2. They had the luxury of waiting a few days until Moose Jaw sidelined Regina in their series, four games to two.

Opening at Moose Jaw's Exhibition Park, the clubs split the first two games, then hurried back to Edmonton for the third game the next afternoon. Renfrew's largest crowd of the year, 4,650 fans, packed the stands on Sunday, giving Ralph Vold a big hand as he received the Sharp-McNeill trophy for their choice as the Esks' most valuable player. The Eskimos then downed the Mallards 9-4, giving Sylvester his thirteenth win of the season.

Monday's game began at 5:00 p.m. to avoid a conflict with the football Eskimos, but the game drew a disappointing crowd of 847 people. Zeigler was brilliant, holding Moose Jaw to four hits through eight innings. The Eskimos combined some clutch hitting and good base running with a bit of luck, scoring five runs to win 5-2.

The league had made travel arrangements for the winners to fly to Detroit at least a day ahead of the first game of the Global World Series. It seemed certain the Eskimos would wrap up the series on Tuesday and have ample time to get to Detroit. Ducey had the new uniforms, purchased the year before, sent out to have the letters "Edmonton" sewn

Manager Tucker with his jubilant Eskimos just after they won the right to represent Canada in the 1957 Global World Series at Detroit. Ron Fairly is the player with his hand on the head of the victorious pitcher, Ralph Vold. Courtesy of the Edmonton Archives EA 524-58.

across the chest. Everything was ready for the Eskimos to catch a flight at midnight Tuesday. Then Mallard ace Ernie Nevers upset the plans with a 3-0 shutout. The charter flight was put on hold. Squeezed for time, league officials named Moose Jaw the home team and scheduled a split double-header at Renfrew on Wednesday in case the series went the full seven games. Only 1,000 fans were in the stands that afternoon as Wayne Tucker decided to start Vold, who had been serving in a relief role in the playoffs. The Mallards had no chance after giving away six unearned runs in a sloppy fourth inning. Vold struck out eight for a three-hit, 7-1 victory and the right to go to the Global World Series.

On to Detroit

Using a bit of boosterism to get the city behind his ball club, Ducey had photographers and Mayor Hawrelak standing by to present Tucker with the National Baseball Congress Trophy, emblematic of the Canadian semi-pro baseball championship. The joyful Esks whooped it up in the clubhouse and left at midnight on their charter flight to Detroit. They arrived tired but happy the next afternoon, scheduled to open the series against Japan on Friday, 13 September. While the club engaged in a light workout at Briggs Stadium that afternoon, Ducey was in his glory, visiting with officials and several major-league scouts. He also renewed ties with Charlie Gehringer, reaching back to the 1932 Edmonton visit by Earle Mack's All-Stars. The former Detroit Tiger star from 1924 to 1942 was one of many who had helped industrialist Dick Falk move the Global World Series from Milwaukee to Detroit.

That night, Ducey's Eskimos took to the field for their long-delayed premiere in the Global World Series. They had been given little chance in the pre-tourney ratings. Tucker planned to start Dale Zeigler but opted instead to pitch Ralph Vold. He had a hunch Vold's superior control would be a better strike-zone match for the smaller Japanese players. It was the right choice. Vold pitched a masterful game, giving up only seven hits with the teams tied 1-1 after twelve innings:

> The Japanese were tough. I never forgot them. They were small and they'd crouch in there, making it really tough to pitch to them. We could see they were a good team, they didn't surprise us. It went on for thirteen innings.

In the top of the thirteenth, Munatones drilled a triple to right-centre field. He scored when Castanon beat out a bad throw to first on a

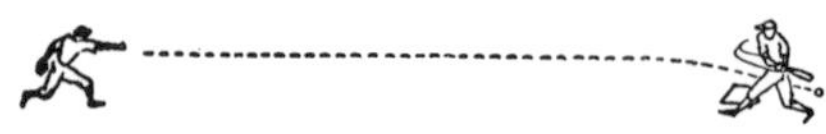

grounder to third. Ducey led a small but delirious Canadian rooting section in the cavernous stadium, now empty of most of the 8,200 fans who turned out some three hours earlier.

In the bottom of the thirteenth, Vold showed no sign of tiring, despite having pitched the Wednesday game in Edmonton. He walked the first batter, then picked him off first base, and struck the second batter out. The Esks were just one out away from an upset. A routine grounder to short looked like the final out. Ducey was rising to his feet to cheer when the ball suddenly took a bad bounce over Ed Sada's shoulder and Japan had a second runner aboard. Ducey felt that sinking feeling again. Vold got two strikes on Japan's first baseman, Yuki Takanouchi, who then slashed a fly ball down the right-field line. Joe Riney got there just as the ball skidded off his glove, dropping in for a double. The winning run scored before Riney could get the throw in to Shollin, and the Esks lost a heartbreaker. Vold had pitched a magnificent game. Although disappointed, the Canadian contingent was cheered by the Eskimos' gutsy performance.

On Saturday, the Eskimos had a well-earned day of rest. Series rules would not allow them to work out, so the lay-off was just what they needed. On Sunday, the team went into a split double-header against two of the top-seeded clubs in the tournament: Hawaii and the United States. Hawaii had been runner-up to the U.S. the two previous years. The day off did nothing for Dale Zeigler's noted lack of control, and the fast-balling pitcher walked three of the Hawaiian players in the third inning, bringing his total to six. Tucker reluctantly took him out and turned the ball over to Moose Jaw's Ernie Nevers, who had been added to the club along with left-fielder Ernie Rodriguez. Nevers pitched a strong game, striking out seven. Joe Riney more than made up for some shoddy work in left field, hitting four for five, as did Shollin. Fairly seemed to be coming out the slump he had been in since returning from exams, knocking in two runs as the Eskimos upset Hawaii 11-6.

By this time, Vold said, the Eskimos had heard a lot about the U.S. club:

> We had heard there were several former major-leaguers on that club [Clint Hartung, former New York Giant was one], older fellows and that they would be the team to beat.

Tucker was concerned and knew the Americans were confident they would roll right over the Canadians:

> We didn't think our makeshift club could measure up to the U.S. and Hawaii. The Americans had loaded up with talent for the series. They were really cocky and thought we would be an easy win. But when we got out on the field, everyone saw that our kids were for real.

Tucker considered pitching Vold in the evening game but felt that Zeigler, who seemed to improve with work, could come back from his bad start in the afternoon. Zeigler was just wild enough that the U.S. batters could not dig in against him. Walking four, he pitched a sparkling one-hitter. The Esks scored five times in the third and added three more in the fourth, going on to win 8-0. In Edmonton, baseball fans, who had been glued to their radios, celebrated. Their club beat the odds and won a semi-final match against Venezuela on Wednesday. The winner would meet Japan that evening for the championship.

Wayne Tucker knew his thirty-fifth birthday would be a memorable one however the day turned out. He was facing the biggest eighteen innings of baseball in his coaching career. He decided to go with the Mallards' Nevers against Venezuela in the afternoon. Nevers rewarded him with a solid three-hit, one-run game. The Eskimos scored only one themselves until the eighth inning. Then a two-run homer by Ken Guffey ignited a four-run outburst. Suddenly, the Eskimos were facing Japan again, but this time for the championship of the Global World Series.

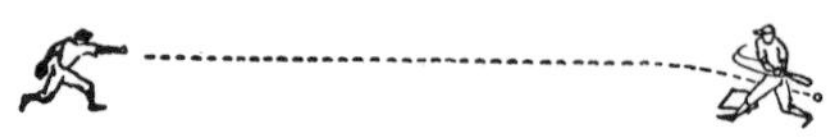

Meanwhile, Ducey spent all his free time lobbying with scouts and baseball officials about the kind of baseball played in Edmonton. He pointed out that the WCBL and its Eskimo representatives were proof that western Canada was fertile ground for organized baseball. All that was needed was some major-league support in terms of player personnel and a rejuvenated Calgary franchise. This was the best chance to showcase his product he would ever get, and he made the most of it. He used Wayne Tucker and Canadian baseball commissioner Jimmy Robison of Indian Head, Saskatchewan to help him. Up in the press box, even Don Fleming proudly extolled the baseball virtues of the Canadian prairies. Tucker said everyone was impressed with the Eskimos:

> There were 32 major-league scouts attending the series. They all praised our hustle and our appearance. They said we looked just like a Yankees' club, with the pinstriped uniforms, the routine and the guts we showed.

Vold could see how important presentation was to Ducey:

> One thing I always noticed about John Ducey was that he organized and kept things better than most pro teams did. After coming out of pro ball, I just admired the way he kept a team in such good shape, with first-class arrangements and neat uniforms. He wanted us to be dressed properly, look respectable and he didn't put up with any foolishness. The way he treated us made you want to win.

Tucker elected to throw Vold at the Japanese club again:

> I was always impressed with Ralph and his attitude and willingness to pitch anytime we needed him. He had tremendous control of his pitches. Sometimes he seemed to be too true with his pitches and I

A somewhat glum-looking Eskimos team, along with Ducey, manager Wayne Tucker, and trainer Dick Bielous (left), just after their heartbreaking loss to Japan in the final game of the 1957 Global World Series at Detroit's Briggs Stadium. Courtesy of the Provincial Archives of Alberta A.7267.

> had to encourage him to be slightly wild at certain times and knock 'em down a bit.

Vold needed all his control that evening. He held the Japanese in check for six innings. Ron Fairly finally came through and smashed a huge two-run homer into the distant upper deck of right-centre field. Vold again had two out in the ninth when Japan battled back to score a run and tie the game at 2-2:

> I'll never forget getting those two strikes against the batter. After pitching two balls, I threw him a curve ball that I swore cut the middle and the umpire called it a ball. So I had to come in with a fast ball and

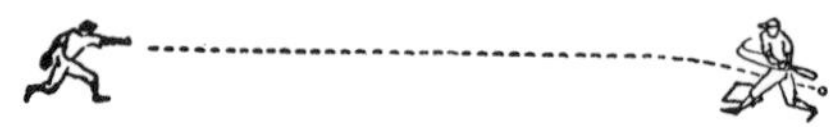

> he hit it. Two out in the ninth, being that close....I had to live with that the rest of my days.

It was as close to winning as Vold and the Eskimos would come. Vold gave way to Ernie Nevers, who struggled for two innings to preserve the tie. In the tenth, Mike Blewett got into trouble with a hit and a balk. Then he served up a pitch that second-baseman Furuta lined into centre field for two runs. Zeigler came in to close out the top of the tenth inning. Ducey and the others hoped the team could pull off a comeback with their last at-bat, but there would be no miracle for Canada in Detroit that night. The Eskimos had given their all but could do nothing against the tough Japanese in the final inning. With Edmonton's last out, Japan had a 4-2 win and the Global World Series championship.

In Ducey's eyes, his club was still a winner, and he made sure everyone in Detroit for the series knew it. Their gutsy performance throughout the series had made them the sentimental favourite going into the final game. They played like champions, barely losing two tough games in extra innings. In both games, one more strike would have won.

The team's overall performance was acknowledged when six team members were selected as series all-stars. Shollin, who led with six extra base hits, was named to the dream team along with Zeigler, Nevers, Riney, Sada, and Rodriguez. Organizer Dick Falk put some icing on the runner-ups' cake, awarding Wayne Tucker the trophy for outstanding sportsmanship. Along with the immense, runner-up trophy, Tucker concluded his birthday with his arms full of brass. But he would have gladly traded it all for a final win:

> Our 1957 club was comparable to a Class-A club when we were at full strength. If Gerst, Oyler, and Elliot had been with us in Detroit, I'm convinced we would have won it all. We were the envy of the league throughout the season. John and I were both thrilled at the chance to help those talented young college kids shape their future careers.

Mayor Bill Hawrelak accepts the runners-up trophy brought back from the 1957 Global World Series in Detroit by Ducey's Eskimos. Courtesy of the Edmonton Archives EA 524-59.

Ducey was full of superlatives about the entire experience. His best was an Olympic-sized tribute to the future potential of the Global World series itself:

> I'm really sold on the Global World Series. It has given Edmonton, Alberta and Canada invaluable publicity and it's just really starting. Frankly, I'm looking forward to the day when the Global Series is next in stature to the Olympic Games.

Industrialist Falk was undaunted, despite taking a financial bath for the third year, stating, "There'll always be a Global World Series as long as

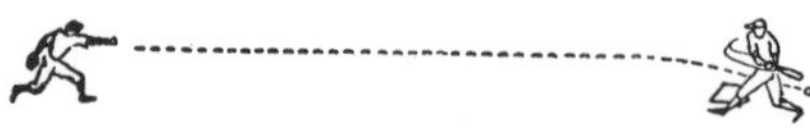

The 1957 WCBL champion Eskimos, most of whom went on to sign professional baseball contracts the following year. Manager Tucker claimed they were comparable to a Class-A team. Courtesy of the Edmonton Archives EA 524-60.

I'm alive." But his accountants must have convinced him otherwise in the cold light of dawn. The Series had been a financial bust and while there was talk of holding the next year's event in a non-major-league city, Falk and his colleagues were never able to re-stage it.

The tired but happy ball players arrived home to a welcoming crowd of some 600 fans on hand at the airport at 2:30 a.m. Saturday—almost as many as had watched their final game in Edmonton ten days earlier.

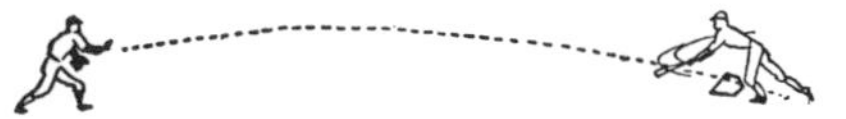

Their effort had caught the imagination of the entire city when the final game was broadcast as NBC television's "game of the day." The team received the first civic parade ever held for an Edmonton baseball team, with the players driven down Jasper Avenue to cheering crowds. Then it was off to a civic luncheon and praise from Mayor Hawrelak and a quickly assembled group of dignitaries. The Eskimos were celebrated for the international honour they had brought the city by doing so well in the eight-nation tourney. In response, Ducey admitted, "My being a part of this team was one of the biggest thrills of a baseball career stretching over many years." Wayne Tucker summed up the club and the season when he said that the 1957 Eskimos had more fight and more spirit, and had conducted themselves better, than any club he had ever coached, played on, or seen in his life.

Ducey and Tucker knew they would not see the likes of this team again. Zeigler was expected to sign a major-league contract. Shollin, Sylvester, and Munatones would graduate the following spring and likely turn professional. Vold was being offered a contract by the Giants' Herman Franks. Few expected that Fairly would be able to keep the swarming major-league scouts at bay for long.

Ducey was immensely proud of his "boys" and with good reason. His 1957 WCBL champions more than made up for all the frustration of past years. They allowed him finally to get a team to the Global World Series and showcase his baseball product for all to see. Despite both early and late season rain-outs, it had been a good season at the gate, drawing 80,000 fans for Edmonton's 33 home games, an average of about 2,500 per game. Yet when the books were balanced, the club recorded another loss.

The league itself had a deficit of $3,104. At the October meeting, Ducey's colleagues asked for his impressions of the Global World Series, officially recorded thus:

> Mr. Ducey informed the meeting that the biggest upset of the series was when the Canadian team defeated the Americans. He pointed out

that the American team was a strong one and that they expected to take the Canadian team out quite handily. He felt that Zeigler had played the best game of his life that day (against the U.S.) and that it was a great thrill for all team members.

Trying again

Ducey faced the 1958 season with a mere shadow of his championship team. Before the season started, a deal was arranged to send first-baseman Ken Guffey and Mike Castanon to Williston. Fairly had not yet signed a professional contract and Ducey expected him to return. Vold signed with the Giants' organization and after working out with them in the spring, spent the early part of the season with their Triple-A club at Phoenix. Ernie Nevers, the talented Moose Jaw pitcher who had joined the Esks for the Global World Series, signed with his hometown Kansas City Athletics and was assigned to the Rochester Americans. With USC in contention for the U.S. collegiate crown, the Eskimos faced the 9 June league opener with a makeshift team that included six local players, two California junior college players, and two Portland University players. Tucker and Ducey were particularly high on home-bred Gene Kinasewich, who was given a chance to start the season at third base.

Some 3,000 fans had turned out to welcome the 1958 edition of the Eskimos, but any similarity to the 1957 club was purely coincidental. Ducey gave the fans their first glimpse of the new Eskimo uniforms, unveiled at Detroit the previous fall. But the Tucker men fell 12-9 to the newly merged Lloydminster-North Battleford Combines as the Slim Thorpe curse worked again. Ten days later, the Esks had tumbled into the league cellar and Ducey burned up the telephone lines looking for reinforcements. From Utah came outfielders Gary LaComb and Roger Tomlinson, joined by catcher Jerry Zuback from Washington. By 21 June, the USC Trojans had captured the U.S. college crown and more help was on the way. First to arrive were left-handed pitchers Bruce Gardner

Pat Gillick, flanked by Don Biasotti and Bruce Gardner, was among the USC Trojan ballplayers brought in by Ducey in 1958. Pitcher Gillick came down with a sore arm and returned home. Some thirty years later, he built the Toronto Blue Jays into World Series champions as their general manager. Courtesy of the Edmonton Archives EA 524-61.

and Pat Gillick, along with third-baseman Don Biasotti. Then came future major-leaguers shortstop Tom Satriano and hard-hitting outfielder Len Gabrielson. But the Williston Oilers now had the bulk of the USC talent, eight players led by Guffey and Castanon. Starring for the Oilers was a spectacular pitcher-outfielder named Jerry Adair, an all-American at Oklahoma State. By late June, he led the league in hitting at a .475 clip, while carrying a 2-0 pitching record.

Ron Fairly was considering a return to Edmonton, reportedly urged to do so by Rod Dedeaux of USC and the Dodgers, who were prepared to let

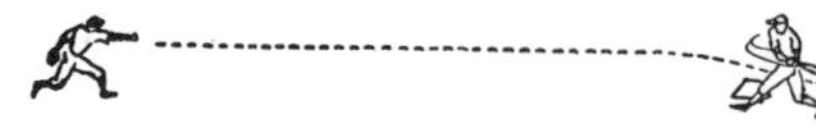

him play another year before signing him. Then a bid by the New York Yankees spurred the Dodgers to offer him a $75,000 signing bonus. Although it was lower than that offered by the Yankees, it included some attractive conditions. In the end, Fairly signed with the newly located Los Angeles Dodgers, believing he would have better chances to move up through that organization. His hunch was right. He was initially sent to Des Moines of the Class-A Western League. Before the summer was out, he joined the Los Angeles roster for the first of twelve seasons with them. Also coming up to the Dodgers late that summer, for his first of ten major-league seasons, was twenty-eight-year-old shortstop Bob Lillis, who had starred for the Eskimos in 1950.

The biggest news for Eskimo fans late that spring was once again the return of Ralph Vold, whose contract with the Giants allowed him to reject a request to move down to a Class-AA farm team. He had pitched extremely well, beating a couple of major-league clubs in the spring, but he became a victim of the economics of baseball:

> After spring training they had decided to keep five of us...Felipe Alou was one of them...and it looked like I was staying in Phoenix. Then they signed Gaylord Perry for a bonus of $100,000 and the business manager came in and talked to me. "You know, this is a tough thing, but we don't have any money in you...you're the only one like that. But if you want to go to Corpus Christi, Texas, you sure can."
>
> By then I had three small children. My wife and I spent a few days debating what to do. I was twenty-seven years old and I decided I didn't have enough time left.

Vold decided to return home to concentrate on his business in Ponoka and pitch for the Eskimos. He promptly snapped a six-game losing streak and got the Eskimos back on the winning path. Pat Gillick, who had an outstanding curve ball, paid the price for throwing too many, coming down with a severe sore arm that forced him to sit out the rest of the season.

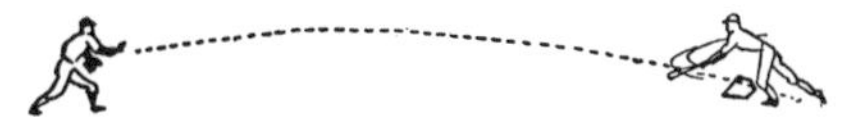

Gillick returned to Alberta the next year, pitching two seasons for the Granum White Sox in the Southern Alberta league. Fortunately for him—and eventually for the Toronto Blue Jays—he soon put his pitching days behind him. He rose through the ranks to become one of major-league baseball's most accomplished administrators: with Gillick as general manager, the Toronto Blue Jays won back-to-back World Series championships in 1992 and 1993.

In the midst of the 1958 season, Ducey was caught in a situation that seemed like a bad dream from the old WIL days. Regina owner Denny Evenson had fired manager Bob Mistele in early July and was having trouble with his players. Dissension had grown over a variety of complaints, including late paycheques. Then a blanket fine levied by Evenson, accusing his players of lax play, caused six of them and playing manager Roland Jones to quit the club. Evenson tried but could not find adequate replacements. After a frenzied series of meetings that caused league president Chuck Henderson of Edmonton no end of discomfort, Evenson decided to withdraw his team from the WCBL. Henderson and the other owners, siding with Evenson, told him he would be welcome to return in 1959. They decided to shorten the 1958 season by three games for each of the remaining teams and begin the playoffs on 12 August.

A few days later after Regina withdrew, the Moose Jaw Mallards announced they too were retiring from the league. Their tenuous financial situation had worsened significantly when Regina withdrew, leaving them with six empty playing dates. President Henderson then had no choice but to move the playoffs up further and have two lengthy, nine-game semi-final series, with Edmonton playing Lloydminster-North Battleford while Saskatoon played Williston.

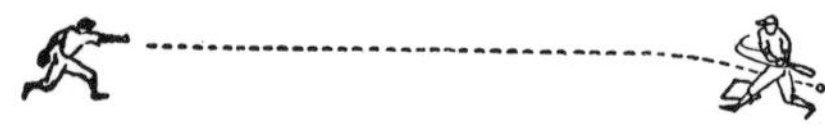

Throughout these struggles, Ducey was central to the league's survival. He counselled the other owners when they ran into trouble, nursed a succession of league presidents as they struggled with technical decisions, but above all, humoured his colleagues to keep soldiering on. Bill Hunter, a Moose Jaw club owner, described one key league meeting when Ducey and the others roared into town to save the league in 1958:

> John was a wonderful baseball man and it was always a pleasure to be around him. He provided encouragement and advice but he was also front and centre when we needed some cheering up. At this particular meeting, with the league's future in serious doubt, someone opened up a big leather case full of liquor and we partied for two straight days. The third day we sat down and settled our problems.

In early August, with the league in disarray after the withdrawal of Moose Jaw and Regina, the Eskimos found themselves again facing the Combines, this time for a lengthy, best-of-nine semi-final playoff. Fortunately, Ralph Vold had rejoined the Eskimos from Phoenix by this time. He and Bruce Gardner quickly chalked up twin victories against the Combines at Renfrew Park. But the gritty Combines battled back, and after eight games the teams were tied at four apiece. That set the stage for the ninth and final game of the series in Lloydminster. Two thousand Lloydminster fans packed Meridian Park hoping to see another Karpinski-like revenge against the haughty Eskimos in their Yankee pinstripes.

The Eskimos jumped into a three-run lead in the first. Then the Combines came right back with three in the bottom of the inning. Tucker juggled the batting order all he could but the club could not score another run. The Combines picked up a single tally in the third. Vold came in as a pinch-hitter in the seventh and lined a single. He shut out the Combines the rest of the way, but his opponent, the ageless Benny Griggs, did the same after relieving in the second inning. In the ninth, the Eskimos got two men on base with two out, but the attack sputtered to an end as LaComb grounded out. The home fans went wild in celebration. Slim Thorpe's team had knocked Ducey's big-city team out of the playoffs for the second time in three years.

It was no consolation for Ducey that the Williston Oilers, who had earlier defeated the Saskatoon Gems, went on to make short work of Thorpe's Lloydminster-North Battleford Combines. The power-packed Oilers won the series in five straight games, bringing the Western Canada League championship over to North Dakota on their first try. If Ducey needed any more bad news, it came with word that the Global World Series, which had been such a spectacular experience for Edmonton in 1957, would definitely not be held in the fall of 1958.

Upset with the precarious state of the WCBL, Ducey searched throughout the winter of 1958-59 to find a home for Edmonton in a permanent, professional league. He again went to Calgary, trying to kindle some interest, but struck out once more. It was soon clear he had no other alternative, so he began working to make the best of the WCBL in 1959. Old friend Chuck Henderson, who had his fill of problems in 1958 after taking on the presidency at Ducey's behest, was relieved to hand over the reins to Keith Erne of Regina, who became the new league commissioner. To recognize the entry of Williston, North Dakota, there was a change of name to the Canadian-American, or Can-Am, League in 1959. Moose Jaw announced it would not return. Then Regina's Denny Evenson said his club would not be back unless he could find the right person to run it.

That threat to the 1959 season led to a discussion between Ducey and Wayne Tucker, now a close friend, about the manager going to Regina to save the franchise and most probably the league. Tucker did not want to leave Edmonton:

> One of the lowest points for me was leaving Edmonton for Regina. John explained to me in detail the reasons that the league was doomed if I didn't take over in Regina. It was a big job to act as a player, manager, and general manager. I guess I did it for John rather than for the

league. The WCBL really didn't know how to appreciate him and all he did for them. He was the organization behind the league and he kept it alive.

Tucker knew that if he did not go to Regina and the league failed, he would have no future in Edmonton. In the end, the two friends agreed, and Tucker signed on as general and playing manager of the Regina Braves, allowing the league to survive another season.

With Tucker in Regina, Ducey's New York Yankee contacts led him to sign Stan Charnofsky of Los Angeles to manage the 1959 Eskimos. Charnofsky was coaching at USC during a spring exhibition game against the 1953 WIL Eskimos, so he at least knew of Edmonton's baseball reputation. Like Sturgeon and Tucker before him, Charnofsky played second base.

The end of an era

In 1959, despite that Wayne Tucker had left to shore up the Regina franchise, Ducey was soon in a better position to line up his team than he had been the season before. He had Vold back again along with Norm Forsythe returning from Loyola for a second season, and by opening day, he had eight USC ballplayers on the team, including Tom Satriano, Len Gabrielson, and John Werhas, all future major-leaguers.

Ducey even got cooperation from the weatherman on opening night as the arch-rival Combines came to town. The now-bitter opponents drew an evening crowd of 3,767 fans, 1,200 above the previous year. With Charnofsky in command, Forsythe and Werhas back with the Eskimos for another year, the omens looked good. The Loyal Edmonton Regiment Band brightened up the festivities and the fans-of-the-year, Mrs. Annie Tyson and Don Cameron, handled the ceremonial duties from their first-base box. On the field, the Eskimos, with Norm Forsythe pitching nine strong innings, ran over the Combines 12-3, sending the fans home in a happy mood.

The clubs were evenly matched in 1959, which made for entertaining baseball. Edmonton fans enjoyed the performance and hustle of players like Vold, Forsythe, Gabrielson, Satriano, and Werhas. When the Combines came to town, Don Buford in centre field provided the excitement, along with a couple of USC team-mates. Pete Estrada of Saskatoon produced the Commodore punch, while Tucker's Senators offered hard-hitting veteran Cliff Pemberton in combination with Bruce Gardner to please the fans. Even Williston, who had tumbled into last place, played exciting baseball with centre-fielder Bill Lynn replacing Jerry Adair as the league's leading hitter. Adair had already begun a nine-season career with the Baltimore Orioles.

Things were going so well that to stir the pot a bit, Ducey enticed the Calgary Dodgers of the Southern Alberta league to meet the Eskimos in a three-game exhibition series. League rules allowed four such matches during the season. Talk of a post-season playoff between the two teams soon faded after Calgary took the rubber match of the intensely fought series 5-4. That caused Ducey no end of distress because he had labeled the Southern Alberta Baseball league as "bush" and said it couldn't hold a candle to the Can-Am league brand of baseball. Still, he was right in one respect. The fans packed Renfrew Park to watch the old Edmonton-Calgary rivalry.

Growing concern

By the time the last two weeks of the season rolled around, the Eskimos and Combines were locked in a see-saw battle for the league lead. Slim Thorpe was boasting about overtaking the Esks during the six games left between the two contending clubs. Ducey was now more concerned about the financial health of his baseball club. After five years of lack-

luster financial performance, despite an entertaining brand of baseball, the directors were increasingly uneasy. As a result, Brant Matthews and Cecil Ross were carrying most of the losses. The Eskimos split two games with Saskatoon, then beat Williston twice. That set the stage for hand-to-hand combat with the Combines, and the two clubs split a two-game series, allowing the Eskimos to come home for a two-day rest with a share of first place.

All was in readiness at Renfrew for the start of the final five-game series between the two deadlocked clubs. It was "Booster Night," with a raft of lucky number prizes awarded—everything from new aluminum doors to a springer spaniel pup—preceded by a three-inning exhibition game between the Edmonton Oldtimers and a similar squad from Morinville. In an effort to bring out larger crowds, Ducey issued a press release saying that a good turnout at the gate as a result of advance publicity could set the Eskimo organization on the road to a new, professional league in 1960:

> I know nothing would please you men more than were we able to bring a high calibre of organized professional baseball to Edmonton. We have tried diligently to accomplish this in the face of many difficulties, odds and problems. We have not yet succeeded in placing Edmonton in a league that we all know must be comprised of prominent cities, in order to draw the attendance needed for a higher classification of professional baseball.

It was a call of some desperation as he ended by saying that if large crowds did turn out for the two games, it could be "the specific and deciding factor in advancing to an alignment of league we have sought for 15 years." It was not to be. The weather intervened and Friday's game was rained out. On a cool, damp Saturday, only 667 fans turned out for the afternoon match, although 1,862 attended that evening; the Esks won both games. The next day in Lloydminster, 1,330 fans watched a Sunday

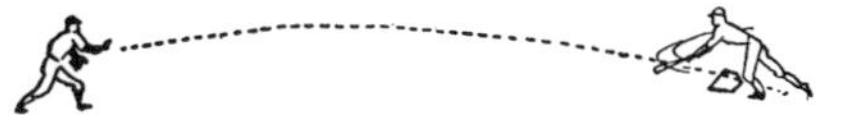

double-header as USC's Jim Withers responded with a three-hit shutout, clinching the pennant for the Eskimos. Ducey could finally relax a bit. It was about the best gift he could ask for on the eve of his fifty-first birthday. The Combines salvaged the final game but it meant nothing, and the Eskimos were happy to get on the bus and out of town, their minds already on the semi-final series against Saskatoon.

In Edmonton, Ducey re-scheduled "Booster Night," which had earlier been rained out, to open the playoffs. The evening was so chilly that the Saskatoon relief corps started a small bonfire in the Renfrew bullpen to keep warm. But warmed by hot coffee peddled by the concessionaires and the odor of rum wafting through the stands, the 1,850 fans present had a merry time, watching some of their former heroes of past seasons perform in a three-inning Oldtimers exhibition match against Morinville. Tommy Brant and Hal Callihan combined for an 8-0 win against Morinville, with Des O'Connor bashing a bases-loaded triple to left field. The colourful George Green was the home plate umpire, giving the fans a chance to warm their lungs at his antics behind home plate. It brought back fun-filled memories from the early days of Renfrew's twenty-six-year history.

This night, third baseman John Werhas was the fans' choice for the Sharp-McNeill trophy as Edmonton's most valuable player for 1959. Werhas, who would go on to a fine career in the Pacific Coast League and play in eighty-nine major-league games with the Dodgers and the Los Angeles Angels, responded by clubbing a double and a home run. Jim Sims kept the Commodores in check, allowing one run in the ninth as the Eskimos hung on to take a 3-1 win. It was the last look Edmonton fans had at big Len Gabrielson. He had to leave for home the next morning to undergo a tonsillectomy before enrolling at USC and had already signed an $80,000 bonus with the Milwaukee Braves. Gabrielson would play with Milwaukee part of the next season, spend two years in the minors, then return to enjoy another seven years in the major leagues.

Edmonton went on to Saskatoon and swept the series in four games. In Lloydminster, Tucker's Regina Senators went up three wins to none, lost

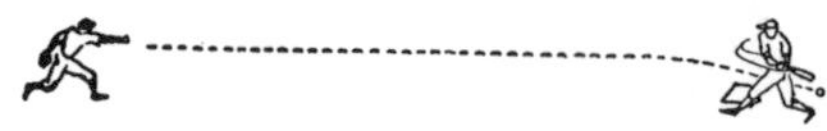

the next game, then moved into the finals by clubbing Lloydminster 9-0. Ducey was greatly relieved that Lloydminster had been put away. He was also pleased his club would be meeting Tucker's team for the league championship.

Cool weather for the opening game of the best-of-five finals drew a disappointing Labour Day afternoon crowd of only 1,300 into Renfrew Park. Many fans preferred to stay at home and keep warm in front of their television sets, watching the football Eskimos defeat Calgary 16-10 down south. It was a reminder to Ducey how much the sports business had changed. When he had taken over Renfrew in 1946, there had been no television, no football, no stock car racing, and no professional wrestling. Now he was competing against all of these for a share of the entertainment dollar, with television giving Edmontonians an even wider choice, particularly on chilly days and nights.

The baseball he offered was every bit as good as it had been in earlier years, and the fans who stayed home that Labour Day missed another fine pitching performance by Norm Forsythe, who chalked up his sixteenth win with an eleven-inning, 3-2 squeaker over Regina. But by then, both clubs were suffering from the annual fall flight of U.S. college players. Forsythe and Werhas left after the game, while Jim Sims and Roland Jones were to leave following the next night's game. In an effort to plug the hole left by Gabrielson, Ducey had picked up another USC ball player, Don Buford from Lloydminster. A few days later, he was joined by team-mate Monte Bond, as the Eskimo roster dwindled to twelve players.

Tuesday night, the temperature was near freezing and only 713 shivering fans watched the Eskimos come from behind to win another thriller. Tucker had the brilliant Bruce Gardner on the hill the next night, and he shut down his former club with a no-hitter through seven innings. His mates backed him up by blasting out twenty hits, which, helped by seven errors courtesy of the collapsing Esks, gave him a 16-3 victory on three hits. Ducey was getting that old sinking feeling again.

Tucker now had some hope that he could even the series and called upon his other former Eskimo ace, Blaine Sylvester. The hope died quickly. Home runs by Don Buford, Stan Charnofsky, and Monte Bond allowed the Eskimos to score seven runs in the first inning. By the time it was over, Ducey and Brant Matthews had their third playoff crown in five years with a 14-4 rout of the Senators. Most fitting of all, perhaps, was that the final outs were credited to Ralph Vold, who came in to relieve in the seventh. "Big Whitey" had been magnificent for the Eskimos over the past four seasons, the major contributor to their successes. As he walked off the mound the night of 10 September to an admiring throng, no one could guess that he would be the last of Ducey's Edmonton Eskimos.

20

Searching for a solution

THE AMERICAN MEMBERS OF THE TEAM WERE HEADED STATESIDE A DAY AFTER THE CHARTERED BUS BROUGHT THEM BACK TO EDMONTON. Ducey had to concede that, although the U.S. college ball players provided hustling entertainment, their early fall exodus back to campus had reached the breaking point. A rush of player replacements for the playoffs cheapened the final product. Cutting the league short by two weeks would not help either, as that would not provide enough home dates to make up most of the airfare expenses, let alone turn a profit. He would have to find a more successful baseball combination for the 1960s. "We just cannot go on the way we have," Ducey said. "We've got to be realistic about things." Don Fleming suggested that the

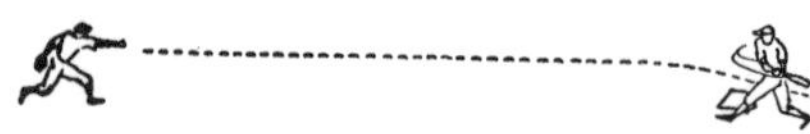

scheduled league meeting a month hence would see a realignment with clubs in the Southern Alberta League for 1960. Lethbridge had defeated the Calgary Dodgers to win the league finals. Ducey felt that the time was ripe for a league made up of Edmonton, Regina, Saskatoon, Calgary, Lethbridge, and Medicine Hat.

As he began to focus his proposed new league, Ducey also addressed his needs at home. The key to improved financial performance would be restoration to the ball club of the food and drink concessions, operated by the city since 1956. He also negotiated with the city for the addition of 180 new box seats down first base and the provision of additional parking on Renfrew's east side. Today these items are critical for successful baseball operation; however, the city turned down his request in a letter from commissioner J. M. Tweddle:

> The commissioners are of the opinion that it would be unlikely that a profitable operation could be conducted under the present circumstances. The lack of adequate capital and a suitable loop in which to play present major obstacles.

Ducey couldn't argue about the last two points. Writing to the thirty-five existing shareholders of the ball club for a $100 contribution to liquidate the 1958 club deficit, Ducey said, "Judging from present indications, it may well be that our darkest days of baseball promotion are about over." But they were not.

Brant Matthews—an unsustainable loss

In late September 1959, the often-ailing Brant Matthews died suddenly. A pioneer Edmonton hotelier, the shy but generous man had loved baseball. He was content to stand off to the side and help in a quiet but major way to see Ducey's dreams for Edmonton baseball realized. He poured a small fortune into the Edmonton baseball club but shunned any recognition for his efforts; joined in later years by lumber magnate Cecil Ross, he was Ducey's financial "angel." Brian O'Hanlon was one of the many who admired Matthews:

> It amazed me how Brant always came through for the ball club. He was always there. Personally, I seldom saw him when I was working at the park. However, the talks I had with him were often more concerned with finance in general rather than with the ballclub. Shy would be a good description of him. He certainly didn't like the spotlight.

In terms of monetary help and moral support, Matthews stuck it through with Ducey from 1946-59, providing financial continuity and serving as a civic-minded example for the other shareholders. At his death, the Edmonton Baseball Club (1955) Ltd. owed him more than $20,000, which he had advanced to cover deficits over the 1955-59 period. In total during the 1950s, the Edmonton club had lost some $130,000. This was very big money in those days, and the largest chunk of it had been made up by Matthews.

In the late fall, Ducey again had to ask the shareholders for money to cover outstanding debts and bankroll operations for 1960. With the support of Saskatoon and Regina, his proposed six-team league looked promising. The southern Alberta clubs, Calgary, Medicine Hat and Lethbridge, felt they could be ready join in for the 1960 season. Ducey saw it as the ideal alignment: competitive cities with low travel costs. Several shareholders responded with financial pledges to cover the losses and field a team for 1960. Without Matthews, however, Ducey had no solid financial foundation. It became clear that he could not raise enough money from the other shareholders to operate in 1960. He was close to his vision of a solid, low-expense league, with the long-sought Edmonton-Calgary alignment. But the time was not right and the money had run out. The Rajah of Renfrew had fielded his last ball club.

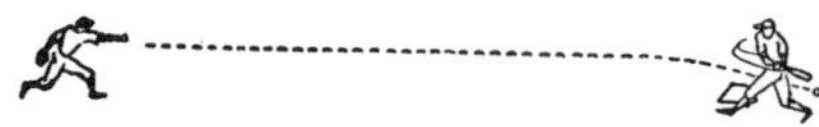

Ducey had scraped along with little personal reward from baseball other than his love of the game. He was recognized in baseball circles as a knowledgeable, first-class administrator, and was on a first-name basis with several big-league general managers, well tied into their scouting networks. For fourteen seasons, he gave Edmonton's loyal circle of regular fans high-calibre baseball, always professionally presented. He had also wrung a considerable amount of money out of Edmonton City Hall to improve the aging Renfrew Park and keep it in the best possible shape. Yet the leagues he was in kept collapsing around him, plagued by distance and poor weather. He had to face the fact that it was time to prepare for the future. At age fifty-one, he had nothing in the bank and his insurance business had been neglected for years. O'Hanlon observed, "He was such a likeable person and a good salesman, I think he really could have done extremely well financially in his insurance business if he had spent the time at it."

Ducey continued to talk about the possibility of a new league, but by the end of January 1960, it was clear that Calgary efforts to finance a new club had failed. Although Don Fleming didn't want to write the story, Ducey finally had to admit publicly that he would not be presenting baseball at Renfrew Park in 1960. The inability of Calgary to develop a solid franchise and the steady financial drain were the main factors in his decision:

> The failure of Calgary to respond, leaves us with no justification to continue any further baseball efforts in Edmonton. The Edmonton Baseball Club, at a heavy financial loss, has carried on the baseball program under difficult conditions, mainly, through the absence of Calgary, our sister city. The traditional rivalry existing between the two cities was always a needed and healthy situation, regardless of the spectator sport involved. Geographically, Calgary is also vital to Edmonton for any future, successful baseball participation, and vice versa.
>
> I have always maintained that Calgary is a good sports city, given good administration of sport, and that other commodity so vital today, first

> class facilities for the fans and the teams. People come to where they are invited and return where they are well accommodated.
>
> There is no further point in urging, coaxing or courting Calgary into the proposed 1960 Western Canada Baseball League. A city must want to be a member of a league, regardless of the sport involved. There is no such thing as civic duty in sport, but there is the matter of civic pride.

He stressed that it was the absence of a dedicated full-time baseball administrator and the failure to provide first-class playing and fan facilities that hurt baseball in the southern city. "Calgary is a good sports city and has excellent potential for baseball if these requirements are met," he added. Despite the efforts of several people, they were not and while Calgary had success with hockey and football in the 1950s, its baseball fortunes languished during Ducey's time.

Boosting baseball

Over the next two years, there was talk of Edmonton and Calgary receiving a bid from the Pacific Coast League, providing Calgary could obtain the proper facilities. Ducey consulted closely with Dewey Soriano, by then PCL president, about the requirements both cities would need to enter an expanded Pacific Coast League. Edmonton could more than hold its own in drawing the fans in that league, Ducey said, providing a full set of attendance statistics to back up his claim. Once again nothing came of it. The PCL was pre-occupied with the possibility of further major-league expansion on the west coast and could not consider northern expansion until the situation cleared.

Ducey continued his quest. He maintained that the city would be ripe for a return to organized baseball once legalized Sunday sport and new park facilities were realized. In 1962, he got the chambers of commerce in Edmonton and Calgary to join forces with him in promoting the potential of

both cities to people from the major leagues. He offered four different league possibilities, from an alignment with the northern cities in the Pacific Coast League, to an inter-city rookie league embracing two clubs made up of "outstanding U.S. college players" in both Calgary and Edmonton. He sent his detailed proposal to the offices of all major-league owners, the commissioner of baseball, and the two major-league presidents. He got encouraging responses from thirteen major-league clubs and another dozen baseball administrators on his proposal for a college league, but none were in a position to offer support until the demand for another such league could be settled. A question of sufficient talent and the decline in working agreements between major-league clubs and minor-league franchises prevented such an eventuality occurring in western Canada in the 1960s.

In 1966, Ducey actively promoted domed stadiums for Edmonton and Calgary after the province turned down a city request for financial aid to build a new coliseum. Eyeing the growing oil revenues held by the provincial government, he sent a needling message to Alberta's politicians:

> Sport is a very important aspect of our western culture, every bit as much as are the arts, which have been endowed with the Jubilee auditoriums by our provincial government. Now that the arts have been properly taken care of, it's time to present the people of southern and northern Alberta with sports complexes.

Ducey felt such a facility could be built then for half the $31 million cost of the Houston Astrodome. He proposed the domed stadiums be part of new convention centres and offer facilities for baseball, football, and hockey. Edmonton city council struggled with the idea of an omniplex for the next three years, but the concept finally died over concerns about infrastructure costs.

In the mid-1970s, Ducey was named to a civic committee to examine the design for a new stadium to be built for the 1978 Commonwealth Games. He quickly found a baseball ally in alderman Ron Hayter:

John and I had discussed the possibility of a new ball park for many years. During our deliberations on Commonwealth Stadium, there was a suggestion from him that the stadium should be made large enough to accommodate baseball. I supported him. We had quite a debate about that, but the idea was shot down. One of the other members said there was no way we would ever have professional baseball back in Edmonton... that anybody who suggested the idea was dreaming.

It would have cost us about a million dollars more to make the stadium large enough for baseball. The idea went to a vote and the vote was three to two not to make it large enough for baseball. Now, looking back, John Ducey was right and those people who didn't have his vision were wrong.

Fighting the Lord's Day Act

Ducey maintained that a new baseball facility for Edmonton was only one key to its return to organized baseball. Another was legalized Sunday baseball, which drew a good deal of his attention. Ever since he had umpired his first baseball game at Diamond Park in 1931, the federal *Lord's Day Act* had galled him. Brought up in a strongly religious home, he willingly gave the church the first part of every Sunday. He accepted the provision that such events could not continue beyond 6:00 p.m. but took issue with the decree that Sunday sporting attractions could not charge a set price. Sunday afternoons had always been the best time for baseball in Edmonton, especially during the war years, when gasoline rationing restricted travel to the local lakes. The *Lord's Day Act* was extremely costly when Edmonton was in the WIL because silver collections didn't pay enough to meet the expenses of presenting professional ball. While Saskatoon owner Spero Leakos and some of his players were served with a court summons for charging Sunday ticket prices in the late 1950s, Ducey could only stand by in frustration at the meagre offerings some fans threw into the silver collections on Sunday afternoons.

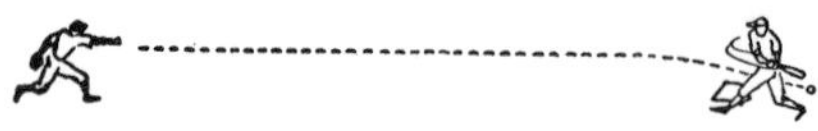

He never missed an opportunity to remind the provincial legislature that it was within its power to provide relief from the restrictions imposed by the 1907 law. By 1964, sensing public support for such a change, Ducey began lobbying the provincial government and the City of Edmonton for an easing of the restrictions. He pointed out that from 1946-59, Sunday silver collections at Renfrew Park averaged only 36¢ per head. (Frustrated by this, a club director had once suggested putting up a sign on the collection tables saying, "We think this game is worth $1.00 What do you think?") Ducey said even that amount was the result of a weekly struggle by his loyal staff, who manned the collection tables and tried to intimidate the more obvious "cheapskates."

He explained that while amateur sports leagues could survive on Sunday collections because of low overhead costs, professional sports, with high salary and travel costs, could not. He pressed for "Sunday legalized sport" between the hours of 1:30 and 5:55 p.m. at the very least, if organized baseball was ever to return to Edmonton and Calgary. He could not understand why the Edmonton Zoo could operate Sunday afternoons "as spectator entertainment at a direct charge of $1.00 for adults, 50¢ for children" while Renfrew Park could not do the same.

City council eventually agreed with him and put Sunday sports on a plebiscite in October 1964. The electorate voted 52,000 to 30,000 in favour of it. In Calgary, 20,000 people signed a petition to the same effect. The City of Edmonton then put the question to the provincial government, but the Social Credit party, with strong rural support, was not ready to give in to the urban centres. To them, the issue was much broader than Sunday sport. Amendments to the federal act could open up the frightening possibility of Sunday shopping.

The argument reached the floor of the Alberta legislature and Ducey sat in on the debate. One government member said opening up Sunday would be a "real attack on the moral fibre of our nation." While denying that it was a religious issue, Premier Ernest Manning was staunchly

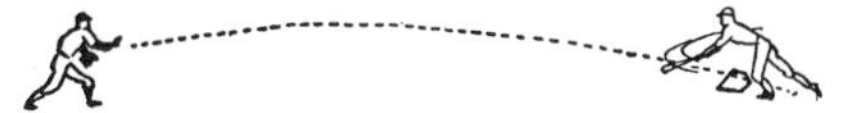

opposed to Sunday sport because it would open the day to encroaching commercialism:

> In my view, it is not wise to take any step toward the commercialization of Sunday beyond what it is today. A society that abandons its respect for the sanctity of the day of worship hastens the trend to ever-increasing commercialism. Rome deteriorated from the inside.

To Don Fleming, it seemed clear that commercial Sunday sport would not come to Alberta without a change of government and he jeered at the Social Credit position:

> It won't be probable as long as Manning and The Sing-Along Gang over at the big house howl an over-powering chorus of "Never on Sunday." The point being how can triple-A players clean their uniforms with the laundromats shut down, so the machines can go to church on the Sabbath?

Ducey pointed out that by 1965, only three cities in North America with populations over 200,000 did not allow "legalized Sunday sport": Edmonton, Calgary, and Ottawa. The issue grew embarrassing to the Social Credit government because they had allowed exceptions for symphony concerts and civic zoos. Ducey worked closely on the issue with an opposition member of the legislature, William Dickie, a Calgary Liberal. Dickie lobbied the point for almost two years. In the dying days of the legislative session in April 1965, with the Premier away in the East, Dickie secured support from government backbenchers to vote in favour of a provincial *Lord's Day Act*. While the word "sport" was never mentioned, the 1966 throne speech said the government would deal with the matter. It did, and the *Alberta Lord's Day Act* was proclaimed during the 1966 session. Municipalities were allowed to approve commercial sports on

Sundays with the exception of horse races, dog races, boxing, and wrestling.

Edmonton soon put the question on a plebiscite, asking voters if they approved "allowing certain public games, contests or sports at which a fee is charged on Sunday afternoons between the hours of half past one and six o'clock." The voters said yes by a margin of 93,310 to 25,258. A bylaw to that effect was passed by city council on 15 November 1966. For the first time since Deacon White had fielded an Edmonton team in 1907, baseball, hockey, and football promoters could charge admission on Sunday afternoons. It was too late for Ducey to turn it into anything other than a moral victory, but he continued to stress that legalized Sunday sport was a necessary step if professional baseball was ever to return to Edmonton. Ironically, the federal *Lord's Day Act* was repealed in 1985 after the Supreme Court of Canada found it offended the new *Canadian Charter of Rights and Freedoms*, on the basis that the purpose of the act had been the compulsion of religious observance.

The changing world of minor-league baseball

Back in 1953, as he turned the presidency of the Western International League over to Bob Brown of Vancouver, outgoing president Robert Abel had one major warning for his successor:

> Television will be a major headache in the future. The problem won't arise tomorrow, or even the next day, but it's coming and it is so great that the time to start heading it off is now! It is our job to get the youngsters outside again, where they can begin throwing baseballs shortly after they start walking.

It had been Ducey's first meeting as a WIL director, and he and his colleagues had differing views about the effect television would have on baseball. Abel was slightly off the mark, but he was right in one respect.

Television, and many other new leisure opportunities, had a deleterious effect on professional sports below the major-league level. Fans who in 1945 had little else to do but attend a ball game at Renfrew Park on a Sunday afternoon had a far greater range of options competing for their time by 1955. The proliferation of paved highways, for example, put all North Americans within easy reach of virtually any place on the continent. By the early 1960s, the conversion to jet aircraft hugely magnified the range of holiday travel for those with growing leisure time. Ducey himself became one of these, regularly travelling to Phoenix to watch the spring training of the San Francisco Giants.

Major-league baseball, which had expanded partly due to the growth in television markets, was soon joined by the sudden rise in popularity of the National Football League and its subsequent growth. Expansion of the six-team National Hockey League, a fixture of the age of radio for decades, was also stimulated by the arrival of network television. Golf, tennis, skiing, and dozens of other participant sports exploded in the 1960s as physical fitness became a personal concern. Suddenly semi-pro and minor-league baseball were not the only summer game in town. The school yards and sandlots that had been developing baseball talent since the start of the twentieth century stood almost empty of scrub teams and youngsters yearning to get in the game.

Just as shifting public attitudes and changing political mores had swept away the restrictions of Sunday sports in Alberta, communications and single-participant pastimes steamrollered over local baseball nines almost everywhere. Baseball's innocence and its "Golden Age" were passing, giving way to major-league access and highly paid professionalism. While many Canadians were becoming more active in their leisure time, most had become sports observers, not participants. Big-league baseball, hockey, and football became free home entertainment.

The situation was the same across the continent, observes Robert Objoski in *Bush League*, his book on minor-league baseball. The minor leagues experienced significant growth in the post-World War Two period,

achieving a peak attendance of 41,872,762 in 1949. Attendance took a huge drop to some 34 million in 1950, and by 1960 had declined to 10,974,084. Television was largely to blame, Objoski writes:

> In 1949, when the minor leagues reached their peak, there were 59 leagues with 464 teams in as many cities.... By 1950, televised big-league games had become an important factor across the baseball spectrum and had begun to pull fans away from minor-league parks in alarming numbers.

Between 1952 and 1962, 300 cities lost their minor-league teams. By 1963, the number of leagues had dropped to eighteen. They stabilized at that level, partly due to various major-league stabilization funds, which provided financial support to designated minor leagues.

The changes sweeping across the baseball landscape hurt Ducey's success in his later years as he grappled with the growing costs of offering professional-level baseball to a declining share of the sports-revenue base. In the end, it was more than distance and weather that conspired to beat him. His time as a local sports promoter had spanned the better part of two decades of rapid social and economic change. Then his time, and the money, simply ran out.

Changing circumstances made it impossible for him to make enough money to put on the kind of baseball he wanted to present in far-off Edmonton. Competition for the sporting dollar had changed baseball at his level forever. Before the end came, he realized that to mount a competitive sports product required financial support from the major leagues. They, in turn, had been slow to respond, until they saw the minor leagues dying all around them. He spoke about that in 1964:

> From 1952 to 1959 it cost my colleagues and myself approximately $150,000 to promote the game in Edmonton. We won't play any more benefits for the major leagues.

He meant that local leagues such as his could not continue to develop players without some kind of return or subsidy. Nine of his college ballplayers from the 1957 WCL Eskimos went on to sign $405,000 worth of bonuses with major-league organizations the next year. By the time the Can-Am league disbanded in 1959, sixty-seven of its players had signed with major-league organizations over a five-year period; at least thirteen made it to the big leagues. As much as he took public pride in these numbers, Ducey and his colleagues received no financial help or compensation for the development of these players.

This led Ducey to conclude that organized baseball could only survive at his level if the clubs had arrangements under which the majors would provide managers and players, and pay their salaries, training costs, and travel to and from the local clubs. The clubs would be responsible for the balance of operational costs, administration, and travel. This is largely how a much smaller minor-league baseball system survives today. It is also the kind of arrangement that helped bring professional baseball back to Edmonton in the 1980s, twenty years after Ducey was forced to give up.

While he believed such an arrangement might occur as early as 1964, it did not. However, Ron Hayter credits Ducey for keeping Edmonton's baseball hopes alive until Mel Kowalchuk and Peter Pocklington brought the Pacific Coast League there in 1981:

> John always maintained that we would eventually get Triple-A baseball and some people used to laugh at him. But he was a visionary, he was a person who saw what other people didn't see.
>
> He was always pushing baseball and he kept his name before the public long after he was officially out of baseball. He was known as

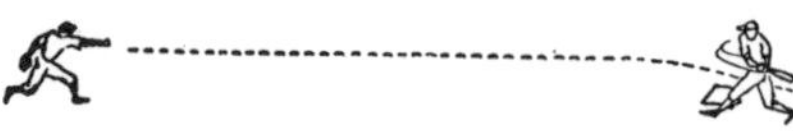

> "Edmonton's Mr. Baseball," and we certainly accepted him as such. He was the person who maintained a strong baseball presence in Edmonton through the lean years, as well as the good years. He lived and breathed baseball...he coached teams, he organized leagues and he kept Edmonton's name in the minds of those in organized baseball. All of this created a foundation for what Edmonton has today...triple-A baseball.

Ducey maintained his links with organized baseball but turned his attention to earning a living as a full-time property insurance agent and commercial real estate broker. He took fierce pride in his former players, staying in contact with them; he could cite batting averages and won-lost records of all those who went on in organized baseball. He stayed in touch with his team managers, Morris, Sturgeon, and Tucker, as he did with life-long friends like Reardon, Herman, and Eddie Shore.

Ducey maintained a large personal baseball network of fans, players, umpires, scouts, and administrators. His memory and his love of both hockey and baseball made him a popular source among several generations of sports reporters in Edmonton and Alberta. This networking made him a catalyst for one of his most enduring and unique efforts, the formation of the Edmonton Oldtimers Baseball Association in 1964.

21

Heading for home

Baseball is a storyteller's sport.

Whenever baseball people get together, they tell baseball stories. If a person has a good memory and years of experience in the game, as John Ducey did, he is usually a good storyteller. Ducey listened to and learned from some of the best in the business, including such men as Lefty Gomez, with whom he often socialized through the years. At Cooperstown one evening, Ducey listened to Casey Stengel spinning yarns to a small group of fascinated hangers-on. Ducey's close friendships with Beans Reardon and Babe Herman also added to his lore, as did the many major-league scouts he met with frequently. He also read everything that he could get his hands on about baseball.

His memory, which held a vast lexicon of statistics, also housed an immense supply of stories about baseball and, to a lesser extent, hockey. Most were original and came from experience. He had a sense of the per-

Ducey with his umpiring mentor, John E. "Beans" Reardon in 1955. Courtesy of the Edmonton Archives EA 524-63.

former's art and could embellish any tale with timing, emphasis, and a range of dialects. The Saturday night parties with a small nucleus of close friends were regular storytelling occasions. Wives were left in the living room. The men gravitated to the kitchen, to be close to the liquor and mix, and to tell stories, each trying to best the other.

During the week, there were frequent encounters with Edmonton's oldtimers on city streets and in coffee shops along Jasper Avenue. There were visits with and calls to his friends of press and radio, and later television. Ducey always had fresh news or a story for anyone who would listen, and they in turn had stories for him. By the early 1960s, having lived

In the mid-1960s, Ducey joined the CBC's Glen Bjarnsson to host a popular World Series "warmup" show for Edmonton television viewers. Courtesy of the Edmonton Archives EA 524-64.

through fifty years of Edmonton's growth, he knew much about the city, its pioneer citizens, and its history. Although he was a prolific letter-writer, his handwriting had been awful since a third-grade penmanship teacher forced him to write with his right hand. After retiring from baseball, he used a portable typewriter to stay in touch with a wide circle of friends and baseball acquaintances. His letters were normally two type-written pages, banged out using the two-finger method learned in his early sports-writing jobs. In the mid-1960s, Christmas cards he received from contacts in major-league baseball alone averaged some forty per year, all of which would receive a written reply.

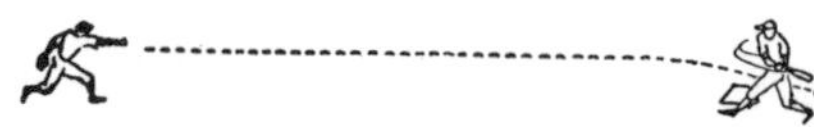

His penchant for writing and storytelling, a lifetime of memories, and a passionate love of baseball led him to wed these elements in a final but long-lasting venture. He had learned of a new kind of baseball organization in some parts of the United States, known as oldtimers baseball associations. Made up of former baseball men who had reached the age of fifty or sixty, they were located in several major-league cities. Some, such as the "Pitch and Hit Club" in Chicago and the "Oldtimers Club" in Cleveland, Ohio, had more than a thousand members. Why not, he wondered, start one in Edmonton? Why not indeed? Edmonton was rich in baseball heritage and he had been part of it for some forty years. If an oldtimers association would work in a big-league city, it could work in Edmonton.

The Edmonton Oldtimers Baseball Association

Ducey received enthusiastic support for the idea. By mid-1964, a plan was hatched; membership requirements, guidelines, and goals were sketched out. The group would be called "The Edmonton Oldtimers Baseball Association," its aims "to foster and maintain a true feeling of sportsmanship, good will and fraternal association among its members." Further, they strove "to perpetuate and to honour the memory of Mr. William Freemont 'Deacon' White, a beloved man who was truly 'Mr. Baseball,' not only in Edmonton but throughout Western Canada from 1906 to 1930."

The initial executive was led by Phil Horn as the first president and the Hon. Justice Hugh John MacDonald as honourary president. Others included Laurel Harney, Louis Podersky, George Mackintosh, Ed McHugh, Norman Dodge, Ken Samis, and Ducey himself. They set the minimum age at fifty and assembled a list of men who had "participated in Edmonton's long baseball history." The role was not that important. Initially, they listed the categories of player, team manager, coach, umpire, trainer, general manager, club president, secretary, treasurer,

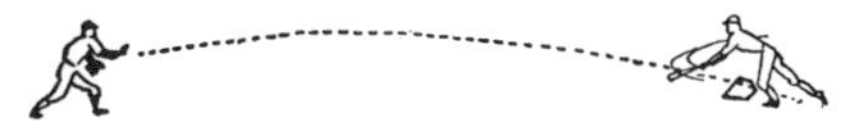

club doctor, team sponsor, league president, and official scorer; membership would eventually be expanded to include just about anyone who participated in baseball in or around Edmonton. It now includes former ballboys, batboys, and even ball park groundskeepers. With time taking a toll on older members, the minimum age today is forty. But the basic requirement remains the same: a love of baseball, along with some association with it in the Edmonton or northern Alberta area. More than 30 years after its founding, it remains a unique organization in Canada with 180 members.

Ducey took on the combined roles of historian and newsletter editor, a job that allowed him to compile and dispense a steady stream of anecdotes about Edmonton's baseball history for almost two decades. The group planned to have four meetings yearly, but eventually held a business meeting in the fall and a social meeting in the spring. In 1964, Ducey simply hoped the first meeting in October would be "an interesting affair and that it could grow into a good group." He and his colleagues compiled a list of forty members, thirty-three of whom attended the first general meeting. The 1963 World Series film was the major attraction, but just as *being there* was important at Renfrew and Diamond parks in the old days, *being there* to swap baseball yarns and visit with old friends was the reason to join the new organization.

Within two years, membership reached 160. Ducey's newsletters, filled with anecdotes and activities of existing members, and sketches of new members, were running a solid five-and-a-half pages. (In recent years that chore has been ably handled by the Hon. Justice Allan Wachowich. Sprinkled with other Edmonton sports highlights, the "letter" now runs some twenty pages—proof that the Oldtimers are still swapping stories and exchanging information.) In 1964, lifetime honourary memberships were given to Henry Roche, J.C. "Chuck" Henderson, whose active Edmonton baseball roots went back to 1915, and Wilbur "Webb" King, who had played in the 1920s and 1930s. Today, lifetime plaques are awarded to members who reach age seventy-five.

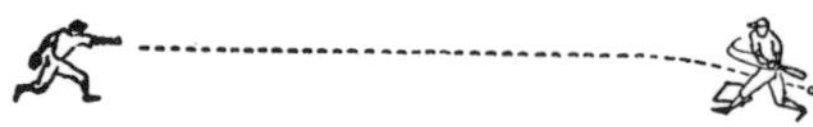

Honouring Edmonton's "King of Sports"

Soon after its founding, Ducey and the original forty members nominated "Deacon" White for membership in the Edmonton Sports Hall of Fame, based on White's contribution to Edmonton sports during his twenty-six years in Edmonton. White, who had left Edmonton more than thirty years earlier and died in 1939, was inducted into the Edmonton Sports Hall of Fame on 21 April 1965. Then Ducey began what turned into almost a two-year quest to see if a living relative could be found so that White's framed scroll could be sent to some member of his family. Working with Walter S. Campbell, an Oldtimer member and White's former Edmonton hockey partner in 1914, Ducey did some long-distance sleuthing.

He enlisted John S. Phillips, owner of the Howe News Bureau in Chicago and long the official statistician for the American League and several minor baseball leagues. Ducey had enrolled Phillips as an early member of the Edmonton Oldtimers. Phillips had handled all of Ducey's league statistics in the 1950s, and the two were good friends. All Ducey could tell Phillips was that Deacon White was born 6 December 1878 in Sheridan, Illinois, information that came from Canadian army records obtained by Henry Roche in 1940.

Phillips first asked former National League star Fred Lindstrom, then a postmaster in Evanston, Illinois, to check with White's alma mater, Northwestern University, to see if it would accept the scroll and hang it in the Athletic Department. The response was negative because White had never played for any of the university's inter-collegiate teams. Lindstrom could find no other traces of White. Phillips checked with the Illinois Bureau of Vital Statistics, the Cook County clerk's office in Chicago, and the village of Sheridan, but could find no living relatives. But from Sheridan he received details of the White family burial plot. It showed that Deacon White had been buried there 2 November 1939, alongside his parents and a sister. However, the plot had room for six graves, sug-

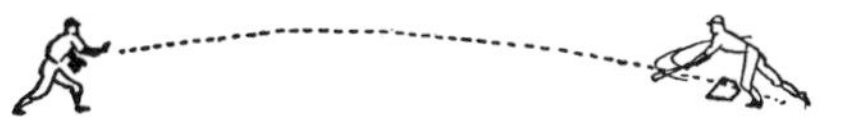

gesting that one or two members of White's family might still be living, if not buried elsewhere.

Phillips turned the information over to Ducey, who contacted the Sheridan village clerk, who had earlier been unable to help locate any of the White kin. Ducey sent him some information about Deacon White and the clerk, then eighty years of age, responded with some additional news. "I was delighted to get the paper as I have been a baseball fan for fifty years—St. Louis Cardinals," wrote T.C. Adams. Then he casually added, "we have just recently had an addition to the [burial] lot." It was the remains of White's second sister, Lou Maud White, who had died and been cremated in Chicago in September 1965.

Adams sent Ducey the burial removal certificate, which contained the name of the Chicago funeral home that dispatched the remains for internment in Sheridan. Ducey wrote them and in late November they advised him that Maud White had died at the Bethany Methodist Home in Chicago and left a sister, Ann D. White, who still resided there. She was then eighty-four years of age, frail and with fading memory, so Ducey carried on correspondence with the Home's administrator.

On 17 February 1967, with some 125 people present, a ceremony was held at the Chicago's Bethany Methodist Home. Deacon White's Sports Hall of Fame scroll from far-off Edmonton was formally presented to his last surviving sister, flanked by some of her younger relatives. Ducey arranged for Phillips and Jack Sheehan to represent the Edmonton Oldtimers Baseball Association and present the scroll to Ann White. In 1920, Sheehan, a shortstop, had been the player-manager of the Winnipeg Maroons in competition with Deacon White's Eskimos. He had just retired in January after thirty years as a major-league executive with the Washington Senators.

It had taken some two years and a volume of correspondence to bring the event about. For Ducey and his colleagues, a long-standing debt to Deacon White was finally paid, thirty-five years after his sad departure from the Alberta city. Many people still remembered his many contributions to Edmonton's sporting history.

The ceremony was heartening to the original forty oldtimers, who represented several Edmonton ballplayers from the 1920s and early 1930s. The oldest was eighty-one-year-old Harold Deeton, who had been playing baseball in Edmonton *before* Deacon White arrived in 1906. From White's era were Con Bissett, who had played before the Prince of Wales in 1919 and ended his baseball career as the president of Wayne Tucker's 1959 Regina team; Chuck Henderson, Jim Enright, and Jack Starky, who played for White in 1920; and Gordon "Deacon" Jones, who played on White's 1921 Eskimos. Others included "Cap" Speissmann, who played through three decades of senior baseball, and of course, Riley Mullen, Ducey's original team-mate and former partner. Major league sports were represented by the likes of Clarence S. Campbell, Leroy Goldsworthy, Babe Herman, Heinie Manush, and Beans Reardon.

From Edmonton teams of the late 1920s and early 1930s were Henry Roche, Webb King, Phil Horn, Norman Dodge, Clint Purvis, Reg "Pep" Moon, George Green, Bert Croft, Ed McHugh, Ken Samis, Ralph Morgan, Clayton Dolighan, John Gerlitz, and Dave Fenton. There were journalists like George Mackintosh, Ken McConnell, Stan Moher, and Bill Lewis. Trainers Cecil "Tiger" Goldstick and Doug Hardy were early members, as was team doctor C.R. "Gig" Dobson. As the Oldtimers' newsletter circulated further afield, the group's membership continued to grow, and by 1967 they were ready to hold their first annual dinner. "Uptown at the Mac" was the only place Ducey would consider. He prevailed on Beans Reardon to come from his home in Long Beach as the group's first guest speaker. Reardon would not accept a dime for his expenses and was in sparkling form, launching the Oldtimers' annual dinner as a tradition that has continued for thirty seasons.

Recognition and rewards

The organization gave Ducey great pleasure during the final two decades of his life. But other honours came his way and meant a great deal to him. In

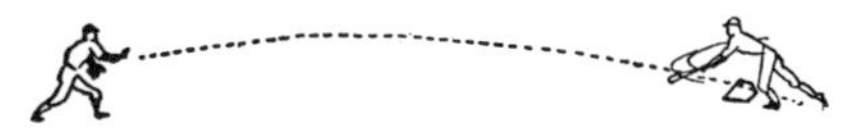

1954 and again in 1958, Don Fleming and his media colleagues arranged for Ducey to be named Edmonton's Sportsman of the Year. He was also inducted into the Edmonton Sports Hall of Fame in 1958. On Alberta's 75th anniversary in 1980, Ducey and wife Grace went to Calgary, where Ducey became a member of the Alberta Sports Hall of Fame.

Ducey struck up a friendship with Peter O'Malley in 1965 when the son of the Los Angeles Dodgers' Walter O'Malley was apprenticing as president and general manager of the Spokane Indians in the Pacific Coast league. O'Malley had heard about Ducey from Rod Dedeaux of USC. Ducey arranged to call on him during a vacation trip to the Spokane area. The two talked about the future of the PCL and the possibility of a northern alignment that would include Edmonton and Calgary. They continued to correspond over the next nine years, culminating in a gracious invitation from O'Malley that took Ducey to the 1974 World Series as a guest of the Los Angeles Dodgers. It was one of Ducey's biggest baseball thrills, for it was his first and only World Series attendance. Unfortunately, that was the Series in which the powerful Oakland A's rolled over the Dodgers in four straight games. However, it gave Ducey a chance to mingle with Reardon and other old friends in Los Angeles and the San Francisco area. O'Malley later saw to it that whenever an Los Angeles Dodgers official passed through Edmonton, a call was made on Ducey and then to Grace, after John's death.

Ducey made three memorable visits to the Baseball Hall of Fame at Cooperstown, which led him to send reference material on Deacon White's 1920-22 Eskimos to the Hall of Fame Library. He also got to several major-league parks, visiting again with Charlie Gehringer at Detroit's Tiger Stadium, with recently arrived Expo Ron Fairly at Montreal's Jarry Park, and with umpire Emmett Ashford at Boston's Fenway Park. At the 1979 All-Star Game at Seattle's Kingdome, he watched as old friend Vernon "Lefty" Gomez was honoured in pre-game ceremonies.

In April 1981, Ducey made his first official visit to Renfrew Park in many years. Organized baseball had finally returned to the city. Edmonton's

Ducey where he loved to be later in life: among Little League ball players at Edmonton's Kinsmen Park. At right is his long-time baseball colleague, Phil Horn. Courtesy of the Edmonton Archives EA 524-65.

Mel Kowalchuk and Peter Pocklington secured a Pacific Coast franchise and brought the Trappers to Renfrew Park. Ducey had not been involved, but his dream of Triple-A baseball for Edmonton had finally come true. Despite his own forecast that the weather would never let baseball open successfully in early April, luck was with the Trappers. On opening night, it was Ducey's turn to throw out the first pitch, to alderman Ron Hayter, by then one of Canada's leading amateur baseball officials.

Kowalchuk also set 31 May as "John Ducey Night" at Renfrew Park. On that occasion, with prices rolled back and tickets set at a "deuce," the Trappers and several other organizations honoured the seventy-three-year old former Rajah of Renfrew. Among the most prized gifts Ducey received that night were two-theatre style box seats behind home place with his name on the back. For the next two seasons, he and his wife took in several Trappers' games when the temperature was to his liking. "At home he falls asleep in his chair at this hour," quipped Grace. "Down here at least he stays awake." Ducey remained good "copy" for Edmonton's new breed of sports reporters, always available for comment on Edmonton's baseball history or the contemporary scene.

In his early seventies, Ducey battled several waves of classic depression. The always-gregarious Ducey was baffled by the ailment, which worked against his outgoing nature. "It got to the point where going downtown I would sit at the back of the bus, just hoping that no one would see or talk to me," he confessed. A shudder went through the Oldtimers group when he missed his first meeting because of it. He suddenly found the newsletter an onerous chore, made more difficult by having to report the passing of so many of his friends and colleagues as time took its toll. However, he fought back with the help of electro-shock therapy. After years of smoking cigars, pipes, and cigarettes, his health deteriorated markedly in 1983, forcing him to give up his duties with his beloved Oldtimers. He continued his passion for writing to those with whom he had shared so many memories, particularly Babe Herman and Beans Reardon, the latter by then incapacitated by a stroke.

Early in 1983, a group of Canadian baseball officials, several of whom were close to the Toronto Blue Jays, established the Canadian Baseball Hall of Fame in Toronto. They canvassed several baseball people across Canada, including baseball historians Bill Humber of Seneca College in Toronto and David Shury of North Battleford, to seek nominees for the first group of inductees. Shury, who for many years was the official and then the

unofficial historian of Saskatchewan baseball, insisted that Ducey be named for his contributions to the game in western Canada. Humber, who had just published his first history of Canadian baseball earlier that year, was keenly aware of Ducey's career, having interviewed him for *Cheering for the Home Team*. Their support was fortified with material supplied by Ron Hayter, who actively backed Ducey's nomination:

> If you're going to put someone forward as a Hall of Fame candidate in any sport, you have to show the commitment of that person and the contributions they made to it. Besides his active career, I mentioned all the efforts he had made on behalf of baseball in Edmonton in the 1960s and 1970s. He was a leader, he was a builder, he was a visionary. You put all those things together and you get someone who is absolutely a candidate for the Baseball Hall of Fame.

Their efforts were successful, and in March it was announced that Ducey would be among the first six Canadians to be inducted into the new Hall. "Your contributions to Canadian Baseball over your lifetime are unparalleled and it is with great appreciation for your dedication that we say 'thank you'," wrote Bruce Prentice, the Hall's president. Named with Ducey in the builders of baseball category was Frank Shaughnessy Sr., former president of the International League for some twenty-four years and a man Ducey had met with at many baseball gatherings. In the player category were James "Tip" O'Neill, of Woodstock, Ontario, who joined the St. Louis Browns in 1887; George "Twinkletoes" Selkirk, who replaced Babe Ruth in the New York Yankee outfield, playing there for the next nine years; and Phil Marchildon, a native of Penetanguishene, Ontario, whose ten-year career with the Philadelphia Athletics and the Boston Red Sox was interrupted by World War Two. Selkirk was the man who smuggled the New York Yankee baseballs across the border and mailed them to Ducey from Toronto in 1946. Marchildon was the Athletics' pitcher Ducey watched on his first visit to Fenway Park in 1942.

The sixth inductee was the late Rt. Hon. Lester B. Pearson, named in an honourary category for his lifetime support of Canadian baseball.

Ducey, still campaigning for a possible 1984 induction of Beans Reardon and Babe Herman into Cooperstown's Hall of Fame, shared his good news with them, again expressing his hope they would soon be deservedly honoured in baseball's "big Hall." Sadly, neither ever was. The lonely, disabled Reardon, whose wife replied to Ducey saying, "the only disappointment in his life that he can't get over is not being chosen for the Hall of Fame," passed away that year, hoping until the end for that elusive honour. Herman had a busy retirement and a rich family life, taking it far better when his own chance at baseball immortality at Cooperstown passed him by in 1984. He died a much happier man than Reardon, in 1987.

Despite his deteriorating condition, Ducey's spirit was buoyed by his impending honour. In August 1983, as he neared his seventy-fifth birthday, his family hoped he could make the trip to Toronto right up to departure time, although he had been in and out of the hospital several times over the summer. His illness had finally been diagnosed as emphysema, brought on by years of heavy smoking. In the end, he could not muster the strength to go to Toronto, so I went in his place. By the time I brought home his trophy, he was back in the hospital to stay. Six weeks later, on 11 September 1983, after receiving the Last Sacrament, he died in Edmonton's General Hospital, just a few blocks down the street from Grandin School, where his long baseball journey had begun. "Thank you very much for all your time," were the last, appreciative words he was able to speak to his family.

His funeral a few days later was attended by what was said to be one of the largest crowds ever seen for such services at St. Joseph's Cathedral. It was his

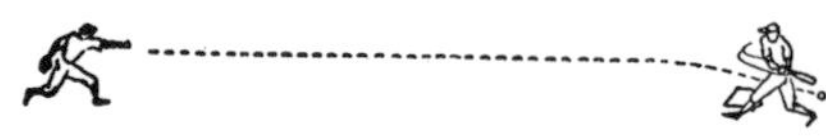

parish church, where his father had helped lay the cornerstone in 1924. The pallbearers included members of the Oldtimers Association, along with Mel Kowalchuk of the Edmonton Trappers and alderman Ron Hayter, representing the City of Edmonton. The church was packed with old friends, colleagues, and people who had known him only from afar. Monsignor Joe Malone neared the end of his eulogy with reference to his character:

> I would like to speak of his friends, but they are too many to mention here, but of enemies he had none. He never bore a grudge. He loved people. He saw good in everyone he met.

Joe then revealed that in fact, he had been one of the first to meet him—as an altar boy playing baseball for St. Anthony's parish—in the early 1920s. It happened when Ducey organized a game between "his guys" from St. Joachim's church and Stan Moher's Holy Trinity team, over on Edmonton's South Side. Discreetly, the Monsignor didn't say which team won that game.

As the service went on, that recollection by Monsignor Malone made me wonder what those days must have been like some sixty years earlier. I thought about how much the city of Edmonton had changed since that time. Ducey's early sandlot ball diamonds had been located only a few blocks from this very church. Close by, he had begun playing his first baseball with his classmates from Grandin School.

This reflection caused me to imagine that perhaps he was still somewhere close, once again organizing those baseball games among his boyhood friends. No doubt he would insist his young club be dressed "like professionals." He would be eager to take on all comers in a joyful

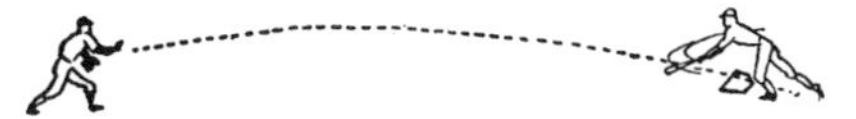

but competitive game. Now, I thought to myself, he was truly home, his long journey over. He would be in a place where the weather-gods could no longer harass him and where he could play baseball all day long, especially on Sundays...unless of course...he decided to umpire.

Epilogue

After the funeral, the pall bearers discussed the possibility of renaming Renfrew Park after John Ducey.

Edmonton city council formally named the old "park below the hill" John Ducey Park on 13 March 1984.

Built in 1933, John Ducey Park was far too small for Triple-A baseball and for a city population that had surpassed half a million. In 1992, another city council, with Hayter still on it, finally approved a proposal for a new baseball park to be built on the old Renfrew Park site. The old park would disappear, to be razed in the fall of 1994 to make way for a new, 10,000-seat facility. The cost to the city was to be $3.5 million, with an equal sum to come from the Edmonton Trappers Baseball Club, owned by Peter Pocklington and headed by Mel Kowalchuk. In the end, Pocklington spent

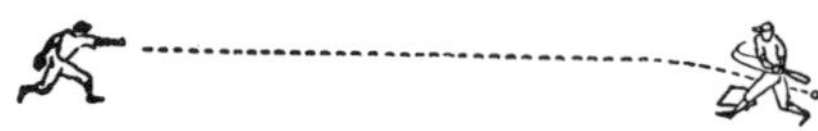

more than $6 million on the new park. The lost opportunity costs from not proceeding earlier with Ducey's baseball proposal for Commonwealth Stadium in the late 1970s were never calculated. Pocklington's PCL club and the Edmonton fans had to struggle with the old, undersized Renfrew Park facility through fourteen seasons.

In a bid to help ensure financial viability of the new park, city council traded to Pocklington the right to name the park; a caveat was that a bust of Ducey be installed in the new structure. Ducey himself would have considered that a small price to pay if it meant finally having a new ball park built for Edmonton baseball fans. "It's sad to say," he observed in 1981, "but this ball park is way below Triple-A standards. I hope I live to see the day when they build a big, brand new Renfrew."

On 28 August 1994, after the final game of the season, the Ducey family was among those who closed Renfrew Park—then John Ducey Park—forever. As he had done on that diamond when it was opened in 1933, my sister and I were asked to make one final tour around its bases to home plate. Crews began demolishing it the next day.

On 2 May 1995, Edmonton celebrated the opening of what is acknowledged to be one of the finer parks in minor-league baseball. In the first season in the then-unnamed park, Edmonton became only the second Pacific Coast League Triple-A team to surpass the 400,000 mark for attendance in the last 25 years. Fans who know about Edmonton's baseball heritage would not have been surprised by that achievement. Now called Telus Field after a corporate sponsor, the park contains a bronze bust of "John Ducey, Edmonton's Mr. Baseball." On the field, the Trappers responded to their new surroundings by winning their second and third

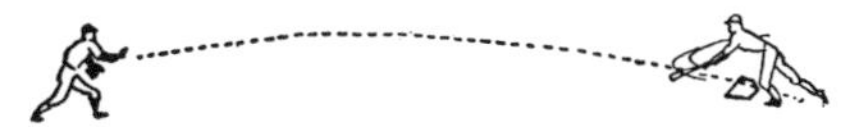

Pacific Coast League championships in 1996 and 1997, adding to the single title they had won in old John Ducey Park in 1984.

In October 1997, just two months before her own death, Grace Ducey returned to the ballpark for the last time. With members of the Oldtimers Baseball Association and Trappers' president Mel Kowalchuk taking part, she watched with pride as the City of Edmonton officially renamed the avenue in front of the ballpark John Ducey Way. To her, and the others, it was a fitting public tribute to "Edmonton's Mr. Baseball."

Appendix One

Edmonton in professional baseball, 1907–1954

1907 - Western Canada League Class D

President: Bruce L. Robinson

Standings	W	L	GB
Medicine Hat	58	32	—
Edmonton	50	35	5.5
Lethbridge	37	45	17
Calgary	26	59	29.5

1909 - Western Canada League Class C

President: C.J. Eckstrom

Standings	W	L	GB
Medicine Hat	68	33	—
Winnipeg	66	38	3.5
Calgary	56	44	11.5
Lethbridge	51	46	15
Moose Jaw	50	50	17.5
Regina	42	53	23
Brandon	37	67	32.5
Edmonton	28	67	37

1910 - Western Canada League Class D

President: C.J. Eckstrom

Standings	W	L	GB
Calgary	69	29	—
Edmonton	60	32	6
Winnipeg	53	50	18
Medicine Hat/ Saskatoon*	46	45	21.5
Lethbridge	40	53	26.5
Brandon	43	60	28.5
Regina	27	70	41.5

**Saskatoon played 2nd half in place of Medicine Hat*

1911 - Western Canada League Class D

President: C.J. Eckstrom

Standings	W	L	GB
Moose Jaw	83	30	—
Calgary	62	39	15
Winnipeg	53	49	24.5
Edmonton	53	50	25
Saskatoon	40	73	43
Brandon	24	75	52

1912 - Western Canada League Class D

Presidents: Fred Johnson, John Dewar

Standings	W	L	GB
Calgary	59	34	—
Bassano	45	46	13
Red Deer	48	52	14.5
Edmonton	40	60	22.5

1913 - Western Canada League Class D

President: Frank M. Gray

Standings	W	L	GB
Moose Jaw	68	35	—
Saskatoon	63	37	3.5
Medicine Hat	59	46	10
Calgary	51	56	19
Edmonton	39	57	25.5
Regina	29	78	41

1914 - Western Canada League Class D

President: James E. Fleming

Standings	W	L	GB
Saskatoon	71	52	—
Moose Jaw	63	52	4
Regina	67	57	4.5
Medicine Hat	61	53	5.5
Edmonton	53	57	11.5
Calgary	37	81	31.5

1920 - Western Canada League Class B

President: Frank H. Miley

Standings	W	L	GB
Regina	68	37	—
Calgary	69	39	0.5
Winnipeg	52	52	15.5
Moose Jaw	53	55	16.5
Saskatoon	42	69	29
Edmonton	37	68	31

1921 - Western Canada League Class B

President: Robert Pearson

Standings	W	L	GB
Calgary	68	38	—
Winnipeg	70	41	0.5
Saskatoon	52	58	18
Edmonton	45	58	21.5
Regina*	25	26	NA
Moose Jaw*	12	41	NA

** played first half only*

1922 - Western International League* Class B

President: William F. White Class

Standings	W	L	Pct.
Calgary	24	16	.600
Edmonton	23	16	.590
Vancouver	22	23	.489
Tacoma	16	30	.348

**League collapsed June 18*

1953 - Western International League

Class A

President: Robert P. Brown

Standings	W	L	GB
Lewiston	78	55	—
Salem	79	58	1
Edmonton	79	61	2.5
Vancouver	77	64	5
Spokane	75	67	7.5
Yakima	70	74	13.5
Calgary	59	75	19.5
Tri-City	59	77	20.5
Wenatchee	59	80	22
Victoria	57	81	23.5

1954 - Western International League

Class A

President: Robert B. Abel

Standings	W	L	GB
Vancouver	74	49	—
Yakima	80	57	1
Lewiston	77	61	4.5
Salem	71	66	10
Edmonton	62	63	13
Tri-City	56	81	25
Wenatchee	54	80	25.5
Spokane*	30	24	NA
Victoria+	43	57	NA
Calgary	19	28	NA

* *Spokane and Calgary withdrew June 21*

\+ *Victoria withdrew August 2*

Sources

Lloyd Johnson and Miles Wolf, eds. *The Encyclopedia of Minor League Baseball.* Durham, North Carolina: Baseball America Inc., 1993.

The Reach Official Baseball Guide. Philadelphia: A.J. Reach and Company, 1921 and 1922.

The Spalding Official Baseball Guide. Canadian edition. Montreal: 1923.

Appendix Two

Major-league players who appeared with teams at Edmonton's Diamond and Renfrew parks in regular or league playoffs through 1959

The author gratefully acknowledges the collaboration and assistance of Mr. Owen Ricker, Regina, Saskatchewan, a fellow member of the Society of American Baseball Research, in the compilation of this appendix. Further assistance was provided by Mr. Ray Nemec of Napierville, Illinois, another SABR member.

Section A

Edmonton roster players who made it to the major leagues

Western Canada League Class C

1910 EDMONTON ESKIMOS

Baxter, John (Moose)
1910, BA .272
Majors: 1907 StLN
G 6, H 4, BA .190

Dell, William George (Slim/Wheezer)
1910, W 16, L 10
Majors: 1912 StLN, 1915-17 BknN
G 92, W 19, L 23, ERA 2.55

Morse, Peter (Hap)
1910, BA .340 (with Medicine Hat 1913, BA .268; with Regina 1914, BA .344)
Majors: 1911 StLN
G 4, AB 8, H 0

1911 Edmonton Eskimos

Pieh, Cy (traded to Brandon 9 Aug)
1911 combined W 12, L 17 (with Lethbridge 1909, W 13 L 6; 1910, W 14 L 15)
Majors: 1913-15 NYA
G 43, W 9, L 9, ERA 3.78

1913 Edmonton Gray Birds

Skeels, Dave (played left field for Edmonton 1913, finished season with Calgary)
1913 combined BA .307 (played left field for Regina in 1910; also pitched for Moose Jaw and Regina in 1910 with combined record of W 10, L 14)
Majors: 1910 DetA
G 1, W 0, L 0, IP 6, ERA 12.00

1914 Edmonton Eskimos

Gregg, Dave (Highpockets)
1914, W 1, L 4**
Majors: 1913 CleA
G 1, W 0, L 0, IP 1, ERA 18.00

Nordyke, Lou (player-manager to 3 July 1914)
1914 BA .348**
Majors: 1906 StLA
G 25, H 13, BA .245

Sutherland, Harvey Scott (Suds)
1914, W 3, L 2
Majors: 1921 DetA
G 13, W 6, L 2, ERA 4.97

Williams, Ken
1914, BA .315 (with Regina 1913, BA .292)
Majors: 1915-16 CinN, 1918-27 StLA, 1928-29 BosA
G 1397, H 1552, BA .319

Western Canada League Class B

1920 Edmonton Eskimos

Dumovich, Nick
1920, W 7, L 13
Majors: 1923 ChiN
G 28, W 3, L 5, ERA 4.60

Standridge, Pete (player-manager)
1920, W 3, L 3 (with Calgary 1909, W 6, L 7; 1910, W 15, L 4; 1911, W 21, L 10; 1912, W 21, L 6)
Majors: 1911 StLN, 1915 ChiN
G 31, W 4, L 1, ERA 3.85

1921 Edmonton Eskimos

Hauger, Arthur
1921, BA .315; 1922, BA .249 (with Moose Jaw 1920, BA .332)
Majors: 1912 CleA
G 15, H 1, BA .056

Herman, Floyd Caves (Lefty/Babe)
1921, BA .330
Majors: 1926-31 BknN, 1932 CinN, 1933-34 ChiN, 1935 PitN 1935-36 CinN
G 1552, H 1818, BA .324

Manush, Henry Emmett (Heinie)
1921, BA .321
Majors: 1923-27 DetA, 1928-30 StLA, 1930-35 WasA, 1936 BosA
G 2009, H 2524, BA .330
**Inducted into Baseball Hall of Fame at Cooperstown, New York in 1964.*

Watson, Charles John (Doc) (also with Saskatoon)
1921 combined W 1 L 7** (with Saskatoon 1920, W4 L 17)
Majors: 1913 ChiN, 1914 ChiFed/StLFed
G 69, W 22, L 21, ERA 2.70

Western International League Class B

1922 Edmonton Eskimos

Whaling, Bert
1922, BA .195 (with Regina 1920 BA .244)
Majors: 1913-15 BosN
G 211, H 129, BA.225

Alberta Big Four Intercity League 1947-50

1949 Edmonton Eskimos

Tappe, Ted
1949 BA .289
Majors: 1950-51 CinN, 1955 ChiN
G 34, H 15, BA .269

1950 Edmonton Eskimos

Lillis, Bob
1950, BA .409
Majors: 1958-61 LAN, 1961 StLN, 1962-67 HouN
G 817, H 549, BA .236

Western International League, 1953-54 Class A

1953-54 Edmonton Eskimos

Caster, George (Ug)
1953 pitching coach, pinch-hitter
Majors: 1934-35, 1937-40 PhiA, 1941-45 StLA, 1946 DetA
G 376, W 76, L 100, ERA 4.55

Partee, Roy
1954, BA .303
Majors: 1943-44, 46-47 BosA, 1948 StLA
G 367, H 273, BA .250

Sturgeon, Bob (player-manager)
1953, BA .237; 1954, BA .269
Majors: 1940-42 ChiN, 1946-47 ChiN, 1948 BosN
G 420, H 313, BA .257

Western Canada League 1955-58/ Can-Am League 1959

1956 Edmonton Eskimos

Henrich, Bob
1956, BA .176
Majors: 1957-59 CinN
G 46, H 2, BA 125

1957 Edmonton Eskimos

Elliot, Larry
1957, BA .339
Majors: 1962-63 PitN, 1964 NYN, 1966 NYN
G 157, H 103, BA .236

Fairly, Ron
1957, BA .388
Majors: 1958-69 LAN, 1969-74 MontN, 1975 StLN, 1976 StLN & OakA, 1977 TorA, 1978 CalA
G 2442, H 1913, BA .266

1958-59 Edmonton Eskimos

Gabrielson, Len
1958, BA n.a; 1959, BA .258
Majors: 1960-63 StLN, 1964-65 ChiN, 1965-66 SFN, 1967 CalA, 1967-70 LAN
G 708, H 446, BA .253

Satriano, Tom
1958, BA n.a.; 1959, BA .350
Majors: 1961-64 LAA, 1965-69 CalA, 1970 BosA
G 674, H 365, BA .225

Werhas, John
1958, BA n.a.; 1959, BA .298
Majors 1964-65 LAN, 1967 LAN-CalA
G 89, H 29, BA .173

1959 Edmonton Eskimos

Buford, Don
Appeared in playoffs for 1959 Eskimos
Majors: 1963-67 ChiA, 1968-72 BalA
G 1286, H 1203, BA .264

Heath, Bill
1959, BA .321 (also played for Williston, 1958)
Majors: 1965 ChiA, 1966-67 HouN, 1967 DetA, 1969 ChiN
G 112, H 47, BA .236

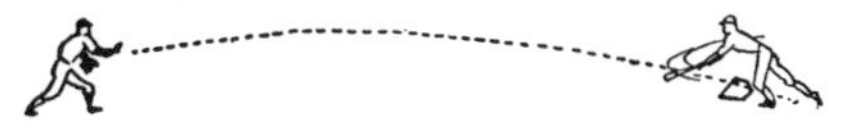

Section B

Other future or former major league players on teams appearing in Edmonton in league or playoff play through 1959

Western Canada League 1907-1914

1907 Calgary Chinooks

Merritt, Bill (manager)
1907, AB 8, H 0 (left team 17 June 1907)
Majors: 1891 ChiN, 1892 LouN, 1893 BosN, 1894 BosN-PitN-CinN, 1895 CinN-PitN, 1896-97 PitN, 1899 BosN
G 400, H 383, BA .272

1907 Lethbridge Miners

Kippert, Ed (Kickapoo)
1907, BA .277; also W 5, L 5
Majors: 1914 CinN
G 2, AB 2, H 0, BA .000

1907 Medicine Hat Gaslighters

Hulen, Billy (aka Hamilton, Billy)
1907, BA .319 (manager Medicine Hat 1909-10, Regina 1913)
Majors: 1896 PhiN, 1899 WasN
G 107, H 1301, BA .287

Works, Ralph
1907, W 26, L 11
Majors: 1909-11 DetA, 1912 DetA-CinN, 1913 CinN
G 99, W 24, L 24, ERA 3.79

1909 Moose Jaw Robin Hoods

Currie, Clarence
1909, W 5, L 6
Majors: 1902 CinN, 02-03StLN 03ChiN
G 53, W 15, L 23, ERA 3.39

1909 and 1910 Calgary Bronks

Carney, Bill (player-manager)
1910, BA .277
Majors: 1904 ChiN
G 2, AB 7, H 0, BA .000

Smith, Wally
1909, BA .339; 1910, BA .303
Majors: 1911-12 StLN, 1914 WasA
G 201, H 117, BA .229

1910 Brandon Angels

Hartford, Bruce
1910, BA .224
Majors: 1914 CleA
G 8, H 4, BA .182

1910 Medicine Hat/Saskatoon

Wilson, Les (Tug)
1910, BA .293 (with Calgary 1911, BA .343)
Majors: 1911 BosA
G 5, AB 7, H 0, BA .000

1910 Regina Bonepilers

Letcher, Tom
1910, BA .288 (with Brandon and Saskatoon 1911, combined BA .226; also umpired part of 1911)
Majors: 1891 Cin-Mil - American Association (considered a major league)
G 6, H 4, BA .190

1910 and 1911 Moose Jaw Robin Hoods

Brown, Paul (Ray)
1910, W 15, L 11; 1911, W 6, L 2** (with Medicine Hat 1913, W 16, L 14; with Moose Jaw, Saskatoon & Regina 1914, W 6, L 4)
Majors: 1909 ChiN
G 1, W 1, L 0, ERA 2.00

Fournier, Jack
1911, BA .377
Majors: 1912-17 ChiA, 1918 NYA, 1920-22 StLN, 1923-26 BknN, 1927 BosN
G 1530, H 1631, BA .313

1912 and 1913 Calgary Bronks

Roche, Jack
1912, BA .352; 1913, BA .317
Majors: 1914-15, 1917 StLN
G 59, H 14, BA .286

1913 Medicine Hat Mad Hatters

Schneider, Peter
1913, W 17, L 7
Majors: 1914-18 CinN, 1919 NYA
G 207, W 59, L 86, ERA 2.66

1913 Moose Jaw Robin Hoods

Steele, Bob
1913, W 17, L 9 (*b. Cassburn, Ont.*)
Majors: 1916 StLN, 1917 StLN-PitN, 1918 PitN-NYN, 1919 NYN
G 91, W 16, L 38, ERA 3.05

1913 and 1914 Regina Red Sox

Smith, Jack W.
1913, BA .239; 1914, BA .281
Majors: 1915-26 StLN, 26-29 BosN
G 1406, H 1301, BA .287

1913 and 1914 Saskatoon Quakers

Cadreau William (Big Chief)
1914, W 10, L 5 (played until 25 July)
Majors: 1910 ChiA (played under name of Choneau)
G 1, W 0, L 1, ERA 3.60

Grover, Roy
1914, BA .261 (with Moose Jaw 1921, BA .317; with Tacoma 1922, BA .241**)
Majors: 1916-17 PhiA, 1919PhiA-WasA
G 207, H 156, BA .226

Kallio, Rudy
1914, W 15, L 12
Majors: 1918-19 DetA, 1925 BosA
G 49, W 9, L 18, ERA 4.18

Walters, Alfred John (Roxy)
1913, BA .270; 1914, BA .311
Majors: 1915-18 NYA, 1919-23 BosA, 1924-25 CleA
G 498, H 317, BA .222

1914 Medicine Hat

Buckles, Jess
1914, W 25, L 12
Majors: 1916 NYA
G 2, W 0, L 0, ERA 2.25

1914 MOOSE JAW

Yohe, Bill
1914, BA .299
Majors: 1909 WasA
G 21, H 15, BA .208

Western Canada League 1920 Class B

1920 CALGARY BRONKS

Christensen, Walter (Cuckoo)
1920, BA .345
Majors: 1926-27 CinN
G 171, H 162, BA .315

Hawkes, Nelson (Chicken)
1920, BA .357
Majors: 1921 NYA, 1925 PhiN
G 146, H 124, BA .316

Kilhullen, Pat
1920, BA .259; 1921, BA .256 (with Tacoma 1922)
Majors: 1914 PitN
G 1, AB 1, BA .000

Mack, Frank (Stubby)
1920, W 16, L 11; 1921, W 0, L 4**
Majors: 1922-23, 1925 ChiA
G 27, W 2, L 3, ERA 5.01

Manda, Carl
1920, BA .284; 1921, BA .295; 1922, BA .294
Majors: 1914 ChiA
G 9, H 4, BA .267

Steengrafe, Milt
1920, W 12, L 4
Majors: 1924-26 ChiA
G 16, W 1, L 1, ERA 5.11

Wirts, Elwood (Kettle)
1920, BA .335
Majors: 1921-23 ChiN, 1924 ChiA
G 49, H 14, BA .163

1920 MOOSE JAW ROBIN HOODS

Leifer, Elmer
1920, BA .326; W 5, L 1,
Majors: 1921 ChiA
G 9, H 3, BA .300

Williams, Denny
1920, BA .322
Majors: 1921 CinN, 1924-25, 1928 BosA
G 120, H 85, BA .259

1920 AND 1921 REGINA SENATORS

Burke, Patrick
1920, BA .271; 1921, BA .320
Majors: 1924 StLA
G 1, H 0, BA 3

Frederick, John
1921, BA .244
Majors: 1921-24 BknN
G 805, H 954, BA .308

Furhman, Alfred (Ollie)
1920, BA .285
Majors: 1922 PhiA
G 6, H 2, BA .333

Harstad, Oscar (Doc) (also with Saskatoon)
1921 combined W 8, L 14**
Majors: 1915 CleA
G 32, W 3, L 5, ERA 3.40

McMullen, Hugh
1921, BA .205
Majors: 1925-26 NYN, 1928 WasA, 1929 CinN
G 64, H 19, BA .176

Pillette, Herman
1920, W 14 L 9
Majors: 1917 CinN, 1922-24 DetA
G 107, W 34, L 32, ERA 3.45

Smith, Marvin (Red)
1920, BA .252
Majors: 1925 PhiA
G 20, H 4, BA .286

Vache, Ernest
1920, BA .335
Majors: 1925 BosA
G 110, H 79, BA .313

1920 and 1921 Winnipeg Maroons

Attreau, Richard
1921, BA .294
Majors: 1926-27 PhiN
G 61, H 31, BA .215

Henion, LaFayette
1920, W 3, L 9 (with Regina 1921, W 6, L 2**)
Majors: 1919 BknN
G 1, IP 3, W 0, L 0, ERA 6.00

Kaufman, Tony
1920, W 5, L 13; 1921, W 22, L 7
Majors: 1921-27 ChiN, 1927 PhiN, 1927-28, 1930-31, 1935 StLN
G 202, W 64, L 62, ERA 4.0

Melillo, Oscar (Spinach)
1920, BA .291; 1921, BA .291
Majors: 1926-35 StLA, 1935-37 BosA
G 1377, H 1316, BA .260

Sheehan, Jack (player-manager)
1920, BA .354
Majors: 1920-21 BknN
G 8, H 2, BA .118

1921 Moose Jaw Millers

Duff, Alba (Larry)
1921, W 4, L 10**
Majors: 1920 WasA
G 3, W 1, L 1, ERA 4.97

Koenig, Mark
1921, BA .202
Majors: 1925-30 NYA, 1930-31 DetA, 1932-33 ChiN, 1934 CinN, 1935-36 NYN
G 1162, H 1190, BA .279

Calgary Bronks 1921

deVivros, Bernie
1921, BA .244
Majors: 1924 ChiA, 1927 DetA
G 25, H 5, BA .217

Gillespie, John (Silent John)
1921, W 12, L 11
Majors: 1922 CinN
G 31, W 3, L 3, ERA 4.52

Mensor, Ed (The Midget)
1921, BA .270
Majors: 1912-14 PitN
G 127, H 54, BA .221

Schnell, Karl
1921, W 21, L 6
Majors: 1922-23 CinN
G 11, W 0, L 0, ERA 4.29

SASKATOON QUAKERS 1921

Grabowski, John
1921, BA .288
Majors: 1924-26 ChiA, 1927-29 NYA, 1931 DetA
G 296, H 206, BA .252

Hummel, John (player-manager)
1921, BA .328
Majors: 1905-15 BknN, 1918 NYA
G 1161, H 991, BA .254

Jude, Frank (Chief)
1921, BA .355
Majors: 1906 CinN
G 80, H 64, BA .208

CALGARY BRONKS 1922

Kerr, John Francis
1922, BA .322
Majors: 1923-24 DetA, 1929-31 ChiA, 1932-34 WasA
G 471, H 388, BA .266

Rodgers, Bill (manager)
1922, BA .285
Majors: 1915 CleA-BosA-CinN, 1916 CinN
G 102, H 65, BA .243

Zamlock, Carl
1922, BA .290
Majors: 1913 DetA
G 17, W 1, L 6, ERA 2.45

VANCOUVER BEAVERS 1922

Marquis, Jimmy
1922, W 2, L 3**
Majors: 1925 NYA
G 2, W 0, L 0, ERA 9.82

Edmonton Senior Baseball League

U.S. ARMY YANKS 1945

Kampouris, Alex
Played in late season 1945
Majors: 1934-38 CinN, 1938-39 NYN, 1941-43 BknN, 1943 WasA
G 708, H 531, BA .243

Alberta Big Four Intercity League 1947-50

1948 AND 1950 CALGARY PURITY 99

Gorbous, Glen (b. *Drumheller, Alberta*)
1948, BA .319; 1950, BA .374
Majors: 1955 CinN, 1955-57 PhiN
G 117, H 66, BA .238

Western International League Class A 1953-54

1953 AND 1954 CALGARY STAMPEDERS

Lillard, Gene (manager)
Majors: 1936, 1939 ChiN, 1940 StLN
G 44, H 8, BA .182

Mead, Charles (b. *Vermillion, Alberta*)
1953, BA .328 (with Yakima 1954, BA .259)
Majors: 1943-45 NYN
G 87, H 64, BA .245

Orrell, Forrest (Joe)
1953, W 13, L 13: 1954 Calgary & Lewiston combined W 12, L 6
Majors: 1943-45 DetA
G 32, W 4, L 4, ERA 3.01

Lewiston Bronks 1953-54

Bockman, J. Edward
1954, BA .290
Majors: 1946 NYA, 1947 CleA, 1948-49 PitN
G 199, H 109, BA .230

Heist, Alfred Lewiston
1953, BA 287; 1954, BA .299
Majors: 1960-61 ChiN, 1962 HouN
G 177, H 126, BA .255

Richardson, Ken
1953, BA .350 (with Vancouver 1954, BA .293)
Majors: 1942 PhiA, 1946 PhiN
G 12, H 4, BA .114

1953 and 1954 Salem Senators

Bevens, Floyd (Bill)
1953, W 0, L 2
Majors: 1944-47 NYA
G 96, W 40, L 36, ERA 3.08

Briggs, Jonathan (John)
1954, W 20, L 8
Majors: 1956-58 ChinN, 1959 CleA, 1960 CleA-KCA
G 59, W 9, L 11, ERA 5.00

Essegian, Charles (Chuck)
1953, BA .240
Majors: 1958 PhiN, 1959 StLN, 1959-60 LAN, 1961 BalA-KCA-CleA, 1962 CleA, 1963 KCA
G 404, H 260, BA .255

Luby, Hugh (player-manager)
1953, BA .316; 1954, BA .357
Majors: 1936 PhiA, 1944 NYN
G 120, H 89, BA .247

Smith, Milton
1953, BA .391
Majors: 1955 CinN
G 36, H 20, BA .196

1953 Spokane Indians

Command, James
1953, BA .321
Majors: 1954-55 PhiN
G 14, H 4, BA .174

Palys, Stan
1953, BA .331
Majors: 1953-55 PhiN, 1955-56 CinN
G 138, H 79, BA .237

Spring, Jack
1953, W 14, L 8
Majors: 1955 PhiN, 1957 BosA, 1958 WasA, 1961-63 LAA, 1964 LAA-CHiN-StLN, 1965 CleA
G 155, W 12, L 5, ERA 4.26

1954 Spokane Indians

Anderson, Andy
1954, BA .234 (combined with Yakima)
Majors: 1948-49 StLA
G 122 H 41 BA .184

Anderson, John
1954, W 10, L 1
Majors: 1958 PhiN, 1960BalA, 1962 StlN-HouN
G 24, W 0, L 0, ERA 6.45

1953 and 1954 Tri-Cities Braves

Dobernic, Andres (Jess)
1953, W 13, L 7; 1954, W 9, L 9
Majors: 1939 ChiA, 1948 ChiN, 1949 ChiN-CinN
G 76, W 7, L 3, ERA 5.22

1953 Vancouver Capilanos

Barrett, Dick (Kewpie Dick)
(pitching coach)
1953, W 0, L 1
Majors: 1933 PhiA, 1934 BosN, 1943 Chi-PhiN, 1944-45 PhiN
G 141, W 35, L 58, ERA 4.28

Fletcher, Alfred Vanoide (Van)
1953, W 17, L 13
Majors: 1955 DetA
G 9, W 0, L 0, ERA 3.00

Marshall, Clarence (Cuddles)
1953, W 2, L 3
Majors: 1946, 1948-49 NYA, 1950 StLA
G 73, W 7, L 7, ERA 5.98

1953 and 1954 Victoria Tyees

Garriott, Cecil (player-manager)
1953, BA .284
Majors: 1946 ChiN
G 6, AB 5, H 0, BA .000

Clark, James (Jim)
1953 (combined with Vancouver) BA .285 (with Vancouver 1954, BA .286)
Majors: 1948 WasA
G 9, H 3, BA .250

Clay, Dain
1954 (combined with Wenatchee) BA .288
Majors: 1943-46 CinN
G 433, H 397, BA .258

Lake, Edward
1954, BA .276
Majors: 1939-41 StLN, 1943-45 BosA, 1946-50 DetA
G 835, H 599, BA .231

Mesner, Steve
1954, BA .243
Majors: 1938-39 ChiN, 1941 StLN, 1943-45 CinN
G 451, H 397, BA .252

Sheridan, Neil
1954 (combined with Vancouver) BA .308
Majors: 1948 BosA
G 2, AB 1, H 0, BA .000

1953 and 1954 Wenatchee Chiefs

Beamon, Charlie
1953, W 10, L 14; 1954, W 7, L 10
Majors: 1956-58 BalA
G 27, W 3, L 3, ERA 3.88

Dasso, Francis
1953, W 1, L 1
Majors: 1945-46 CinN
G 18, W 4, L 5, ERA 3.91

Green, Elijah (Pumpsie)
1953, BA .245; 1954, BA .297
Majors: 1959-62 BosA, 1963 NYN
G 344, H 196, BA .246

Kelly, George (Highpockets)
Manager for part of 1953
Majors: 1915-17 NYN, 1917 PitN, 1919-26 NYN, 1927-30 CinN, 1930 ChiN, 1932 BknN
G 1632, H 1778, BA .297

McCormick, Myron (Mike) (player-manager)
1953, BA .318
Majors: 1940-43, 1946 CinN, 1946-48 BosN, 1949 BkN, 1950 NYN-ChiA, 1951 WasA
G 748, H 640, BA .275

1953 and 1954 Yakima Bears

Lodigiani, Dario
Manager
Majors: 1938-40 PhiA, 1941-42 ChiA, 1946 ChiA
G 404, H 355, BA .260

Stringer, Lou (player-manager)
1954, BA .289
Majors: 1941-42, 1946 ChiN, 1948-50 BosA
G 409, H 290, BA .231

Wellman, Bob
1953, BA .350 (with Vancouver 1954, BA .293)
Majors: 1948, 1950 PhiA
G 15, H 7, BA .280

Western Canada League 1955-58

1956 Bismarck Barons (Mandak League)

Cihocki, Al (player-manager)
Appeared in one interlocking game at Edmonton on 7 August
Majors: 1945 CleA
G 92, H 60, BA .212

1956 Lloydminster Meridians

Perranoski, Ron
W 1, L 0 (playoffs only)
Majors: 1961-67 LAN, 1968-71 MinA, 1971-72 Det, 1972 LAN, 1973 CalA
G 737, W 79, L 74, ERA 2.79

1959 Lloydminster-North Battleford Combines*

Buford, Don (*appeared with Edmonton in playoffs)
1959, BA .284
Majors: 1963-67 ChiA, 1968-72 BalA
G 1286, H 1203, BA .264

1957 Moose Jaw Mallards

Haller, Tom
1957, BA .300
Majors: 1961-67 SFN, 1968-71 LAN, 1972 DetA
G 1294, H 1011, BA .257

1957 Regina Senators

Gregory, Leroy
1957, W 0, L 3 (with Moose Jaw 1958, W 4, L 4**)
Majors: 1964 ChiN
G 11, W 0, L 0, ERA 3.50

Tartabull, Jose
1957, BA .301
Majors: 1962-65 KCA, 1966 KCA-BosA, 1967-68 BosA, 1969-70 OakA
G 749, H 484, BA .261

1958 Williston Oilers

Adair, Jerry
1958, BA .399
Majors: 1958-66 BalA, 1966-67 ChiA, 1967-68 BosA, 1969-70 KCA
G 1165, H 1022, BA .254

***Note:** records marked ** are unofficial*

Section C

Special Category*

Western International League 1953

Edmonton Eskimos

Day, Leon* rhp
1953, G 23, GS 10, W 5, L 5, ERA 4.84
Negro Major Leagues 1934-1950: Bacharach Giants, Brooklyn Eagles, Newark Eagles, Baltimore Elite Giants
W 67, L 29
*Inducted into Baseball Hall of Fame at Cooperstown, New York 1995.

Section D

Umpires who worked at Diamond and Renfrew Park through 1959 who went on to work in the major leagues.

Reardon, John Edward (Beans)
Umpired in Edmonton and Calgary, Western Canada League, Class B, 1920 and 1921; Pacific Coast League Class AA, 1922-25; National League 1926-49; World Series Games: 1930 (6), 1934 (7), 1939 (4), 1943 (5), 1949 (5).

Ashford, Emmett
Umpired in Southwest International League, Class C, July 1951-July-1952; Arizona-Texas League, Class C, August-September 1952; Western International League, Class A 1953; Pacific Coast League, Class AAA, 1954-65; American League 1966-70; World Series Games: 1970 (5).

Sources

Major-league statistics

The Baseball Encyclopedia. Ninth edition. New York: MacMillan Publishing Co., 1993.

Montangue, John, ed. *The Major League Year and Notebook.* Lexington, Kentucky: Sportsource Inc.

Neft et al. *The Sports Encylopedia:Baseball.* New York: Grosset & Dunlap, 1974.

Thorn, John and Pete Palmer, eds. *Total Baseball.* Second edition. Warner Books, 1991.

Minor-leagues statistics

Johnson, Lloyd, ed. *The Minor League Register.* Baseball America, 1994.

The Reach Official American League Baseball Guide. Philadelphia: A.J. Reach and Company, 1921 and 1922.

The Spalding Official Baseball Guide, 1922-23. Canadian edition. Montreal: 1923.

Leon Day

Edmonton Journal (various issues 1953).

The Baseball Encyclopedia. New York: MacMillan, 1993.

Saskatchewan teams and players

Hack, Paul and Dave Shury. *Wheat Province Diamonds: A Story of Saskatchewan Baseball.* Regina: Saskatchewan Sports Hall of Fame and Museum, 1997.

Umpiring

Gerlach, Larry R. *The Men In Blue: Conversations with Umpires.* New York: Viking Press, 1980.

Appendix Three

Some selected Edmonton baseball rosters, 1900–1959

1900

Edmonton vs Strathcona

Ball, W.	c	Jackson
Ball, F.	p	Buckee
Carney	1b	Dodd
Knox	2b	Worth
Wilson	3b	Steeves
Ball, Billie	ss	Shire
Wood	rf	Grabowski
Campbell	cf	Buckell
Carr	lf	Blaine

Edmonton's first "regular" baseball team, led by the three Ball brothers, played on a rough diamond near "the bush," a block north of Jasper Avenue between 103 and 104 streets on what were then the Hudson's Bay Lands. Opponents included Strathcona, Sturgeon River, and Wetaskiwin.

1906

Edmonton Capitals vs Calgary Bronks

Gouchee	c	Ford
Howard	p	Crist
Dobson	1b	Painter
Deeton	2b	Rochon
Berry	3b	Moyne
Bradley	ss	Donovan
Till	rf	Watson
Grady	cf	Dickson
McGurl	lf	McCartney

This was the first year of intense rivalry between the two cities. Both stacked their lineups with players imported from eastern Canada and the United States. Edmonton games took place on a temporary diamond at the Rossdale fairgrounds.

1907 - Western Canada Baseball League
Edmonton Legislators vs Calgary Bronks

Ford	c	Driscoll
Blexrud	p	White
Lussi	1b	O'Donnell
Wessler	2b	Farrell
Baker	3b	Chandler
Grimes (also lf)	ss	Barrett
Wheeler	rf	O'Neil
Adams	cf	Taylor
McQuicken	lf	Russell

Staffed mainly with Americans, these two teams played the first professional baseball game in Edmonton at the new Diamond Park on May 30, 1907. Edmonton placed second in the four-team Alberta league, Calgary last.

1909 - Western Canada League
Edmonton Eskimos vs Calgary Bronks

Nye	c	Kelly
McNeil	p	Standridge
Gragian	1b	Kwickler
McGuire (mgr.)	2b	Chandler
Brennan	3b	Mills
O'Brien	ss	Rochon
Shea	rf	Parkes
Murphy	cf	Wheeler
Burridge	lf	Baker

The Edmonton club was assembled in Toronto by Dennis "Dinny" McGuire and made up mainly of players from the eastern United States. They arrived in Edmonton on a Canadian Northern Railways train on the eve of the opening game.

1914 - Western Canada League
Edmonton Eskimos vs Saskatoon Quakers

Lemieux	c	Walters
Russell	p	Cadreau
Nordyke (mgr.)	1b	Hurley
Redmond	2b	Chick
Ruell	3b	Grover
O'Brien	ss	Harper
Povey	rf	Wilson
Fortier	cf	Harley
Goldie	lf	Mills

After drawing a record 5,000 fans on opening day, Edmonton played so poorly that club directors ordered Deacon White to find some new players. One of those brought in was Ken Williams (rf), who went on to an outstanding major-league career.

1919 - Edmonton Senior Baseball League
Knights of Columbus vs Dekan Grotto

Mountfield	c	Dewney
Murphy	p	Nehring
Kenny	1b	Drayton
Speissmann	2b	Martin
Carrigan	3b	VanNorman
Starky	ss	Thompson
Howard	rf	Kelso
Siska	cf	Arseneau
Isan	lf	Arnold

Following World War One, Edmonton could not organize in time to rejoin the Western Canada League, so a four-team amateur league was formed to play at Diamond Park. The other two teams were the YMCA and Deacon White's Great War Veterans.

1920 - Western Canada League
Edmonton Eskimos vs Calgary Bronks

Ritchie	c	Kilhullen
Bonner	p	Sweeney
Gleichman	1b	Gregor
Eagleson	2b	H.Christenson
Starky	3b	Manda
Wiley	ss	Lammara
Monroe	rf	W.Christenson
Schultz	cf	Hawkes
Nelson	lf	Tobin

John "Beans" Reardon made his professional debut by umpiring opening games in both Edmonton and Calgary. The slight twenty-two-year-old was then described as "the last person in the world one would take as a professional ball umpire." He went on to umpire in the National League for twenty-three years.

1921 - Western Canada League
Edmonton Eskimos vs Calgary Bronks

Leake	c	Sullivan
Fairbanks	p	Sweeney
Herman	1b	Anhier
Stokke	2b	deViveros
Giola	3b	Manda
Miller	ss	Hamilton
Forsythe	rf	Griffith
Apperson	cf	Nelson
Manush	lf	Mooney

Although unknown when they first arrived from spring training in California, Manush and Herman were to become big-league stars. Manda and deViveros of Calgary also made it to the majors but only for brief appearances.

1924 - Busher King Tournament
Edmonton Outlaws vs Mirror CNR

Batey	c	A. Ray
Dodge	p	Turner
Henderson	1b	Ryan
Sibbetts	2b	Adams
Starky	3b	Lapp
Hamilton	ss	Busby
Forman	rf	Cairns
Brown	cf	Murray
Enright	lf	Wagner
Grady	c	—
—	p	Walker

Deacon White organized the "Busher King" tournament and was said to have bet heavily on his veteran Outlaws. However, they were upset by the pitching heroics of Mirror's Cliff Turner, whom White had released after a pre-season professional try-out in 1921. His performance earned Turner a Detroit Tigers contract.

1930 - Edmonton Senior Baseball League - Diamond Park
Edmonton Imperials vs Young Liberals

McHugh	c	Van Camp
Hall	p	Moebe
Horn	1b	Dingle
Young	2b	Hinchclyffe
Croft	3b	McDonald
Dolighan	ss	Kennedy
Ducey	rf	Berg
Mahar	cf	Martell
McGillis	lf	Lammie

This was John Ducey's sixth and last season as a senior amateur player. His notoriously poor hitting led him to follow a career as an umpire; that fall he went to Hollywood, California to train under Beans Reardon.

1933 - Edmonton Senior Baseball League
Renfrew Park Cubs vs South Side Athletics

Henderson	c	Stewart
Speissmann	p	Loblick
Horn	1b	Hambly
Wilkie	2b	Moon
Robinson	3b	Fenton
Dolighan	ss	Luna
Gerlitz	rf	Lammie
McCready	cf	Green
Maher	lf	Lewis

Led by Pete McCready, the talent-laden Cubs dominated the first baseball season at Renfrew Park and were finally the league champions. This was a four-team city senior league and various combinations of it played in the ball park throughout the 1930s.

1943 - Provincial Senior Intercity Championship
Edmonton U.S. Army Yanks vs Calgary Navy

Lolla	c	McDonald
Gray	p	Wynn
Adams	1b	Lane
Phillips	2b	Ornest
Knonpka	3b	Kanik
Miller	ss	Bentley
Baldwin	rf	Hansen
Misosky	cf	Albin
Valenti	lf	Dahl

The first year of wartime baseball featuring U.S. service clubs in Edmonton. A four-game playoff between the Yanks and the Canadian Navy team, based in Calgary, drew 23,000 fans to Renfrew Park. The Yanks end up as both city and provincial champions.

1945 - Edmonton Senior Baseball League
U.S. Army Yanks vs Dodgers

Crumley	c	McCauley
Gray	p	Tougas
Meyers	1b	Morgan
Hackney	2b	Phifer
—	2b	Ornest
Burchfield	3b	Carney
Galvin	ss	Shandro
Schumacher	lf	Governale
Valenti	cf	Superstein
Baldwin	rf	Green

The Yanks powered their way through the final year of wartime baseball at Renfrew Park and went on to become western Canada champions just as most of the players on several service teams were being discharged and sent home.

1948 - Big Four Intercity Baseball League

Morris	c	Buono
Belter	p	Hawkey
Seaman	p	—
McGill	1b	Lane
Price	2b	Stevenson
Morgan	3b	Clovechok
Gonzales	ss	Enjaian
Johnston	rf	Chulla
Brockie	cf	Canepa
Perani	lf	Bailey

Fierce rivalry between the league champion Eskimos and the Cubs, as well as with Calgary's Buffaloes and Purity 99, drew a record 115,000 fans to Renfrew Park. The next year, however, baseball would have to contend at the gate with the newly resurrected Edmonton Eskimo football club.

1950 - Big Four Intercity Baseball League
Eskimos vs Dodgers

Morris	c	Kortgard
Seaman	p	Hawkey
Belter	p	—
Lowe	p	—
Bradish	1b	Ryan
Enjaian	2b	McInerney
Granato	3b	O'Connor
Lillis	ss	Stewart, Don
Johnston	rf	Stewart, Doug
Brockie	cf	Robertshaw
Karlson	lf	Anderson

Cal's Dodgers, made up mainly of local players, upset John Ducey's favoured Eskimos, dominated by U.S. imports, in the final season of the Big Four League. The league marked the end of Edmonton-Calgary baseball rivalry until the arrival of the Pacific Coast League in the early 1980s.

1951 - Edmonton Oilers - Exhibition and Tournament team.

Warwick	c
Belter	p
Devine	p
Seaman	p
Thorseth	p
Wynn	1b
McInerney	2b
Karlson	3b
O'Connor	3b
Freeman	ss
Gadsby	rf
Robertshaw	cf
Stewart	lf
Ken Samis	mgr.

The Oilers beat most of the best barnstorming teams that appeared in western Canada—when they played at Renfrew Park. But they could not win in any of the lucrative tournaments held that season. As a result, the players, working on a profit-sharing plan, made almost no money.

1953 - Western International League
Edmonton Eskimos vs
Calgary Stampeders

Prentice	c	Bricker
Morgan	c	—
McNulty	p	Levinson
Conant	p	—
Day	p	—
Widner	p	—
Tisnerat	p	—
Sturgeon (also mgr.)	1b	Mellinger
Weaver	1b	—
Kanelos	2b	Hunter
Meisner	3b	Tedesco
Thompson	ss	Whitehead
Campbell	lf	Stathos
Skurski	cf	Bonebrake
Herman	rf	Mead
—	mgr.	Gene Lillard

The ten-team WIL began to falter soon after Calgary and Edmonton joined. High travel costs and poor weather plagued the league for two years. After Calgary, Spokane, and Victoria withdrew during the season, the league disbanded at the end of 1954.

1957 Western Canada Baseball League
Edmonton Eskimos vs
Lloydminster Meridians

Michaels	c	Tanner
Vold	p	Kuodis
Guffey	1b	B. Williams
Castanon	2b	Birk
Munatones	3b	C. Williams
Sada	ss	Maxey
Shollin	rf	Moriarty
Fairly	cf	Roberts
Riney	lf	Zayas

After finishing in second place, the Eskimos won two playoff series to take the championship and send the team to represent Canada at the Global World Series in Detroit. Ponoka's Ralph Vold was the only Canadian in this lineup, dominated by University of Southern California players.

1959 Can-Am League
Edmonton Eskimos vs
Lloydminster Combines

Vold	p	Nelson
—	p	Powell
—	p	Ford (also rf)
Heath	c	Tanner
Ersepke	1b	Kosteniuk
Charnofsky	2b	Stone
Werhas	3b	Bergeron
Scott	ss	Buford
Gillespie	rf	Bond
Gabrielson	cf	Mousalam
Satriano	lf	Bryson

The last Edmonton Eskimos Baseball club finished in first place and won the league playoffs. General manager Ducey announced his retirement from baseball the following spring. It would be 1981 before regular inter-city baseball returned to Renfrew Park in the form of the Pacific Coast League Trappers.

Sources

The Edmonton Bulletin.
The Edmonton Journal.

Sources

1 The Beginnings

Cashman, Tony. *The Edmonton Story*. Edmonton: Institute of Applied Art, 1956.

______. *Edmonton Exhibition—The First 100 Years*. Edmonton: Edmonton Exhibition Association, 1979.

______. A *Picture History of Alberta*. Edmonton: Hurtig Publishers, 1979.

Danzig, Allison and Joe Richler. *The History of Baseball*. Englewood Cliffs, New Jersey: Prentice Hall, 1959.

Ducey, Agnes C. *The Ducey Story, A Historical Record of a Family's Migrations, 1100 A.D.-1900 A.D.* Nebraska, 1966.

Enger, Arnold. "The History of Baseball in the Province of Alberta." Paper prepared for the University of Alberta, 1986.

Gruneau, Richard S. and John G. Albinson. *Canadian Sport: Sociological Perspectives*. Don Mills: Addison-Wesley, 1976.

Hack, Paul and Dave Shury. *Wheat Province Diamonds: A Story of Saskatchewan Baseball*. Regina: Saskatchewan Sport Hall of Fame and Museum, 1997.

Hesketh, Bob and Frances Swyripa, eds. *Edmonton: The Life of a City*, Edmonton: NeWest Press, 1995.

Howell, Colin D. *Northern Sandlots: A Social History of Maritime Baseball.* Toronto: University of Toronto Press, 1994.

Howell, Nancy and Maxwell Howell. *Sports and Games in Canadian Life, 1700 to the Present.* Toronto: MacMillan, 1969.

Humber, William. *Diamonds of The North: A Concise History of Baseball In Canada.* Don Mills: Oxford University Press, 1995.

______. *Cheering for the Home Team, The Story of Baseball In Canada.* Erin, Ontario: Boston Mills Press, 1983.

James, Bill. *The Bill James Historical Baseball Abstract.* New York: Villard Books, 1986.

Kirwin, Bill. "A Colony Within a Colony: The Western Canada Baseball League of 1912," *NINE* 4,2 (Spring 1996).

LaCasse, Geoff. "The Development of Professional Baseball in Vancouver" and "Early Professional Baseball in Vancouver: The Northwestern League, Vancouver Beavers and R.P. Brown." Papers presented to the B.C. Studies Conference, 1990.

MacGregor, James G. *A History of Edmonton.* Edmonton: Hurtig Publishers, 1981.

Metcalfe, Alan. *Canada Learns to Play, The Emergence of Organized Sport, 1807-1914.* Toronto: McClelland & Stewart, 1987.

Mott, Morris. "The First Pro Sports League on the Prairies: The Manitoba Baseball League of 1886." *Canadian Journal of History of Sport* XV,2 (December 1984).

Neft et al. *The Sports Encyclopedia: Baseball*, New York: Grosset & Dunlop, 1974.

Palmer, Howard. *Alberta, A New History.* Edmonton: Hurtig Publishers, 1990.

Shearon, Jim. *Canada's Baseball Legends.* Ontario: Malin Head Press, 1994.

Shury, David W. *Play Ball Son: The Story of the Saskatchewan Baseball Association.* North Battleford, Saskatchewan: Turner, Warwick Printers, 1986.

Solomon, Burt. *The Baseball Timeline: The Day-by-Day History of Baseball from Valley Forge to the Present Day.* New York: Avon Books, 1997.

Thorn, John and Pete Palmer, eds. *Total Baseball.* Second edition. New York: Time Warner Books, 1991.

Voisey, Paul. *Vulcan, The Making of a Prairie Community*, Toronto: University of Toronto Press, 1988.

Ward, Geoffrey and Ken Burns. *Baseball, An Illustrated History.* New York: Alfred A. Knopf, 1994.

Weaver, Angela, student-at-law. "Memorandum re The Lord's Day Act." Paper prepared for the University of Alberta.

Newspapers

Edmonton Bulletin: 1881, 1883, 1884, 1888, 1889, 1899, 1900, 1901, 1904, 1905, 1906, 1907, 1908, 1911.

Edmonton Journal: 1907.

Calgary Herald: 1884, 1893, 1907.

Interviews

"The John Ducey Story," CJCA Radio, 1954.

John Ducey, September 23, 1959.

John Ducey, September 23, 1979.

Other materials

Certificate of Baptism, of John Ducey, Buffalo, New York, September 3, 1908.

Affidavit of Execution concerning birth and residences, by Thomas Ducey, sworn at Edmonton, 21 July 1934.

City of Edmonton Population Statistics, 1952.

2 Edmonton's Early Innings

Newspapers

Edmonton Bulletin: 1881, 1883, 1884, 1891, 1892, 1893, 1894, 1899, 1900, 1901, 1903, 1904, 1905, 1906, 1907, 1909.

Calgary Herald: 1884, 1903, 1906.

Calgary Eye Opener: 1906.

Other materials

Certificate of Baptism of Thomas James Ducey, Lindsay, Ontario, August 11, 1871.

Abstract on the career of Henry F. O'Day, John Ducey Collection, Alberta Archives.

City of Edmonton Population Statistics, 1952.

3 The Deacon White Era

Anderson, Robin John. "'On the Edge of the Baseball Map' with the 1908 Vancouver Beavers." *Canadian Historical Review* 77,4 (December 1996).

Artibise, Alan F.J., ed. *Town and City: Aspects of Western Canadian Urban Development*. Regina: Canadian Plains Research Centre, 1981.

Betke, Carl. "The Original City of Edmonton: A Derivative Prairie Urban Community." In *Town and City*, Artibise, ed.

______. "Sports Promotion in the Western Canadian City: The Example of Early Edmonton." *Urban History Review* XII,2 (October 1983).

Bowman, John S. *The Encyclopedia of Baseball Managers*. New York: Crescent Books, 1990.

Cashman, Tony. "Early Days of Baseball in Edmonton." *The Edmontonian Magazine*, undated, circa 1964.

Lamb, Paddy. *Deacon White: Founder of Modern Sport in Edmonton*. City of Edmonton Archives, 1995.
MacGregor, J.G. *Edmonton, A History*. Edmonton: Hurtig Publishers, 1967.
Objoski, Robert. *Bush League: A History of Minor League Baseball*. New York: MacMillan Publishing, 1975.
Palmer, *Alberta: A New History*.
Voisey, *Vulcan*.
Weatherall, Donald with Irene Kmet. *Useful Pleasures: The Shaping of Leisure In Alberta, 1896-1945*. Regina: Canadian Plains Research Centre, 1990.

Newspapers

Edmonton Bulletin: 1907, 1908, 1909, 1910, 1911, 1913.
Edmonton Capital: 1912, 1914.
Edmonton Journal: 1906, 1907, 1908, 1912, 1913, 1914.

Correspondence

Department of Defence, Ottawa, Canada, to Henry J. Roche, May 30, 1940, re Deacon White's birth date and military career.
Ducey, John to G.V. Carveth, December 29, 1968, re Cliff "Tiny" Turner.
Reardon, Beans to John Ducey, July 14, 1981.

Other materials

City of Edmonton Archives files on Deacon White: undated clipping, the *Edmonton Bulletin*, 1906; Deacon White, letter to the Sports Editor of the *Winnipeg Free Press*, undated, 1906; pamphlet, *Edmonton: Gateway to the North*, "World War One and the End of the Boom," undated; City of Edmonton Police Report 1928, concerning Deacon White.
Abstract of Deacon White's Career, John Ducey to the City of Edmonton, 1965.
Government of Canada, *An Act Respecting the Lord's Day*, March 1, 1908.
"President's Report to the National Baseball Congress, 1907"; "President's Report, Western Canada, 1909"; "President's Report, Western Canada League," 1910, 1911, 1912, 1913 and 1914. All contained in the National Baseball Hall of Fame Library, Cooperstown, New York. Cited in Arnold Enger, "The History of Baseball in the Province of Alberta."

4 Edmonton's "King of Sports"

Cashman, *The Edmonton Story*.
______, "Early Days of Baseball in the Early Days of Edmonton."
Filichia, Peter. *Professional Baseball Franchises*. New York: Facts on File, 1993.

Lorenz, Stacy J. "'A Lively Interest on the Prairies': Western Canada, The Mass Media and 'A World of Sport,' 1870-1939." Paper delivered at the Northern Great Plains History Conference, Brandon, Manitoba, September, 1995.
Neft et al., *The Sports Encyclopedia: Baseball.*
Palmer, *Alberta:* A *New History.*
The Reach Official American League Baseball Guide. Philadelphia: A.J. Reach and Company, 1921 and 1922.
Thorn and Palmer, *Total Baseball.*

Newspapers
Edmonton Bulletin: 1911, 1919, 1920, 1921.
Edmonton Journal: 1919, 1920, 1921, 1939, 1971.
Victoria Times: 1972.

Correspondence
Ducey, John to Duke Keats, January 14, 1970.

Other materials
Abstract of Deacon White's Career, John Ducey to the City of Edmonton, 1965.
Jack Starky, "Thumbnail Sketch to Edmonton Oldtimers Baseball Association," May 1973.

5 Manush, Herman, and Reardon

Bowman, *The Encyclopedia of Baseball Managers.*
Danzig and Richler, *The History of Baseball.*
Davis, Ralph. "Reardon Became Ump, Without Being Player." *The Sporting News*, undated, circa 1932.
Gerlach, Larry R. *The Men in Blue: Conversations with Umpires.* New York: The Viking Press, 1980.
Hack and Shury, *Wheat Province Diamonds.*
Holmes, Tot. *Brooklyn's Babe: The Life and Legends of Babe Herman.* Gothenburg, Nebraska: Holmes Publishing, 1990.
Munro, Neil and Stats Inc. *STATS Canadian Players Encyclopedia*, Stats Publishing, 1996.
Neft et al., *The Sports Encyclopedia: Baseball.*
Page, J. Percy, on the death of Deacon White. *Edmonton Journal* November 9, 1939.
The Reach Official Baseball Guide, A.J. Reach Company, Philadelphia, 1921 and 1922.
Ritter, Lawrence S. *The Glory of Their Times*, New York: Collier Books, 1966.
Skipper, James K. Jr. *Baseball Nicknames, A Dictionary of Origins and Meanings.* Jefferson, North Carolina and London: McFarland & Company, 1992.

Snelling, Dennis. *The Pacific Coast League: A Statistical History, 1903-1957*. Jefferson, North Carolina and London: McFarland and Company, 1995.
Solomon, *Baseball Timeline*.
The Spalding Official Baseball Guide, Canadian Edition, 1923.
Thorn and Palmer, *Total Baseball*.

Correspondence

Ducey, John to Warren Giles, Chairman, Committee on Veterans, National Baseball Hall of Fame, Cooperstown, New York, November 1, 1976, re Beans Reardon.
Reardon, Beans to John Ducey, July 14, 1981, re Mae West.

Newspapers

Edmonton Journal: 1919, 1922, 1924, 1936, 1937, 1939, 1941, 1950, 1971, 1972.
Edmonton Bulletin: 1919, 1920, 1921, 1922, 1939.

Other materials

The Canadian Encyclopedia. McClelland & Stewart Inc., CD ROM Version, 1996.
Abstract on the career of Henry F. O'Day by John Ducey.
John Ducey, "Introductory Notes to the Edmonton Oldtimers Baseball Association on the career of Duke Keats," 1972.

6 From Player to Umpire

Cashman, Tony. "When Wages Were Two Dollars a Game," *Edmonton Journal* August 3, 1974.
______. *Edmonton's Catholic Schools*. Edmonton: Edmonton Roman Catholic Separate School District No. 7, 1977.
Collins, Tom. "Appleton's Hockey Hero, Roger Jenkins," *View Magazine* (Appleton, Wisconsin) June 8, 1980.
Fischler, Stan and Shirley Walton Fischler. *The Hockey Encyclopedia: The Complete Record of Professional Ice Hockey*. New York: MacMillan, 1983.
Gerlach, *The Men In Blue*.
Neft et al., *The Sports Encyclopedia: Baseball*.
Shatzkin, Mike, ed. *The Ballplayers—Baseball's Ultimate Biographical Reference*. New York: Arbor House, 1990.
Thorn and Palmer, *Total Baseball*.
Weaver, Angela. "Memorandum re The Lord's Day Act."

Newspapers

Edmonton Bulletin: 1907, 1919, 1928, 1930, 1931, 1932.
Edmonton Journal: 1925, 1930, 1931, 1932, 1960, 1980.

Correspondence
Ainlay, H.D. to the editor of the *Edmonton Bulletin*, September 1931.
Ducey, John to Brant Ducey, April 22, 1972.
Filkin, J.O. to the editor of the *Hollywood News*, December 1930.
Reardon, Beans to John Ducey, July 14, 1981.

Interviews
John Ducey, undated, August 1946 (notes).
John Ducey, City of Edmonton Archives, September 23, 1979.
Riley Mullen at John Ducey Park, August 28, 1994.
Cecil Goldstick, March 1, 1995.
Mary Broderick, April 15, 1995.
Dick Noon, June 23, 1995.

Other materials
Official Handbook & Scorecard, Edmonton Senior Baseball League, 1933.
Clarence S. Campbell, "Report on the History and Development of Renfrew Baseball Park," to the City of Edmonton Commissioners, 1937, City of Edmonton Archives.

7 Renfrew Park

Cashman, *The Edmonton Story*.
______, "When Wages Were Two Dollars a Game...".
______, *The Best Edmonton Stories*.
______, *Edmonton Exhibition*.
Fischler and Fischler, *The Hockey Encyclopedia*.
Hamilton, F.F. Jr. *Ice Capades, Years of Entertainment*. Washington: Penchant Publishing Company Limited, 1974.
Hurdis, John. *Speedskating In Canada, 1854-1981, A Chronological History*, Montreal: Canadian Printco Company, 1980.
Ward and Burns, *Baseball, An Illustrated History*.
Gary Zeman, *Alberta On Ice*. Edmonton: GMS Ventures, 1985.

Newspapers
Edmonton Bulletin: 1919, 1933.
Edmonton Journal: 1953, 1974, 1979.

Interviews
Cecil Goldstick, March 1, 1995.

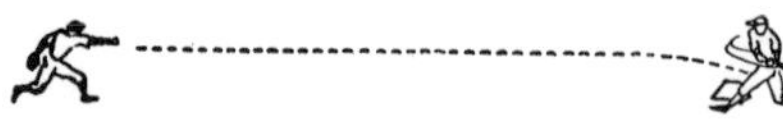

Other materials

Con Bissett, "Thumbnail Sketch to the Edmonton Oldtimers Baseball Association," re Prince of Wales visit, undated, 1977.

City of Edmonton Council Decision regarding Renfrew Park, April 24, 1933, City of Edmonton Archives.

Clarence S. Campbell, "Report on the History and Development of Renfrew Baseball Park," to City of Edmonton Commissioners, 1937.

Official Handbook and Scorecard, Edmonton Senior Baseball League, 1933.

8 Baseball Battles

Bruce, Janet. *The Kansas City Monarchs, Champions of Black Baseball*. Lawrence, Kansas: University Press of Kansas, 1985.

Hjolway, John B. *Black Diamonds: Life in the Negro Leagues from the Men Who Lived It*. Westport, Connecticut: Meckler Books, 1989.

Rogosin, Donn. *Invisible Men: Life in Baseball's Negro Leagues*. New York: Atheneum, 1987.

Ruck, Rob. *Sandlot Seasons: Sport In Black Pittsburg*. Urbana, Illinois: Illini Books, 1993.

Ward and Burns, *Baseball, An Illustrated History*.

Newspapers

Edmonton Bulletin: 1933, 1934, 1949.

Edmonton Journal: 1934, 1934, 1973, 1980.

Correspondence

Boone, Lute to John Ducey, telegram, July 4, 1934.

Ducey, John to the editor of *Baseball Magazine*, undated, 1933.

Interviews

Des O'Connor, February 26, 1995.

Cliff Johnston, February 27, 1995.

Doug Darrah, March 1, 1995.

Hon. Allan H. Wachowich, May 3, 1995.

Dick Noon, June 23, 1995.

9 Settling Down

Fischler, Stan. "Shore Inspired Hatred and Devotion." *The Hockey News*, March 21, 1970.

Graham, Walter. "Along Memory Lane with John Ducey." *Springfield Republican* March 20, 1976.

"John Ducey's umpiring career." *U.S. Army Post* undated, 1944.
Jones, Terry, on John Ducey Nite at Renfrew Park. *Edmonton Journal* May 30, 1981.
"Report of the 20th Annual New York Baseball Writers Meeting." *The New York Times* February 8, 1943.
Turner, Dan. *Heroes, Bums and Ordinary Men*. Toronto: Doubleday, 1988.

Newspapers
Edmonton Bulletin: 1932, 1935, 1936, 1937, 1938, 1940, 1941, 1942, 1943.
Edmonton Journal: 1932, 1935, 1937, 1939, 1941, 1942, 1943, 1972.
Saskatoon Star: 1937, 1938.

Correspondence
Boone, Lute to John Ducey, April 20, 1935.
Boone, Lute to Ken McConnell, May 9, 1935.
Ducey, John to Brant Ducey, Jan. 5, 1982.
Johns, Sid W, Saskatoon Industrial Exhibition, to John Ducey, August 13, 1935.

Interviews
John Ducey, undated, August 1946 (notes).
Cliff Kilburn, June 17, 1994.
Grace J. Ducey, June 22, 1995.

Other materials
Profile of skater Marion "Red" McCarthy, *Springfield Indians Hockey Review* 1941-42.
Official 5 Cent Score Card, New York Baseball Writers Eating and Oratorical Contest, New York, New York, 1942 and 1943.

10 The Yanks Invade Renfrew

Newspapers
Edmonton Bulletin: 1943.
Edmonton Journal: 1943.
Vancouver Province: 1942.
Springfield Republican: 1943.

Correspondence
Department of Munitions and Supply to John Ducey, March 4, 1944.

Other materials
City of Edmonton Population Statistics, 1952.

11 On The Move Again

Browne, Lois. *Girls of Summer.* Toronto: HarperCollins Publishers, 1992.
Johnson, Susan. *When Women Played Hardball.* Seattle: Seal Press, 1994.
Neft et al., *The Sports Encyclopedia: Baseball.*
Thorn and Palmer, *Total Baseball.*

Newspapers

Edmonton Bulletin: 1944, 1945, 1946.
Edmonton Journal: 1934, 1943, 1944, 1945, 1946.
Calgary Albertan: 1944, 1945.
Calgary Herald: 1946.
San Francisco Chronicle: May 1946.

Correspondence

Ducey, John to Dave Little, April 30, 1945, re umpiring fees.
Hansen, Bill to John Ducey, Sept. 4, 1944, re the Calgary baseball situation.
Hansen, Bill to John Ducey, telegram, May 12, 1945, re umpiring offer.
Weiss, George to John Ducey, June 17, 1946.

Interviews

Riley Mullen, May 1, 1995.
Ken Awid, June 23, 1995.

Other materials

Ducey's service award from Bechtel, Price Callahan.
Formation of Joint Stock Company, Memorandum of Association under *The Companies Act*, Province of Alberta, April 18, 1946.
Minutes of Directors of Edmonton Senior Baseball League, Ltd., April 18, 1946 and May 6, 1946.

12 Back to Baseball

Newspapers

Edmonton Bulletin: 1946, 1947.
Edmonton Journal: 1946, 1947.

Interviews

Des O'Connor, February 27, 1995.
Doug Darrah, March 1, 1995.

13 The Big Four League

Newspapers

Edmonton Bulletin: 1947.
Edmonton Journal: 1947.
Calgary Herald: 1947.

Interviews

Cliff Johnston, February 27, 1995.
Des O'Connor, February 27, 1995.
Doug Darrah, March 1, 1995.
Dick Noon, June 23, 1995.

Other materials

1947 Edmonton Big Four League Program, Dick Noon collection, Medicine Hat, Alberta.

14 The Rajah of Renfrew

Beddoes, Dick. "Jonathan Ducey's Band." *Edmonton Bulletin* May 10, 1950.
Halberstam, David. *Summer of 1949*. New York: Avon Books, 1990.
Jenkins, *Heroes, Bums and Ordinary Men*.
Neft et al., *The Sports Encyclopedia: Baseball*.
Thorn and Palmer, *Total Baseball*.

Newspapers

Edmonton Bulletin: 1947, 1948, 1949, 1950.
Edmonton Journal: 1947, 1948, 1949, 1950.
Calgary Herald: 1947, 1948.
Calgary Albertan: 1947.

Interviews

Don Fleming, March 1, 1995.
Des O'Connor, February 25, 1995.
Cliff Johnston, February 27, 1995.
Hon. Allan H. Wachowich, May 3, 1995.
Dick Noon, June 23, 1995.

Other materials

Minutes of the Alberta Big Four League, 18 March 1947, 20 April 1947, 26 October 1947, 11 January 1948, 8 May 1948, 7 June 1948, 12 August 1948, 4 September 1948, 7 October

1948, 8 August 1949, 22 September 1949, 24 January 1950, 8 February 1950, 17 November 1950.

15 Pinch Hitting

Bruce, Janet. *The Kansas City Monarchs: Champions of Black Baseball*. University Press of Kansas, 1985.
Fischler and Fischler, *The Hockey Encyclopedia*.
Hjolway, John B. *Black Diamonds: Life in the Negro Leagues from the Men Who Lived It*. Westport, Connecticut: Meckler Books, 1989.
Rogosin, Don. *Invisible Men: Life in Baseball's Negro Leagues*. New York: Atheneum, 1987.

Newspapers

Edmonton Journal: 1951, 1952.

Interviews

Des O'Connor, February 25, 1995.
Don Fleming, March 1, 1995.
Ralph Vold, June 25, 1995.

16 Organized Baseball Returns

The Baseball Encyclopedia. Ninth edition. New York: MacMillan Publishing, 1993.
Holway, John B. *Blackball Stars: Negro League Pioneers*. Westport, Connecticut: Meckler Books, 1988.
Objoski, *Bush League*.
Rogosin, *Invisible Men*.
Shatzin, *The Ballplayers*.

Newspapers

Edmonton Journal: 1953, 1953.
Compton California Herald American: March, 1953.

Other materials

Minutes of the Western International Baseball League, 10 November 1952, 9 November 1953, 20 January 1954, 12 June 1954.
Minutes of the Edmonton Baseball Club, 23 December 1952, 30 December 1952, 26 January 1953, 16 March 1953, 19 May 1953, 10 August 1953, 19 September 1953, 6 October 1953.

17 Renfrew Reminiscences

Gerlach, *The Men In Blue.*
Neft et al., *The Sports Encyclopedia: Baseball.*
Thorn and Palmer, *Total Baseball.*

Newspapers Consulted

Edmonton Journal: 1953, 1954.

Interviews

Des O'Connor, February 25, 1995.
Cliff Johnston, February 27, 1995.
Doug Darrah, March 1, 1995.
Don Fleming, March 1, 1995.
Mary Broderick, April 15, 1995.
Ken Awid, June 23, 1995.
Dick Noon, June 23, 1995.

18 Striking Out

Newspapers

Edmonton Journal: 1953, 1954.

Other materials

Edmonton Sr. Baseball Club Ltd., Financial Statements, 1952-60

19 The Western Canada League

Neft et al., *The Sports Encyclopedia: Baseball.*
Stubbs, Lewis St. George. *Shoestring Glory: Semi-Pro Baseball on the Prairies 1886-1994.* Winnipeg: Turnstone Press, 1996.
Thorn and Palmer, *Total Baseball.*

Newspapers

Edmonton Journal: 1955-60, 1965, 1995.
Calgary Albertan: 1954, 1955, 1956.
Calgary Herald: 1955.
Regina Leader-Post: 1955.
Saskatoon Star-Phoenix: 1954.
Vancouver Province: 1955.

Correspondence

Dedeaux, Rod to John Ducey, July 27, 1962.
Ducey, John to Directors of the Edmonton Baseball Club Ltd., October 9, 1954.
Ducey, John to Edmonton Sportswriters Chapter, August 26, 1959.
Ducey, John to Robert E. Smith, President, U.S. Baseball Federation, February 19, 1981.
Ducey, John to Rod Dedeaux, February 25, 1981.
Tucker, Wayne to Brant Ducey, June 27, 1995.

Interviews

Mary Broderick, April 15, 1995.
Ralph Vold, June 25, 1995.
Brian O'Hanlon, August 21, 1997.

Other materials

Edmonton Eskimos, Home Team Rules, 1957.
Edmonton Sr. Baseball Club Ltd., Financial Statements, 1952-60.
Minutes of the Western Canada Baseball League, 14 April 1956, 19 October 1957, 11 October 1958.

20 Searching for a Solution

Abel, Robert, on the impact of television on baseball. *Vancouver News-Herald*, January 19, 1953.
Ducey, John. "No more benefits for the major leagues," *Edmonton Journal*, Jan. 11, 1963.
Johnson, Arthur T. *Minor League Baseball and Local Economic Development*. Urbana and Chicago: University of Illinois Press, 1993.
Objoski, *Bush League*.
Weaver, Angela. "Memorandum re The Lord's Day Act."

Newspapers

Edmonton Journal, 1959, 1960, 1963, 1965, 1966.

Correspondence

Dickie, William, M.L.A. to John Ducey, March 23, 1965.
Ducey, John to Directors of the Edmonton Baseball Club, March 10, 1959.
Ducey, John to Dewey Soriano, September 8, 1960.
Ducey, John to Directors of the Edmonton Baseball Club, undated, October 1960.
Ducey, John to major league baseball owners and officials, July 24, 1962.
Ducey, John to Mayor William Hawrelak, December 14, 1964.
Ducey, John to William Dickie, M.L.A., March 25, 1965.

Ducey, John to Brant Ducey, April 2, 1965.
Soriano, Dewey to John Ducey, September 12, 1960.
Tweddle, J.M. to John Ducey, undated, 1959.

Interviews

Ron Hayter, June 23, 1995.
Brian O'Hanlon, August 21, 1997.

21 Heading for Home

Fleming, Don. "Death Takes Edmonton's Mr. Baseball." *Edmonton Journal* September 12, 1983.
Shury, David. "Prairie Diamonds." *North Battleford Telegraph* September 23, 1983.

Newspapers

Edmonton Journal: 1965, 1966, 1983, 1995.

Correspondence

Adams, T.C., Clerk of Sherman, Illinois, to John Ducey, undated, June 1965.
Campbell, Walter to John Ducey, February 23, 1966; May 9, 1966.
Department of National Defence to Henry Roche, May 30, 1940.
Ducey, John to Brant Ducey, October 19, 1964, re objectives of the Edmonton Oldtimers Baseball Association.
Ducey, John to members of The Edmonton Oldtimers Baseball Association, March 1, 1965.
Ducey, John to members of the Edmonton Oldtimers Baseball Associations, March 19, 1965, meeting reminder.
Ducey, John to John S. Phillips, April 29, 1965.
Ducey, John to Brant Ducey, August 21, 1965.
Ducey, John to Karl Schlerf. Nov. 19, 1965.
Ducey, John to Ann D. White, May 1, 1966.
Ducey, John to Fred Lindstrom, May 2, 1966.
Ducey, John to B.W. Shelin, September 14, 1966.
Ducey, John to Mel Kowalchuck, June 7, 1981.
Ducey, John to Brant Ducey, re fellow nominees to Hall of Fame, March 8, 1983.
Ducey, John to Beans Reardon, March 11, 1983.
Ducey, John to Babe Herman, March 24, 1983.
Kowalchuck, Mel to John Ducey, March 24, 1981.
Phillips, John S. to John Ducey, May 14, 1965.
Prentice, Bruce President of Canadian Baseball Hall of Fame, to John Ducey, February 26, 1983.

Reardon, Genie to John Ducey, April 18, 1980.

Other materials

Program, Pitch and Hit Club of Chicago, Jan. 27, 1963.
Newsletter of the Edmonton Oldtimers Baseball Association, March, 1965 and March, 1966.
Minutes of the Annual Meeting of October 28, 1965, Edmonton Oldtimers Baseball Association.
Member Profiles of The Edmonton Oldtimers Baseball Association.

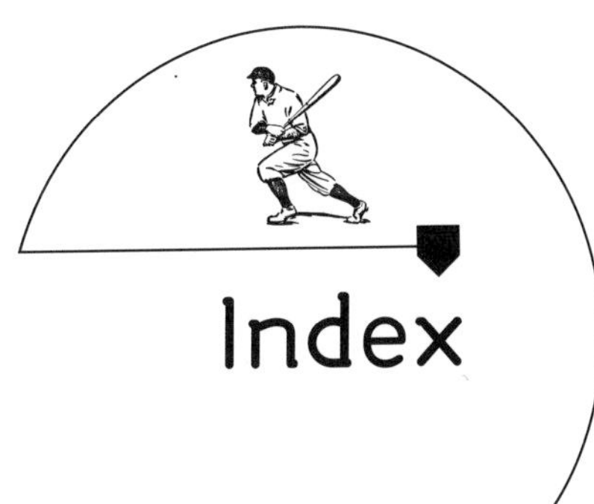

Index

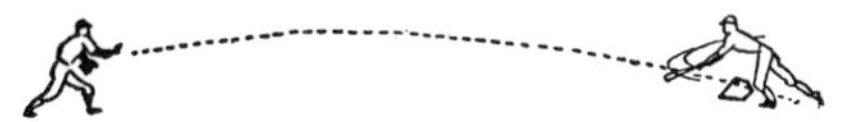

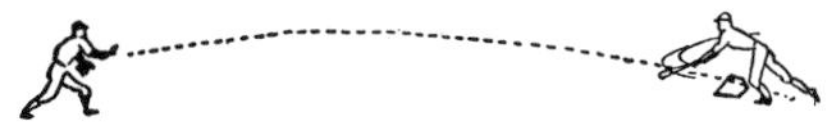

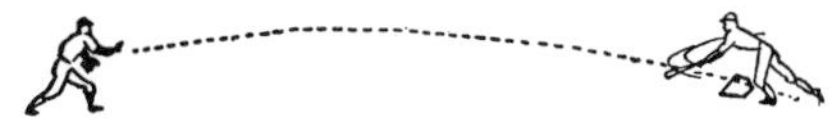

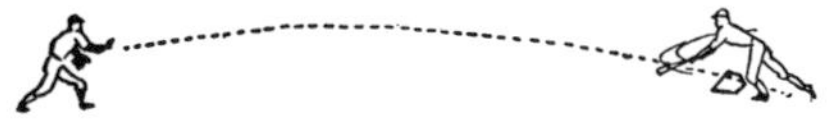

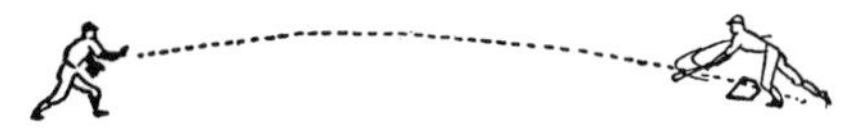